ARE YOU ENTERTAINED?

**SIMONE C. DRAKE &
DWAN K. HENDERSON**
EDITORS

ARE YOU ENTERTAINED?

BLACK POPULAR CULTURE
IN THE TWENTY-FIRST CENTURY

DUKE UNIVERSITY PRESS *Durham and London* 2020

Printed in the United States of America on acid-free paper ∞
Designed by Matthew Tauch
Typeset in Portrait by Westchester Publishing Services

Library of Congress Cataloging-in-Publication Data
Names: Drake, Simone C., [date] editor. | Henderson, Dwan K., [date] editor.
Title: Are you entertained? : Black popular culture in the twenty-first century /
    edited by Simone C. Drake and Dwan K. Henderson.
Other titles: Black popular culture in the twenty-first century
Description: Durham : Duke University Press, 2020. | Includes bibliographical
    references and index.
Identifiers: LCCN 2019016289 (print)
LCCN 2019981471 (ebook)
ISBN 9781478005179 (hardcover)
ISBN 9781478006787 (paperback)
ISBN 9781478009009 (ebook)
Subjects: LCSH: African Americans in popular culture. | Racism in popular culture—
    United States. | African American arts. | Popular culture—United States. | Politics
    and culture—United States. | United States—Civilization—African American
    influences.
Classification: LCC E185.625 .A74 2020 (print)
LCC E185.625 (ebook)
DDC 305.896/073—dc23
LC record available at https://lccn.loc.gov/2019016289
LC ebook record available at https://lccn.loc.gov/2019981471

Cover art: Still from Beyoncé, *The Formation World Tour.* Photo by Matthew Tauch.

Duke University Press gratefully acknowledges The Ohio State University, which provided
funds toward the publication of this book.

FOR JESSE . . .

.

CONTENTS

MORE THAN ENTERTAINMENT / BLACK
CULTURE AND SUBJECT MAKING

In an August 2016 interview for *Vulture*, Rembert Browne asked musician, writer, actor, director, producer, and creator Donald Glover to "[explain] the genesis of [his soon-to-be television phenomenon] *Atlanta*." Glover replied, "I wanted to show white people, you don't know everything about black culture. I know it's very easy to feel that way. Like I get it, you can hear about the Nae Nae the day it comes out. You follow Hood Vines, and you have your one Black friend and you think they teach you everything." But they do not, and Glover's reproof is fitting. Perhaps more than at any time in history and more visibly because lives are so technologically intertwined in real time, the "popular" in Black popular cultural productions is commodified, consumed, appropriated, and then, often, mass-produced with startling simultaneity through the very lens that Glover references, as if "white people . . . know everything about black culture."

Tellingly, Glover's words recall Stuart Hall's seminal question about Black popular culture and bring it into the twenty-first century: "What is this 'black' in black popular culture?" In his provocative and widely anthologized 1992 essay, Hall asserts that the answer to the question he poses is never the same; similarities and continuities surely exist over time, yet we can always identify Leroi Jones's (a.k.a. Amiri Baraka) "changing same." Far more so now than when Hall composed his essay, Black popular culture occupies a central space in mainstream popular culture and the public sphere. As we approach the twilight of the second decade of the twenty-first century, we are twenty-five years removed from the first edited collection attending to the place, space, and weight of Black popular culture in 1992. When a three-day conference at the Studio Museum in Harlem spurred the production of Michele Wallace's project *Black Popular Culture*, co-edited by Gina Dent, Black cultural productions were only beginning their crossover into the mainstream. When those crossovers yielded corporate wins, Black cultural producers rode the waves of a particular type of progress—one that simultaneously illustrated Black culture's marketability and the price of commodification. Take, for example, Berry Gordy's refashioning of soul music and Black artists for a crossover audience during the 1960s and 1970s. Or, consider Motown wunderkind-turned-pop-icon Michael Jackson's "Billie Jean" becoming the first music video by a Black artist to air on MTV IN 1983. In fact, according to Rob Tannenbaum, if not for the commercial success of Jackson's videos in the 1980s, MTV would have been shut down by its parent company due to a $50 million loss when only a $10 million loss prior to profit had been expected.[1] As the *Root.com* conjectures, and justifiably so, Jackson's musical genius resulted in MTV experiencing their first ever quarterly profit during the first three months of 1984. The move away from whitewashed rock and roll saved the network, and that lesson was not taken lightly. Five years later, though not without reservation, MTV executives aired *Yo! MTV Raps* as an "experiment," and "the ratings were phenomenal and resulted in a significant programming change."[2] Notably, Jackson's integration of MTV occurred just one year before *The Cosby Show* would hit primetime television in 1984, introducing many to a positive visual representation of an upper-middle-class and highly educated professional Black family and becoming one of the world's most beloved sitcoms. Just two years later, in 1986, Spike Lee premiered his first feature-length film, *She's Gotta Have It*, launching a career of politicized filmmaking that would extend through the 1990s and begin to carve out a space for Black directors and writers in Hollywood.

As increased representation met the increased visibility of the Information Age, the 1990s brought expansion of Black representation and influence; but, it also generated a burgeoning insistence on multiplicity as well as historicity in portraying Black identity. For example, Michael Jordan's preeminence on the basketball court presented an image of blackness that was perhaps a historically comfortable one for those who could objectify his Black body, marvel in its athleticism, and understand his celebrity. Yet, the corporate branding of Jordan and his subsequent shoe and apparel game renegotiated the reach and power of athletes, particularly Black athletes, in the popular sphere. Simultaneously, televisions around the nation previously privy to the visual, if not societal, normalization of the Huxtables in *The Cosby Show* had also "seen inside" a Huxtable child's journey from suburban space to a fictional historically Black college in the spinoff *A Different World*. This world, for Denise Huxtable and the viewer, was one in which singular definitions of blackness were necessarily consistently defied. On the stage in 1990, August Wilson won a Pulitzer for *The Piano Lesson*, the fourth play in his "Pittsburgh Cycle," which began with a seminal question about identity: "Can one acquire a sense of self-worth by denying one's past?" In 1993, Toni Morrison would win a Pulitzer for *Beloved*, a novel that also delves into the effects of denial and, in Angela Davis's words, makes it "possible to humanize slavery, to remember that the system of slavery did not destroy the humanity of those whom it enslaved."[3] Evoking gendered realities of slavery and the potentially disabling weight of the past's ghosts, Morrison allows readers room to lay claim to the strength of ancestors in newly imagined ways. Each of these texts would necessarily speak differently to Black audiences seeing or revisioning themselves than to white audiences who might engage blackness superficially but not *feel* the impacts of representation.

In 2020, it is likely safe to say that discourse on Black popular culture in the academy has less investment in debates of high versus low culture or of justifications for allotting critical, academic attention to Black popular cultural forms than it once did. But, the proliferation of Black culture in the age of the internet lends credence to Ellis Cashmore's insistence that Black culture has been subsumed by white corporations and converted into an exceptionally profitable commodity.[4] And it is this truth that makes Hall's articulation of Black popular culture as an "area that is profoundly mythic" all the more relevant. "It is where we discover and play with the identifications of ourselves, where we are imagined, where we are represented," Hall argues, "not only to the audiences out there who do not get the message, but to ourselves for the first time."[5] As a result, the steroidal commodification of Black popular culture has long raised a different set of concerns about value, consumption, and incorporation into the U.S. body politic for contemporary Black cultural producers, as accompanying mass consumption is a phenomenon of deracination that has sometimes shifted the meaning of "Black" in Black popular culture. For example, in 2013 the American Music

Award for Best R&B album was presented to Justin Timberlake, which, pundits quipped, infuriated Robin Thicke, another white R&B artist. That same year, the Best Hip-Hop album was awarded to Macklemore and Ryan Lewis. To add insult to injury, just a few months later, the 2014 Grammy for Best Rap Album, Best Rap Song, Best Rap Performance, and Best New Artist were also awarded to Macklemore and Ryan Lewis, creating dismay among many Kendrick Lamar fans—dismay that Macklemore's "shout-out" to Lamar did little to console. And Jay-Z only won in the Best Rap/Sung Collaboration category for "Holy Grail," a collaboration with Justin Timberlake.

What does the "Black" in Black popular culture mean when white male artists not only win but dominate music awards in categories that are historically Black genres? What does the "Black" in Black popular culture constitute when the newly elected mayor of New York City, Bill de Blasio, performs a choreographed "smackdown" dance on stage with his Black wife and two biracial children? And how have the politics of Black popular culture metamorphosed when the hip-hop mogul Jay-Z launches an exorbitantly priced clothing and accessory line at an establishment (Barney's) notorious for racial profiling (a.k.a. shop-and-frisk), around the same time Macklemore chooses to forgo a traditional acceptance speech at the AMA and instead speak bluntly to the murder of Trayvon Martin?[6] A baseline response to all of these questions is that the stakes have shifted in Black popular cultural production. Propaganda remains alive and well, but the development of new models for engaging Black art and its relationship to power, capitalism, and consumption demands critical dialogue on how white corporations have hijacked Black culture for their own profit. Where that is normalized, Miley Cyrus is twerking and employing Black identity tropes to give herself street cred, and Kylie Jenner seemingly "discovered" cornrows in 2013. These examples demonstrate the "changing same" of white corporate ownership of Black culture and artistic production. Whether it was during slavery or after emancipation, through minstrelsy and blackface, that legacy repeatedly manifests in the Black culture industry, as Black people and their cultural productions are locations of "entertainment" that dominant culture has strategically manipulated to represent Black pathology and a presumed knowledge of Black identity.

The renewed national activism spurred by white violence and, particularly, police violence has shaped many Black cultural productions in the space between the police shooting of Michael Brown in 2014 and the 2017 white supremacist rally in Charlottesville, Virginia. The twenty-four-hour news cycle, social media, and other technologies have changed forms of

Black protest within popular culture and made them more visible. In fact, technology is integral to the Movement for Black Lives. Perhaps the most prominent indicator of the phenomenon occurred at the 2015 Super Bowl and Grammy Awards; both illustrated the potential for dominating social media, news cycles, and cultural conversations to influence culture broadly. One day prior to her scheduled Super Bowl halftime performance with Coldplay, Beyoncé released the "Formation" music video on Tidal, the subscription-based music streaming platform that she and her husband, Shawn Carter (a.k.a. Jay-Z), founded and, in large part, own. The music video, with its critique of the devaluation of Black lives through conjoining images of police violence and Hurricane Katrina, was simultaneously an instant success and the subject of negative scrutiny both in conversation and online. Her live performance of "Formation" the next day at the fiftieth Super Bowl added insult to injury for haters as she and her crew of Afro-coiffed sistahs rocked black leather leotards and berets, paying homage to the fiftieth anniversary of the Black Panther Party. At the conclusion of her performance, she announced her Formation World Tour, and just two months later released her equally earthshaking *Lemonade* studio album—an album that she somehow kept under wraps until its release. In spite of All Lives Matter and Blue Lives Matter protests and boycotts in response to both the music video and Super Bowl performance, her tour sold over two million tickets and grossed over $250 million between April 27, 2016, and October 7, 2016.[7]

Before all had settled around the Super Bowl controversy, Kendrick Lamar performed "The Blacker the Berry" and "Alright" at the 2016 Grammys clad in "prison blues" and chains on a stage set with a literal prison cage, pyrotechnics, and African dancers. Although *Rolling Stone* declared Lamar "stole the show" in their headline, it was not a national sentiment. His performance, combined with Beyoncé's just weeks earlier and Colin Kaepernick's protests against police brutality in fall 2016, reinserted a disruptive trope of fiercely resistant blackness into the popular realm.[8] Their performances came at a moment in which resistance was increasingly swift, loud, and furious. With the election of the forty-fifth president of the United States in November 2016, fear and anger as a result of his administration's support for racist, sexist, anti-LGBT, xenophobic, and otherwise bigoted action and policy reached a fever pitch. Lin-Manuel Miranda, who had taken the nation by storm one year earlier with his revolutionary marriage of hip hop and musical theater in *Hamilton*, used his platform to combat discrimination. With a predominantly nonwhite cast, Miranda reframed U.S. national history visually and aurally, penning a reclamation story of founding father Alexander

Hamilton, "a bastard, orphan, son of a whore and Scotsman, dropped in a forgotten spot in the Caribbean," "another immigrant comin' up from the bottom" whose "enemies destroyed his rep [while] America forgot him."[9] His reiteration of Hamilton's occupation of such socioeconomically and sociopolitically beleaguered identity spaces, the melding of genres long perceived both artistically and culturally incongruous, and his race-blind casting are symbolic and literal manifestations of inclusion and defiance of norms. But, it was a statement collectively prepared by the cast and read to then Vice-President-elect Mike Pence at the November 18, 2016, performance in New York City that went viral, showing the power of cultural productions and cultural producers in the digital age. In a profoundly divided and divisive post-2016 election moment, Miranda and the cast expressed hope that President-elect Trump and Mr. Pence would indeed embrace a diverse America and "work on behalf of all of us."[10]

Stuart Hall's questioning of the "Black" in Black popular culture spoke to his theorizing about the nonlinearity and multiplicity of African diasporic cultural identity. Fred Moten revisits the shifting, changing nature of blackness across time and space that Hall addressed. Thinking about resistance and the history of blackness, Moten defines blackness as "the extended movement of a specific upheaval, an ongoing irruption that anarranges [sic] every line—[blackness] is a strain that pressures the assumption of the equivalence of personhood and subjectivity."[11] In this sense, LeVar Burton's chains in the 1977 Roots television miniseries reflect an "extended movement of a specific upheaval" or "an ongoing irruption" that manifests again in Lamar's 2016 Grammy performance. Twenty-first-century iterations and productions of blackness are disruptive and repetitive. They are synchronous, and importantly, they increasingly refuse to serve white consumers and interlopers as "purveyors of pleasure" through their own subjection to degradation and violence and the consequential "transubstantiation of abjection into contentment," as Saidiya Hartman theorizes about the sordid "nexus of pleasure and possession" that pervaded chattel slavery.[12]

The disruptive trope of blackness in the twenty-first century often weds resistance to pleasure, not for the white audience but for the Black audience in need of catharsis. Evidence of this resurfaced at the 2017 Grammys. Beyoncé was once again at the forefront, centering an unapologetic blackness. Pregnant with twins, Queen Bey dramatically performed "Love Drought" and "Sandcastles" from Lemonade, nominated for Album of the Year. Decked out in a gold bikini, invoking the Yoruba Orisha Oshun, Beyoncé embodied both Black pleasure and resistance—both the pleasure of reproduction and children heightened by the significance of twins in Yoruba culture and the insertion of an Africanness that traversed the Atlantic during the Middle Passage. After a hiatus, she followed that with #Beychella, her performance as the first African American woman to headline Coachella in 2018. Her mid-set words perhaps best capture the purposeful resistance and "education in black expression" that she undertook: "Coachella, thank you for allowing me to be the first Black woman to headline. Ain't that 'bout a bitch?"[13] Proceeding to combine couture and elements of Black culture from Nefertiti to the HBCU, as well as a tribute to the artistic journey that led her to become Beyoncé—with all the weight that moniker carries, reinforced by the scope of her production—the artist and performer created a spectacle that played on the largely white audience's consumption of Black expression without background knowledge; it made the set, as Hall argues, the identification, imagination, representation, of ourselves. With sixty-two Grammy nominations, she is the most nominated female artist in history and a music goddess in her own right.[14] Her calculated performances during a two-year period are about much more than Black people occupying prominent spaces in the popular realm. They position Black cultural productions in this epic moment as moving beyond the corporeality of the black flesh and representing and interrogating blackness as embodiment, performance, and resistance.[15]

The 2018 film *Black Panther*, directed by Ryan Coogler, manifests resistance, pleasure, and pain, bringing Black audiences from the United States to Africa to tears. Why? It features not only the first Black Marvel superhero in a lead role on the big screen but also Black women visibly catapulted beyond victimhood to intellectual and physical badassery, a theorized African continent untouched by colonizers' pillaging of the continent, its people, and its varied cultures, and juxtaposition of that theoretical space with the varied seen and lived impacts of colonization in both the Black family and in the United States as a whole. In contrast to *Black Panther*'s creation of imagined space, in 2018, Lamar's *DAMN*, winner of the 2018 Pulitzer Prize for Music, and the release of Childish Gambino's (a.k.a. Donald Glover) "This Is America" pointedly negotiated the complex and often stark realities of varied Black experiences without effacing them. As critic Matthew Trammell notes and as Lamar's 2016 Grammy performance visually and lyrically testified, where Lamar excels is in his ability "to articulate, in human terms, the intimate specifics of daily self-defense from [his] surroundings."[16] Through his art, he speaks his own truth, the ways in which his blackness and American experiences shape his own life. And that, perhaps, is what links Lamar's text to Childish Gambino's. The lyrics and video for the latter code and historicize the complex subjectivit(ies) of blackness in a United States of America that simultaneously celebrates and criminalizes melanin, often relishes performances rather than realities of Black lives, and is prone to violence and destruction. Where Lamar's music is heavily downloaded on platforms like Spotify, YouTube made Gambino's video viral with over fifty million views.

In the digital age and beyond, newer avenues by which artists and consumers push back against continued, rampant marginalization and discrimination in the culture industry are cultural productions to be reckoned with in themselves. The significant role once held by Black radio and Black print culture in the Black political sphere has been displaced in many ways by social media and the digital explosion. Even though, according to a 2018 report published by the Pew Research Center, YouTube can claim the highest number of online American adult users (73 percent), Instagram, Snapchat, and Twitter usage by demographic reveals the power of social media to activate, politicize, resist, and consume in the contemporary moment. Compared to YouTube's white (71 percent) versus Black (76 percent) usage, separated by only five percentage points, the report noted a significant difference in white versus Black Instagram usage (32 vs. 43 percent) and white versus Black Snapchat usage (24 vs. 36 percent), as well as a shrinking difference in white versus Black Twitter usage (24 vs. 26 percent).[17]

Disproportionate usage is also evident in terms of age, where the eighteen-to-twenty-nine-year-old demographic is the most inclined to use Facebook (81 percent), YouTube (91), Instagram (64), Snapchat (68), and Twitter (40).[18] Social media, then, functions as an important communication platform for Black Americans in the twenty-first century in spite of the "digital divide" in other areas of technology. In a February 2018 report also published by Pew, the fifteen percentage-point difference between Black (57) and white (72) home broadband usage adjusts to only a three-point difference—Black (75) and white (77)—for smartphone usage.[19] These numbers explain the degree to which young Black users have adopted social media as a platform for activism and resistance. The "clapback" christened "Black Twitter" in particular as an entity that the mainstream media and Black cultural critics must acknowledge.

Black Twitter became "a strain"—invoking musical expression or outburst (aesthetics) and excessive exertion or labor (force)—as it vocalized its displeasure with the absence of blackness (and all other racially and ethnically marginalized folk) in the 2016 Academy Awards nominations. The refusal of the Academy to recognize both Black labor and Black genius catalyzed the hashtag #OscarsSoWhite. A similar discontent was echoed on social media after the 2017 Grammys and the widespread perception that Beyoncé was snubbed, particularly in the coveted category of Record of the Year. Even Adele, who won the category, was confused and contrite, as she proclaimed in her acceptance speech, "The artist of my life is Beyoncé, and this album to me, the 'Lemonade' album, was just so monumental." Off-stage, still dubious of her win, Adele followed up with "I felt like it was her time to win. What the f*** does she have to do to win album of the year?" As Adele left the ceremony with awards in all five of the categories for which she was nominated, Beyoncé, who was nominated in nine categories, won only two, Best Music Video and Best Urban Contemporary. While few would deny that Adele is talented in her own right, discourse on white mediocrity and the limits of recognizing Black genius permeated Black Twitter and even some mainstream media at the conclusion of the award ceremony. Although clearly more incorporated, blackness in the popular realm continues to hit ceilings and obstacles.

In spite of the continued challenges, sometimes blackness is blue. When film director and writer Barry Jenkins (*Medicine for Melancholy*) collaborated with Tarell Alvin McCraney to adapt the latter's play *In Moonlight Black Boys Look Blue*, neither may have imagined that the film adaptation, *Moonlight*, originally showing almost exclusively at art houses, would take home an Oscar for Best Picture, Best Writing Adapted Screenplay, and Best Supporting Actor at the 2017 Academy Awards. *Moonlight* disrupted the whiteness of the Oscars, generally and particularly during the previous year, when it, along with *Hidden Figures, Fences,* and *Loving,* inserted Black narratives into the mainstream. This was particularly true given that, in nearly every possible category, *La La Land* was nominated. As the supreme exemplar of revived tropes and nostalgia for Hollywood's Golden Age and thus, perhaps, white artistic mediocrity in 2016, *La La Land* was boldly nominated in fourteen categories and won six (after a bizarre fiasco in which it was wrongly awarded Best Picture). *La La Land*, a musical whose leading actress is neither a singer nor a dancer but won Best Actress, and whose leading actor's claim to singing and dancing fame was *The Mickey Mouse Club* alongside Justin Timberlake, Britney Spears, and Christina Aguilera, was the critics' hands-on favorite to win Best Picture. *Moonlight* was second; its win, then, over a film that checked all of the academy's go-to boxes for success was somewhat shocking.

Moonlight's disruption extends further than its win, however, because it offers a story that challenges the familiar, complicating poverty and masculinity and their intersections with race and gender. Jenkins and McCraney disallow blackness to be defined in the hegemonic manner Hollywood so often imposes upon Black bodies. Pleasure and pain converge, as the story is both empowering and probes deeply the pain and hate that human beings can inflict upon other human beings. The narrative, sound, and aesthetics embody the beauty and pain of the coming of age of a gay Black boy in the Liberty City neighborhood of Miami during the Reagan-Bush era. Jenkins masterfully develops the narrative around three stages of the protagonist Chiron's life through portrayals by three different actors. Growing up with a single, drug-addicted mother in abject poverty, Chiron spends his childhood and youth being bullied and abused by his peers and his mother. Although the film received critical acclaim both before and after its release, in an Academy whose membership is dominated by white men, it would be easy to expect merit would not outweigh whiteness. Appropriately, though, representing Black pain and pleasure during an epoch of hateful rhetoric and opposition to difference outside of white, heterosexual, middle-class manliness, *Moonlight* continues a legacy of Black cultural producers embracing culture and performance as disruptive tools.

What constitutes "Black" in Black popular culture, then, becomes a more complex discussion than ever before in the twenty-first century because nearly 150 years after emancipation, Black cultural production is always already still linked to the affirmation of Black humanity. Whether a Black independent film like Barry Jenkins's *Medicine for Melancholy*, a film franchise like Tyler Perry's *Medea* films, YouTube-producer-turned-HBO-creator Issa Rae's interest in "telling a very specific, authentic story, not trying to answer for all Black people" through *Awkward Black Girl* or *Insecure,* Janelle Monáe's futuristic, cyber-girl, pansexual blackness, the new-money, "ghetto fabulousness" of T.I. and Tiny, the respectability politics resistance of Tiffany Haddish or Cardi B., or the seeming endless spectacle of blackness in the sports arena, Black cultural producers respond to stakes of Black art that continue to be inextricably linked not only to the entertainment of white folk but also to the dependence of dominant culture upon static notions of Blacks as hypersexual, primitive (premodern), violent, lazy, feckless, conniving, childish, and ultimately lacking humanity.[20]

And their responses can be quite complex. What might seem like a simple contrast of positive versus negative cultural producers in pairing a Black indie film with Tyler Perry and Janelle Monáe with T.I. can never be so simplistic when the stakes are so high. As propaganda in the twenty-first century, Black popular cultural products resist static representations through alternative realities. But, there also must be space for articulations and representations of Black life and culture that embrace the pleasure, joy, and freedom embodied in the production of what some call the "buffoonery" of Perry and the oft-perceived degeneration of contemporary rap and hip-hop music. Such appellations create quite the paradox—the Black masses, including professional Black women who seem to never escape being objects of punishment in Perry's storylines, support the "low-down folk" culture represented in Perry's theatrical and filmic productions. Perry, then, emerges as a controversial figure, and the controversy is rooted in the high stakes of Black representation in a nation that readily accepts blackness as synonymous with pathology. Plenty of white directors traffic in buffoonery and misogyny, but their art does not suffer from the same high stakes of representation. Perry epitomizes the challenges of producing Black art in a space and time in which the stakes of representation are high precisely because the rules of the game change depending upon who is producing the images.

The same can be said for Black athletes and the multiple levels of performance they engage and are subjected to on the playing fields and public stage; their bodies, physical prowess, and voices have permeated popular culture and become propagandistic in their own right. Venus and Serena Williams, for example, have had to negotiate an often ugly dialectic of entertainer and spectacle. In particular, Serena's unapologetic display of her curves and musculature in elaborate, unconventional tennis attire and her vocal declarations of self-confidence and self-love have thwarted the efforts of mass media and many opponents to diminish her. In August 2018, for instance, the French Tennis Federation, through its president Bernard Guidicelli, attempted to make her Black body a site of pathology, banning a high-compression, black catsuit inspired by *Black Panther* and designed to prevent blood clots—a chronic condition that nearly killed her both in 2011 and during childbirth only one year earlier. In words that seemed a metaphor for Serena, herself, Guidicelli told *Tennis* magazine, "It will no longer be accepted. One must respect the game and the place."[21] In short, her body and need for self-care were disrespectful to a game that she has enhanced through her skill, perseverance, presence, and brand. Fittingly, one year later, with multiple August 2019 covers and an accompanying first-person essay for *Harper's Bazaar*, Williams boldly claimed the beauty and grace in her powerful "unretouched" Black body, as well as her space and place in the world that forged her equally powerful spirit. Well aware of the hard-won influence and inspiration that she and her brand represent, both in the game and outside of it, she writes: "As a teenager, I was booed by an entire stadium

(I took the high road and even thanked those who didn't want to see me win). I've been called every name in the book. I've been shamed because of my body shape. I've been paid unequally because of my sex. I've been penalized a game in the final of a major because I expressed my opinion or grunted too loudly.... And these are only the things that are seen by the public. In short, it's never been easy. But then I think of the next girl who is going to come along who looks like me, and I hope, 'Maybe, my voice will help her.'"[22]

While perhaps the earliest example of the influential power of Black male athletes on Black popular culture was Allen Iverson's appeal to the hip-hop generation, Lebron James's widespread cultural influence rivals that of any artistic entertainer.[23] For example, his tweet calling the forty-fifth president of the United States "a bum" was one of the "[Nine] Most Retweeted Tweets of 2017."[24] His reach challenges that of Michael Jordan within Black culture, largely because James has gradually grown keenly aware of the cultural, social, and political responsibility that his success and visibility bring in ways that Jordan seemed unwilling to do at the dawn of personal corporate branding. The historic political activism of athletes, like Muhammad Ali's outspoken denunciation of the Vietnam War and Tommie Smith's and John Carlos's Black power salute on the medal stage at the 1968 Olympic games, stands in bleak contrast to Michael Jordan's explaining that he chose to be silent regarding the 1990 North Carolina Senate race between Jesse Helms (R) and Harvey Gantt (D) because "Republicans buy shoes." In contrast, LeBron James's awareness of his immense leverage is increasingly on display as he evolves. For example, in a February 15, 2018, joint interview with fellow NBA star Kevin Durant on YouTube's "UNINTERRUPTED," both men railed against social injustice and the political climate in the United States that continues to disproportionately harm people of color. James, cognizant of how his Black maleness is perceived despite his success and conscious of the reparative work that he can do with his platform, professed, "I'm a black man with a bunch of money and havin' a crib in Brentwood and havin' the word 'nigger' spraypainted over my gate.... That lets you know ... I still have a lot more work to do. And no matter how far, money or access or how high you become in life as an African American man, female, they will always try to figure out a way to let you know that you still beneath them, and it's either one of two things at that point. You either cave in to that notion or chalk it up and say, 'You know what? Imma paint over this goddamn gate and Imma make it taller.'" More pointedly, in the same interview, James publicly censured the forty-fifth president of the United States, arguing that "the No. 1 job in America, the appointed person, is someone who doesn't understand the people and really don't give a fuck about the people."[25] In response, recalling the tired trope of Black male bodies as mindless physical specimens, the president called James "dumb" in a tweet; similarly, Fox News host Laura Ingraham suggested that James was "ignorant" and should "shut up and dribble." James's reply was two-fold and fully rejected the labels and directive: an Instagram post with a neon image of the words, "I am more than just an Athlete" and artful taunting of his detractors in a subsequent interview during 2018 NBA All-Star Week. In that interview, he both reiterated his own journey and fully claimed the powerful impact of his celebrity at Ingraham's expense: "You know, to be an African American kid and grow up in the inner city with a single parent, mother, and not being financially stable and to make it where I've made it today, I think I've defeated the odds. I want every kid to know that . . . all these other kids that look up to me for inspiration who are trying to find a way out, finding some leeway on how they can become as great as they can be and how those dreams can become a reality. [Ingraham] did the best thing to help me create more awareness. So I appreciate her for giving me even more awareness."[26] His words reify the truth that in the twenty-first century, sports function as a critical space for negotiating Black culture and the high stakes of representation. Thus, the disruption of static notions that Toni Morrison positions as necessary to substantiate white supremacy in *Playing in the Dark* are part of the challenge Black popular culture must negotiate as it contends with white consumerism—as it is subjected to the white gaze that depends upon not seeing the full humanity and complexity of Black folks.

Endlessly, concertedly, meticulously, Black cultural producers have had to combat historical efforts to diminish their experiences and their identities; current explorations of Black popular culture cannot be divorced from that history. Significant effort was made by European Enlightenment pseudo-science and white supremacist ideologies to prove African-descended people lacked culture and civilization, and many of those arguments were intricately linked to artistic production. Thomas Jefferson, for example, in *Notes on the State of Virginia*, denigrates Phillis Wheatley and Black artists generally when he insists that religion enabled Wheatley to produce something that "kindles the senses" but lacks imagination. Jefferson insisted on an inherent inferiority in Black thought and creativity: "But never yet could I find that a black had uttered a thought above the level of plain narration; never see even an elementary trait of painting or sculpture. In music they are more generally gifted than the whites with accurate ears fortune and time, and they have been found capable of imagining a small catch."[27] Sentiments like Jefferson's made it impossible for discourse on the social uplift of African Americans to be divorced from culture, since culture was deeply entwined with racist ideologies of what constitutes civilization and humanness.

The reality of art and culture being inextricably linked to white supremacist rhetoric and violence is precisely why African American cultural movements have coincided with African American social movements. There are, in fact, three distinct cultural movements in which such critical discourse has not only been closely linked to social and political change, but the critical discourse has also informed the production of the art: the New Negro Movement, the Black Arts Movement, and the Post-Soul Aesthetic. Historicizing these movements is critical for understanding Black popular culture as not simply entertainment but an integral space for Black intellectual debate around Black subject making.

The publication of Alain LeRoy Locke's anthology *The New Negro* in 1925 functioned as the definitive text of the cultural revolution popularly referred to as the Harlem Renaissance and known by academics as the New Negro Movement. Locke served as a mentor to Black artists and ultimately as dean of black letters and art during the New Negro Movement. Coining the term "New Negro" as a way of recognizing the production of Black art *by* Black artists as opposed to previous work *about* Black artists, Locke argues that his anthology concentrates on self-expression and agency. By letting the Negro have her own voice, Locke proposes that a New Negro displaces the Old Negro, who is "more a myth than man," and humanizes Black people who had theretofore been represented as a formula. He also suggests that urban migration from the South to northern and midwestern industrial centers accounts for the shift from discourse on the "Negro problem" to the recognition of class differentiation among U.S. Blacks.

Ethnic diversity, then, also informs the metamorphosis from Old to New Negro, as Harlem itself represented an African diasporic population of African, Caribbean, and both southern and northern African Americans. While, on one hand, Locke calls for race cooperation, on the other, he offers an Afrocentric manifesto calling for Black artists to appreciate and incorporate "African representation of form." According to Locke, "A more highly stylized art does not exist than the African," and he uses that assertion for his ultimate mandate: a "racial school of art" to be composed of the younger Black artists of the era. "It is not meant to dictate a style to the young Negro artists," Locke concedes, "but to point the lesson that contemporary European art has already learned—that any vital artistic expression of the Negro theme and subject in art must break through the stereotypes to a new style, a distinctive fresh technique, and some sort of characteristic idiom."[28] The Eurocentric, middle-class dictates how Locke is engaging Black art. Like many of his contemporaries—most notably Langston Hughes, Zora Neale Hurston, and Aaron Douglas—Locke was largely dependent upon financial support from his white benefactor; in both Hughes's and Locke's cases, the benefactor was Charlotte Osgood Mason. The ideology of pursuing "social or racial uplift" by embracing middle-class values and decorum was, however, a vexed pursuit. The mimicry of European modernism and its infatuation with primitivism helped to distinguish Black art and artists as capable of full citizenship and incorporation into the body politic. But the formalist approach to Black production of primitivism-influenced art reified racial stereotypes and worked against Locke's cultural and national agenda. Arguably, the central paradox of patron-based artistic production during the New Negro era continues to hold true for many Black cultural producers today.

A year after the publication of *The New Negro* anthology, George Schuyler published his essay "The Negro Art Hokum" in the June 16, 1926, edition of *The Nation*. His essay takes to task the very notion of a "racial school of art." Though not stated explicitly, Schuyler's essay responds to the cultural agenda laid out in Locke's *The New Negro*. He offers an anti-essentialist argument that resonates more with post–civil rights rhetoric than the rhetoric of his time period. Schuyler insists that geography and the influence of (European) educational institutions is what determines the content and style of Black art, rather than some shared ancestral essence. He declares, "This, of course, is easily understood if one stops to realize that the Aframerican is merely a lampblacked Anglo-Saxon," and he points to the assimilation of European immigrants as evidence that the "American Negro is just plain American." Arguing that Black and white Americans of the same socioeconomic class invest in the same material culture and ideologies, Schuyler asks, "How, then, can the black American be expected to produce art and literature dissimilar to that of the white-American?" Failing to account for class disparities along racial lines, he concludes that when considering the cultural production of a conglomerate of esteemed international Black artists, one finds the influence of nation—not race.[29] In many ways, the goals of Schuyler intersect with those of Locke. Both seek to debunk racial stereotypes of the Old Negro, yet Schuyler's advocacy for assimilation directly contradicts Locke's espousal of Afrocentrism and primitivism. Moreover, where Locke turns to ancestral heritage to prove humanness, Schuyler proposes that national identity, region, and social class debunk stereotypes.

Just one week after Schuyler's article appeared, Langston Hughes's "The Negro Artist and the Racial Mountain" was also published in the *Nation*. Departing from the theorizations of both Locke and Schuyler, Hughes privileges Black folk culture in a way that suggests an artistic freedom surely informed by his break from his patron. Hughes repudiates racial assimilation, mourning the urge by certain Black artists to understand *real* art as American art and therefore devoid of any Black aesthetics. He locates the privileging of white culture and aesthetics within the realm of the Black middle class, claiming that within it, "there will perhaps be more aping of things white than in a less cultured or less wealthy home." This broad generalization sets up his argument in praise of the "low-down folks" who, to use the contemporary vernacular, "keep it real." He praises a Black folk culture that, unlike the Philadelphia clubwoman, is not ashamed of jazz and Negro spirituals. Painting Schuyler's argument as mere "race shame," he unequivocally rejects the proposition that there is such a thing as de-raced American art. His manifesto for younger Black artists, then, is to embrace their blackness, recognize its beauty, *and* do so without fear or shame.[30]

A couple of months later, the preeminent W. E. B. Du Bois offered his own Black art manifesto in the October 1926 edition of the *Crisis*. In what would later be published as an essay at the annual NAACP conference in Chicago celebrating the twelfth recipient of the Spingarn Medal, Carter G. Woodson, Du Bois makes clear that, in his mind, Black politics and art are inextricably linked. He implies that white U.S. materialism results in the inability to appreciate Beauty, and he proposes Black youth might help stir "the beginning of a new appreciation of joy" by tapping into the usable past Woodson emphasized in his work. By accentuating a history that elicits racial pride, Du Bois is not echoing Locke's Afrocentric rootedness for Black art. Instead, he suggests that if Black America accepts its "duty" to create, preserve, and realize Beauty, those artists "become the apostle of Truth and Right." Art, therefore, is and always must be propaganda, according to Du Bois: "I stand in utter shamelessness and say that whatever art I have for writing has been used always for propaganda for gaining the right of Black folk to love and enjoy." Du Bois ultimately calls for an unbound Black artist who is free to debunk white stereotypes, as well as to ignore the conservative politics of a Black public that wishes to distort "Truth."[31]

The political manifestos of the Black Arts Movement, the sister movement of the Black Power Movement, register Hughes's embrace of Black as beautiful and his rooting of Black artistic production in the "low-down folk"; in it, however, there is also a healthy dose of Du Bois's insistence that

Black art be produced as truth-telling propaganda and not simply art for art's sake. Amiri Baraka's 1969 poem "Black Art" defines a Black aesthetic that goes beyond functioning as a material object or cultural product, demanding revolutionary art:

> We want "poems that kill"
> Assassin poems, Poems that shoot
> guns. Poems that wrestle cops into alleys
> and take their weapons leaving them dead
> with tongues pulled out and sent to Ireland.[32]

Similarly, Nikki Giovanni's 1967 poem "For Saundra" demands a violent militancy, questioning the possibility of producing any art that is not political:

> so i thought again
> and it occurred to me
> maybe i shouldn't write
> at all
> but clean my gun
> and check my kerosene supply
> perhaps these are not poetic
> times
> at all.[33]

Poems by artists like Baraka and Giovanni dictated the Black aesthetic, serving as mini manifestos that, in 1970, found a voice in Gil Scott-Heron's spoken-word performance "The Revolution Will Not Be Televised." Insisting that the revolution will not be something you watch—something co-opted by the white media and white values even when featuring Black people—but something that happens in your mind, Heron offered a truncated version of treatises on the Black aesthetic by Hoyt Fuller in "Toward a Black Aesthetic" (1968) and Addison Gayle Jr. in *The Black Aesthetic* (1971). Fuller, like Baraka and Heron, locates the streets as a central space for revolt and observes, "The serious black artist of today is at war with the American society as few have been throughout American history." He declares in earnest:

> Few, I believe, would argue with my assertion that the black artist, due to his historical position in America at the present time, is engaged in a war with this nation that will determine the future of black art. Likewise, there are few among them—and here again this is only conjecture—who would disagree with the idea that unique experiences produce unique

cultural artifacts, and that art is a product of such cultural experiences. To push this thesis to its logical conclusion, unique art derived from unique cultural experiences mandates unique critical tools for evaluation.[34]

Hughes's assertion that a particular experience produces a particular type of art resonates loudly.

After the civil rights era, discourse on the Black aesthetic became grounded in anti-essentialist critiques. These critiques also began to be more cognizant of "Black popular culture" as a space in which the Black aesthetic is produced. The controversial yet seminal essay by Trey Ellis, "The New Black Aesthetic," lays the groundwork for a significant shift in how the Black aesthetic is defined. Playing on the concept of a racial mulatto, Ellis conceives of the "cultural mulatto," Black people like himself whose socioeconomic privilege troubles notions of both Black aesthetics and Black authenticity. His argument, rooted in class and gender privilege, has been the recipient of much critique, but his intervention in the discourse has been foundational for millennial discourse on race and cultural production.

Take, for example, Harlem's Studio Museum director and chief curator Thelma Golden and visual artist Glenn Ligon coining the expression "post-black." Describing the Studio Museum's *Freestyle* (2001) exhibition, the museum's website explains how this exhibition of work by a young group of artists "brought into the public consciousness the concept of 'post-black.' . . . It identified a generation of Black artists who felt free to abandon or confront the label of 'Black artist,' preferring to be understood as individuals with complex investigations of blackness in their work. Post-black art became a transitional stance in the quest to define ongoing changes in African-American art; it ultimately became part of the perpetual redefinition of blackness in contemporary culture."[35]

Golden and Ligon's application of "post-black" to a particular type of Black art and its subsequent application to Black popular culture is similar to the use of "post-soul aesthetic" by the popular culture scholar Mark Anthony Neal in *Soul Babies: Black Popular Culture and the Post-Soul Aesthetic* (2001). Focusing on film, television, music, and cultural criticism, Neal explains how he struggled to find a language to address the postmodern realities of African American communities. He selects the concept of "post-soul aesthetic" (borrowing from the cultural critic Nelson George) to do that work, explaining, "In the post-soul aesthetic, I am surmising that there is an aesthetic center within contemporary Black popular culture that at various moments considers issues like deindustrialization, desegregation, the corporate annexation of black popular expression, cyberization in the workforce, the globalization of finance and communication, the general commodification of black life and culture, and the proliferation of black 'meta-identities,' while continuously collapsing on modern concepts of blackness and reanimating 'premodern' (African?) concepts of blackness."[36] Both concepts—post-black and post-soul aesthetic—are rooted in a rethinking of modernity and the *production* of the concept of blackness.

Stuart Hall's essay wrestles with the challenges of defining postmodern blackness and cultural production at the close of the twentieth century. He concedes that the signifier "Black" in the term "Black popular culture" denotes the Black community—a space he describes as the locus for archiving Black struggle, the Black aesthetic, and Black counternarratives. However, he warns that attention must be turned to the diversity of the Black experience, not its supposed homogeneity.[37] Post–civil rights discourse on Black popular culture privileges heterogeneous experiences, ideas, and resistant practices; therefore, it diverges from the preceding cultural movements. A common framework among all three movements, however, is either an explicit assertion that Black artists produce Black cultural products (the New Negro and the Black Arts Movement) or an implied understanding that it is Black people who produce Black popular culture (post-Black and post-soul aesthetics).

The notion that art is propaganda was and continues to be real, if history is any indicator. It affects how Black people move through the world. For this reason, it is imperative to develop new models for engaging Black popular culture and its relationship to power, capitalism, gender identity, presidential politics, and countless other forces that work to marginalize, dehumanize, and strip Black people of full citizenship—especially in a nation that struggles, visibly and vocally, to see them as complex and human. In many ways, the "'Black' in Black popular culture" that this volume addresses is authentic representation of the lived experience of blackness in an always increasingly politicized and commodified U.S. space.

For that reason, *Are You Entertained?* offers a dynamic, interdisciplinary analysis of contemporary shifts, trends, and debates in Black popular culture. The volume is divided into five thematic sections, each composed of analytical and creative essays and an interview with a scholar who has been influential in public dialogues on Black popular culture. Part I, "Performing Blackness," explores the creative spaces of cabaret, television, and radio as theories of performance and performativity have become central to the theaters of Black popular culture. Ralina Joseph proposes that the Obama era created a space to position mixed-race blackness as comedic fodder. She considers how this trope, intended to be humorous, is reflective of how audiences understand mixed-race African Americans and the idea of the post-racial. Emily Lordi uses the metaphor of "Black radio" to explore the reason and function of a recent trend in Black musicians releasing albums that thematize Black radio and position the diverse range of voices, styles, and sometimes experimentation as odes to free(r) airwaves. Vincent Stephens considers how racializing cabaret as white, or "campy," excludes African American cabaret singers from studies of Black popular music. Drawing on the dichotomies of Black/white and straight/queer, Stephens reads the careers of key Black cabaret singers as constituting Black popular musical production. H. Ike Okafor-Newsum presents an analysis of the visual art selected for this volume. Varied in media as well as historicity and focus, the pieces capture not only links to a Black cultural past but elements that complicate that culture presently. This section concludes with an interview with Lisa B. Thompson on theorizing and writing performance.

Because Black popular culture is, as Hall aptly states, always a space of contestation and politicizing, part II, "Politicizing Blackness," explores ways in which blackness and popular culture have been deliberately politicized, for varied public arenas have long served as opportune spaces for disseminating political ideologies. Kelly Jo Fulkerson-Dikuaa turns to the journalism and cartoons of Jackie Ormes to question how media images of Black women and girls operate in fights for racial equality. Moving the Black woman from foil to subject, Fulkerson-Dikuaa demonstrates how Ormes's cartoons were about more than protest and political commentary; they also provided an avenue for a Black woman to harness a form of Black womanhood often left unexamined in dominant discourses surrounding Black women of the 1940s and 1950s. Delving into digital literacies and platforms, Eric Darnell Pritchard explores video blogs (vlogs) and web series as spaces where Black queer people create, represent, and potentially alter realities. He demonstrates the limitations and possibilities of these specific texts and the digital sphere to story, witness, and archive diverse representations of Black queerness. David J. Leonard considers the phenomenon of "blerd ballers" and the intersection of race and masculinity as Black NBA players use off-court spaces for sartorial protests against racialized dress codes. An interview with Tracy Sharpley-Whiting ends this segment and offers insight on how diasporic blackness outside of the United States is consumed.

Part III, "Owning Blackness," explores the problem of ownership that has plagued Black life in slavery and freedom. Once physical property during slavery, upon emancipation, Black people found not only their personhood and labor production exploited and consumed but also their creative and intellectual production. To begin the section, Sheneese Thompson demonstrates how Black Twitter teeters between humor and pleasure and outrage and pain, avowing the blackness that hegemonic society hates. A foray into the evolution of signifying practices, Thompson's essay offers Twitter as a space of ownership and identity proclamation. Richard Schur undertakes a legal-cultural analysis of trademark law to map a debate about trademark and authenticity in Black popular culture productions. Schur explores the question of who profits from racial trademarks by bringing hip-hop studies, critical race theory, and contemporary African American art into dialogue. Turning to dance, Imani Kai Johnson continues the interrogation of ownership and hip hop. She pushes for a movement beyond the language of appropriation and minstrelsy to examine the experiences of Africanist aesthetic sensibilities in the absence of Black bodies in breaking (breakdancing) culture worldwide. What better way of owning blackness than to produce your own cultural productions. Breaking from the traditional academic essay, Nina Angela Mercer offers a meditation on Black cultural production that, with creativity and sharp insight, defines Black ritual theater. Through prose and poetry tapping out a polyrhythmic beat, Mercer explores how ritual theater practitioners build community and define theater as every day and everywhere there are lives touching other lives. This section closes with an interview with Mark Anthony Neal, a formidable scholar who laid much of the groundwork for Black popular culture being a serious field of academic study.

Part IV, "Loving Blackness," pays homage to cultural productions that catalyze a genre of Black love and romance in print and visual culture: self-love, the proliferation of Black heterosexual love narratives, and the stylized emergence of the Black queer love narrative. Takiyah Nur Amin examines how popular dances that emerge from Black cultural contexts function as a site for pleasure, agency, and resistance. She posits Black popular dance as a site for meaning-making and self-love and considers the contours of embodied epistemology in twerking, the Harlem shake, j-setting, and similar movement practices. Simone Drake explores soundscapes, queer interiority, and Black boyhood in the film *Moonlight*. She considers how attention to the nuances distinguishing silence and quiet troubles heteromasculinist coming-of-age narratives and how the film's musical score transports viewers deep into the interior life of a queer Black boy who says very little. Kinohi Nishikawa studies urban fiction's disturbance of traditional literary traditions. Studying both the contradiction of urban fiction emerging after culture wars brought African American literature into the American literature canon and the divergent responses to it, Nishikawa considers the topics and roles of African American women in the urban fiction arena. This section concludes with an extended interview with Patricia Hill Collins, a trailblazer in interdisciplinary scholarship in Black women's studies.

As a whole, *Are You Entertained?* addresses social and cultural shifts and changes, considering what "culture" means in the context of a capitalist, consumer economy. Hall's question "What is this 'Black' in Black popular culture?" still has relevance, but the culture wars and neonationalist identity politics that framed *Black Popular Culture* have given way to postnational identity formations, individualism, and new avenues for expression. Ultimately, Black popular culture is uniquely different now. We hope that this volume fulfills our aims: to bring together essays that engage the politics that created the shifts, as well as the products that have emerged as highly influential in the construction of a national identity for all U.S. citizens both at home and around the globe.

Notes

1   Palmer, "How the 'Billie Jean' Video Changed MTV."

2   Palmer, "How the 'Billie Jean' Video Changed MTV."

3   Quoted in White, "'Beloved' Author Speaks about Writing."

4   Cashmore, *The Black Culture Industry.*

5   Hall, "What Is This 'Black' in Black Popular Culture?," 113.

6   See Jacob Bernstein, "Jay-Z and Barneys Announce Substantial Changes in Their Partnership, *New York Times*, November 18, 2013; and K. C. Orcutt, "Each One, Teach One: How JAY-Z Continues to Evolve His Philanthropic Blueprint," *REVOLT*, February 20, 2019. Under fire to respond publicly to Barney's racial profiling in 2012, Jay-Z reconfigured his agreement with the clothier, mandating leadership input, a seat on a council designed to address racial profiling, and proceeds from sales benefitting the Shawn Carter Foundation. While the Barney's episode does highlight absences in Black popular cultural politics, Jay-Z cannot be fully dismissed as an agent of change. His propensity for activist and philanthropist anonymity puts him at odds with an older generation of activists who believe that the struggle should be lived out loud, often at great risk to oneself—most notably icon Harry Belafonte, who claimed in the August 7, 2012, *Hollywood Reporter* that Jay-Z, "like other high-profile artists . . . had turned his back] on social responsibility." The perceived egotism in Jay-Z's response, "my presence is charity," was both acknowledged and

regrettable. But, it seems integral in this twenty-first-century cultural space to allow that his "presence" as newly minted billionaire, corporate entity, and brand is often reformative. His behind-the-scenes work and fundraising is well documented: for criminal justice reform, college and study abroad scholarships for disadvantaged youth, bail for BLM protesters in Baltimore, and supplies of "millions of pounds of aid" during Hurricane Maria. While he must negotiate the power of his voice beyond just spitting rhymes, his positioning underscores the complex relationship between Black culture makers, money, and cultural change—particularly when previously unheard of levels of success and power in the capitalist machine are in play, and blackness is not monolithic.

7 Palmer, "How the 'Billie Jean' Video Changed MTV."

8 Although it is not addressed fully in this introduction, quarterback Colin Kaepernick's protest of police brutality by kneeling for the anthem and his ongoing efforts to use his brand (which only increased in value, visibility, and influence post-NFL blackballing and public callout by the president and others) has been a catalyst in the fight for social justice since 2016.

9 Miranda, "Alexander Hamilton."

10 Quoted in Politi, "The Slatest."

11 Moten, *In the Break*, 1.

12 Hartman, *Scenes of Subjection*, 23.

13 St. Félix, "Beyoncé's Triumphant Homecoming."

14 Minsker, "Grammys 2017."

15 Kendrick Lamar also offers another provocative performance that reshapes the popular cultural landscape, opening the 2018 Grammy Awards by performing "XXX" and other songs from his LP *DAMN,* along with the very outspoken and sociopolitically conscious Bono and The Edge of U2. As Dave Chapelle, who served as a sort of "Greek chorus" in Lamar's performance argues, "the only thing more frightening than watching a black man be honest in America is being an honest black man in America. Rumble young man, rumble." See Madison Vain, "Kendrick Lamar, Bono, the Edge Open the Grammys with a Fiery 'XXX' Performance," *Entertainment Weekly*, January 28, 2018, https://ew.com/grammys/2018/01/28/grammys-2018-u2-kendrick-performance/

16 "The 2018 Pulitzer Prize Winner in Music," https://www.pulitzer.org/winners/kendrick-lamar. Note that Lamar also composed and cultivated the soundtrack for Coogler's *Black Panther*.

17 Smith and Anderson, "Appendix A."

18 Smith and Anderson, "Appendix A."

19 "Mobile Fact Sheet"; "Internet/Broadband Fact Sheet."

20 Nadeska, "Issa Rae Talks."

21 See Laurel Wamsley, "'One Must Respect the Game': French Open Bans Serena Williams's Catsuit," *NPR.org*, August 24, 2018. During the French Open, Bernard Giudicelli, president of the French Tennis Association, targeted Serena Williams's attire in an interview with *Tennis* magazine, although she had given birth in 2017

and wore a high-compression, black catsuit inspired by *Black Panther* to prevent blood clots.

22   Harpersbazaarus, "August Cover Reveal." Instagram photo, July 9, 2019. https:// www.instagram.com/p/BzssfHDFnFM/.

23   During his NBA career (with the Philadelphia 76ers), Iverson was notorious for rule breaking (i.e., practicing while hungover, missing team events, disobeying the league's dress code) and an unwillingness to follow societal rules. His tattoos, cornrows, and single-arm sleeve combined with a rule-shirking attitude produced a public persona that many urban youth—both male and female—embraced.

24   Twitter (@Twitter), "Top 9 Most Retweeted Tweets of 2017," Twitter, December 5, 2017. https://twitter.com/i/moments/937834305920700416. James was responding to the president's rescinding of the Golden State Warriors' invitation to the White House after they won the 2017 NBA Championship (via Twitter). Although Steph Curry previously indicated that most of the Warriors would not be going as a result of the president's policies and behavior, the president's tweet was a means of "saving face" for his rabid base. LeBron James threw shade in response.

25   UNITERRUPTED, "Kevin Durant x LeBron James x Cari Champion: Rolling with the Champion." Uploaded on February 15, 2018. YouTube video, 16:44 min. https:// www.youtube.com/watch?v=HtNWc1AIU20&feature=youtu.be.

26   "LeBron James fires back at Laura Ingraham." *The Boston Globe*, February 17, 2018, https://www.boston.com/sports/nba/2018/02/17/lebron-james-fox-news-laura -ingraham. And as if her words lit an activist fire in James, in August 2018, Akron public schools opened the I Promise School with significant funding from James's foundation—a school that aids at-risk youth, largely children of color, guarantees free college tuition to graduates, and embraces the lived reality that without family education to accompany child education, many at-risk youth and their families will not break the cycles they traverse. Later in November of that same year, James co-executive produced a three-part documentary exploring the history of intersections between the NBA and civic responsibility, titled appropriately *Shut Up and Dribble* (Showtime).

27   Jefferson, *Notes on the State of Virginia*, chapter 15.

28   Locke, *The New Negro*, 259, 256, 266–67.

29   Schuyler, "The Negro Art Hokum," 1172–73.

30   Hughes, "The Negro Artist and the Racial Mountain," 1268.

31   Du Bois, "Criteria of Negro Art," 296.

32   Baraka, "Black Art," *Transbluency*, 142–43.

33   Giovanni, "For Saundra," *The Collected Poetry of Nikki Giovanni*, 80.

34   Fuller, "Journey toward a Black Aesthetic," 1872, 1876.

35   "Frequency."

36   Neal, *Soul Babies*, 2–3.

37   Hall, "What Is This 'Black' in Black Popular Culture?," 28, 29.

References

Baraka, Amiri. "Black Art" (1965). *Transbluency: The Selected Poetry of Amiri Baraka/LeRoi Jones (1961–1995)*. New York: Marsilio, 1995, 142–43.

Bernstein, Jacob. "Jay-Z and Barneys Announce Substantial Changes in Their Partnership." *New York Times*, November 18, 2013. https://www.nytimes.com/2013/11/18/fashion/jay-z-and-barneys-announce-substantial-changes-in-their-partnership.html.

Browne, Rembert. "Donald Glover's Community: The Comic Turns His Eye to His Hometown—and Black America—in *Atlanta*." *Vulture*, August 23, 2016. http://www.vulture.com/2016/08/donald-glover-atlanta.html.

Cashmore, Ellis. *The Black Culture Industry*. New York: Routledge, 1997.

Demby, Gene. "Harry Belafonte, Jay Z, and Intergenerational Beef." NPR, July 30, 2013. http://www.npr.org/blogs/codeswitch/2013/07/30/207068455/harry-belafonte-jay-z-and-inter-generational-beef.

Du Bois, W. E. B. "Criteria of Negro Art." *The Crisis*, 32 (October 1926): 290–97.

Duggan, Maeve. "The Demographics of Social Media Users." *Pew Research Center*, August 19, 2015. http://www.pewinternet.org/2015/08/19/the-demographics-of-social-media-users/.

"Frequency." Studio Museum Harlem. N.d. http://www.studiomuseum.org/exhibition/frequency.

Fuller, Hoyt. "Journey toward a Black Aesthetic." PhD diss., University of Massachusetts, Amherst, 2011.

Giovanni, Nikki. "For Saundra" (1966). *The Collected Poetry of Nikki Giovanni: 1968–1998*. New York: William Morrow, 2003, 80.

Hall, Stuart. "What Is This 'Black' in Black Popular Culture?" *Social Justice*, 20, no. 1–2 (spring 1993): 104–15.

Harpersbazaarus. "August Cover Reveal." Instagram photo, July 9, 2019. https://www.instagram.com/p/BzssfHDFnFM/

Hartman, Saidiya V. *Scenes of Subjection: Terror, Slavery, and Self-Making in Nineteenth Century America*. Oxford: Oxford University Press, 1997.

Hughes, Langston. "The Negro Artist and the Racial Mountain." *The Nation*, 122 (June 23, 1926): 692–94.

"Internet/Broadband Fact Sheet." Pew Research Center, February 5, 2018. http://www.pewinternet.org/fact-sheet/internet-broadband/.

LeBron James Fires Back at Laura Ingraham." *The Boston Globe*, February 17, 2018. https://www.boston.com/sports/nba/2018/02/17/lebron-james-fox-news-laura-ingraham.

Locke, Alain, ed. *The New Negro* (1925). New York: Atheneum, 1992.

Minsker, Evan. "Grammys 2017: Beyoncé's 'Daddy Lessons' Rejected by Country Committee." *Pitchfork*, December 8, 2016. https://pitchfork.com/news/70299-grammys-2017-beyonces-daddy-lessons-rejected-by-country-committee/.

Miranda, Lin-Manuel. "Alexander Hamilton." *Hamilton: An American Musical*. New York: Atlantic, 2015.

"Mobile Fact Sheet." Pew Research Center, February 5, 2018. http://www
.pewinternet.org/fact-sheet/mobile/.

Moten, Fred. *In the Break: The Aesthetics of the Black Radical Tradition*. Minneapolis:
University of Minnesota Press, 2003.

Nadeska, Alexis. "Issa Rae Talks 'Insecure' Season 2, Old TV Execs Dying Off, and
Life Goals." *Complex*, July 23, 2017. http://www.complex.com/pop-culture/issa
-rae-interview-2017-cover-story.

Neal, Mark Anthony. *Soul Babies: Black Popular Culture and the Post-Soul Aesthetic*.
New York: Routledge, 2001.

Palmer, Tamara. "How the 'Billie Jean' Video Changed MTV." *The Root*, March 10,
2013. http://www.theroot.com/how-the-billie-jean-video-changed-mtv
-1790895543.

Politi, Daniel. "The Slatest: Watch *Hamilton* Cast Deliver Message to Mike Pence:
'Uphold Our American Values.'" *Slate*, November 19, 2016. http://www.slate
.com/blogs/the_slatest/2016/11/19/watch_hamilton_cast_deliver_message_to
_mike_pence_uphold_our_american_values.html.

Pulitzer Foundation. "The 2018 Pulitzer Prize Winner in Music." https://www
.pulitzer.org/winners/kendrick-lamar

Schuyler, George S. "The Negro Art Hokum." *The Nation*, 122 (June 16, 1926):
662–63.

Smith, Aaron. "Detailed Demographic Tables." Pew Research Center, January 6,
2014. http://www.pewinternet.org/2014/01/06/detailed-demographic-tables/.

Smith, Aaron, and Monica Anderson. "Appendix A: Detailed Table." Pew Research
Center, March 1, 2018. http://www.pewinternet.org/2018/03/01/social-media
-use-2018-appendix-a-detailed-table/.

St. Félix, Doreen. "Beyoncé's Triumphant Homecoming at Coachella." *New Yorker*,
April 16, 2018. https://www.newyorker.com/culture/culture-desk/beyonces
-triumphant-homecoming-at-coachella.

Twitter (@Twitter). "Top 9 Most Retweeted Tweets of 2017." Twitter, December 5,
2017. https://twitter.com/i/moments/937834305920700416.

UNINTERRUPTED. "Kevin Durant x LeBron James x Cari Champion: Rolling with
the Champion." Uploaded on February 15, 2018, 16:44 min. YouTube. https://
www.youtube.com/watch?v=HtNWc1AIU20&feature=youtu.be.

Waddell, Ray. "Beyonce's Formation Tour Sold over 2 Million Tickets and Made
over $250 Million." *Billboard*, October 14, 2016. http://www.billboard.com
/articles/business/7541993/beyonce-formation-tour-2-million-tickets-250
-million-dollars.

Wamsley, Laurel. "'One Must Respect the Game': French Open Bans Serena
Williams's Catsuit."

Catsuit." *NPR.org*, August 24, 2018. https://www.npr.org/2018/08/24/641549735/one
-must-respect-the-game-french-open-bans-serena-williams-catsuit.

White, Dan. "'Beloved' Author Speaks about Writing, Revelations, and Good and
Evil." *UC Santa Cruz Newscenter*, October 22, 2014. https://news.ucsc.edu/2014
/10/rev-fall-14-beloved-author.html.

I. PERFORMING BLACKNESS

CH.1   **"MUTTS LIKE ME"** / MIXED-RACE JOKES
AND POST-RACIAL REJECTION IN THE
OBAMA ERA

Ralina L. Joseph

In November 2008, the halcyon days of the first Black
president-elect, euphoria swept many progressive and liberal enclaves of the
United States. For perhaps the first time in his impending presidency, Barack
Obama let the entire country glimpse his then-well-guarded sense of humor.
In his very first presidential press conference, flanked by his vice president,
chief of staff, and other senior advisors (see figure 1.1), Obama fielded a reporter's question: "I'm wondering what you're doing to get ready?" After the
president-elect delineated a laundry list that included consulting with former presidents and choosing a school for his daughters, the reporter asked
a follow-up question: "Everyone wants to know what kind of dog you want
to buy for your girls." Obama smiled genially, looked down, and responded
with a reverential tone:

FIG.1.1 More serious moments at Obama's first press conference. Source: Getty Images, USA 2008 Presidential Election: President-elect Obama's First Press Conference, accessed August 21, 2017. http://www.gettyimages.ca/detail/news-photo/president-elect-barack-obama-holds-his-first-press-news-photo/534289284?#president-elect-barack-obama-holds-his-first-press-conference-in-picture-id534289284.

With respect to the dog, this is a major issue. I think it's generated more interest on our website than just about anything. We have two criteria that have to be reconciled. One is that Malia is allergic, so it has to be hyper-allergenic. There are a number of breeds that are hyper-allergenic. On the other hand our preference would be to get a shelter dog. But obviously a lot of shelter dogs are *mutts like me* [my emphasis]. So whether we are going to be able to balance those two things is a pressing issue on the Obama household.[1]

When Obama straight-faced but winkingly referred to himself as a "mutt," he ushered in some much-needed levity to the dawn of his presidency and to a then little joked-about but highly debated topic: Barack Obama's mixed-race African American background. In his first election campaign, the press framed Obama as *either* African American *or* mixed-race but never *both* African American *and* mixed-race. I use the cumbersome but inclusive phrase "mixed-race African American" to buck such either/or dichotomization and

FIG. 1.2 Obama enlightens and delights the ladies of *The View*. Source: Wikimedia, accessed August 21, 2017, https://upload.wikimedia.org/wikipedia/commons/d/d9/Barack _Obama_guests_on_The_View.jpg.

stake a claim for mixedness in blackness and blackness in mixedness, a move I believe twenty-first-century mixed-race African American figures such as Obama make through such "mutts like me" moments.[2]

Obama's joke reclaimed a racialized slur, the misfit animal created by crossing two "pure breeds." Nearly two years later, Obama applied a similar word not just to multiracial folks of African descent but to all African Americans. On the daytime talk show *The View* he commented, "The interesting thing about the African-American experience in this country is that we are sort of a mongrel people. I mean we're all kinds of mixed-up" (see figure 1.2). He continued, "Now that's actually true for white America as well, but we just know more about [black folks being mixed]."[3] On the one hand, by asserting mixture further into whiteness, Obama blasphemously sullied an assumed-to-be-pure entity; on the other hand, he neutralized the potentially threatening nature of racial mixture by inserting it into whiteness.

By reclaiming terms such as "mutt" and its closely related cousin "mongrel" as "us" terms for Black people, whether multiracially or monoracially identified, and even tucking whites under the Black American rubric of historical mixture, Obama ensured that these words would fail to stay hurtful "them" epithets. This remained the case even as they continued to be hurled at Obama via anonymous missives online; it was even so in the face of celebrity attacks such as when the aging rocker and rabid Republican Ted Nugent described the president at a January 2014 gun expo in Las Vegas as a "communist-raised, communist-educated, communist-nurtured, subhuman mongrel."[4] "Mongrel," while perhaps more scientific sounding and certainly more vitriolic in tone than the colloquial and lovable "mutt," is the historical term used by defenders of enslavement for mixed-race African Americans and by eugenicists for Jews in Nazi Germany.[5] Obama's use of these two words showed a simultaneous embrace of his mixedness and blackness as an effort to cast race as a still central, and not post-racial, issue.

In this essay I examine how the Obama era ushered in a certain brand of masculine, mixed-race, African American humor perhaps best performed by Obama and two famous comedic impersonators, Keegan-Michael Key and Jordan Peele. This utterly twenty-first-century iteration of mixed-race African Americanness represented by Obama, Key, and Peele knits together blackness with mixed-race (and vice versa) for a complicated, fluid, and inclusive conception of mixed-race blackness for two ultimate purposes: a rejection of hegemonic, troublesome, and ultimately false ideas that the United States is now post-racial, and an assertion that mixed-race blackness must be understood as one of the many iterations of what it means to be African American.

Mixed-Race (Black), Not Post-Racial (American)

Obama's joke set the stage for other comics to gently rib the president. For example, at Obama's first White House Correspondents' Dinner, in 2009, Wanda Sykes jokingly suggested that Obama's being a "mulatto" complicated other African Americans' claiming him as "the first black President."[6] While the term "mutt" might appear to be solely about Obama's assumed racialized biology—as if race and biology were actually paired anywhere outside of spurious science—that biology also complicated perceptions of his political and personal allegiances. Where did his loyalties lie, as a sellout mulatto or as a down-for-the-cause race man? Throughout his two presidential terms, Obama exhaustingly answered the question of racial identification—not least by disclosing that he checked "Black, African Am., or Negro" on the 2010 census and did not choose to "mark one or more."[7] Obama's results for his litmus test of authentic blackness were still up for debate, however, in many circles throughout his presidency.

With Obama, "mixed" (not paired with African American) was not deployed in the popular press as a mere description of family lineage. It was a Rorschach test of racial allegiance. Not coincidentally, as Obama ascended to presidential heights in 2008, so did two race words: post-race and mixed-race. Obama's "mutts like me" joke occurred at the moment in which much of the country was still grappling with the question of whether he identified as (in that very narrow formulation) mixed-race *or* (not *and*) Black. At this same moment, Catherine Squires points out, the word "post-race" was peaking in public discourse, and the media iterated an imagined "multiracial America," not the least embodied by our new president as the magical means to achieve a "post-racial" state.[8] While popular discourses link these terms, race scholars and critics refute the connection. The artist and activist Louie Gong puts it best: "Mixed race isn't post-race. It's not less race. It's more race. . . . In order to dialog about mixed race, we need more understanding. It's not a dialog to forget about issues of race."[9]

Understanding mixed-race as more race, or what Greg Carter describes as "an abundance of race," provides us with an opportunity to engage with the structuring and multiple ideologies of racialization. We can then reject, again, in Carter's words, "racelessness, color-blindness, or post-raciality" and instead form "a racial identity [as] a preliminary step towards antiracist activity."[10] In a similar vein, Michele Elam explains, "Mixed race prompts us to consider that race, too, is an image that is never perceived as 'one thing' or the possession of just one person. Rather, mixed race functions as a relation among things and people."[11] What Carter and Elam suggest in the burgeoning field of critical mixed-race studies is that mixed-race does not have to be the way out of discussions of race but can be a way deeper into them. Extrapolated further, Obama's "mutt" and "mongrel" references provide us with a path toward each other; being "purebred," the mythical state available to only a select few, isn't offered as even a rhetorical possibility.

Yet, unlike Obama's frame, the media often situates mixed-race African American figures away from larger African American communities by describing them as exceptional or pathological. This is precisely the separation Obama refused with his "mongrel" comment on *The View* and what Sika Dagbovie-Mullins calls "black sentient mixed-race identity . . . [that] intimates a mixed-race subjectivity that includes a particular awareness of the world, a perception rooted in blackness."[12] The isolation of mixed-race figures in media works against a "black sentient mixed-race identity" through the conflation of mixed-race and post-race and through efforts to excise blackness from mixedness. Popular discourse offers that mixing races makes them diminish, become irrelevant, or even disappear as they descend into this strange prefix, "the post." The idea of being after, being away from, being released from race circulates through ideas on racial mixing as the media posit the browning of America as the answer to our racial ills.

One strain of post-racial logic presents the notion that mixing, and in particular mixing blackness and whiteness, the two far-flung poles on our social distance scales, cancels out real (read: monoracial) races and all of the entrenched racial histories that accompany perceived monoraciality. Because, as Brandi Catanese notes, "twenty-first century social graces dictate that reference to race always be issued *sotto voce*, so as not to cause any undue discomfort," race is treated as "the unruly chin hair on the face of an otherwise unblemished America: only bad manners would compel anyone to bring it up, and the politest among us will instead do others the favor of not mentioning a thing that can only cause embarrassment, discomfort, or shame."[13] What is shaming for white Americans, or what causes what Robin DiAngelo calls "white fragility" or the inability to deal with race-based stress, is that racial difference equates to racial disparity, and that one's racialized privilege operates in direct relation to another's racialized oppression.[14]

However, in the popular U.S. imagination, mixture remains untethered from racial disparity; it becomes a way out of the race talk. In other words, instead of mixed-race providing an opportunity to deal with the realities of structural racism, as critical mixed-race studies scholars enjoin us, it becomes the imagined panacea to all race ills. Mixed-race creates a blank slate akin to "the post," two new beginnings for race—the dawn that arises after the postapocalyptic racial explosion. LeiLani Nishime asserts, "Multiracial people [are invoked] as an emerging racial category to argue that they act as a stepping-stone to a race-free future."[15] Thus the pain of racial wounds is magically healed by the salve of mixed-race without the infection of racism ever being treated. This false and dangerous idea is not, as David Ikard puts it, "a radical shift in racial thinking but rather an updated version of white supremacist ideology."[16]

Obama's "mutt" and "mongrel" references refuted such post-racial "white supremacist ideology" in the manner in which these terms are very much attached to primordial, old-school notions of mixed-race. He took an old stereotype and robbed it of its power by reclaiming it. In his first presidential election campaign, Obama's mixed-race African Americanness enabled both overtly racist images of him as an ape, thug, or terrorist, as well as post-racial, inferentially racist images of him as messiah, whites' "black best friend," or a mythical creature.[17] However, Obama's public negotiation of his mixed-race African Americanness did not migrate into post-racial territory even as he benefited from the association between mixed-race and post-race. In the first election campaign, he rhetorically transcended his blackness by dropping a mixed-race joke or reference to his white family's Kansas roots, thereby assuring mainstream accessibility. At the same time, he consistently signified on his blackness, maintaining allegiance to African American audiences.

Obama's public *naming* of his whiteness and *claiming* of his blackness was consistent with his *joking embrace* of his mixedness. Our forty-fourth president managed to exhibit a racial fluidity with racial narratives that became familiar and even comfortable because of his performance of a mixed-race African American masculinity that sutured together blackness and mixedness.[18] Obama's public race negotiation enabled an African American mixed-race form of what Catanese deems "transgression," which acknowledges "the histories of social location that people wear on their bodies and inform all of our interpretive frameworks."[19] The lesson for audiences remains that certain performances of mixed-race African Americanness can indeed be powerful rejections of post-racialism. While Obama is not the sole architect of such a performance, his enactment of it has brought discourses of anti-post-racialism and mixed-race African American masculinity to the public sphere in a more mainstream manner than ever before.

Key and Peele

Obama's rise to fame set the stage for the ascension of two mixed-race African American comics, Keegan-Michael Key and Jordan Peele. Unlike mixed-race stars of past decades such as Vin Diesel, who coyly avoided disclosing their racial makeup, the comics have freely shared their biographies with the press, noting that they both have a white mother and a Black father.[20] Because the most famous person in the world shared a racial background with the two comics, the time was right for their biographies to become a part of their public image. Peele notes that in their pitch for their show, one line that made the network president's "eyes light up" was his sharing that, "because of Obama, people are realizing that there's this mixed community that has a very interesting perspective."[21] Like Obama, both comics are regularly called *either* but not *both* Black or mixed-race in the press fairly interchangeably. After the two costarred on the sketch-comedy television show *MADtv*, they began hosting their own highly successful sketch-comedy series *Key & Peele* (2012–15) on the cable television network Comedy Central.[22]

FIG.1.3 Key and Peele as President Obama and his anger translator Luther. Source: Jennifer Konerman, "Watch Key and Peele's Farewell Address as Obama and His 'Anger Translator,' Luther," *Billboard*, January 6, 2017, http://www.billboard.com/articles/news/7647624/key-and-peele-farewell-address-as-obama-anger-translator-luther.

Both on and off the show, Key and Peele freely played with stereotypes about their own mixed-race blackness, both literally (in exaggerated versions of themselves during on-stage bits between skits) and metaphorically (in characters like Obama and Luther, his "anger translator," who said all that controlled, straight-laced Obama could not; see figure 1.3).

The duo have become darlings of the critics as well, described by Emily Nussbaum in the *New Yorker* as "the best, most transgressive comics [who] treat human behavior as a form of drag, shape-shifting with aggressive fluidity." The critic added, "Key and Peele's biracialism is central to their comedy. . . . It is expansive, not constricting, a Golden Ticket to themes rarely explored on television."[23] A racialized "look" didn't matter in Key and Peele's racialized formulation; while Key would read to many audiences as more racially ambiguous and Peele as unambiguously African American, their explicit mixed-race African American race talk expansively claimed both of their phenotypes as authentically mixed-race *and* African American. If Obama's "mutt" joking was reclaiming an old stereotype—putting it front

and center in developing an ultimately transgressive, anti-post-racial ethos—
Key and Peele's mixed-race African American jokes skewered the very idea
of the post-racial and made all aspects of mixed-race African American masculinity available for comedic fodder.

"It Literally Doesn't Get Any More Impartial Than That"

Key and Peele played up their mixed-race blackness most explicitly not in
the sketches on their show *Key & Peele* but when they played versions of
themselves outside of the sketches. To kick off the beginning of their third
season, in November 2013, Key and Peele were guests on Comedy Central's
The Daily Show with Jon Stewart.[24] In addition to joining Stewart at the desk,
as is traditional for his guests, the two participated in a segment befitting
their sketch-comedy background, "Racist or Not Racist." They were joined
by a panel of *The Daily Show* contributors: the African American Jessica
Williams (whose race is underscored by her satirical title, "junior black
correspondent"), the South Asian American Aasif Mandvi (underscored as
"senior Asian" and "senior Middle Eastern correspondent"), and the white
Jason Jones (whose whiteness is certainly played with in this skit, but not
in the same way as for the correspondents of color; for example, never in
the show is Jones—or any of the white contributors, for that matter—called
"white correspondent").

In this bit, Stewart skewered the flatness of cable news networks' reporting on stories pertaining to race and how the rush to label a person or action
as "racist" shuts down conversation, much less complex analysis. Stewart
presented different media stories, the first being an early elementary school-
age white boy dressing up as a Ku Klux Klan member for Halloween. Stewart
asked the panelists to weigh in on whether they believed the story to be
"RACIST" or "NOT RACIST." The capital letters on the cards accentuate the
emphatic nature of any proclamation: there are no grays in assessments of
racism. For this particular case, both Williams and Mandvi vehemently
flipped their "RACIST" cards, whereas a smiling, clueless Jones flipped his
to "ADORABLE." For another racialized incident both Williams and Mandvi flipped to "RACIST," while Jones flipped his card to "CREATIVE" (see figure 1.4). This satire played with notions of post-racialism and, in particular,
one of post-racialism's offshoots, so-called reverse discrimination. The cards
could be read as rhetorical iterations of "race cards," conversation halters believed to be thrown down by sensitive or delusional people of color to claim
victim status. But this was not exactly what was happening here.

FIG.1.4 Playing the "race cards." Source: "Racist or Not Racist?," *The Daily Show with Jon Stewart*, November 13, 2013, http://www.cc.com/video-clips/2jhh5v/the-daily-show-with -jon-stewart-racist-or-not-racist-.

Jones's frustration mounted as he saw the disconnect between his responses and those of the two people of color flanking him; he sputtered, "It would be nice if we could get some impartial judges here." With that line, Key and Peele sauntered onto stage. Jones, eyes wide, voice high and stuttering, balked, "Jon, they're, they're, they're not impartial." Key responded, "What are you talking about, we're both mixed-race," and Peele tag-teamed, "It literally doesn't get any more impartial than that." Jones stammered further, "You're both, you're both—" to which Key and Peele exclaimed, "Whoa, whoa, whoa right there, racist right there, racist." The comics teased out the notion that they would silence their so-called biased blackness and spotlight their impartial mixed-race. This move played against some viewers' visual understandings of race. According to U.S. racial literacy, Key and Peele do not pass for white. Their blackness (or, in the case of Key, nonwhiteness) is visible—despite their claims to mixed-race—and so it has to be their "real race." But the audience was not allowed to read blackness monolithically or monoracially because of the comics' highlighting of their mixed-race.

Read through the white male auteur lens of *The Daily Show*, Jones, the scapegoat white guy, could not iterate a racialized label for the two mixed-race African American men before getting cut off and labeled racist. This was the true post-racial move; as Eduardo Bonilla-Silva argues, the confused logic of post-racialism—or what he deems colorblind racism—suggests that real racism comes through the mere naming of race and from white claims of discrimination.[25] *The Daily Show*'s parody of post-racialism, then, surged when Jones suggested that he was the genuine casualty.

To continue, Stewart gave the duo the story they were instructed to weigh in about: "A *Washington Post* columnist named Richard Cohen . . . recently defended the Tea Party against charges of racism by suggesting that the country is just changing faster than they can adapt, which he phrased thusly, 'People with conventional views must repress a gag reflex when considering [Bill de Blasio] the mayor-elect of New York—a white man married to a black woman and with two biracial children.'" The two initially responded, as the audience was set up to expect, in just the same way as Williams and Mandvi: with people of color primordialism, they chose their "natural" sides. Key scoffed, "That guy is straight-up racist." Peele seconded his sentiment: "Oh yeah. He is a volcano of hate." But the show flipped the audience's assumptions of racial loyalty. After a long beat Peele continued, "Against white people." Key added, "He's giving white people no credit." Peele tag-teamed, "Basically he's saying, hey, you've got to cut the Tea Party some slack because they can't think straight because they're trying too hard not to vomit when they see a black guy with a white girl."

This bit flipped the audience's racial assumptions. With the card set up, they were primed to believe that Key and Peele would go with their visibly raced—that is, Black—sides. But the two did not fall into racialized assumptions. They toyed with notions of assumed partiality and the role of racial loyalty, or rather what racial fluidity meant in the Obama era, in a world with a mixed-race Black president. While primordial racialism and post-race attempted to delimit the representational space, Key and Peele broke out of it and, in doing so, pushed the ideological boundaries of post-racialism. Interestingly, they scripted themselves into the de Blasio bit, flipping the white man–Black woman pairing to a "black guy with a white girl," their own parental configurations and romantic pairings with white women.

This skit was part of their comedic bag of tricks where Black men were just as likely to do cosplay befitting a Renaissance fair as they were to be football players named Javaris Jamar Javarison-Lamar or African American survivors of a zombie apocalypse in which the racist zombies refused to eat Black people. Their mixed-race African American characters included a teenage boy who fretted over what he described as the diminutive Halloween candy "fun size" bar of his "white penis," due to the fact that he was not monoracially Black, as his friend had read him, but "biracial. All the white went straight to my penis."[26] Key and Peele regularly outed themselves as mixed-race in their biographical bits between sketches and examined how issues of Black authenticity entered into their lives. But they didn't isolate issues like "hav[ing] to adjust our blackness" as mixed-race problems. Instead, they skewered their "white talk," or how "we sound whiter than the black dude in the college a capella group" and how "we sound whiter than Mitt Romney in a snowstorm" for all "white-sounding black guys" regardless of their identifying as mixed-race. Such significations of allegedly inauthentic blackness, of how "you gotta dial [blackness] up a bit" because "you never want to be the whitest-sounding black guy in a room," were not the sole purview of mixed-race African Americans.[27] In all of these messy negotiations, Key and Peele were unabashedly African American *and* mixed-race, and their blackness and mixed-ness, their "white talk" and "black adjustment" served to illustrate the vast diversity of what it means to be both African American and mixed-race.

Key and Peele's mixed-race blackness was performed in codes where it enabled their racialized fluidity and skewering of racialized stereotypes; such coding also allowed the comics to flip (and in doing so, occasionally perform) controlling images of all African Americans. But when their multiraciality was made explicit, as it was on *The Daily Show with Jon Stewart*, they scoffed at the conflation of mixed-race and post-race. Post-race became a comedic enabling device to explicitly connect mixedness and blackness and to return to, rather than run away from, race. In the Obama era, mixed-race offered performers like Key and Peele, and even our forty-fourth president himself, the opportunity to negotiate with and through post-racialism without being trapped in its ideological prison.

Conclusion

Michael Omi and Howard Winant's theory of racial formation tells us that race is imagined, but it's not imaginary; just because it's constructed doesn't mean we don't live it.[28] Or, in the words of Stuart Hall, identities are not "armor-plated against other identities" and "are not tied to fixed, permanent, unalterable oppositions." Instead, identities are "historically specific" and a "set of practices."[29] Hall is explicating a contradiction about race that is also a truism. We believe racial differences. We see them. We hear them. We even sense them. Representations act as our barometer of and guide for popular sentiment; examining them illuminates the degree to which race is attached to—and untethered from—its primordial roots.

Mixed-race African American jokes, whether told by our president or by the comedians Key and Peele, are neither "racial" nor "post-racial" in and of themselves. The jokes move to the (post)racial realm with the question of audience. Audiences of all racial stripes chuckled together in a race conscious and not post-racial fashion, albeit perhaps uncomfortably, during Obama's press conference. In other words, audiences can laugh because mixed-race African American men remind us about the continued significance of race while providing us with the permission to simply laugh at our nation's greatest struggle: race. We can joke together while reclaiming the "mutt" or "mongrel" slurs, whether or not they have ever been applied to us, but we cannot forget why we are laughing. The materiality of race comes up too often in jokes by and about mixed-race African Americans for the end-game to be post-raciality. Our birth rates, our death rates, our education, health care, mortgages—all are racialized. None are post. One can only flip or reclaim a stereotype if that controlling image still holds weight—it can't be neutral. Obama's "mutt" joke, while contingent upon flipping old-school notions of race, activates post-racialism to slyly reference racism in the process of reclaiming racial stereotypes and prompting all of us to laugh together. Seeing the play and the parody with which mixed-race blackness is represented provided audiences with an accessible and playful model for how to reject post-racial ideology in what now feels like the long-ago moment of the Barack Obama era.

Notes

A preliminary version of this paper, "Does 'Mixed' Mean 'Post-Race'?: An Examination of 21st Century Media Representations of African American Multiraciality," was shared on February 27, 2014, at Macalester College as the keynote talk for the Mixed-Race America: Identities and Culture conference.

1 TwoEyesX, "Obama Prefers 'Mutt Like Me.'"
2 I use the terms "African American" and "Black" and the terms "mixed race" and "multiracial" interchangeably.
3 Youngman, "President Obama Calls African-Americans a 'Mongrel People.'"
4 Barabak, "Ted Nugent Apologizes, Somewhat."
5 Scales-Trent, "Racial Purity Laws," 273–74.
6 I discuss this particular joke in Transcending Blackness, 8–9.
7 Roberts and Baker, "Asked to Declare His Race." See also Williams, Mark One or More.
8 Squires, The Post-Racial Mystique, 25.

9 Quoted in Kina and Dariotis, *War Baby/Love Child*, 17.
10 Carter, *The United States of the United Races*, 227.
11 Elam, *The Souls of Mixed Folk*, 161.
12 Dagbovie-Mullins, *Crossing B(l)ack*, 2.
13 Catanese, *The Problem of the Color(blind)*, 5.
14 DiAngelo, "White Fragility," 54.
15 Nishime, *Undercover Asian*, 2.
16 Ikard, *Blinded by the Whites*, 8.
17 I argue this in my article "Imagining Obama."
18 In my book *Postracial Resistance: Black Women, Media, and the Uses of Strategic Ambiguity* (2018), I argue that Michelle Obama is actually a queen of the type of strategically ambiguous posturing that her husband enacts here as racial fluidity.
19 Catanese, *The Problem of the Color(blind)*, 22.
20 See Nishime, *Undercover Asian*; and Carter, *The United States of the United Races*.
21 Weiner, "Comedy Central in the Post-TV Era."
22 Siek, "'Key & Peele.'"
23 Nussbaum, "Color Commentary."
24 "Racist or Not Racist."
25 Bonilla-Silva, *Racism without Racists*.
26 Comedy Central, "Key & Peele: Mixed Wiener."
27 Comedy Central, "Key & Peele: White-Sounding Black Guys."
28 Omi and Winant, *Racial Formation*.
29 Hall, "Subjects in History," 292.

References

Barabak, Mark Z. "Ted Nugent Apologizes, Somewhat, for Calling Obama a 'Mongrel.'" *Seattle Times*, February 22, 2014.

Bonilla-Silva, Eduardo. *Racism without Racists: Color-Blind Racism and the Persistence of Racial Inequality in America*. Lanham, MD: Rowman and Littlefield, 2013.

Carter, Greg. *The United States of the United Races: A Utopian History of Racial Mixing*. New York: New York University Press, 2013.

Catanese, Brandi Wilkins. *The Problem of the Color(blind): Racial Transgression and the Politics of Black Performance*. Ann Arbor: University of Michigan Press, 2011.

Comedy Central. "Key & Peele: Mixed Wiener." YouTube, October 17, 2012. http://www.youtube.com/watch?v=klSMoAwjXJs.

Comedy Central. "Key & Peele: White-Sounding Black Guys." YouTube, January 31, 2012. http://www.youtube.com/watch?v=kO-EwelnvxU.

Dagbovie-Mullins, Sika A. *Crossing B(l)ack: Mixed-Race Identity in Modern American Fiction and Culture*. Knoxville: University of Tennessee Press, 2013.

DiAngelo, Robin. "White Fragility." *International Journal of Critical Pedagogy* 3, no. 3 (2011): 54–70.

Elam, Michele. *The Souls of Mixed Folk: Race, Politics, and Aesthetics in the New Millennium.* Stanford, CA: Stanford University Press, 2011.

Hall, Stuart. "Subjects in History: Making Diasporic Identities." In *The House That Race Built*, edited by Waheema Lubiano. New York: Vintage Books, 1998.

Ikard, David. *Blinded by the Whites: Why Race Still Matters in 21st-Century America.* Bloomington: Indiana University Press, 2013.

Joseph, Ralina L. "Imagining Obama: Reading Overtly and Inferentially Racist Images of Our 44th President, 2007–2008." *Communication Studies* 62, no. 4 (2011): 389–405.

Joseph, Ralina L. *Postracial Resistance: Black Women, Media, and the Uses of Strategic Ambiguity.* New York: New York University Press, 2018.

Joseph, Ralina L. *Transcending Blackness: From the New Millennium Mulatta to the Exceptional Multiracial.* Durham, NC: Duke University Press, 2013.

Kina, Laura, and Wei Ming Dariotis, eds. *War Baby/Love Child: Mixed Race Asian American Art.* Seattle: University of Washington Press, 2013.

Nishime, LeiLani. *Undercover Asian: Multiracial Asian Americans in Visual Culture.* Urbana: University of Illinois Press, 2014.

Nussbaum, Emily. "Color Commentary: The Shape-Shifting Masterminds of 'Key and Peele.'" *New Yorker*, September 23, 2013. http://www.newyorker.com/arts /critics/television/2013/09/30/130930crte_television_nussbaum?currentPage=all.

Omi, Michael, and Howard Winant. *Racial Formation in the United States: From the 1960s to the 1980s.* New York: Routledge, 2014.

"Racist or Not Racist." *The Daily Show with Jon Stewart*, November 13, 2013. http:// www.cc.com/video-clips/2jhh5v/the-daily-show-with-jon-stewart-racist-or-not -racist-.

Roberts, Sam, and Peter Baker. "Asked to Declare His Race, Obama Checks 'Black.'" *New York Times*, April 2, 2010. http://www.nytimes.com/2010/04/03/us/politics /03census.html?_r=0.

Scales-Trent, Judy. "Racial Purity Laws in the United States and Nazi Germany: The Targeting Process." *Human Rights Quarterly* 23, no. 2 (2001): 260–307.

Siek, Stephanie. "'Key & Peele': The Color of Funny." *CNN*, February 24, 2012. http://inamerica.blogs.cnn.com/2012/02/24/key-peele-the-color-of-funny/.

Squires, Catherine. *The Post-Racial Mystique: Media and Race in the Twenty-First Century.* New York: New York University Press, 2014.

TwoEyesX. "Obama Prefers 'Mutt Like Me' [First Press Conference]." YouTube, November 7, 2008. http://www.youtube.com/watch?v=4uHn6ydl6TM&feature =related#t=01m34.

Weiner, Jonah. "Comedy Central in the Post-TV Era." *New York Times Magazine*, June 18, 2015. https://www.nytimes.com/2015/06/21/magazine/comedy-central -in-the-post-tv-era.html?_r=0.

Williams, Kim M. *Mark One or More: Civil Rights in Multiracial America.* Ann Arbor: University of Michigan Press, 2008.

Youngman, Sam. "President Obama Calls African-Americans a 'Mongrel People.'" *The Hill*, July 29, 2010. http://thehill.com/homenews/administration/111611 -obama-calls-african-americans-a-mongrel-people-.

BLACK RADIO / ROBERT GLASPER,
ESPERANZA SPALDING, AND
JANELLE MONÁE

Emily J. Lordi

This is not a great moment for U.S. radio. Streamlined and corporatized since the 1996 Telecommunications Act, radio stations have been displaced by new listening technologies like MP3s and streaming systems like Spotify.[1] Black-oriented stations, which since the mid-1970s have been driven more by "preprogrammed formats" than by DJs, are rendered invisible by *Billboard* metrics that consistently show white artists topping the R&B/Hip-Hop chart.[2] And on the AM side of the dial, National Public Radio canceled its one program aimed at African American listeners, *Tell Me More*, in spring of 2014.

It was therefore especially curious that, between 2012 and 2013, a period that might generously be called the twilight of American radio, three young and critically acclaimed African American musicians released four guest-star-studded radio-themed albums. The jazz pianist Robert Glasper and his quartet, the Robert Glasper Experiment, released his album *Black Radio* in the winter of 2012 and won the Grammy for Best R&B Album that year. The jazz bassist Esperanza Spalding's *Radio Music Society* appeared just one month later, following on the heels of Spalding's own Grammy Award for Best New Artist in 2011.[3] The musical polymath and sci-fi wiz Janelle Monáe released her radio-centric *Electric Lady* in September 2013. And Glasper's sequel album, *Black Radio 2*, appeared the following month. Despite their salient differences, Glasper, Spalding, and Monáe all share commitments to virtuosic musicianship, collaboration, and historically Black musical forms. I suggest that all three artists engage radio as a means and metaphor through which to explore tradition and innovation and to recalibrate their relationship to an imagined audience and industry. A detailed analysis of their "radio albums," from cover art to sound production, reveals how these leading African American artists are redefining Black music while negotiating their ambitions for musical excellence, popular appeal, and commercial success in the twenty-first century.

Why radio, and especially Black radio, now? We might begin by noting the crucial role Black radio outlets have historically played as what William Barlow calls "the 'talking drums' of their respective communities"—sources not only of music but also of otherwise inaccessible information about politics, fashion, sports, arts, and culture. A crucial space for community debate and mobilization, especially during the long civil rights movement, Black radio has been "a major force in constructing and sustaining an African American public sphere."[4] This role has been increasingly hard to sustain in our own era of massive corporate consolidation, but it nonetheless shapes Glasper's, Spalding's, and Monáe's work. All born between 1978 and 1985, these artists came of age just before the 1996 Telecom Act resulted in the consolidation that now allows Clear Channel to control over one thousand radio stations, while Radio One—one of the few black-owned stations to survive and thrive in an era of deregulation—dominates the "urban market."[5] Their resultant relationship to radio suggests a more specific way of periodizing Black musical production in what Mark Anthony Neal and others have called the "post-soul" era.[6] While Neal's work in the early 2000s was concerned with artists born after the formal civil rights movement (after 1968), Glasper, Spalding, and Monáe also indicate what is unique about artists born in the late-1970s, after the Telecom Act: they invoke Black radio partly in order to express nostalgia for and renewed commitment to the pre-1996 model of musically and economically free(r) airwaves. For instance, in 2012 Spalding explained her concept for *Radio Music Society* by describing her formative experience of hearing a variety of music on the radio as child, an experience she wanted to evoke for her listeners.[7] While African American artists and intellectuals have critiqued corporate control of black radio at least since Nelson George lamented "the death of rhythm & blues" in 1988, these emerging artists respond to this phenomenon in specific and ingenious ways: their radio albums expand perceived boundaries of black music, re-centralize and hail black radio, and revise the album as a form of collective compensation for musicians of color.[8] Black women musicians' work with this concept additionally regenders the male-dominated medium of radio, as I explain in more detail below.

All three projects display the expansiveness of black music by curating a diverse array of guest artists and styles, which they present as part of a DJ's cohesive playlist. What Neal writes of Glasper's *Black Radio* applies as well to Spalding's and Monáe's work: "The genius of [his] new recording is its willingness to expand the range of what we consider Black music and what Black radio might consider as appropriate for Black or so-called 'Urban' audiences."[9] In addition, by centralizing and revaluing black radio as a specific site with its own values and history, these artists can be seen to contest industry metrics that render black radio invisible. As opposed to "the old, black-radio-driven system" by which *Billboard* measured sales and airplay at black music–oriented record stores and radio stations, Chris Molanphy explains, the system launched in 2012 tracks undifferentiated digital sales and multiformat radio airplay of songs the company decides are R&B or hip hop.[10] Consequently, the R&B/Hip-Hop Chart loses its subcultural specificity and overrepresents white artists. In this context, black radio–themed albums are not only representative of but also *representing for* black radio, as well as the black artists and a core fan base that the industry ignores.

Glasper's, Spalding's, and Monáe's evocation of black radio is symbolic but also pragmatic: it signals their aspirations to actually *get on the radio.*[11] Their albums aim to critique and reform the system whereby, as Yasiin Bey (formerly Mos Def) sings on Glasper's title track, quoting Chuck D, "radio—suckas never play me."[12] In 1988, Chuck D was addressing black radio in particular, and while Glasper, Spalding, and Monáe have all expressed their desire to cross over from the jazz or R&B margins to a broader audience that we might associate with adult contemporary or Top 40 radio formats, black radio is also a key target for their work.[13] Nearly all the guest vocalists on Glasper's albums, from Ledisi to Musiq Soulchild and Brandy, are those whose careers have been sustained by contemporary R&B radio and black listeners—much as that audience once sustained Parliament, Teddy

Pendergrass, and Anita Baker. Lalah Hathaway's cover of Sade's "Cherish the Day" on *Black Radio* is one reminder of this history, as it pertains to Sade's own success; Monáe's decision to feature Prince on her lead single "Q.U.E.E.N." is another.[14]

Even if these albums do not result in singles that get radio play, the albums themselves constitute an innovation too powerful to be called a "plan B." In the midst of the single-download system, these artists use the theme of radio to revive the concept album and ask that all guest artists get paid—and not only for their work on the album but also for their own solo work, which these radio albums might prompt listeners to buy. In short, the radio album is a unique format through which post–Telecom Act African American artists present a unified vision of musical diversity that privileges artistic collaboration and collective compensation.

"Lift Off": Radios, Boomboxes, and Floating Studios

The first track of Glasper's *Black Radio*, "Lift Off," conjures an ethereal sonic space, half–radio station/half–floating recording studio. As is the case with the other lead tracks I will discuss, the form and production of this first song teaches us how to listen to the album as a whole. "Lift Off" opens with the Golden Age of Soul Radio DJ patter that artists have used to introduce their albums since Jimi Hendrix's *Axis Bold as Love* (1967) and Parliament's *Mothership Connection* (1975):

> *Coming to your mind*
> *live and direct from the ethers*
> *now it's all in your speakers,*
> *down to your sneakers."*[15]

The surround-sound production, which seems best suited for privatized listening through headphone "speakers," ultimately places the listener in the midst of a recording studio. The album's guest artists do a simultaneous mic check in which certain voices come through distinctly. This kaleidoscopic mix, the sonic counterpart to the cover image that fragments Glasper's face into several panels, serves myriad functions. First, it emphasizes the artists' musicianship and professionalism: Erykah Badu warms up with vocal exercises, Yasiin Bey asks for more sound in his left ear, and Glasper plays scales. In addition to evoking the "high art" setting of a chamber music performance, the warm-ups also serve to highlight the fact that the Robert Glasper Experiment recorded all tracks live in the studio.[16] But the layered composition additionally makes the logistically impossible suggestion that all the guest artists were in the studio at the same time, recording on different tracks or coming in through different stations. This is the fantasy of the album as radio.

What this radio album will do, the production implies, is prize both live acoustic instrumentation and electronic manipulation. Glasper's piano occupies the lowest part of the mix, which includes the warm male voice of Shafiq Husayn in the middle range and, at the top, a synthesized piano-voice admixture in which a vocoded voice sings a melody mimicking and contrapuntally interacting with Glasper's piano line. While the use of synthesizers in jazz and R&B initially aroused widespread anxieties about inhuman "coldness," with this introduction Glasper stakes his place in a generation of listeners raised on the synthesized sounds of the 1970s and 1980s—those who have paradoxically "grown used to connecting *machines* and *funkiness*," in Andrew Goodwin's terms.[17] Thanks to artists like Stevie Wonder, whom Glasper channels through a cover version of "Jesus Children of America" (1973) and who "tapped into [synthesizers'] obscured potential as human empathizers," the Moog synthesizer now evokes the sound of soul and funk and the bodily experience of dance.[18]

Thanks to West Coast hip-hop producers such as Dr. Dre, it also connotes the physical sensations created by car audio technology.[19] The evocation of Dr. Dre reveals a more contemporary reference point for Glasper's mix of high-pitched synthesizer and live instrumentation.[20] Describing the spatial aspects of hop-hip production, Justin Williams writes, "Dr. Dre's interest in synthesizers may be influenced by a nostalgia for funk music, a fascination with earlier technologies, or his general feeling that they are 'warmer' than sound sampled from a record. While any attempt to locate his exact reasoning would be speculative, the timbres of synthesized sounds are strikingly compatible with car audio technology and the driving experience."[21] In Glasper's track, the radio DJ patter and the synthesized voice evoke the mobile listening environment of the car, while the live instrumentation and the staging of the recording studio simultaneously evoke a stationary space. The production thus asks us to imagine a floating or flying studio. "Lift Off" takes the traditional space of the recording studio and flies it toward an unknown future.

Next is Erykah Badu's version of "Afro Blue." Composed by the Cuban American artist Mongo Santamaria in 1959, set to lyrics by Oscar Brown Jr., and covered by Abbey Lincoln before being recorded by John Coltrane in 1963, "Afro Blue" embodies the dense, international network that characterizes the history of jazz. The tracks that follow Badu's showcase such undersung or emerging talents as Ledisi, KING, and Chrisette Michele, before closing with Bilal's cover of David Bowie's "Letter to Hermione" and Meshell Ndegeocello's cover of Nirvana's "Smells Like Teen Spirit." If these artists, like those featured on *Black Radio 2*, "aren't heard much on 'urban' radio," according to NPR, "the point is that they [should] be."[22] Glasper's taste-making project becomes clear in a dialogue staged at the album's midpoint ("Gonna Be Alright") in which he and his friends agree that "people are just so brainwashed" that they can't tell good from bad music anymore.[23] The *Black Radio* project is motivated as much by their desire to reach new fans as by a condescending urge to save them from their own ignorance, as induced by corporate radio. Therein lies the final meaning of black radio that Glasper invokes: the one destruction-proof archive on an aircraft that is, as Yasiin Bey sings, "built to last." As Glasper explains it, "When music is crashing around us, when you hear the same five songs on the radio that aren't really saying much, we can always go back to great music. Great music always lives on."[24]

Whereas Glasper wants his music to replace what is currently on the radio, Spalding seeks to cultivate a taste for her music in addition to what people might already (justifiably) like. Thus, for Spalding, the radio is less archive than broadcasting system. Released by Heads Up International in March 2012, *Radio Music Society* was designed to ride the exposure Spalding received with her Best New Artist Grammy win and to distribute that exposure to others. In fact, she noted, "I want to take a lot of the players that I know that are really phenomenal jazz musicians right now, put them in these songs, and format it in a way that will end up on the radio without compromising the soul and the core of improvised music."[25] Like Glasper's, her album features a mix of originals and covers, as well as what *All Music* calls "truckloads of players" from across generations: Q-Tip helps produce some tracks; jazz veterans like Terri Lyne Carrington and Jack DeJohnette play drums; and emerging singers such as Gretchen Parlato and Algebra Blessett contribute vocals.[26] Still, as Nate Chinen writes, Spalding is "front and center at every turn."[27]

Her emphasis on exposure or access reflects Gabriel Rossman's contention that, despite radio's decline since the 1990s, radio still plays a crucial role in alerting listeners to new music and thus in driving record sales.[28] As Spalding told NPR, "The benefit of the radio is, something beyond your realm of knowledge can surprise you, can enter your realm of knowledge."[29] Whereas Glasper's collaborations with hip hop and R&B artists aim to make jazz more *aesthetically* accessible—he tells NPR that "the music is going to die if you don't tap into something that people today can relate to"[30]—Spalding views jazz accessibility in more pragmatic or logistical terms. She explains, "[*Radio Music Society*] stems from my concern about the accessibility of jazz, just how people can access it. If you don't already know about jazz music, how would you be exposed?"[31] By implying that innovation and mass appeal are compatible concepts, Spalding conveys an inviting trust and respect for her imagined listening community.

This is true of the self-reflexive opening track, "Radio Song," which shrewdly expresses Spalding's desire to reach listeners where they are—to acquaint jazz novices with song structure and experimental variation—as well as a playful refusal to bend to the demands of corporate radio. The video for the song features everyday people listening in via transistor and car radios and singing as they perform janitorial work or deal with rush-hour traffic. In this sense, the song seeks to shape its own future: it is about how much people will enjoy listening to it on the radio. At the same time, Spalding's evocation of radio play is a joke; clocking in at six-and-a-half minutes, "Radio Song" is twice the length of a radio-formatted song. What's more, aside from its consistent dynamics and looped refrain, the song does not possess characteristics of car-oriented pop production such as synthesizers and heavy bass.[32] Thus we might say that Spalding revises listener-friendliness as a function of repetition rather than brevity: her song is long because it is designed to teach the listener how to sing along with it.

If Glasper's opening track engages the tradition/experimentation nexus through production, Spalding's does so through composition. "Radio Song" opens with a repeated mellow "la la" that introduces Spalding's smooth contralto sound and establishes the song's layered harmonies and syncopated groove.[33] From here, Spalding sings two verses and a chorus that both musically and lyrically resolve the problem the verses outline:

> *Right now you need it,*
> *driving yourself through the hard times,*
> *traffic won't speed up*
> *so you turn the radio on. . . .*
>
> *Well somehow he feels it*
> *And the DJ at the station*
> *sends sweet salvation*
> *when he starts to play this song:*

Now you can't help singing along,
even though you never heard it, you keep singing it wrong!
This song will keep you grooving (keep traffic movin')
Played to lift your spirits (soon as you hear it)
Words are speakin' to you (as if they knew you)
Ooh, this song's the one!

The chorus is looped so that Spalding's lyrical statement that you "can't help singing along" is couched in a musical structure that helps keep you from "singing it wrong." Aiming to familiarize the listener with the song while also opening her to innovation, Spalding creates a song about movement that keeps moving. She gives the listener a playful heads up—"and then they start mixing it up!"—before launching into a B-section that features a saxophone solo and wordy vocal runs. At the three-and-a-half-minute mark, she cuts back to the intro, and just as the song seems about to end, she revives it so that, soon enough, "Here comes the part you know!" She then repeats the chorus three times, features the piano in an improvised third section, and reprises the chorus in counterpoint to a funky vocal hook that takes us out into the fadeout. While the possibility of ending the song at the midpoint suggests that it could work as a radio single, Spalding's decision to double it bespeaks both a desire to meet listeners where they are (to teach them the song) and a desire to reform the radio system from within. In short, Spalding makes a point musically that Glasper makes rhetorically: this music *should* be on the radio, whether or not it is likely to be heard there.

Spalding's claim to authority in this domain has raced and gendered implications. The cover of *Radio Music Society*, which shows her seated atop a giant boom box, regenders the male-dominated medium of radio, both as broadcasting system and as mobile device. Stationed at the helm of her radio/world, Spalding is in control of her music and, in "Radio Song," of the airwaves. Her cover art also regenders the image of Radio Raheem, the character who lays a sonic claim to the urban landscape of Spike Lee's *Do the Right Thing* through his boom box broadcast of Public Enemy's "Fight the Power." Thus, at a moment when the mobile audio technology of the boom box has been displaced by laptops and iPhones, Spalding's use of this "vintage" technology signals a means of building community and of marking one's space within it. As Gaye Theresa Johnson writes, "Sonic expressions of spatial entitlement constitute some of the most eloquent articulations of the right to space."[34] And Spalding's album iconography reminds us that, as Alexander Weheliye writes, "black and Latino youth have been early adopters of 'street technologies,' especially portable music players such as the boom box and Walkman"—and, today, the mobile phone—that allow users "to occupy public space."[35] The giant Afro she sports on her cover marks her space as culturally black, even as her defiant posture suggests that music is her own means of "fighting the powers" of colonization in general and the corporatization of radio in particular.

Like Spalding and Glasper, Monáe collaborates with a diverse range of musicians—both her Atlanta-based collective, the Wondaland Arts Society, and her guest artists—to figure radio as a site of plurality and multiplicity. But while her album *Electric Lady* in some ways anticipates the radio play of its own singles, it also considers the expressive and ideological limitations of radio as a public medium. The album features several interludes at the imagined radio station 105.5 WDRD (an acronym suggesting multiple meanings, including "word," "wired," and "weird"). These skits preface Monáe's songs just as they might on actual radio. Indeed, the first skit on the album precedes her most radio-ready song, a standard verse-chorus-verse seduction duet with Miguel called "Prime Time." In this sense, the album reveals not only the fantastical aspects of Monáe's futurism but also the material, practical ways in which she aims to shape the future of her own work.

She also aims to shape the future of R&B. Whereas Glasper speaks of saving jazz by working with R&B and hip-hop artists, Monáe seeks to revive R&B. She tells Carrie Battan of *Pitchfork* that "somewhere along the way, R&B got lost—gatekeepers have recycled sounds . . . musicianship has declined."[36] In this 2013 interview, she expressed her ambition to "make one of the greatest R&B albums of this year" and to "[get] great music on the radio."[37] The three singles she has released—"Q.U.E.E.N.," "Dance Apocalyptic," and "Prime Time"—did not chart, although the album debuted at number five on the Billboard 200 chart.

Electric Lady itself stages a more ambivalent relationship to radio than Monáe's comments suggest. The album's orchestral overture, which fuses a surf-music guitar riff with Ennio Morricone's spaghetti western sound à la Quentin Tarantino's *Pulp Fiction* (1994), is a far cry from a pop single.[38] Like Glasper's introduction, Monáe's symphonic sound echoes the orchestral opening of her 2010 album, *The ArchAndroid*, and signals a chamber music standard of musicianship. But it offers a quite different sonic vision of "the West." If Glasper's live-and-synthesized production pays homage to Dr. Dre's West Coast car culture, Monáe's evocation of Morricone and surf music conjures a vision of the West as open sea and plain. Her sonic allusion to the cinematic western sets the scene for the entrance of the Stagger Lee–style outlaw, the role Monáe plays in the opening rock track "Givin 'Em What They Love."[39] Steeped in the musical and cinematic past—Monáe's front and back album covers evoke French New Wave film, *Star Wars*, and Michael Jackson's *Captain EO*—the album is initially geared more toward film than radio. Yet the album's production also recognizes radio as well as newer mobile technologies. "Prime Time" and the final track, "What an Experience," recall 1980s pop radio hits while also anticipating playback through laptops or smartphones. Exploiting synthesizers and drum machines, including the TR-808's ability to simulate tinny handclaps, both tracks reflect what Wayne Marshall calls the "trebly zeitgeist" of popular music geared toward mobile listening devices.[40]

If Monáe's skits court radio play, as I have said, they also de-romanticize radio as a site of communal transmission. Not only is the radio station a male space run by the funky "DJ Crash Crash" and shared by his ostensibly male cohort, but the call-in program he hosts also elicits violent, homophobic comments that reveal the threat of public airwaves. On the ironically titled "Our Favorite Fugitive," one caller declares herself "disgusted" by (fugitive) androids like Monáe's alter ego, Cyndi Mayweather; another sneers that "robot love is queer!," to which the DJ offers an unsatisfying rejoinder by wondering "how you would know it's queer . . . if you haven't tried it." Through such moments, Monáe exposes the heterosexist discourse sustained in the male-dominated radio space.

The album as a whole resists this patriarchal, homophobic space both musically and collaboratively. Monáe shares the spotlight with other black women artists, collaborating with Spalding on "Dorothy Dandridge Eyes" and with Badu on "Q.U.E.E.N." Both songs express same-sex desire and celebrate female beauty. Indeed, *Electric Lady* makes more space for black female (homo)sexual desire than do Monáe's other albums—and far more than does corporate radio. Although "Prime Time" is one of the album's least interesting tracks, the sensual performance marks a break from Monáe's own asexual android mold. In this respect, Monáe expands the range of performance choices available to black women artists, whether or not they end up on the radio. Her performance of desire also attunes us to Lalah Hathaway's sensual cover of "Cherish the Day," as well as Spalding's seduction song, "Kissed & Crowned": "Lay your burdens down, don't make a sound, don't worry about a thing, I'm here to love you." Those listeners who wished to hear more explicit expressions of black female desire in mainstream pop would have to wait for the December 2013 release of BEYONCÉ—although that is a subject for another day.

Conclusion: Sovereign Souls

Black radio has been figured as a repository for cultural memory at least since the Commodores' 1985 hit "Nightshift" elegized Jackie Wilson and Marvin Gaye. The musicians I have analyzed here, however, signal new modes of imagining radio as a cultural force. By staging their albums as radio broadcasts, Glasper, Spalding, and Monáe expand the contours of black music, express their commitment to black radio and desire for radio play, privilege group compensation, and make the album do the work that American listeners once expected of radio: introducing them to a broad range of voices and styles.[41]

Glasper, Spalding, and Monáe, as "post-Telecom babies" whose albums explicitly thematize radio at threshold career moments when they navigate or approach popular mainstream success, most clearly (and surprisingly) exploit the waning medium of radio as a model for revitalizing the album format and redistributing their own growing consumer base. But these three artists' vision of the album-as-radio is representative, not exceptional. Their radio albums also illuminate the aesthetic and economic politics of other, similarly diverse and curatorial albums. Recent albums that host several musicians and producers of color include Faith Evans's Grammy-nominated *Divas* (Prolific/EI, 2012); Meshell Ndegeocello's Nina Simone tribute, *Pour une Âme Souveraine* (For a Sovereign Soul; Naïve, 2012); Bruno Mars's *Unorthodox Jukebox* (Atlantic, 2012); and Mariah Carey's *Me. I Am Mariah . . . The Elusive Chanteuse* (Def Jam, 2014). Whether working with independent or major labels, these artists make the album function in ways that evoke the radio they grew up hearing. While their musical diversity expands the boundaries of "race music," their reconstitution of the album as a source of collective promotion and compensation also reflects a model of black economic nationalism for the twenty-first-century culture industry.

Notes

1 Rossman, *Climbing the Charts*, 92.

2 George, *The Death of Rhythm & Blues*, 130; Molanphy, "I Know You Got Soul."

3 Given that *Black Radio Society* is Spalding's fourth studio album, her designation as a "new artist" is subjective, not to say ironic.

4 Barlow, *Voice Over*, 294, xi.

5 For more on this phenomenon see Rose, *The Hip Hop Wars*, 18–19; Rossman, *Climbing the Charts*, 15; Barlow, *Voice Over*, 262.

6 Neal, *Soul Babies.*

7 Esperanza Spalding, EMP Pop Conference Keynote, New York University, March 22, 2012. Both Mark Anthony Neal and Guthrie Ramsey describe this mid-twentieth-century experience of black radio in their respective analyses of Glapser's first album. See Ramsey, "The Power of Suggestion"; Neal, "Liberating 'Black Radio.'"

8 George, *The Death of Rhythm & Blues,* 167.

9 Neal, "Liberating 'Black Radio.'"

10 Molanphy, "I Know You Got Soul."

11 Although these artists' albums have sold relatively well, singles from those albums seldom charted in the United States. Exceptions are Glasper's "Ah Yeah," which spent several weeks on Adult R&B and Hot R&B-Hip-Hop charts, and Spalding's cover of Michael Jackson's "Can't Help It," which charted on Smooth Jazz stations. Glasper's cover of "Afro-Blue" spent seven weeks on the Japan Hot 100 list.

12 Robert Glasper Experiment feat. Yasiin Bey, "Black Radio," *Black Radio* (Blue Note, 2012); Public Enemy, "Rebel without a Pause," *It Takes a Nation of Millions to Hold Us Back* (Def Jam/Columbia, 1988).

13 Battan, "Mind Control," calls *The Electric Lady* "Monáe's boldest bid for pop superstardom to date."

14 See Molanphy's conclusion to "I Know You Got Soul."

15 The introduction to Bilal's debut album, *First Born Second* (Interscope, 2001), is another intertext here, especially as Bilal and Glasper are longtime collaborators.

16 Nakiska, "Robert Glasper and the New Jazz Age."

17 Quoted in Williams, *Rhymin' and Stealin',* 85.

18 Lundy, *Songs in the Key of Life,* 51–52. For more on Wonder and the synthesizer, see 76–82.

19 For a discussion of technological expressiveness in contemporary R&B music, see Weheliye, "Rhythms of Relation."

20 Williams, *Rhymin' and Stealin',* 82.

21 Williams, *Rhymin' and Stealin',* 86.

22 "Robert Glasper Experiment: Tiny Desk Concert."

23 *Black Radio 2* contains a similar preachy interlude by Michael Eric Dyson, who bemoans the loss of "black individuality" and thanks God that "we've still got musicians and thinkers whose obsession with excellence and whose hunger for greatness remind us that we should all be unsatisfied with mimicking the popular, rather than mining the fertile veins of creativity that God placed deep inside each of us" ("I Stand Alone," *Black Radio 2* [Blue Note, 2013]).

24 "Robert Glasper: A Unified Field Theory." The album's liner notes by Angelika Beener stress this meaning, as Glasper does in several interviews.

25 In "Who Is Esperanza Spalding?" Vozick-Levinson writes, "The Grammys exposure should help Spalding with her next project, a more mainstream-oriented album called *Radio Music Society.*"

26 Thom Jurek review of Radio Music Society, AllMusic.com.

27 Chinen, "Rookie of the Year." Spalding also comments on the tendency of the press to isolate her as a star, apart from her collaborators, in this story.

28 Rossman, *Climbing the Charts*, 22–23.

29 "Esperanza Spalding: Jazz as 'Radio Music.'"

30 "Robert Glasper: A Unified Field Theory." See also Nakiska, "Robert Glasper and the New Jazz Age."

31 "Robert Glasper: A Unified Field Theory." See too Spalding's remarks to Chinen in "The Rookie of the Year."

32 See Suzanne Smith on Motown and automotive listening, quoted in Williams, *Rhymin' and Stealin'*, 79.

33 Spalding, "Radio Song," *Radio Music Society* (Heads Up International, 2012).

34 Johnson, *Spaces of Conflict*, 85.

35 Weheliye, "Rhythms of Relation," 362.

36 Battan, "Mind Control."

37 Battan, "Mind Control."

38 This and all other tracks cited are from Janelle Monáe, *The Electric Lady* (Wondaland Arts Society/Bad Boy, 2013).

39 For a more detailed reading of this track and others on the album, see Lordi, "Calling All Stars."

40 Marshall, "Treble Culture," 63.

41 The obvious drawback to refiguring the album rather than reforming radio is that albums (if legally downloaded) are not free. Still, file-sharing does allow music to move beyond the single consumer—and in this case to move entire albums, rather than the singles that would be broadcast on radio.

References

Barlow, William. *Voice Over: The Making of Black Radio*. Philadelphia: Temple University Press, 1999.

Battan, Carrie. "Mind Control." *Pitchfork*, September 4, 2013.

Chinen, Nate. "The Rookie of the Year, One Year Wiser." *New York Times*, March 16, 2012.

"Esperanza Spalding: Jazz as 'Radio Music.'" NPR.org, March 17, 2012.

George, Nelson. *The Death of Rhythm & Blues*. New York: Penguin, 1988.

Johnson, Gaye Theresa. *Spaces of Conflict, Sounds of Solidarity: Music, Race, and Spatial Entitlement in Los Angeles*. Berkeley: University of California Press, 2013.

Lordi, Emily J. "Calling All Stars: Janelle Monáe's Black Feminist Futures." *Feminist Wire*, September 25, 2013.

Lundy, Zeth. *Songs in the Key of Life*. New York: Continuum, 2007.

Marshall, Wayne. "Treble Culture." In *Oxford Handbook of Mobile Music Studies*, vol. 2, edited by Sumanth Gopinath and Jason Stanyek. New York: Oxford University Press, 2014.

Molanphy, Chris. "I Know You Got Soul: The Trouble with *Billboard*'s R&B/Hip-Hop Chart." *Pitchfork*, April 14, 2014.

Nakiska, Tempe. "Robert Glasper and the New Jazz Age." *Interview*, October 31, 2013.

Neal, Mark Anthony. "Liberating 'Black Radio': The Robert Glasper Experiment." *New Black Man (in Exile)*, March 6, 2012.

Neal, Mark Anthony. *Soul Babies: Black Popular Culture and the Post-Soul Aesthetic.* New York: Routledge, 2001.

Ramsey, Guthrie. "The Power of Suggestion/The Pleasure of Groove: Robert Glasper's Post-Genre Black Radio Project, Part 3." *Musiqology*, February 22, 2012.

"Robert Glasper: A Unified Field Theory for Black Music." NPR.org, February 24, 2012.

"Robert Glasper Experiment: Tiny Desk Concert." NPR.org, January 20, 2014.

Rose, Tricia. *The Hip Hop Wars.* New York: Basic/Civitas, 2008.

Rossman, Gabriel. *Climbing the Charts: What Radio Airplay Tells Us about the Diffusion of Innovation.* Princeton, NJ: Princeton University Press, 2012.

Vozick-Levinson, Simon. "Who Is Esperanza Spalding?" *Entertainment Weekly*, December 3, 2010.

Weheliye, Alexander. "Rhythms of Relation: Black Popular Music and Mobile Technologies." In *The Oxford Handbook of Mobile Music Studies*, vol. 2, edited by Sumanth Gopinath and Jason Stanyek. New York: Oxford University Press, 2014.

Williams, Justin A. *Rhymin' and Stealin': Musical Borrowing in Hip-Hop.* Ann Arbor: University of Michigan Press, 2013.

**CAMPING AND VAMPING ACROSS
BORDERS** / LOCATING CABARET SINGERS
IN THE BLACK CULTURAL SPECTRUM

Vincent Stephens

When historians document black popular music production,
cabaret singers such as Pearl Bailey, Mae Barnes, Jimmie Daniels, Eartha Kitt,
Mabel Mercer, and Bobby Short are rarely included. Other than a brief ex-
cerpt in Eileen Southern's *The Music of Black Americans: A History*, you would
not know that black performers were central to the genre.[1] Comparatively,
black performers figure very heavily into James Gavin's definitive 1991 account of mid-twentieth-century New York cabaret culture, *Intimate Nights*.
The genre, however, has a deep and underexplored role in providing professional opportunities for black performers during the 1920s to the 1950s,
when the genre thrived.

This omission overlooks the significant impact of these performers as recording artists, concert performers, cabaret fixtures, actors, and political actors. Their absence from the black popular music canon reflects a perceived

gap between cabaret and black aesthetics, notably the dominance of "soul" as the defining lens for framing black cultural production. In *Soul Babies*, Mark Anthony Neal defines "soul" as "the most vivid and popular expression of an African-American modernity." He notes how

> soul challenged the prevailing logic of white supremacy and segregation in ways that were disconcerting and even grotesque to some, regardless of race or ethnicity. Premised on the construction of 'positive' black images that could be juxtaposed against the overextended influence of Western caricatures of black life, the soul aesthetic dramatically altered the projects of Harlem Renaissance artists and critics by sanctioning both vernacular and popular expression largely valued within the black community without concern for the reactions of mainstream critics or institutions.[2]

Presumably, the most canonical images of blackness fulfill this notion of positive images reflecting authentic black expression, yet the absence of cabaret would suggest something was amiss in the genre. As Jack Hamilton notes in *Just around Midnight*, "The policing of racial authenticity in music gained new energy in the late 1960s. During this period the concept of 'soul' became a fixation of popular discourse."[3] This policing manifests itself in a tendency to essentialize blackness, black people, and the music they produce.

Cabaret provides a critical space to interrogate the artificial racial and musical boundaries implied by the omission of cabaret from conversations about black music. Keith Negus, drawing from Paul Gilroy's work, proposes approaching "black music" in a vein that incorporates "the diaspora of the black Atlantic world and the idea of a changing same" that links performers to social history without reducing them to a singular sound.[4] Building from this notion, I ask readers to consider the following. Cultural historians continue to broaden understandings of African American popular music and performance toward an anti-essentialist definition. They do so by asking critical questions about what constitutes the black music canon and the reasons behind certain inclusions and exclusions. While similar inquiries are applicable regarding blacks in country music, punk music, and other genres coded traditionally as white, cabaret is an essential genre for addressing these questions.

Two elements that have historically kept cabaret on the historical margins of black music are its association with affluent white consumers and the ways queer culture, especially "camp" sensibilities, inflect the genre. David Bergman identifies four aspects of camp: "First, everyone agrees that camp is a style . . . that favors 'exaggeration,' 'artifice,' and 'extremity.' Second, camp exists in tension with popular culture, commercial culture, or consumer culture.

Third, the person who can recognize camp, who sees things as campy, or who can camp is a person outside the cultural mainstream. Fourth, camp is affiliated with homosexual culture, or at least with a self-conscious eroticism that throws into question the naturalization of desire."[5] I focus on the camp element because it opens up a space to challenge racial and sexual binaries. The scholar Pamela Robertson quotes Dennis Altman's notion that what camp is to gay men, soul is to black culture—a cultural code—and she explores its implications, but I see a closer connection between these qualities and view cabaret as a unique site of cultural fusion.[6]

In the popular imagination, camp is the inverse of soul, in the same way we commonly perceive races and sexual orientation categories as opposites. The intersection of blackness and queerness that cabaret frequently represents, however, allows us to reimagine the ways that they speak to each other. I argue that the combination of soul and camp provides cabaret with a unique flavor that also deconstructs artificial boundaries between black and white musical expression, and straight and queer expressive cultures. I explore the import of this fusion by examining the roots and aesthetics of U.S. cabaret, articulating important parallels between soul and camp for their respective communities of origin, and illustrating how black cabaret performers have fused soul's cultural politics and camp's expressive aesthetics in innovative ways that defied the racial politics of authenticity. I conclude by placing my argument in the context of the post-soul critical paradigm that argues for a more decentered notion of identity.

Defining the Genre, the Scene, the Singers

Cabaret rooms originated in the Parisian neighborhood of Montmartre in the late nineteenth century and reached the United States after American expatriates developed a particular affinity for cabaret culture in the 1920s and 1930s. Critics estimate that U.S. cabaret began around the 1930s and peaked from 1945 to 1963.[7] Robert Connolly generally concurs with this timeline, noting, "The 1930s through the 1950s was perhaps the heyday of nightclubs and night-club singers. After the theater or a dinner party, New Yorkers liked to top off the evening by dropping into a club to hear some favorite performer. There was an entertainer, an ambiance, and a price tag to fit every taste." Described as "an intimate art, one intended to be enjoyed by a smaller number of people in a small space," cabaret has been dominated by female performers, who "concentrate on projecting the music and lyrics with a minimum of gestures and theatrics rather than on pushing their own personalities" and "choose their songs with the greatest care from the best popular music of the past and present which puts them above changing fashions."[8] Yet Larry Kart argues that cabaret as a U.S. phenomenon "lasted until that indeterminate point in the late 1950s or early 1960s when the notion that there was such a thing as an aristocracy of taste, let alone an actual aristocracy to support it, finally began to seem out of date."[9] In the late 1950s, the rock generation's desire for a separate culture from their parents and television's growing appeal were key aspects of cabaret's decline.[10]

New York was the epicenter of the American cabaret scene, though Boston, Chicago, Detroit, and San Francisco also had prominent venues. One of the most comprehensive cabaret boxed sets, 1987's *The Erteguns' New York*, features recordings from nineteen artists from the Atlantic Records label; ten are primarily featured as vocalists and nine as instrumentalists.[11] The collection also maps out forty-six venues associated with "the New York Cabaret scene," including forty-two primarily in Manhattan near Central Park and four divided among Downtown and Greenwich Village. These locations are key; despite the era's racial stratification, African Americans were mainstays in shaping cabaret culture as performers, club owners, hosts, and patrons. Thus the cabaret circuit arguably offered one of the most progressive spaces for black performers. The *Erteguns' New York*, in its breadth, provides a representative snapshot of the scene's cultural diversity. In addition to Chris Connor, Carmen McRae, and Mel Tormé, who are commonly included in vocal jazz guides, there are three African Americans, Barnes, Jimmie Daniels, and Short, as well as Mabel Mercer, who is of Welsh and African American lineage.

More than merely players on the scene, each of these latter performers was a staple of urban cabaret venues. Barnes was a fixture at the Bon Soir; Daniels opened his own club in Harlem and was a well-respected host and performer, especially at the Bon Soir; Mercer was revered as the "definitive café singer," adored by songwriters and singers; Short is the most iconic male singer in cabaret via influential recordings and his twenty-eight-year stint at the Café Carlyle. Moreover, urban cabaret venues factor very prominently in biographical and autobiographical accounts of performers such as Bailey, Kitt, Mercer, and Short, and other black celebrities of their generation.[12]

Shifting Perceptions: Soul, Camp, Class, and Authenticity

Soul and camp perform similar expressive functions for their communities of origin. The ways critics and historians artificially separate camp culture from black culture, and soul from certain forms of classed and gendered black expression distorts our ability to understand their overlaps. *Perceived* social class differences are integral to this gap as well. The 1950s is the commercial and cultural heyday for African American cabaret singers, and those mentioned have a unique relationship to the concept of soul, as defined by Neal, in black culture. Cabaret performers fulfilled a portion of his definition by projecting a unique combination of talent, cosmopolitanism, and professional savvy. In this sense, they projected a "positive" image of blacks as successful, dignified entertainers. The controversial aspect of cabaret performers is the "sophisticated" nature of their expression in terms of gender expression and social class.

Soul is often interpreted as an expression of working-class black values far removed from the boîtes of New York, Paris, and London. For example, according to Neal, "soul singularly emerges in its role because of its conscious deconstruction of black church music, effectively reanimating the most politically benign aspects of the mid-twentieth century black church, to reconnect the social functions of the black church with the populist demands of the black working class."[13] Whereas soul music fused gospel music with secular lyrics and occasional musical elements drawn from the blues and jazz, European cabaret, torch singing, swing jazz, and Broadway primarily influence cabaret. While an iconic black American genre (jazz) is an important ingredient in cabaret, it is a multicultural and multinational hybrid. Essentially, cabaret seems less culturally rooted in the black idiom.[14]

Though cabaret performers typically sang American songbook standards before affluent, predominantly white audiences in sophisticated performing venues, there is no clear correlation between their acceptance as individual performers by white audiences and white attitudes toward the social plight of blacks in general.[15] For example, Café Society Downtown, which opened in 1938, was the first integrated nightclub in America. Further, certain clubs, such as the Blue Angel ("one of the foremost showcases for black talent"), were known for welcoming racially diverse performers and audiences.[16] As I discuss later, urban cabaret scenes were some of the few genuinely multicultural social milieus of the 1950s where musicians, composers, artists in various mediums, and their acquaintances seem to have interacted harmoniously. The general association of cabaret with white culture, however, extends to black cabaret performers who seem elite and out of touch with "common" black men and women by association, even though the "common" person is a reductionist fiction.

The influence of camp in cabaret is especially important, as it represents another layer seemingly removed from the black mainstream. Cabaret culture appealed strongly to gay men. Certain clubs had a heavy gay male clientele. For example, the Bon Soir actually featured a gay bar on one side of the room, and clubs like the Spotlight had a palpable gay ambiance.[17] Gavin argues, "Intimate clubs gave men the freedom to express 'feminine' emotions; within the nightclub culture they were surrounded by other homosexuals with similar interests; they could bask in the presence of the old leading ladies they loved."[18] The theater scholar John Clum connects Broadway musicals (an important source of cabaret repertoire), gay men (a central class in composing and consuming Broadway musicals), and camp (a cultural sensibility primarily associated within gay male taste) by noting, "The gay voice in the musical's spectacle and presentation speaks with some irony, some awareness of its artificiality. In discussing that gay voice, one must discuss camp, an over-theorized but crucial term that explains many of the links between musical theater and gay culture."[19] The most iconic discussion of camp is Susan Sontag's 1964 essay "Notes on 'Camp,'" where she observes, "The essence of Camp is its love of the unnatural: of artifice and exaggeration. And Camp is esoteric—something of a private code, a badge of identity even, among *small urban cliques*." She also notes Camp's strong affiliation with gay culture: "While it's not true that Camp taste is homosexual taste, there is no doubt a peculiar affinity and overlap. . . . *Homosexuals, by and large, constitute the vanguard—and the most articulate audience—of* Camp."[20] The italicized phrases point to the association of camp with urbanity, wit, dandyism, and homosexual as well as homosexual-adjacent culture. Sontag popularized camp, but drawing on Bergman's definition, gay men have since redefined and politicized camp as a form of cultural resistance.

Clum elaborates on camp's unique role in gay spectatorship, noting, "Camp allows gay spectators to find gayness in shows that are ostensibly heterosexual and heterosexist. It allows us to identify with the indomitable, odd women, whom Ethan Mordden calls 'amiable freaks,' who are often at the center of musicals. For show queens, the musical offers a reading against its own ostensible heterosexuality."[21] These definitions and connections are essential for placing cabaret in a cultural context. Well before Sontag's essay, the iconic Stonewall Riots of 1969, and academic theories of camp, gay men had immersed themselves in camp culture.

Ebony magazine's 1952 profile of Mabel Mercer described her fan base this way:

Miss Mercer's devotees are mostly artistically minded folk who behave very much like disciples at a shrine. For them the superbly dignified Miss

Mercer can do no wrong. A delicate wisp of a crew-cut youngster was heard to murmur as he left the By-Line Room, "Wasn't Mabel too, too divine tonight?"

Miss Mercer exerts a strange fascination for hordes of young men, all very delicate and sensitive. They come to see her regularly, kiss her hand and embrace her tenderly. They ask her to sing their favorite songs and moon over her starry-eyed while she rocks regally on her chair. No valid psychological explanation for this unusual phenomenon has yet been offered but it is one of the more curious features of New York's night life.[22]

The article "outs" her audience as gay men via euphemisms like "artistically minded," "delicate wisp," "delicate and sensitive," and "curious," quoting gay argot and singling out the men's fascination as defying "psychological explanation." Indeed, Gavin quotes maître d' Archie Walker's comment, "Who could have a gayer following than Mabel Mercer? Every old queen with four days to live came to see her."[23] The article does not specify their race, but it is easy, given the historical context, to imagine that it was predominantly white.

Writers commonly use camp to describe classic cabaret performers. For example, a profile of Mercer notes, "Mercer filled in for Bobby Short, an ardent admirer who could be as camp as she was sincere, at the chic Carlyle Hotel when he was absent."[24] Camp also surfaces as a descriptor for other cabaret performers. The New York Times obituary for Eartha Kitt referenced her "camp appeal."[25] Her role as Catwoman on the 1960s Batman series was the height of her camp persona.[26] The producer behind Batman integrated camp elements into the series consciously to appeal to adults, who would recognize its tongue-in cheek nature, and their kids, who would enjoy its adventurous elements.[27]

Camp was clearly understood as an "open secret" that informed the careers of classic cabaret singers. There's no clear marker of when camp became less explicit within cabaret, though the late 1960s birth of liberationist politics is often understood as a turning point, when gay culture abandoned some of its unique subcultures for more assimilationist forms of expression.[28] This arguably coincided with changing aesthetics in black popular culture. Whereas campy figures like the singer Diana Ross and the actor Antonio Fargas's various roles as gay comedic foils (e.g., Lindy in Car Wash) thrived in the 1970s, by the late 1970s and early 1980s, a hypermasculine strain also emerged in black music that narrowed room for genderplay.[29]

While camp is not the cornerstone of every recording classifiable as cabaret, an über stylization and lightness of tone defines much of the black cabaret canon. Camp is not necessarily something one looks for; it tends to reveal itself and is most detectable and affecting when seen and heard directly rather than described secondhand. However, a few recordings illuminate some of the camp aspects in the careers of certain singers. For example, the cover of the 1998 collection *Eartha Kitt—Greatest Hits: Purr-Fect* nods to her camp iconicity as Catwoman. The punning title and the vintage image of her lying in a reclining chair, dressed in a leopard-skin dress, wearing a bouffant wig, and staring with an amused "come hither" look signify to those in on the joke.[30] In the liner notes Joseph R. Laredo describes her persona as "feline seductress" who "knows exactly how to wield her unique vocal instrument for maximum effect." Winking innuendos define many of her interpretations on the compilation's twenty-two songs, as she sings in a nasally voice with a coquettish tone—somewhere between seduction and amusement.

Alternately, Pearl Bailey's use of "mother wit" informs the comedy style of multiple generations of black performers, ranging from "Moms" Mabley to Whoopi Goldberg. Like Kitt's, her style blends camp's artificiality with distinctly black forms of expression. Having gained fame with winking spoken asides that softened the content of risqué material, her 1960s album *Naughty but Nice* reveals a clear camp moment in her spoken coda to the song "Never Give Anything Away," which gently flirts with prostitution.[31] In the last fourteen seconds of the 1:54 song, she speak-sings a dollop of mother wit:

> *Don't give it away honey!*
> *Ain't worth it*
> *I tell ya*
> *Put a price on it*
> *Always comes out better*
> *Well make it cheap . . .*
> *Somebody'll buy it.*

The cumulative effect of listening to the album leaves listeners envisioning her performing beyond the recording itself and easily visualizing her black matron's demeanor delivering these lines.

Mercer and Short are synonymous with distinctive stylistic quirks that inflect virtually all of their recordings. Mercer, who was raised in Wales, sings in a regal, almost anachronistic style, rolling her "r"'s and enunciating all of her words clearly. Leslie Gourse writes, "With her rolled *r*'s and restrained accent, she sounded like a mischievous dowager, not seeking an audience but granting one."[32] The idea of a matronly looking black woman opening her mouth and singing with such an über European accent is ironic to the point of almost being perverse. There is an almost exotic fascination with her Welsh affect that defies American and British stereotypes about blacks, and she is more of a storyteller than a comedian—even though her songs often have a subtle humor.

Short, however, sings in a hoarse timbre that often sounds like he is on the verge of laryngitis. His broad repertoire often features novelty songs punctuated by songs with bite. His penchant for camp tropes like irony and sly comedy comes through most clearly on his 1975 *Live at the Café Carlyle*.[33] Most of his performances on the album are American songbook love songs that demand a modicum of sincerity and reverence, but the fourth, "Mister and Missus Fitch," has an edge. He prefaces the performance with a telling introduction: "Here's a Cole Porter song about America's favorite pastime. That of social climbing." The song details the story of peasant farmers who discover oil and are soon the toast of the town, until the stock market crash upends their fortune. Notably, after their change of fortunes, he sings:

> Men who once knew Missus Fitch
> Referred to her as a bitch
> And the girls who all loved Mr. Fitch
> Said he was always a son of a bitch
> So love and kisses . . . Mr. and Missus . . . Fitch.

In camp fashion, the song's affect unmasks the underlying truth of social climbing, the divisions inherent in society, and the false motivations underlying friendships of convenience. Just as soul challenges racist constructs of blackness, camp exposes things for what they are.

The aesthetics of the most dominant black commercial music forms of the post-1960s era (e.g., R&B, hip hop) seem only tangentially related to the campiness intrinsic to cabaret genres. A closer look reveals how performers ranging from Millie Jackson and Toni Braxton to Busta Rhymes and the hip-hop group OutKast integrate discernibly campy elements into their music and personae. Jackson's winking style, Braxton's languorous reading of "Unbreak My Heart" and its melodramatic video, Rhymes's clownish persona, and Andre 3000's gender-ambiguous fashion constitute a camp continuum if we consider definitions of camp as a form of exaggeration. Black variations of the camp tradition endure in multiple forms of contemporary black expression. In 2015 the writer Daniel Mallory Ostberg coined the term "camp heterosexuality" and listed a number of performers from within black music.[34] Camp has never disappeared from black pop; it has merely gone unnamed—hence the perception of earlier performances of camp as somehow unrelated to black culture. This perceived gap possibly shapes the absence of cabaret from most black music histories and rests on a political gap between camp (understood as white and gay) and soul (understood as black and straight).

Related to the queer nature of the campiness of cabaret is a perception of cabaret artists as elites. Camp is a symptom of a broader elitism and distance from a class-specific version of blackness. Autobiographies written by cabaret performers, including Bailey, Kitt, and Short, are key sources for understanding their own sense of their identities and relationships to black communities. While their autobiographies do not respond exclusively to issues of cultural authenticity, these and various other public statements demonstrate an astute awareness that blacks perceived them negatively.

Kitt's writing illustrates the policing of blackness as an element these writers have responded to frequently through autobiography. One of the key functions of black celebrity autobiographies that Kwatkiutl Dreher identifies is recuperation. She describes Kitt as "a celebrity autobiographer making the most of the dance of autobiography to 'take up for herself' against the bully of defamation." Among the defenses Kitt's books address are challenging perceptions that she is "aloof" and haughty, characteristics signified by her light ("yella") skin color, tendency to speak foreign languages among her cast mates, a voice perceived as "too weird," and her tendency to push boundaries. Her ability to see through Katherine Dunham's pretenses during her mid-1940s stint with the famed choreographer generated tension between them because of their parallel backgrounds. Kitt's willingness to challenge Lady Bird Johnson on issues related to poverty, the Vietnam War, and the generational malaise of young people at an infamous White House dinner in 1968 also signified her willingness to go against the grain. Dreher reiterates Kitt's boldness, asserting that "Even though Kitt comes to us as an outrageous performer willing to gamble her status in the entertainment industry at the highest level, she unapologetically takes up for her actions. They are her challenges to the national home to make good on its promise to explore the conditions of America's underprivileged children living in cultures of poverty"[35]

Arguably, the emergence of autobiographies like Kitt's contributed to rhetorical challenges to the notion of a singular black experience. Black celebrities represented the crossover dream of social acceptance on one's own terms and conformed to black modernity. These qualities aligned cabaret singers within the confines of soul. The budding late 1960s nationalist element shifted the landscape toward narrower conceptions of blackness that espoused rigid notions of authentic blackness, frequently in heteronormative terms.[36] Neal writes of nationalist infusions during the "soul" era, "The soul aesthetic was the cultural component to the most visible black nationalist ideas of the twentieth century."[37] Short, Bailey, and Kitt developed their talent in mostly integrated cultural environments. Each has remarked on the ire directed toward them along political lines from other blacks. Kitt painfully recounts blacks' perceptions that she thought she was white; she was harassed and threatened by members of the Black Panthers.[38] In *Raw Pearl* Bailey recounts her response to an inquiry on the *Mike Douglas Show* regarding why she had not marched for civil rights:

> No I haven't marched any place physically, but I march every day in my heart. I live with humanity every day, and when you live with humanity then you have walked—and the road is not easy, necessarily.
>
> People are so quick to point out the favors a Negro gets because he is an entertainer. We have paved the way for many, and, too, have paid with blood, sweat, and tears.[39]

Similarly, in *American Singers*, Short responds very pointedly to black consciousness rhetoric:

> It was never in me to be the best colored singer or the best colored student. I simply wanted to be the best singer and the best student. But I have a respect for my race that might surprise *some of the people who discovered just six months ago that they are black*. I was brought up in such a way that doesn't allow any head-banging. . . . A long time ago, I discovered that the best advertisement for a minority is that member who, without being Uncle Tom, takes the time to mesh with whatever exists socially. He makes it that much easier for the next member who comes along.[40]

Both speak to an ethic of paving the way for others and frame themselves consciously in relation to future generations of black performers. The issue of authenticity related to camp, class, and nationalism that the performers address partially explains the perceived distance between them as performers and personalities and "authentic" black culture—a notion tied to the soul era.

Homophobia is an implicit thread that the symbolic annihilation of cabaret and camp traces from black cultural memory. Homophobic ideologies predate black nationalism, and while many of its leading voices opposed it, notably the Black Panther Party's leader Huey P. Newton, heteronormativity characterized much of its rhetoric. An outgrowth of such masculinist rhetoric is a chasm between inauthentic and authentic black culture. The clash between the camp and elitist overtones of cabaret and the rigid ideology of the mid- to late 1960s black nationalism was influential enough to create a historical gulf in black cultural memory.

Overlooked Overlaps: Camp as a Cross-Cultural Bridge

The soul era birthed enduring tropes about authentic blackness that aimed to elevate blackness but threatened to narrow the contours of black expression. As a multiracial genre largely rooted in New York's integrated nightlife, cabaret is useful for exploring the tonal shift in 1960s politics. One of the overlooked aspects of cabaret was the social fusion it modeled in its frequent mixing of racial and sexual cultures. Jimmie Daniels (1907–1984)—a singer, performer, club manager, and host—symbolizes these overlaps better than anyone does. Born in Laredo, Texas, he left business school for New York, where he performed on Broadway in the late 1920s before finding success in the 1930s in Monaco and London. After relocating to New York, he gained a reputation as a party host. In 1935 he met the club owner Herbert Jacoby, who invited him to Paris, where he worked as an entertainer in Le Boeuf Sur le Toi. He vacillated between New York and Paris until the late 1930s.[41]

From 1939 to 1942 he managed Jimmie Daniels's Nightclub in Harlem, before leaving for the military. Daniels was openly gay and a staple of European and American social circles. Esther Newton writes, "Even while working in Harlem, Jimmie Daniels moved in a smart interracial milieu, and by the late 1940s his large duplex apartment in Greenwich Village had become a social hub for his many friends and acquaintances."[42] In 1950 he became the host at the Bon Soir, where he worked for the next decade. The Bon Soir was "a chic supper club. Known as a place where African Americans and Whites, as well as gay and straight clientele, interacted without tension, the club was described as having a balance of elegant, intimate, risqué, and respectable ambiance."[43] In the early 1960s Daniels managed the Tiffany Room and performed occasionally. He died in 1984, and Bobby Short arranged his memorial.

Daniels's prominence in Greenwich Village matters because New York's interracial and pansexual revolution in the 1950s represented an experiment in multiculturalism. As Marlon Ross outlines, Le Roi Jones (Amiri Baraka), a key icon of black nationalism, was one of the more outspoken critics of the scene where Daniels thrived. Baraka's objection was rooted in his life in Greenwich Village and his adaption of nationalism in the mid-1960s. In the middle of the "classic" civil rights era, the Village-centered cabaret scene was an interracial social space. The scene was also intersexual and symbolized the burgeoning urban gay social movement. By the mid-1960s, the nationalist strain had grown increasingly divested from integration and moved toward separation. Ross's perspective on nationalism's blunt attempts at disentangling African and European elements is that such efforts have always been "a problem in black cultural nationalist theory."[44] Nationalists rejected interracial socializing and pathologized homosexuality as deviant behavior outside of authentic blackness.

Ross's analysis of Baraka's rhetoric during his transition from beatnik to nationalist addresses the artifice of separating cultures by exposing the interconnectedness between queer culture and black culture.[45] Baraka, who moved to the Village in 1957, was once intimately acquainted with gay figures like the poets Allen Ginsberg and Frank O'Hara, but he eventually rejected the scene as the opposite of authentic blackness. In his 1960s rhetoric, homosexuality, particularly the white middle-class artistic milieu where he developed his voice, was "both a sign of advancing European-focused high culture" and "a sign of the most degraded, decadent, abhorrent descent into legally punishable impulses of pathological self-destruction." Ross frames this shift by defining "cultural *identification* as a *temporal* process" in which we constantly revise and reconstitute ourselves. Ross argues that Baraka attacked black gay writers (notably James Baldwin) in a homophobic language akin to the African American verbal tradition of "the dozens." Yet, for Ross, this attempt to disaffiliate with gay culture is tempered by Baraka's intimate knowledge of the gay verbal mode of camp that Ross identifies as a *cross-cultural gay mode* rather than a *white gay mode*. In other words, black people can camp as well as anyone as both performers and interpreters. Baraka's access to camp served as a tool for deconstructing whiteness since camp "calls out the artifice, hypocrisy, parasitism, and queerness buried within the backside of high white culture."[46] As much as Baraka attempted to revise himself by disparaging homosexual culture, its influence is inseparable from his work.

Ross's critical intervention is radical for linking the dozens and camp as "verbal contests involving feats of creative insider name-calling always with a sexual edge in which individuals from socially marginalized groups enact their ideological complicity with and resistance to the dominant norm." He illustrates how queer men were integral to urban black communities;

thus the Village was not Baraka's *first* exposure to homosexuality but merely a variation. In this sense, homosexuality is clearly not a "white" development, nor is camp, "for black homosexuals' inventive use of identity invective reveals a specific interaction between the dozens and camp so indeterminate that defining where one 'site' or 'role' begins and the other ends in their verbal contests would be absolutely impossible." These critical observations transcend Baraka and point toward how black *and* queer cultures were not inherently discrete, and illustrate how they developed ways to challenge hypersexual images of their cultures by turning the tables and "making sexual talk itself a playful weapon." As such, camp and the dozens "refuse to accept the embarrassment of shame cast onto their communities by a dominant culture that desires to keep sex a dirty secret practiced deviantly only by society's suppressed others."[47] Camp, the dozens, and even soul's manifestations (e.g., jive talk) are highly stylized sociolinguistic responses to marginality. Their origins differ, but they serve similar functions and cannot be severed from each other for political convenience. Metaphorically, this reasoning applies to my effort to historicize campy black performers within the black performative milieu.

Kitt's playfulness, Mercer's rolled r's, and Daniels's all-around fabulousness are intersections of blackness *and* camp in cabaret. Cabaret was a space for artists to express black subjectivity outside of culturally and sexually "straight" modes. By sitting on the periphery of R&B, jazz, and soul, these artists differed from the black musical mainstream, making their expression (e.g., mannered gestures, quirky repertoire) difficult to integrate into the political moment. During a time of harsh social transitions toward civil rights and equity, they may have seemed out of touch and indulgent. In the nationalist conception perpetuated by writers like Baraka, blackness was limited to functionality and certain forms of productivity, but it was too narrow.[48]

Ironically, many of these performers engaged in unheralded forms of "soulful" activism. Bailey pioneered the all-black casting of a "white" musical (*Hello Dolly!*) on Broadway in 1967. Kitt was outspoken about many social issues and was one of the first performers to challenge South African apartheid and relate it publicly to U.S. racial conditions. Short championed black composers such as Duke Ellington throughout his career, wrote the foreword for the definitive book on the black composer Andy Razaf, and coproduced the all-black revue *Black Broadway*, focused on black veteran performers like Eubie Blake and Adelaide Hall.[49] Collectively, these gestures place them within a notably black mode of cultural production.

Listening with Post-Soul Ears

When viewed collectively in historical terms, the careers of classic cabaret icons represent a distinctive fusion of "soul" politics, cabaret, blackness, and camp that happened at a time when social and cultural integration was idealized. The shifting political winds have made it difficult to place them historically. Fortunately, writers and scholars like Nelson George and Neal have opened this door critically by articulating the parameters of a "post-soul paradigm" that moves away from a segregation-era modernist notion of blacks as a monolith toward a more expansive view of what blackness meant historically and what it can mean today.

George marks 1971's premier of Melvin Van Peebles's film *Sweet Sweetback's Baadasssss Song* as a post-soul benchmark that challenged the "positive-image canon" that traditionally confined black artists. He views the flowering of different "character types" in post-1970s African American culture as signifying a more decentered notion of identity. According to George, "The soul world lingers on, but for the current generation it seems as anachronistic as the idea of a National Association for the Advancement of Colored People and as technologically primitive as a crackly old Motown 45."[50] Neal also discusses this expanded frame for understanding post-70s African American consciousness, describing post-soul as an aesthetic that "ultimately renders many 'traditional' tropes of blackness dated and even meaningless; in its borrowing from black modern traditions, it is so consumed with its contemporary existential concerns that such traditions are not just called into question but obliterated."[51] George and Neal offer a more open, anti-essentialist lens for reflecting on black popular culture of the present and the past and appreciating the diverse musical expressions possible within the black diaspora.

Collectively, the post-soul perspective clarifies the strongholds that integrationist and separatist politics have had in shaping contemporary black thought. If neither perspective is monolithic, we can also recognize how they continually bifurcate our thinking into imagining that black and white music and black and gay culture are opposites. This perspective shortchanges the interplay between these cultures and the complex ways blacks have expressed themselves historically.

Cabaret's historical obscurity threatens to limit our attention to contemporary black cabaret vocalists, such as Darius de Haas, Norm Lewis, Audra McDonald, and Paula West. They are the inheritors of a longstanding, black expressive tradition that has an essential role in understanding black American musical history accurately. These vocalists extend the achievements of their predecessors and have the potential to influence future performers. Renewing critical attention to the historical role of blacks in cabaret could make it a more visible tradition and increase the genre's appeal as a branch of black musical expression. The commercial marginality of cabaret music certifies it as an independent genre. As such, its greatest hope for survival is a combination of performances as well as support from the academic and journalistic communities. Independent music (e.g., punk, modern rock) has long had cachet within rock criticism for standing outside of rock conventions. There is no reason a campy form of expression such as cabaret cannot achieve similar status in critical accounts of black popular music.

Notes

1   Southern, *The Music of Black Americans*, 596.
2   Neal, *Soul Babies*, 18.
3   Hamilton, *Just around Midnight*, 21.
4   Negus, *Popular Music in Theory*, 105–6, draws from Gilroy's *The Black Atlantic* and *Small Acts*.
5   Bergman, introduction to *Camp Grounds*, 4–5.
6   Robertson, "Mae West's Maids," 394.
7   Gavin, *Intimate Nights*, 7, 9.
8   Connolly, "Cabaret!," 71, 72.
9   Kart, "Back to the Cabaret."
10 Gavin, *Intimate Nights*, 67.
11 *The Erteguns' New York: New York Cabaret Music*, CD 782308-2 (Atlantic Records, 1987).
12 Bailey, *The Raw Pearl*; Bailey, *Talking to Myself*; Bailey, *Between You and Me*; Kitt, *Thursday's Child*; Kitt, *Alone with Me*; Kitt, *Confessions of a Sex Kitten*; Short, *Black and White Baby*; Short and Mackintosh, *Bobby Short*. Also see Haskins, *Mabel Mercer*.
13 Neal, *What the Music Said*, 40.
14 For example, Hemming and Hadju describe criticism Bobby Short received for his style, "especially by some African-American separatists for seemingly abandoning his African roots by performing 'white' music in a 'white' style. Short explained that his approach is 'color blind.' After all, as he often notes, classic pop has been influenced by a variety of cultures, including African-American, Italian, Jewish, and many others, and he certainly plays it all" (*Discovering Great Singers*, 222–23).
15 Regarding audiences, Short notes, "Even in New York in those days it was an uncommon sight to find a group of black people sitting in an East Side cabaret. Then, no city was without its unspoken 'no blacks' rule, particularly when it came

to eating and sleeping. I had heard of the archaic edicts that existed even up in Harlem. Despite the overwhelmingly black population, it was customary for a 'Whites Only' sign to be put out by uptown businessmen. It was the patronage of the white tourists that they looked for—not only at the legendary Cotton Club, but in other establishments as well" (Short and Mackintosh, *Bobby Short*, 76).

16 Gavin, *Intimate Nights*, 33, 83.
17 Gavin, *Intimate Nights*, 87, 264.
18 Gavin, *Intimate Nights*, 303.
19 Clum, *Something for the Boys*, 7.
20 Sontag, "Notes on 'Camp,'" 54, 64, emphasis added.
21 Clum, *Something for the Boys*, 8.
22 "Mabel Mercer," 41, 43.
23 Gavin, *Intimate Nights*, 286. Archie Walker was maître d' at the club Downstairs.
24 Lander, "A Champagne World," 56.
25 Hoerburger, "Eartha Kitt, a Seducer of Audiences, Dies at 81."
26 Kitt, *Confessions of a Sex Kitten*, 259-62.
27 Spigel and Jenkins, "Same Bat Channel," 125.
28 Harris cites the rise of gay liberationist politics as a form of identity that diminished the relevance of cultural codes like camp among gay men (*The Rise and Fall of Gay Culture*, 33-34, 269).
29 Gamson describes pressure on the openly gay singer Sylvester to tone down his image to appease his record label and black radio stations in the early 1980s (*The Fabulous Sylvester*, 192, 194-95).
30 Eartha Kitt, *Eartha Kitt—Greatest Hits: Purr-Fect*, CD 782308-2 (BMG Special Products, 1998).
31 Pearl Bailey, *Naughty but Nice*, digital album (Stage Door Records, 2012). Originally released 1960 on Roulette Records.
32 Gourse, *Louis' Children*, 240.
33 Bobby Short, *Bobby Short Live at the Café Carlyle*, CD 7771 (Atlantic Records, 1975).
34 Mallory Ostberg, "Syllabus."
35 Dreher, *Dancing on the White Page*, 92, 91, 94, 97, 99, 106-7, 109-16, 117.
36 Williams, "Living at the Crossroads," 145-47.
37 Neal, *Soul Babies*, 44.
38 Kitt, *Confessions of a Sex Kitten*, 123-24.
39 Bailey, *The Raw Pearl*, 118-19.
40 Baillett, *American Singers*, 138, emphasis added.
41 Short, *Life and Times*, 80.
42 Newton, *Cherry Grove*, 156.
43 Galatowitsch, "Jimmie Daniels (1908-1984)"; Short, *Life and Times*, 80.
44 Ross, "Camping the Dirty Dozens," 301.
45 Harper also discusses Baraka's homophobic rhetoric in *Are We Not Men?*, 49-52.
46 Ross, "Camping the Dirty Dozens," 296, 293, 296, 297, 291, 297.
47 Ross, "Camping the Dirty Dozens," 304, 298-99, 305, 304.

48 Ross, "Camping the Dirty Dozens," 297.

49 Regarding Bailey, see Gill, *No Surrender!*, 138; Kitt, *Confessions of a Sex Kitten*, 227–42, 248; Short, foreword to *Black and Blue*, xi–xv; Short, *Life and Times*, 232–34.

50 George, *Buppies*, 3, 7.

51 Neal, *Soul Babies*, 67.

References

Bailey, Pearl. *Between You and Me: A Heartfelt Memoir on Learning, Loving, and Living.* New York: Doubleday, 1989.

Bailey, Pearl. *The Raw Pearl.* New York: Harcourt, Brace and World, 1968.

Bailey, Pearl. *Talking to Myself.* New York: Houghton Mifflin Harcourt, 1971.

Baillett, Whitney. *American Singers.* New York: Oxford University Press, 1979.

Bergman, David. Introduction to *Camp Grounds: Style and Homosexuality.* Amherst: University of Massachusetts Press, 1993.

Clum, John M. *Something for the Boys: Musical Theatre and Gay Culture.* New York: Palgrave, 1999.

Connolly, Robert. "Cabaret!" *Stereo Review,* February 1975.

Dreher, Kwakiutl L. *Dancing on the White Page: Black Women Entertainers Writing Autobiography.* Albany: State University of New York Press, 2008.

Galatowitsch, Diane. "Jimmie Daniels (1908–1984)." Amistad Research Center, 2014. http://www.amistadresearchcenter.org/archon/index.php?p=creators /creator&id=63. Accessed March 30, 2019.

Gamson, Joshua. *The Fabulous Sylvester: The Legend, the Music, the Seventies in San Francisco.* New York: Picador, 2005.

Gavin, James. *Intimate Nights: The Golden Age of New York Cabaret.* New York: Grove Weidenfeld, 1991.

George, Nelson. *Buppies, B-Boys, Baps and Bohos: Notes on Post-Soul Black Culture.* New York: Harper Collins, 1992.

Gill, Glenda E. *No Surrender! No Retreat! African American Pioneer Performers of Twenti- eth Century American Theater.* New York: St. Martin's, 2000.

Gilroy, Paul. *The Black Atlantic: Modernity and Double Consciousness.* London: Verso, 1993.

Gilroy, Paul. *Small Acts: Thoughts on the Politics of Black Cultures.* London: Serpent's Tail, 1993.

Gourse, Leslie. *Louis' Children: American Jazz Singers.* 2nd ed. New York: Cooper Square Press, 2001.

Hamilton, Jack. *Just around Midnight: Rock and Roll and the Racial Imagination.* Cam- bridge, MA: Harvard University Press, 2016.

Harper, Phillip Brian. *Are We Not Men? Masculine Anxiety and the Problem of African- American Identity.* New York: Oxford University Press, 1996.

Harris, Daniel. *The Rise and Fall of Gay Culture.* New York: Hyperion, 1997.

Haskins, James. *Mabel Mercer: A Life.* New York: Atheneum, 1987.

Hemming, Roy, and David Hadju. *Discovering Great Singers of Classic Pop*. New York: New Market Press, 1991.

Hoerburger, Rob. "Eartha Kitt, a Seducer of Audiences, Dies at 81." *New York Times*, December 25, 2008. http://www.nytimes.com/2008/12/26/arts/26kitt.html ?module=Search&mabReward=relbias%3As&_r=0.

Kart, Larry. "Back to the Cabaret." *Chicago Tribune*, January 31, 1988.

Kitt, Eartha. *Alone with Me: A New Autobiography*. New York: H. Regnery, 1976.

Kitt, Eartha. *Confessions of a Sex Kitten*. London: Barricade Books, 1989.

Kitt, Eartha. *Thursday's Child*. London: Cassell, 1957.

Lander, David. "A Champagne World." *American Legacy*, Summer 2006.

"Mabel Mercer." *Ebony*, September 1952.

Mallory Ostberg, Daniel. "Syllabus for the Course on 'Camp Heterosexuality' I Have Not Yet Been Asked to Teach." *The Toast*, March 13, 2015. http://the-toast .net/2015/03/13/syllabus-course-camp-heterosexuality-not-yet-asked-teach/.

Neal, Mark Anthony. *Soul Babies: Black Popular Culture and the Post-Soul Aesthetic*. New York: Routledge, 2002.

Neal, Mark Anthony. *What the Music Said: Black Popular Music and Black Public Culture*. New York: Routledge, 1999.

Negus, Keith. *Popular Music in Theory: An Introduction*. Hanover, NH: Wesleyan University Press, 1996.

Newton, Esther. *Cherry Grove, Fire Island: Sixty Years in America's First Gay and Lesbian Town*. Boston: Beacon Press, 1993.

Robertson, Pamela. "Mae West's Maids: Race, 'Authenticity,' and the Discourse of Camp." In *Camp: Queer Aesthetics and the Performing Subject: A Reader*, edited by Fabio Cleto. Ann Arbor: University of Michigan Press, 1999.

Ross, Marlon B. "Camping the Dirty Dozens: The Queer Resources of Black Nationalist Invective." *Callaloo* 23, no. 1 (Winter 2000): 301.

Short, Bobby. *Black and White Baby*. New York: Dodd, Mead, 1971.

Short, Bobby. Foreword to *Black and Blue: The Life and Lyrics of Andy Razaf*, by Barry Singer. New York: Schirmer Books, 1992.

Short, Bobby, with Robert Mackintosh. *Bobby Short: The Life and Times of a Saloon Singer*. New York: Clarkson Potter, 1995.

Sontag, Susan. "Notes on 'Camp.'" In *Camp: Queer Aesthetics and the Performing Subject: A Reader*, edited by Fabio Cleto. Ann Arbor: University of Michigan Press, 1999.

Southern, Eileen. *The Music of Black Americans: A History*. 3rd ed. New York: Norton, 1997.

Spigel, Lynn, and Henry Jenkins. "Same Bat Channel, Different Bat Times: Mass Culture and Popular Memory." In *The Many Lives of Batman: Critical Approaches to a Superhero and His Media*, edited by Roberta E. Pearson and William Uricchio. New York: Routledge, 1991.

Williams, Rhonda. "Living at the Crossroads: Explorations in Race, Nationality, Sexuality, and Gender." In *The House That Race Built*, edited by Wahneema Lubiano. New York: Vintage Books, 1998.

CH.4   THE ART OF BLACK POPULAR CULTURE

H. Ike Okafor-Newsum

Understandably, in the past, fine art in the form of painting and sculpture was not included in the discussion of popular culture in the modern age as these art forms were thought to be limited to museums and private galleries and to the gaze of cultural elites. Religious iconography, which is hegemonic in the popular imagination, may be an exception, but for many, painting and sculpture are not believed to be products for mass consumption as are music, dance, fashion, cuisine, movies, and video. In the 1970s and 1980s the phenomenon of pop art was an opportunity for formally trained artists to participate in mass consumption through the production and presentation of graphic-commercial-iconographic imagery. It brought to the public awareness artists like Roy Lichtenstein, Andy Warhol, and Jean-Michel Basquiat. The graphic art that accompanied Black Power and the Black Arts Movement, made popular by political organs like the Black Panther Party newspaper, entertained the imagination of everyday, common folk who respected and revered the organization and those who benefited from its various programs. The political art of Black social movements also included public murals, most notably the Africobra *Wall of Respect* in Chicago that inspired social activists internationally. Murals like the *Wall of Respect* were intended for public consumption in order to provide opportunities for artists to interact with community folks in collaborative projects, for viewers to imagine themselves in various roles and occupations, and for artists to make art relevant for everyday, common folk. Mural art was also popular in the mid-1930s in Mexico; the images of Mexican muralists inspired African American artists like Hale Woodruff, John Biggers, and Corey Barksdale.

Today the tendency to exclude fine art from the study of popular culture begs the question, "What is the *pop* in popular culture?" How, for example, do we talk about the long-running television show *The Joy of Painting* that made art educator Bob Ross a household name and aired for thirty-one seasons, from 1983 to 1994? Imagine how many Americans were inspired by the show, which featured master painters and techniques of the trade. Certainly among the mass consumers of this show were African American viewers.

In 1992, in an attempt to define Black popular culture, Michele Wallace and Gina Dent published a collection of essays under the title *Black Popular Culture*. The contributors to this award-winning collection read like a slate of the top cultural studies scholars of our time and set the bar for works of this kind that would follow. Five years later, the University of Pittsburgh Press published Joseph K. Adjaye and Adrianne R. Andrews's *Language, Rhythm, and Sound: Black Popular Cultures into the Twenty-First Century* (1997), which, like the earlier collection, is erudite and thought provoking, offering an eclectic collection of essays that presents theoretical approaches and critical commentary about cultural phenomena in Africa and its diaspora. These works reestablish a tradition of revisiting cultural events as they are understood by Black artists and academics. Edited by Alain Locke with illustrations by Aaron Douglas, *The New Negro* is the grandparent of these more recent works, an early treatment of Black cultural expression directed to an academic audience. Given its limited consumption, it begs the question of how effective the Black intelligentsia has been in popularizing the phenomenon we call Black cultural studies. To put it another way, are the masses as receptive to the academic study of Jay-Z as they are to his performances?

For those who think critically about cultural expression, such publications are important tools that allow us to entertain diverse and divergent views and approaches to Black cultural events. The graphic illustrations in *The New Negro* suggest the important role of formally trained artists in the study and discussion of Black cultural expression; however, little attention is paid to fine art, painting, and sculpture in the two contemporary collections.

In their contributions to *Black Popular Culture*, Judith Wilson and Michele Wallace acknowledge the existence of this problem, and while their contributions broach the subject of fine art produced by African American artists, only one or two images of artwork appear in the anthology. To her credit, Wilson's essay, "Getting Down to Get Over: Romare Bearden's Use of Pornography and the Problem of the Black Female Body in Afro-U.S. Art," is an interesting discussion of Bearden's representation of Black women and the paucity of the Black female nude in art by African American artists prior to the 1960s. Wallace's afterword, which asks the question "Why are there no great Black artists?," offers little on the subject of Black art or Black artists. And there are no art images and little discussion of fine art in the Black cultural context in the collection edited by Adjaye and Andrews, an oversight for which I share some responsibility as one of the anthology's contributors. Hence the present work seeks to fill this gap in the current discourse on Black popular culture by discussing the work of seven artists: Lehna Huie, Shani Jamila, Soraya Jean-Louis, April Sunami, Jason Wallace, Ike Okafor-Newsum, Leonardo Benzant, and Simone Drake.

Present-day technology makes possible the mass consumption of images in ways that surpass the efficacy of television. A search for images via social media platforms like YouTube, Facebook, Instagram, Squarespace, and Twitter will yield instant results. Formally trained artists have discovered the ease of self-promotion with the use of technology, creating their own online galleries, and, in doing so, make fine art more accessible to a general audience. The production of contemporary Black art, like the art of the Harlem Renaissance, the Black Arts Movement, and the Post-Black Movement, takes place under a condition of racial hierarchy and white supremacy that is perpetuated by a Eurocentric, capitalist hegemony. Echoing Stuart Hall, Lawrence Grossberg has suggested that the idea of hegemony is "a struggle over the popular." In the realm of visual art this concerns the power to control the symbolic matrix that constitutes visual experience in the most diverse and comprehensive sense—within and between civil society, the state, and the economic sector.[1] How can Black art be an arbiter of identity politics and an advocate for social equality and economic justice?

Lehna Huie's painting *Say Her Name* (figure 4.1) serves as one example of imagery contributing to the public discourse that usually imagines racialized police brutality as violence against African American men. Huie was commissioned to create this work for the African American Policy Forum's "Say Her Name" cultural event, honoring the mothers who lost their daughters to senseless police violence. The centerpiece of Huie's contribution is a

FIG.4.1 Lehna Huie, *Say Her Name*. Mixed media.

saintly depiction of the face of Sandra Bland, a twenty-eight-year-old African American woman who was found hanged in a jail cell in Waller County, Texas, on July 13, 2015, three days after being assaulted and arrested by state trooper Brian Encinia during a traffic stop.[2] *Say Her Name* represents the ongoing demand for accountable policing. Surrounded by the faces of fifteen figures, potential mourners, victims of state-sponsored violence, or potential activists calling for justice, Sandra Bland symbolizes opposition against police brutality. She also represents a list of Black female victims (Charleena Lyles, Sharday Hill, Tanisha Anderson, Natasha McKenna, et al.). However, Bland's activism in the Black Lives Matter movement has made her more than just another victim. Bland is an inspirational figure in the lexicon of protest art.

Black women artists like Shani Jamila use their images and social media networks to advocate for social-economic justice and for gender and racial

FIG.4.2 Shani Jamila, *Lit*. Photograph.

equality. Her photograph *Lit*, with its intense blue background and spots and shards of light (white, blue, violet, and pink; figure 4.2), captures what appears to be a performance, like those organized by the photographer, who regularly employs the arts for consciousness raising. Jamila's social media presence and activism in cyberspace, in prisons, and in local communities, along with her extensive travels around the world, have afforded her, according to *Essence*, recognition as "One of the 35 Most Remarkable Women in the World."[3] A collagist, fiber artist, and creative writer, Jamila is also director of the Urban Justice Center in New York City, where she curates exhibits and develops programming for social justice. *Lit* captures the multimodality of Black popular performance. An electric guitar strap on the performer's shoulder as he stands on a literal "lit" stage illuminated by white, blue, violet, and pink, incandescent light conjures eruptions of funk. The hybrid sounds of funk invoked by the image speak to the more contemporary vernacular use of "lit" as something that is hot and exciting—something that gives one life.

Soraya Jean-Louis's surrealistic collage painting *See Them Now* (figure 4.3) uses iconographic imagery to refer to the historical roots of racial injustice

FIG.4.3 Soraya Jean-Louis, *See Them Now*. Collage.

and the oppression of women. The familiar icon *The Brookes*, an eighteenth-century British slave ship, infamous for its depiction of the cramped conditions to which the slave cargo was subjected, echoes the visual lexicon of racial violence in the United States. Also among its symbolism are references to Black women's labor, the freedom quest, the exoticization of Black women, and fertility set against a sunbaked urban backdrop. The reclining figure, seemingly lying on a bed of coal, is reminiscent of the *Roots* paintings and the *Henry Ford Hospital* series by the Mexican surrealist Frida Kahlo, another female artist of color and social activist, whose work addressed the hegemonic devices used to subjugate racially marginalized women.

Dream Logic, a mixed-media painting on canvas by April Sunami, features a batik-like textile design using splashes of squiggles, curlicues, parallel lines, squares, and sprinkles of dots that complement the central figure, a beautiful woman with extravagant hair of fabric-like leaves (figure 4.4). This image not only accentuates the beauty of Black women; it also brings to mind textile artists, like the weavers of Bonwire, "a cluster of some eight villages lying about twelve miles from Kumase . . . the Kente weaving capital of Ashante."[4] While emphasizing Black female beauty, the fabric design in this painting connects the central figure to a history of fabric workers who create wearable art. In this dreamscape that exalts Black women's natural beauty Sunami insists upon a logic that privileges the brown skin and billowy afro that are foregrounded in the frame.

An African ancestral beauty aesthetic was introduced in the Americas during the 1960s and 1970s that challenged mainstream white standards of beauty and brought traditional artifacts like the afro pick into the modern Black protest movement. Jason Wallace's sculpture *Crosshairs*, in the words of Adjaye, serves "simultaneously as a cultural artifact of an external past that has been lost but must be recovered and as a symbolic representation that is pregnant with new meaning, new possibilities for self-recreation" (figure 4.5).[5] The continuum of being and becoming is marked by reinvention. Elements of ancestral memory are deployed in modern strategies of resistance in a continuing culture war between the West and the rest of us. As a public art installation in Harlem, *Crosshairs* plays upon the fact that what makes you powerful can also make you a target.

My mixed-media collage *Nkisi: Head Hair* represents a counterhegemonic discourse (Bakongo cosmology) of indigenous people in contradistinction to Western rationalism and Christianity (figure 4.6). More than defiance, the recognition of the authority of indigenous thought contrary to Western paradigms is an act of cultural identification. Based on the Nkondi power

FIG.4.4 April Sunami, *Dream Logic*.

FIG.4.5 Jason Wallace, *Crosshairs*.

FIG.4.6 H. Ike Okafor-Newsum, *Nkisi: Head Hair*. Mixed-media collage on corrugated cardboard, 21×36 inches.

figures of Congo, *Head Hair* represents an aesthetic rooted in ancient beliefs about creation, relationships among the living and between the living and the dead, and about the power of art-artifacts and the everyday role of art in civil society and sacred spaces. Often presented as protectors, the Nkondi figures (armed with the power of indigenous medicine and a knife) are apt for the genre of resistance art.

Leonardo Benzant's large (each nine to ten feet tall) paper cut forms are colorful, moving, asymmetrical quadriptychs that feel more like sculptures than two-dimensional work (figure 4.7). Produced after a six-day road trip from Galveston, Texas, to New York City, they simultaneously invoke ancient and futuristic aesthetic worlds, the urban and primal, Western art, and African-Caribbean culture, ritual, and archetypes. Accordingly, the color combinations evoke the sea or other watery places from which all living things evolve. Some of the shapes appear to perform an acrobatic dance; others seem to march; and some appear to be evolving entities, new forms of life. These entities are shifting identities that suggest possibilities of change and the ability to morph into a better self—the idea of identity formation as a process of becoming. These colorful, rhythmic entities embody the constant negotiation—continuity and disjuncture—the changing and unsettling metamorphosis of blackness.

Are You Entertained?, fabric art (batik) by Simone Drake, calls attention to one of the precursors to the internet, television, which along with radio popularized the cultural products of politics, commerce, and social life, including products of leisure from African American communities in the form of fashion, cuisine, lore, dance, and music (figure 4.8). It can be said that television is the spark that ignited the field and study of popular culture. The commercialization and commodification of Black cultural products and the corollary influence of television on individual and group concepts of self describe a condition under which resistance and self-determination are a priori. The mass consumption of negative, dehumanizing stereotypes of Black people and the degradation of Black culture by mainstream mass media have made necessary an audio-visual counterculture that dispels and corrects distorted characterizations of African Americans and other peoples of color. The absence of clenched fists and protest signs in this scene of Black subjects simply going about their day brings to mind the way that hegemony works in making (through a subtle co-optation) the oppressed accept the domination of a ruling group, a process that uses mass media effectively.

The popular in Black popular culture continues to be a struggle against hegemonic white racist representations of Black people on the one hand,

FIG.4.7. Leonardo Benzant, *Afrosupernatural: Entities and Archetypes.* Installation mixed media on paper.

and for public access to technology on the other. The popularity and celebrity of President Barack Obama and First Lady Michelle Obama, combined with the efficacy of social media, has called public attention to two artists whose self-promoting media savvy had already made them celebrities in their own right. The Obamas' portraits were painted by the New York–based artist Kehinde Wiley and the Baltimore-based artist Amy Sherald. Masters of the European tradition of painted portraiture, these artists and their artwork, like the others discussed here, push against the historical depictions of African-descended subjects as savages, buffoons, brutes, and Jezebels by rendering dignified images of Black bodies in familiar but unexpected locations with meticulous attention to color and racial detail. I don't know how many viewers will experience the Obama portraits in the National Gallery or on the internet. What I do know is that the potential and endless possibilities of cyber galleries are within reach with a stroke of the keyboard.

FIG.4.8 Simone Drake, *Are You Entertained?* Batik.

Access to technology and the ability to traverse the inner and outer limits of cyberspace are key to the efficacy of Black popular culture. It is possible to produce disciplined, sophisticated Black art while at the same time creating a counterhegemonic vocabulary of expressions—a culture of resistance that also mitigates white supremacy and social-economic injustices. This should be the role of self-conscious Black popular culture—of art and artists committed to the struggle for justice, equality, freedom, and peace. Resistance is the "black" in Black popular culture.

Notes

1　Grossberg quoted in Adjaye, "The Discourse of Kente Cloth," 6.
2　Within minutes of the encounter between Bland and Encinia, the videotaped event flooded social media, and concerns about the mysterious circumstances around her untimely death fueled the controversy surrounding the problem of racial bias and policing in the communities of the poor and people of color.
3　Jamila, "About."

4 Adjaye, "Discourse of Kente Cloth," 25.
5 Adjaye, "Discourse of Kente Cloth," 36.

References

Adjaye, Joseph K. "The Discourse of Kente Cloth: From Haute Couture to Mass Culture." In *Language, Rhythm, and Sound: Black Popular Cultures into the Twenty-First Century*, edited by Joseph K. Adjaye and Adrianne R. Andrews. Pittsburgh: University of Pittsburgh Press, 1997.

Benzant, Leonardo. "Artist Statement." *Claire Oliver Gallery*. www.claireoliver.com. Accessed March 24, 2018.

Jamila, Shani. "About." *Shani Jamila*, 2016. www.shanijamila.com. Accessed March 24, 2018.

Locke, Alain, ed. *The New Negro*. 1925. New York: Atheneum, 1968.

Wallace, Michelle. Afterword. In *Black Popular Culture: Discussions in Contemporary Culture*, edited by Michele Wallace and Gina Dent. Seattle, WA: Bay Press, 1992.

Wallace, Michele, and Gina Dent. *Black Popular Culture: Discussions in Contemporary Culture*. Seattle, WA: Bay Press, 1992.

Wilson, Judith. "Getting Down to Get Over: Romare Bearden's Use of Pornography and the Problem of the Black Female Body in Afro-U.S. Art" In *Black Popular Culture: Discussions in Contemporary Culture*, edited by Michele Wallace and Gina Dent. Seattle, WA: Bay Press, 1992.

AN INTERVIEW WITH LISA B.

THOMPSON / JANUARY 9, 2016

*What is the state of black pop culture in the public sphere and as an
intellectual field of inquiry in the twenty-first century?*

The public sphere is a site of—and for—blackness. I mean it—I think people
may not identify the public sphere as one of the main sites for black popular
culture, but it undoubtedly is and has been since we entered the abolition-
ist and Reconstruction print and performance cultures. Currently, we black
creators and critics seem to be ubiquitous, powerful, game-changing. Black
popular culture consumes the public sphere at every turn (and is consumed
by it), whether it is folks obsessing about poor Kanye West trying to down-
load his song yesterday to the most recent dragging or live tweeting of *Empire*
on Black Twitter. There is the Kendrick Lamar explosion—folks cannot get
enough of him—to the latest and greatest in black film. I think there are
sixteen black films at Sundance this year, or some crazy number like that. Yes,
black popular culture is everywhere, and yet at the same time, there is still concern about how much we are able to control, who speaks/blogs/publishes/
guest-stars and for whom; that anxiety exists in the academy as well. Who

gets to teach black life and its cultural products and producers? Who owns these topics, especially in the context of efforts to centralize a shared public sphere where black lives matter? How do we frame analyses of black pop culture now that we have decided that TV shows, music downloads, status updates, and tweets should be taken seriously and critically examined? How do we as scholars relax, chill, as the kids used to say, and just do what we're doing and still receive support, funding, get published and speaking venues across the social spheres of black and intellectual life? When I began my career black popular culture as a justifiable academic field was still questionable. Luckily, this is not true for my students, and hopefully it will not be the case for future black studies scholars. The current generation does not seem worried about whether other people feel comfortable with these topics, and I am pleased about that. We [Thompson and Mark Anthony Neal] came up in a different era, when Tricia Rose's *Black Noise: Rap Music and Black Culture in Contemporary America* got dropped in 1994 and reverberated across the country in grad programs and black studies courses. We were junior faculty at the time when people began teaching classes on Spike Lee, and now students are like "Who? That old guy? Okay. Cool." So it is both wonderful and challenging in that black popular culture is now part of academia and somewhat legitimized, but I still worry about people not having historical knowledge about black popular culture or black cultural criticism. I am worried because, while our students or our colleagues outside the field may know the hot song, TV show, book, or movie, they often do not know the tradition of black literature, music, or theater that it is built on, that the artists they love are referencing.

> *How do you see Stuart Hall's theorization of the" black" in black popular culture influencing your intellectual engagement with black cultural productions?*

What is still useful about Hall's piece is the insistence on always making sure your thinking is grounded in historic specificity. The historical moment has so much to do with what we were dealing with in terms of what is considered popular, what is considered black. Talking about blackness in an ahistorical way just does a disservice to our notions of art and culture and black folk throughout the diaspora. Even in a particular historical period, there is never one way folks understand their blackness. And that is why we are often interested in artists who upend and disrupt. I have been teaching an undergraduate course called Rethinking Blackness for over a decade now. Blackness is a fascinating thing to think about (and to rethink). So folks like Issa Rae and Donald Glover basically came out of the closet about black awkwardness while simultaneously celebrating "black cool"—I call it the "black nerd aesthetic," or blerd aesthetic—and now that is a dominant thing in the public sphere. But I do not think it comes out of nowhere. It comes out of folks being second- or even third-generation integrated, college-educated, once the only black kid in the class and now trying to make their way, who runs into their tribe of other black folk who had the same kind of experience. . . .

And please let's not forget Trey Ellis's groundbreaking 1989 essay, "The New Black Aesthetic." He laid this all out very early, and we are still seeing his theory's relevance. We need to start being honest about how different performances of blackness are linked to region and class. What I mean is, there is not enough work being done to unpack how awkward blackness in the 'hood is different than awkward blackness in the burbs when your dad is a doctor (like for Issa Rae). But maybe you get a little bit of that with *Everybody Hates Chris*. With Chris Rock's sitcom you start to get a sense of what it is like when you are a working-class black kid, but very little ink has been dropped—or spilled—to talk about that. The other thing that he [Hall] emphasizes are notions of marginality—thinking about the margins of black popular culture and how they influence the center of black popular culture. I have always hung out in the margins because, for one, the other spaces are already so occupied and often overdetermined. Besides that I always like to try to intervene in new terrains. Is that because I'm a Cali girl and our blackness has always been contested by those from the more "racially authentic" sites, such as the South or the East Coast? Perhaps. Maybe it also has to do with my being an artist/scholar, as well as a first-generation college graduate and a child of the urban black working class. I guess it is probably also because of feeling, as someone who creates and writes about black culture, I am homeless—feeling like I do not belong in many of the spaces where my work is disseminated, be it academia or in the theater.

> *Do you feel the digital age affects the production, reception, and dissemination of black pop culture in ways that compel us to both continue revisiting Hall's piece but to also build upon it? If yes, how do you see contemporary theorists and critics building upon Hall's work given the changes the digital age has produced? If no, why do you feel the digital age does not compel scholars to revisit Hall and build upon his work?*

That is an interesting and complex question. . . . I think this notion of the digital is really the question of the moment. But as a playwright and critic I mostly work with ephemeral performance. That show is gone after it closes. The only recorded theatrical performance that I am willing to show students is Stew's *Passing Strange*, because Spike Lee had so many cameras on that stage and really knew that musical so well, so intimately that the show lost very little in translation. He truly captured the feeling and the moment of that musical's closing weekend. But, for the most part, videos are such a flat, horrible way for people to experience black theater and performance. So I think that theater often ends up being—I call it the baldhead stepchild of black culture. Look at the *Norton Anthology of African American Literature*. How many plays are in there relative to poetry and short stories and novel excerpts? We continue to ignore the impact and power and importance of black theater. Soon there will be two shows—*Sweat* by Lynn Nottage and a new play by Suzan-Lori Parks—opening in DC. There is one place that archives many of the Broadway shows, which is the New York Public Library's Theatre on Film and Tape Archive. It is a palace, but not everything is there. You can only see those shows once as a scholar, because they have protected the rights of the performers, designers, and directors (as they should). The digital age sometimes fails us, because we think we can always see the video. When teaching or lecturing I do show clips here and there of plays, but for the most part, I think we are missing out on something crucial if we do not sit for the live performance of a play (or a concert). We need to consider the fact that some cultural products cannot be experienced digitally. So how do we make an effort to get out there to see and support work? I often say let's champion the work we love or want to see instead of expending so much energy blasting what offends us. The stages of New York are about to be lit up with all these amazing shows. You know, for the first time, there is a show about African women being directed by an African woman, written by African women, and performed by African women, opening on Broadway. The production of Danai Gurira's *Eclipsed* is historic. Then there is the revival of *The Color Purple* as well as George Wolfe's *Shuffle Along* opening on Broadway soon too. These shows are on stages within the same block or within blocks of each other. Epic.

[Mark Anthony Neal: And critics have to be able to write about them.]

And which critics are there? . . . That's another thing. Right now, there is no black performing arts critic at the *New York Times*. . . .

[Mark Anthony Neal: . . . and that's where the digital piece is also important because now there are at least spaces for black theater critics to write about it and not have to go through the *New York Times* or the *New Yorker*. . . .]

But let me tell you, when it comes to the money, a producer wants to know what the *New York Times* said. It is not going to go up. Period. We have to create our own version of Broadway—or green-light our own works. That is why the Ava DuVernay model is so powerful. She understands not only what it means to publicize her work but also to create some kind of mechanism to get the work in the theaters, and to support other folks who are producing good work. That is what cultural producers must think about. So I think digital is wonderful for us to be able to use as a teaching tool so students can better understand some references from the text. . . .

[Mark Anthony Neal: And ironically for all the critiques that we might have of Tyler Perry, he actually has very successfully figured out how to do that. . . .]

True, we have to acknowledge Perry's success there. So yeah, there is a lot going on now, as far as digital access to black popular culture—almost to the point where it is too much. Right, so how do you get through all of Spike Lee's work, all of Toni Morrison's work, and know your Miles Davis and Cassandra Wilson plus know your Nicki Minaj and your Drake? Black folks are prolific. Period. Oh, can we go back to black, though, too? The black in black popular culture that Stuart Hall taught me was transnational. So, to be knowledgeable about black culture diasporically you also need to also know your Teju Cole, Wangechi Mutu, Fela Kuti, Chimamanda Ngozi Adichie, Miriam Makeba, and Akon too.

You straddle the realms of critic, scholar, and cultural producer in ways that resonate with early theorists of black popular culture, such as Langston Hughes, Zora Neale Hurston, and W. E. B. Du Bois. Can you discuss the relationship between producing cultural products that circulate in the public sphere yet are also situated in an academic discipline? As an artist-scholar, how do you negotiate the centrality of black pop culture to neoliberal consumerism in the twenty-first century?

Yes, I always find it difficult to figure out how I am going to name myself: am I an artist-scholar, or am I a scholar-artist? It depends on the room. The challenge, I think, mostly is to make sure that neither voice takes over. So when I'm trying to craft a new play, the challenge is to keep the critic from scaring the artist off from doing the work that the artist wants and needs to do. It also is important for the artist in me to possess a sense of history, theory, form, and a sense of responsibility to the subjects I am writing about— whether it is the black middle class, black female sexuality, or intraracial conflict. I do not know if it is always possible, but it is important to nurture that balance between my artist self and my scholar self. I am interested in conveying black life, not as perfection or pathology but in all its messy, fragile, urgent, gorgeous, humorous, sexy complexity and glory. My work as an artist-scholar is to help clear the way for those coming behind me. I want to be in conversation with other folks who are straddling the fence in this way. I want us to talk about what it means to be a black artist-scholar. I want to ask, "What do you give up? What do you gain? What does it mean?" I want to share our stories so the next generation does not have to reinvent the wheel. We need to leave them a blueprint. Besides, like you said, this is not new. We are not new. Langston Hughes, W. E. B. Du Bois, and Zora Neale Hurston enjoyed varying degrees of success doing both things. How many people here—raise your hand if you read *Dark Princess* [Du Bois] and loved it! [*Laughter*] Or, read all of Zora Neale Hurston's scholarly work? Unless you are researching them for a project, then I think the list of folks who read it *all* is very short. It is challenging to do both—be an artist and a scholar—but it is also a blessing. I definitely like being where I am located right now in the academy, where both things I do are encouraged, honored, and respected.

> *Langston Hughes in "The Negro Artist and the Racial Mountain"*
> *insists that the masses, what he called "the low-down folk," produce*
> *organic black cultural products. What interplay do you see between*
> *the low-down folk, cultural production (and consumption), and*
> *participatory democracy in the twenty-first century?*

Well, I am so glad you brought up Langston Hughes's "The Negro Artist and the Racial Mountain," because it is one of my favorites. I think Hughes's essay resonates just as much as Hall's "The Black in Black Popular Culture." I love talking about it with my students and juxtaposing it with George Schuyler's "The Negro Art Hokum" and, of course, Du Bois's "Criteria for Negro Art." I have them [students] work through several questions: What is black art? Who does it serve? Represent? What is this concern with authenticity? I keep returning to them and this idea of the working class, the underclass, the black "po"—meaning *poor* in black English—being central. But I think we are seeing a move now where the black middle class dominates certain elements of black popular culture, particularly the viral video sensation, Issa Rae's *Awkward Black Girl*, and Kenya Barris's *Black-ish*. Those shows, like *Being Mary Jane*, are about the black middle class, but they show the way the black middle class actually operates, which is among and between these different worlds. A world where it is not strange if you have a cousin in jail and you are off to Harvard in the fall. The audience sees there really is not this huge divide between the black masses and more economically privileged black folks. We get to see what is being produced with that knowledge and that kind of wink toward self-awareness of being a part of a privileged generation but at the same time really aware of and frustrated by the restraining limits of blackness. It has been wonderful—I just presented a keynote at the musicology conference last month about how artists respond to Black Lives Matter. A lot of older black folks think that the current generation is unaware of what is really important and that they lack a sense of urgency and a political sensibility. Actually seeing these new artists like Kendrick Lamar, J. Cole, and Janelle Monáe, in particular, and Jill Scott being very much willing to put their careers on the line to engage around these kind of issues—not just songs they are going to sell but also just speaking out. It has been exciting to think about how the black public sphere has been really enriched by these protests despite the trauma that we are all experiencing. I love the theater of protest that has been an exciting place for black working class and black middle class, upper class, if you will, to meet on that ground of contention and struggle—even struggling with each other around who is going to lead or "own" the movement. Is anyone gonna try to trademark it? What's the role of black popular figures—the Jay-Z's and the Bey's and John Legend's and other kind of prominent folks? People are happy to see you there but also want to assure you do not take up all the oxygen in the room, right? What happens with Netta [Johnetta Elzie] and DeRay [Mckesson], and these other folks who emerged, and then the challenges around—what's the brotha's name? People kept questioning whether he was black or not? [the journalist Shaun King]. So I guess this is a very messy mix but a very exciting time to be an artist, to be a scholar, to be an activist, but there is also a lot of fatigue. Overall, I am happy to see how all these things are converging. I try to help my students understand that what we are seeing with black artists is nothing new. I am making them aware that during the civil rights movement Harry Belafonte and Sammy Davis Jr. were there, too, it was not just Baldwin—it was also, these black popular figures: Nina Simone, Ruby Dee, Sidney Poitier, Eartha Kitt [Mark Anthony Neal: Quincy Jones, Donald Goines, Chester Himes] who used their visibility and put their careers on the line to resist.

In the next twenty years, do you foresee everyday practical action becoming more central to black cultural productions?

So, if you mean will most people see themselves as poets, rappers, dancers, or singers? Probably not. I do hope that more black folks will begin to see themselves as artists even if they do not plan to make a living through art. In the artist's hustle mentality, the measure of art has often been about how many "likes" you get or your big box-office draw or how much you are getting paid for a piece of work.

But those who labor in the archives know that the song, the poem, the dance, the photograph is actually what lives on, not the money. Nobody really knows how much—unless they are researching it—how much Alvin Ailey made in his lifetime, but he left a legacy that is priceless. What is exciting to me is that my son, who is ten years old, loves Michael Jackson, but he came to know his body of work posthumously. In fact, the day he died, I had him listen to his catalogue with me, so that he knows his work; he listened to his music and watched his videos nonstop and became an instant fan. To me, that is transcendence. That is otherworldly. He had no idea of the dead man's global reach—he just knew he loved the music. I learned then that because of his artistry, Jackson's reach across time, generation, and even death was precise and undeniable. We are all artists and consumers of art. As soon as we allow art to be part of the quotidian in our consciousness, perhaps we will also be transcendent. Everyone, not just those that get trained to become a particular kind of artist. It is important that we all think of ourselves as artists. Now once you leave fourth grade, there is no space for you to draw or paint or sing or write poems anymore. And really, I think at some point I would like to write a piece about those who engage in multiple kinds of artistic practices. And what does that tell us about the artist's soul? We are led to believe that the only way to be considered an artist is to be paid for it, and the only audience members who matter are the critics. I think that both of those ideas are false and dangerous. That thinking put us in a situation where we do not really get a chance to appreciate all that the world has to offer us, as black folks. The beauty of August Wilson's work is that he understood the everyday poetry of urban poor black folk in a way that I hope to see on stages again, and I think we are seeing some of that with Dominique Morisseau's plays. Not that she is the new Wilson. Morisseau has her own vision and her own legacy to leave. Keep an eye out for her. Her latest play, *Skeleton Crew*, is starting previews. It is about Detroit faculty workers. She is from Detroit, she's reppin' Detroit hard. I'm writing about her in my new book, and I think she is brilliant. Morisseau's work proves that the current generation also understands that there is poetry in the lives of everyday black folk, post–August Wilson. She also believes in the beauty of black popular culture—now ain't that hot?

II. POLITICIZING BLACKNESS

REFASHIONING POLITICAL CARTOONS / COMICS OF JACKIE ORMES, 1938–1958

Kelly Jo Fulkerson-Dikuua

> Who will revere the black woman? . . . Who will glorify and proclaim her beautiful image? · ABBEY LINCOLN, "Who Will Revere"

In a 1955 single-panel comic run by the *Pittsburgh Courier*, a young girl tells her older sister, "I don't want to seem touchy on the subject . . . but that new little white tea-kettle just whistled at me." The young girl, Patty-Jo, stands with one hand on her hip and waving a finger at her curvaceous, pin-up-like sister, Ginger, who hides a newspaper behind her back. Looking closely at the newspaper cover, the words "Till" and "Boy" become apparent as Ginger tries to hide the news from her kid sister. The cartoon artist Jackie Ormes drew this comic in response to an all-white jury's failure to convict the murderers of Emmett Till, a fourteen-year-old boy mutilated and lynched in Mississippi in 1955 for allegedly whistling at a white woman. Ormes's cartoon joins the broader tradition of making visible that which mainstream media often rendered invisible. Till's death, often cited as a catalyst for the civil rights movement, received widespread attention particularly as his mother insisted upon an open casket at his funeral to display her son's mutilated body. Images of Black men being murdered or brutalized by the police have permeated recent social justice movements as well, including Black Lives Matter. Supporters of Black Lives Matter have taken to uploading videos on social media of instances of police brutality and government responses to Black resistance. Just as Mamie Till insisted that her son's casket remain open at his funeral "to let the world see what it is like," the viral nature of these videos ensures that Americans must reckon with the idea that Black men find themselves in a "perpetual state of crisis."[1] The spectacle of violence and police brutality point both to the tragic deaths of Alton Sterling, Tamir Rice, and Philando Castile, and also to the undercurrents of racism that paint Black men in the United States as "phobogenic objects."[2]

These visual images not only reference what is seen but also gesture at and substitute for what is and has been largely unseen in popular media. In a recent graduate seminar I attended, a student raised her hand and said, "I am all for Black Lives Matter, but what about our girls? Where are the protests for our girls?" While Black Lives Matter has certainly addressed the violence enacted upon specific women by the police, this particular student felt dismay that the case against Daniel Holtzclaw, a police officer who stalked and raped thirteen Black women in Oklahoma City, had not been brought to the fore of Black Lives Matter as other cases of police violence had. Simone Drake similarly points out that the "narratives [of a state of crisis] consistently leave out Black women and girls who, presumably, are not in crisis." Drake argues that even the concepts of racial equality and Black manhood have been so deeply intertwined that women have become marginal elements in the struggle for social change.[3]

Given the powerful nature of visual imagery to spark social change, the question arises as to how media images of Black women factor into the fight for racial equality. Traditionally, as bell hooks posits, images of Black women often act as a "foil" either to "soften the image of the black man" or to maintain the position of white womanhood in society.[4] Abbey Lincoln, however, demands that we confront this positioning of the Black woman, asking, "Who will glorify and proclaim her beautiful image?" For hooks, the answer lies not in attempting to resist this "foil-dom" or essentializing gaze of white heteropatriarchy but in focusing on forms of Black female spectatorship that do not "reflect what already exists . . . but [find] a form of representation . . . focused on black femaleness."[5] This chapter explores the visual imagery of cartoon artist Jackie Ormes, not to undermine the powerful images of Black men and boys in driving social change but rather to look at Ormes as an example of a visual artist repositioning Black women outside of this category of foil and focusing on "black femaleness" in and of itself. As Toni Morrison writes, "she [the Black woman] had nothing to fall back on: not maleness, not whiteness, not ladyhood. And out of the profound desolation of her reality she may very well have invented herself."[6] With the deluge of imagery focusing on Black male bodies, this chapter positions Ormes's cartoons as powerful visual inventions and interventions of Black femaleness in mid-twentieth-century America.

Ormes's intervention particularly explores a Black femaleness focused on mobility, fashion, and political commentary. Published in both the *Pittsburgh Courier* and the *Chicago Defender* from 1937 to 1956, her work comprises a significant though often overlooked form of visual artwork: protest and political commentary that underscored social unrest but also provided an avenue for a Black woman to harness a form of Black womanhood often left untreated in dominant discourses surrounding Black women of the 1940s and 1950s. Ormes's work presents well-dressed, politically savvy Black women who migrated in and out of spaces commonly reserved for men and white women. Her comic canon consists of four main strips: *Torchy Brown in "Dixie to Harlem"*; *Candy, Patty-Jo, and Ginger*; and *Torchy Brown in Heartbeats*. *Torchy Brown in "Dixie to Harlem"* ran from 1937 to 1938 in the *Pittsburgh Courier*. This character, Torchy, is a young woman who moves from the segregated South to New York in search of fame. Ormes's next comic, *Candy*, ran for four months over 1945–46 in the *Chicago Defender*, and portrays a subversive domestic worker who provides a definitive critique of the politics of race relations in domestic servitude, complaining about rolling her madame's cigarettes and joking about planting meatballs in her Victory Garden. Ormes's longest running comic, *Patty-Jo and Ginger*, ran from 1946 to 1956 in the *Courier*. This comic strip reveals a strong political consciousness as Ormes uses five-year-old Patty-Jo to critique foreign policy, World War II, segregation, racism, voting, and race relations in general. Finally, *Torchy in Heartbeats* documents a love story between the stylish Torchy and a mystery man revealed only in the final panels. Ormes's comics are political by nature, in their overt political critique, in visual cues that signal a social mobility for her characters, and a strong sense of sartorial flair. The mobility of her characters emanates from their movements either geographically, such as when Torchy moves from the South to the North, to a social mobility in which Candy, a domestic worker, transverses space in her white employer's home and proffers critiques of white female domesticity. Torchy, Candy, Patty-Jo, and Ginger all resist the generally silent political stance expected of Black women during the 1940s and 1950s by offering strong commentary and positioning themselves in traditionally male realms such as sporting events and professional endeavors.

Ormes's Life and Work: Reworking Racism in Comic Art

Ormes herself embodied this mobility, breaking into the world of print media as the first Black female syndicated cartoon artist. By utilizing the medium of the comic, Ormes appropriates a dominantly white male space to produce her artwork, thus redefining the parameters of cartoons, a media imbued with a deeply racist, patriarchal history and canon. While most researchers of comics focus on white male artists, such as Will Eisner or Frank Miller, little work has been conducted on the work of Ormes. Aside from Nancy Goldstein's monumental biographical piece on Ormes and references to her in Trina Robbins's *A Century of Women Cartoonists*, sundry mentions of Ormes appear in volumes about Black comics, such as Fredrik Strömberg's *Black Images in the Comics* or in Frances Gatewood and John Jennings's *The Blacker the Ink*. Ormes has not been canonized in anthologies of Black visual artists in America. Her notable absence from these pages may be due to either the relegation of comics as "low art" or the paucity of space allotted for Black female visual artists in contemporary collections on visual art. In either case, this chapter seeks to build on the work done by Goldstein and Robbins in highlighting the life and oeuvre of Jackie Ormes by approaching comics as "sequential art," to borrow the term used by Will Eisner, to describe cartoons as a series of images arranged for graphic storytelling.[7] Adilifu Nama's *Super Black* fights against the narrow reading of comics as superficial art, reading comics in a "critically celebratory" perspective that "reclaim[s] black super-heroes from . . . clichéd assumptions" and argues that Black superheroes proffer a "futuristic and fantastic vision of blackness."[8] For Nama, comics, or art that appears mundane, reveals cultural and social transformations over time as well as the promise of future ideological shifts. This chapter departs from his note of optimism, reading the transformative in the mundane. Ormes's comic creations Torchy Brown, Candy, Patty-Jo, and Ginger offer depth to the idea of the Black woman as superhero. In a world dominated by what Robbins calls *"white,* white shirted-men," Ormes navigates not only racial barriers but also her transformative power as a woman drawing within a world dominated by anti-Black racism and patriarchy.[9]

Portrayals of Black people in European and American comics reflect the complicity of the mainstream media with the racist and segregated history of global white supremacy. In fact, some of the largest producers of comic media today remain complicit with creating and promoting narrow, raced comics. Disney, for instance, has been indicted for portrayals of villains as Black, including Scar from *The Lion King* and Jafar from *Aladdin*, both of whom are cast next to ambiguously raced heroes: the light-skinned Aladdin, with a decidedly white American accent and Simba, the lighter-colored lion who partners romantically with an even lighter lioness with green eyes. These media stereotypes are embedded within a broader history of media-based racism and syndicated discrimination. As Kheli Willetts argues, just after the introduction of Mickey Mouse in 1928's *Steamboat Willie*, Disney produced "caricatured images of Africans and African Americans" that joined ranks with "a history of drawings informed by racism . . . in existence for almost 500 years." Willetts explains that these drawings arose as a result of travel journals and diaries from colonial enterprises and slave trade routes as well as artwork portraying Black people as subservient to white Europeans. These works of art, Willetts claims, served to "validat[e] the notion of African people as direct descendants of 'the missing link'" or primates and thus to justify the transatlantic slave trade as well as the subordination of people of color to white people.[10] Mainstream comics reinforce and toy with ideas of nativism and primitivism when it comes to Black characters.

Cannibalism and African nativism, for instance, captured the minds and imaginations of white European and American cartoon artists in the nineteenth and early twentieth centuries. Disney's *Cannibal Capers* depicts half-duck, half-human African natives dancing around and attempting to cook each other and Mickey Mouse. The African characters are portrayed as stupid and easily tricked by non-African characters. Betty Boop is featured in a cannibal piece called *I'll Be Glad When You're Dead You Rascal, You*, released in 1932. In this film, Louis Armstrong's head begins chasing Betty Boop and Felix around Africa and morphs into a cannibal who attempts to eat Betty Boop. This cannibalism and African nativism relates to Willetts's assertion that Africans have been viewed as subhuman and portrayed as such in art, including comics. Aside from movies, a fraught relationship has long existed between white cartoon artists and the Black characters in their art. Fredrik Strömberg's extensive history of Black comics highlights the various stock characters Black cartoon figures have embodied, including the cannibal, the Sambo, the mammy, and the pickaninny.

In the introduction to their edited collection, Frances Gatewood and John Jennings disparage the attempt by many white comics to create Black characters, arguing that these characters pandered to mainstream white expectations. In the 1930s and 1940s, for instance, characters like "Whitewash and Ebony White" depicted Black Americans as "dim-witted buffoons" in need of a "white male either to save them or guide them." Marvel, for instance, owned by Warner Bros., has produced fifty-two comics, only five of which feature Black characters: *Batwing, Static Shock, Mister Terrific, Voodoo*, and *The Fury of Firestorm: The Nuclear Men*. Several of these issues were canceled due to low circulation, and none of them features a Black female character. Of these characters, only Batwing survived; he is a former child solider from the Democratic Republic of Congo who works as an African Batman under the supervision of Batman. Such a relationship between Black and white characters is not unusual in a history of comics in which the superhero is a "white-male dominated fantasy." Part of this stereotyping arises from the nature of comics themselves: "Comics traffic in stereotypes and fixity. . . . Comics abstract and simplify." Gatewood and Jennings thus argue for a broader reading of comics, stating that "comics, when created by a skillful and informed hand, can speak with the power of text and words combined."[11]

Ormes rises to this challenge, creating characters who break gender and racial norms. She comments on deep-seated political issues alongside claiming a space in the fashion industry, which is largely dominated by white men and women. As Goldstein explains, "at a time when images of African-Americans in mainstream newspaper comics portrayed only derogatory stereotypes," Ormes's characters "commented on all manner of contemporary topics, from US nuclear armament in the Cold War to the vagaries of Christian Dior's hemlines."[12] Ormes's work, often described as autobiographical, reflects her own life experiences, her enjoyment of fashion, and the political climate of the *Chicago Defender* and the *Pittsburgh Courier*.

Jackie Ormes was born Zelda Mavin Jackson in 1911 in Pittsburgh, Pennsylvania. Her father, William Jackson, owned and operated a printing press until his death in 1917. Zelda's mother then worked as a head housekeeper for a wealthy widow until she remarried in 1918. The extended family began calling Zelda "Jackie" at this time, a gender-neutral name that proved valuable when she entered the world of print media. Ormes landed her first job in print media working as a freelance writer for the *Pittsburgh Courier*.

Edwin Harleston founded the *Courier* in 1907 and by the 1930s it had grown into one of the most widely circulated Black-owned newspapers in the United States.[13] Ranking in sales alongside the *Chicago Defender*, the *Afro-American*, and the *New York Amsterdam News*, the *Courier* remained a significant member of the Black press in the United States. It was "the most influential and significant" of Black newspapers; its "weekly publication [in the 1940s] could boast of having editions in fourteen major cities and a readership of over one million. . . . It carried stories of the United States' racial terror—of lynching, of Jim Crow Laws, and of other indignities and outrages against Blacks."[14] The newspaper offered mobility of ideas and practices often meant to be confined and contained by broader social practices.

Despite the progressive racial politics of the *Courier*, Ormes's editor decided not to print her name "Zelda" in the paper, instead opting for the gender-neutral "Jackie" to be run next to her columns on boxing and court cases. Ormes married a banker, Earl Clark Ormes, in 1931 and gave birth to a daughter a few years later, who tragically passed away at the age of three-and-a-half due to a brain tumor. It is believed that Ormes created the character Patty-Jo in honor of her daughter. In 1937, a year after her daughter's death, she began writing the comic strip *Torchy Brown in "Dixie to Harlem."* The strip ended after one year, and as the Great Depression struck, the Ormes family was forced to move to Salem, Ohio, and then Chicago in search of employment. Ormes took some classes at the School of the Art Institute of Chicago in the early 1940s but felt inadequate next to her largely white classmates, who were better trained. In a comic strip she depicts herself shrunken in a chair as a white male instructor says, "Hmm you may have it little lady, but for the present I'd say it's still unexpressed." Her gender critique and critique of race relations in the United States was heightened during World War II, when she began reporting for the *Chicago Defender* about Black soldiers at the Great Lakes Naval Training Center and Paul Robeson's talks about interracial relations. Her politics and activism within Chicago's Black community prompted the FBI to investigate her as a communist sympathizer. Though in her FBI interviews Ormes denied being involved in the Communist Party USA (CPUSA), her "acquaintance with party members and her participation in what were considered CP front events" filled her 287-page dossier on file with the FBI.[15] Ormes was, however, a declared member of the National Association for the Advancement of Colored People (NAACP) and participated in various theater productions with the support of the NAACP. Given her own rather unconventional path through both womanhood and politics, it is unsurprising that her comics feature strong female leads with defined senses of self and political ideologies. The mobility that both literally and figuratively surrounded her life, whether her move from Pennsylvania to Ohio, her break into the comic world, or her political mobilization, informs the social, sartorial, and political mobility of her characters.

Claiming Social Space: Social Mobility

While "social mobility" often refers to class mobility, in this instance I am deploying the phrase to refer to a physical mobility or repositioning of Ormes's characters as Black women into spaces generally reserved for white men, white women, and Black men. These movements, or repositionings, often convey a specific political message or social commentary. Ormes depicts the character of Torchy Brown, for instance, as being an active spectator at boxing matches. In one panel, a February 26, 1938 comic strip entitled "Excited! Who's Excited?" Torchy cheers on Joe Louis, world heavyweight boxing champ from 1937 to 1949. In this panel, Ormes draws Torchy, a well-dressed, feisty woman, standing as the single Black person and woman amid a crowd of white men watching the boxing match. Torchy screams wildly for Louis, and Torchy herself is named "De Champ" after pouncing on the head of one of the audience members, a bald white man. The visual image of Torchy positioning herself over his head inverts the social order that centers white men as beacons of power and knowledge. Torchy visibly irritates the white male audience members and even unwittingly knocks out one of the men in her excitement. Her physical and verbal domination over the white men in the panel speaks to her lack of concern for white male comfort and imagines a public space in which Black women are able to assert dominance over white men. The inclusion of Louis is especially important as Louis fought the German boxer Max Schmeling and was defeated in 1936. Nazi propagandists used this defeat as evidence that Aryans were physically superior to other races.[16] Though Louis would beat Schmeling in a July 1938 rematch, Ormes's inclusion of Louis in the *Dixie to Harlem* cartoon critiques the codification of white supremacist arguments that initially emerged after Schmeling's 1936 defeat of Louis.

In another instance of mobility, Ormes uses Torchy's character to address the mass migration many Black Americans underwent after World War I, moving from the South to the North. Torchy moves from her home in Mississippi to New York City. Ormes explains that though she never lived in a segregated state, she read about it working for the newspaper and drew inspiration from the segregated South in her Torchy Brown comics: "I had never been to Dixie, but I worked in a newspaper office, and I read everything that was in the paper. It was a whole lot about struggles. Segregation."[17] The first installment of *Dixie to Harlem* introduces Torchy alongside her Aunt Clemmie and Uncle Jeff, who "raised 'Torchy' along with the cows and chickens on a little Dixie farm." The provincial nature of Ormes's southern characters could be read as reflective of her own lack of exposure to the South outside of dominant stereotypes surrounding a lack of education and limited economic opportunities. Torchy's cousin Dinah Dazzle appears in subsequent installments, and she encourages Torchy to consider moving to New York City. Torchy tries on Dinah's clothes and dreams of flying on a fireworks rocket to the city. Eventually she sells off her pig, some chickens, and her horse to purchase a train ticket to pursue her dreams of city life. In this depiction, Ormes positions Dinah Dazzle, whose name reflects her glamorous appearance, as the embodiment of a Black woman leaving behind her farm life and moving into other professional and personal opportunities. Ormes imagines a life outside of farming and sharecropping and insists upon the ability of Black women to enter alternative career spaces as unmarried, independent women.

Interestingly, Torchy does not face racism in the South until attempting to leave her hometown on the train. The transitional space of the train, moving Torchy from the farm to the city reveals itself as a highly segregated space. Torchy, however, outwits the conductor and, as in the boxing arena, subverts racial assumptions and hierarchies. In this panel, Torchy comes upon two arrow-shaped signs while boarding the train to New York. One reads "Colored" and the other "White." Torchy initially pretends she cannot read and slips into the much more comfortable "White" section. As the train conductor approaches she begins to sweat nervously. An Italian man notices her plight and ensures the conductor that she is with him, thus allowing Torchy to remain in the whites-only seating area. Torchy herself assumes an Italian accent and pretends to be Italian as well. The character appears to be rather light in complexion, though not perhaps light enough to be considered Italian. The sympathy she elicits from her travel companion comments upon the mobility of racial identities at this time and the hierarchies found within constructions of whiteness and blackness. Italian immigrants, for instance, received the status of "whiteness" in the United States to increase the white marital pool and ensure that phenotypically lighter-skinned people rather than people of color would receive access to suburban housing. By drawing Torchy in this space and allied with an Italian man, Ormes points to the tenuous nature of racial classification during this period

as well as the absurdity of a system of segregation based on these classifications. Torchy's mobility into a white space undermines segregation laws and
practices. Her ability to "trick" the white conductor, similar to her physical
dominance over the men in the boxing arena, undermines his authority and
calls his judgment and intelligence into question.[18]

While *Torchy* often enters traditionally white male spaces, *Candy*, a single-
panel comic, undermines the subservience that generally characterized the
relationship between wealthy white women and their household employees.
Candy's mobility into a white home allows her to proffer scathing critiques
of her employer, Mrs. Goldrocks. Though the readers never see Mrs. Goldrocks, her name alone indicates her social and financial privilege. Candy, a
signification on the dominant "mammy trope" in popular media of the time,
makes jokes about Mrs. Goldrocks purchasing items on the black market.
In a particular comic from June 16, 1945, Candy is perched on the edge of a
table wearing a black dress and heels. She is stretching a piece of fabric and
says, "Mrs. Goldrocks admits her biggest thrill is black-market 'bargains'—
That's because she's convinced they're really exclusive!" Candy is referring
to the black market that emerged during World War II as the government
rationed food, fabric, and other goods in order to combat the barricade made
on U.S. ports. The black market served as means for those wealthy enough to
maintain a certain standard of living. Candy's joking about Mrs. Goldrocks
"exclusivity" highlights the ways in which people were swindled on the black
market, and her defiance of her employer reverses the image of the mammy
as loyal and subservient. Ormes especially seems to be poking fun at white
housewives who found some sort of "thrill" by shopping on the black market
and flaunting their wealth while simultaneously being ripped off by sellers.

Candy constantly outsmarts Mrs. Goldrocks. In another panel, Candy is
shown hoeing in a garden and saying, "Mrs. G. is telling all her friends about
my Victory Garden. Wait till she sees the meat balls I planted last week."
Women in the United States were encouraged to grow victory gardens during World War II to provide their own vegetables and fruit. These gardens
were seen as an effort by women to contribute to the war cause and lessen
the burden on the government to provide food while supplies were cut short.
The reference to meatballs could have one of two meanings. The Japanese
flags carried by soldiers in battle were often known as "meatball flags" due
to the large red sun in the middle. Ormes may be referencing the burying
of Japanese or other U.S. opponents. Given Candy's cheeky demeanor and
clear disdain for Mrs. Goldrocks, however, the comic reads more as a jab at
her employer. Mrs. Goldrocks enjoys the accolades she receives for having

a victory garden, but she sends Candy to do the actual work of planting. Candy's planting of meatballs reflects her throwing away meat, which was rationed during World War II, to underscore Mrs. Goldrocks's hypocrisy in claiming her altruism by having a victory garden and not actually taking part in war-time sacrifices.

Mobilizing Change through Political Commentary

While much political commentary in *Torchy Brown* and *Candy* remains embedded in the characters' actions or joking quips, Ormes adopts a far more directly political stance in *Patty-Jo and Ginger*. In one comic panel, Patty-Jo takes roller-skates to Montgomery, Alabama, in response to the bus boycott of 1956. In others, Patty-Jo watches "Cinamacarthy" in criticism of the McCarthy era, and says she feels "proud to flunk" her history courses because there is no "right text book on Negro Americans." In this single-panel comic, Patty-Jo is an outspoken little girl with pigtails, big eyes, and a glamorous wardrobe. Approximately five years old, she critiques everything from the U.S. education system to the plight of children, the Cold War, polio, racism, and racial uplift. Patty-Jo's outspoken nature and political acuity contrast with the mechanisms that silenced much of the violence enacted against Black women and Black girls during the Jim Crow era. LaKisha Simmons notes, for instance, that in contrast to the heavily rotated symbol of the noose and lynching tree as forms of white violence, systemic and sexual violence against Black women and girls often remained "in the shadows" and out of the public eye.[19] Patty-Jo further allows Ormes to move outside of the ways in which "Black girls' moral and social fitness became an indicator of race progress" during this period.[20] Patty-Jo's political and intellectual commentary, rather than her ability to conform to a specific respectability politics or ethics of sexual chastity, becomes the marker of progress.

The precocious tot also offers some lighthearted humor; one panel, for instance, depicts Patty-Jo peeking out of a mailbox and jokingly begging Ginger not to be mad at her for hiding there. In another panel, Patty-Jo asks Ginger for a doll for her birthday that won't outtalk Patty-Jo herself. Dolls become a central feature of the *Patty-Jo and Ginger* comic strip; these dolls emphasize the youthfulness of Patty-Jo, whose cutting political commentary makes it easy to forget her age, and demonstrate the ways in which children were affected by anti-Black racism in the 1940s and 1950s. In one panel, Patty-Jo stands next to a sign that reads "Elementary Chalk Dusters Union" and informs Ginger that the "Blackboard workers" are going to strike and that she hopes there is no trouble from the apple polishers. By positioning Patty-Jo within the union strike, Ormes reveals her own position fighting for workers' rights. In addition to a few panels directly addressing the labor unions, Ormes also critiques inflation and the high taxes demanded of workers after World War II. In one panel Patty-Jo is seen floating in the sky while the cow jumps over the moon. She whimsically asks, "Why not? Everything else is [rising]." As Goldstein explains, "an electric washing machine that costs forty-five dollars in 1943 now costs eighty dollars" in 1948.[21] This exorbitant inflation and high taxes appear in several of Ormes's comics, including a 1951 panel that shows Patty-Jo standing near the window viewing a line of picketers. She tells Ginger that her friend Benjie's dad says that jobs are "okay" but that workers "want to eat after taxes." High taxes, coupled with postwar inflation and a minimum wage of seventy-five cents—roughly six dollars today—spurred Ormes's critique of financial inequity.

One of the more salient, longer-running critiques Ormes proffers through *Patty-Jo and Ginger* addresses the American education system and its unbalanced perspective on Black history in the United States. In multiple panels, Patty-Jo complains to Ginger about learning the wrong history in class. In an October 1948 panel, she claims the history textbooks are incorrect because they state that all races are equal. As Goldstein explains, this panel emerged during an election year in which Senator Strom Thurmond's platform fought for segregation and racial integrity.[22] In a similar panel from 1951, Patty-Jo argues that she proudly failed her history class because her textbook's discussion of African Americans was inaccurate. Ormes pushes her critique of the schools further with comics that point to the racial inequality children face. In one panel, Patty-Jo is depicted in a classroom looking at an American flag. The caption reads, "One naked individual with liberty and justice for all." On the chalkboard behind her are the names of a few states and "Dixie" with equal signs and question marks. The state names refer to the *Brown v. Board of Education* ruling in May 1954 that forced school desegregation. The malapropism of "naked individual" instead of "nation indivisible" from the Pledge of Allegiance indicates that Patty-Jo, as a young Black woman in a segregated country, felt like a vulnerable individual and not part of a broader national concern. Ormes often plays on words in this way, such as in a 1949 panel about school registration. In this comic, Ginger registers Patty-Jo for school and Patty-Jo states that they left the "color" (race) line blank because she doesn't want to be "incriminated" for being Black or denied a spot at school. Ormes points to the structural government racism, such as in schools, that disadvantage children based on racial bias.

Patty-Jo also critiques the U.S. government's policies on segregation and the surveillance of organizations such as the CPUSA and the NAACP that fought for civil rights and social change. In a 1947 panel, Patty-Jo writes a letter to her congressional representative, asking whether the "American way of life" is the life that exists in Georgia or New York, referring to the segregation of the South. In a later comic, she grabs her suitcase and dons traveling clothes to head to Montgomery to join the bus boycott in 1956. Ormes also draws several panels criticizing the development of the hydrogen bomb and the use of the atomic bomb in Japan. In one panel, Patty-Jo stands in the dilapidated apartment of a family with an eviction notice on their door and sarcastically encourages them to be comforted that the government is working on a hydrogen bomb rather than attending to substandard housing conditions. Ormes drew several comics encouraging her viewers to vote and fight against these policies. She suggests the politics of the CPUSA as the means to spur social change, though she treads lightly on criticism of the government for its communist witch hunt. In one Halloween panel, Patty-Jo and Ginger are dressed as witches, and Patty-Jo makes a joke about Hollywood scouts hunting for witches. In another panel, Patty-Jo asks Ginger about wearing a red feather to a meeting to reveal her allegiance to the CPUSA. Patty-Jo's child-like innocence in making these claims represents a new generation of Black women who increasingly move into social and political spaces to claim their own terrain and mark themselves as agents of social change and justice. Further, her presence becomes predictive of the emergent trope of the politically savvy Black adolescents in comics, such as Huey from Aaron McGruder's *The Boondocks*.

Fashion-Forward Sensibilities

In a final shift in her work, Ormes moves away from her direct political commentary and presents the life of Torchy Brown as a world traveler, heroine, and fashion-savvy woman. In this incarnation of Torchy, Ormes embraces a Black womanhood not focused on making direct political statements or reclaiming social space but embodying a lifestyle and humanity often denied to Black women. She responds to Abbey Lincoln's question of who will "make them beautiful" by adorning her characters in elaborate wardrobes with meticulous hairstyles and accessories. Tanisha C. Ford explains that fashion is "crucial to defining liberation on one's own terms." The practice of dressing her characters in couture gave Ormes the opportunity, even on the heels of the Great Depression and during World War II fabric rations, to imagine an economic and aesthetic liberation in which Black women become empowered to self-fashion and break out of "intraracial notions of feminine propriety."[23] Ormes's fashion and aesthetic choices visually signal an economic mobility and counter images of poor Black women that often permeated media.

Physically, Ginger and Candy resemble each other, with their pin-up like physiques and similar facial features. Their wardrobes, however, reflect their disparate economic situations. Candy is the buxom domestic worker whose fashion is regulated by war-time material restrictions. Her employer, Mrs. Goldrocks, however, always manages to finagle nicer clothing than permitted, and Candy is given the castaway clothes of her employer. Ginger, in *Patty-Jo and Ginger*, escapes war-time regulations and instead is reminiscent of a Gibson girl with "flared skirts and practical shirt-blouse . . . tailored for clerical work in a business office . . . a woman who was at once modern and feminine, independent and alluring."[24] Goldstein suggests that Christian Dior, in particular, caught Ormes's eye; his 1947 "New Look" promoting "an hourglass silhouette of prominent bust line, small waist and bouffant skirt" provided a renewed sense of femininity to her "austere" wartime fashions.[25] In addition to Ginger's modern wardrobe, Patty-Jo boasts a sizable wardrobe of petticoats, dresses, cowgirl costumes, and a range of seasonal clothing, such as swimwear and winter coats.

Ormes revived the Torchy character in 1950–54 in a cartoon entitled *Torchy in Heartbeats* and a paper-doll section called *Torchy's Togs*. This series, published in color, maintained a far less political tone and instead told the story of Torchy falling in and out of love and eventually becoming a nurse's aide, working in the South and getting engaged to Paul, her longtime love. The *Courier* hoped the series would increase readership as it presented an ongoing story week to week.[26] This final installment of Torchy emphasized the centrality of fashion to Ormes's work. In "Fashion in the Funny Papers," Nancy Goldstein traces the changing fashion trends from the 1940s to the 1950s that influenced how Ormes dressed her characters. Torchy's glamorous nightlife style, for instance, draws on the style of Hollywood's Letty Lynton, whose dresses had "sensational wide, flounced sleeves" and whose hairstyles were reminiscent of those worn by Lena Horne, who was a personal friend of Ormes and her sister, Delores Jackson.[27]

Conclusion

Ormes's characters became a reflection of herself and a projection of Black womanhood that was often hidden during the 1940s and 1950s. As Goldstein explains, "without the ways or means to realize her dreams, [Ormes] let her cartoon characters do the talking, traveling, dressing up, and strutting. As her doppelganger Torchy said in 1937, "'I've got to get away from here. I belong in big places.'"[28] Ormes's characters allowed for an imagining of Black womanhood that was political, fashionable, and independent. Few male characters feature in her work, with the exception of boxers, politicians, and Torchy's lovers in *Torchy in Heartbeats*, but even these men are background pieces to Torchy's life and work. Ormes's characters tackle political topics and social justice issues such as war, voting, equal medical care, education, and domestic servitude. From Torchy's entering the boxing arena to Candy's stealing her employer's clothes, Patty-Jo's defiant refusal to say the Pledge of Allegiance, and Ginger's posing nearly nude in the bathtub, Ormes's creations speak to the boundaries set in place by society and embody a Black femininity beyond the restrictions of the time. bell hooks argues that when Black women take up the role of spectator and artist, the process of "looking and looking back" at images, they are able to "know the present and invent the future."[29] Ormes provides a mobility for her characters not just within social, political, and sartorial bounds but one that permits them to mobilize into a new, uncharted terrain that will "glorify and proclaim" the image of Black womanhood.

Notes

1 Drake, *When We Imagine Grace*, 3.
2 Fanon, *Black Skin*, 72.
3 Drake, *When We Imagine Grace*, 3.
4 hooks, *Black Looks*, 120, 131.
5 hooks, *Black Looks*, 130–31.
6 Morrison, "What the Black Woman Thinks."
7 Eisner, *Comics and Sequential Art*, 1.
8 Nama, *Super Black*, 6.
9 Robbins, *A Century of Women Cartoonists*, 113.
10 Willetts, *Cannibals and Coons*, 10.
11 Gatewood and Jennings, *The Blacker the Ink*, 5, 2, 4.
12 Quoted in Gatewood and Jennings, *The Blacker the Ink*, 95.
13 Vann, *The Pittsburgh Courier*.
14 Gatewood and Jennings, *The Blacker the Ink*, 9.
15 Goldstein, *Jackie Ormes*, 30.
16 Runstedler, *Jack Johnson*, 258.
17 Quoted in Goldstein, *Jackie Ormes*, 17.

18 Torchy's "trickster" nature provides a strong parallel to Henry Louis Gates's "trick-
    ster figure," who is "full of guile, who tells lies . . . who is a rhetorical genius . . . in-
    tent on demystifying" the power of those in positions of dominance (*The Signifying
    Monkey*, 56).
19 Simmons, *Crescent City Girls*, 3.
20 Chatelain, *Southside Girls*, 20.
21 Goldstein, *Jackie Ormes*, 57.
22 Goldstein, *Jackie Ormes*, 100.
23 Ford, *Liberated Threads*, 16, 6.
24 Goldstein, *Jackie Ormes*, 107.
25 Quoted in Gatewood and Jennings, *The Blacker the Ink*, 110.
26 Goldstein, *Jackie Ormes*, 135.
27 Goldstein, "Fashion in the Funny Papers," 102.
28 Quoted in Gatewood and Jennings, *The Blacker the Ink*, 101.
29 hooks, *Black Looks*, 31.

References

Chatelain, Marcia. *Southside Girls: Growing Up in the Great Migration.* Durham, NC:
    Duke University Press, 2015.
Drake, Simone C. *When We Imagine Grace: Black Men and Subject Making.* Chicago:
    University of Chicago Press, 2016.
Eisner, Will. *Comics and Sequential Art: Principles and Practices from the Legendary
    Cartoonist.* New York: W. W. Norton & Company, 2008.
Fanon, Frantz. *Black Skin, White Masks.* New York: Grove Press, 2008.
Ford, Tanisha. *Liberated Threads: Black Women, Style and the Global Politics of Soul
    (Gender and American Culture).* Chapel Hill: University of North Carolina
    Press, 2017.
Gates, Henry Louis. *The Signifying Monkey: A Theory of African-American Literary Criti-
    cism.* Oxford: Oxford University Press, 1988.
Gatewood, Frances, and John Jennings, et al. *The Blacker the Ink: Constructions of
    Black Identity in Comics and Sequential Art.* New Brunswick, NJ: Rutgers Univer-
    sity Press, 2015.
Goldstein, Nancy. *Jackie Ormes: The First African American Woman Cartoonist.* Ann
    Arbor: University of Michigan Press, 2008.
hooks, bell. *Black Looks: Race and Representation.* Boston, MA: South End Press, 1992.
Lincoln, Abbey. "Who Will Revere the Black Woman?" *Negro Digest*, 1966. https://
    www.ebony.com/black-history/who-will-revere-the-black-woman-405/.
Morrison, Toni. "What the Black Woman Thinks of White Women's Lib." *The New
    York Times*, August 22, 1971. Accessed: https://www.nytimes.com/1971/08/22
    /archives/what-the-black-woman-thinks-about-womens-lib-the-black-woman
    -and.html.

Nama, Adilifu. *Super Black: American Pop Culture and Black Superheroes*. Austin: University of Texas at Austin Press, 2011.

Robbins, Trina. *A Century of Women Cartoonists*. North Hampton, MA: Kitchen Sink Press, 1993.

Runstedler, Theresa. *Jack Johnson, Rebel Sojourner: Boxing in the Shadow of a Global Color Line*. Los Angeles: University of California Press, 2013.

Simmons, LaKisha Michelle. *Crescent City Girls: The Lives of Young Black Women in Segregated New Orleans*. Chapel Hill: University of North Carolina Press, 2015.

Strömberg, Fredrik. *Black Images in the Comics: A Visual History*. Seattle, WA: Fantagraphics Books, 2005.

Vann, Robert Lee. "The Pittsburgh Courier." PBS.org, n.d. http:// www.pbs.org /blackpress/news_bios/courier.html.

Willets, Kheli. "Cannibals and Coons: Blackness in the Early Days of Walt Disney." *Diversity in Disney Films: Critical Essays on Race, Ethnicity, Gender, Sexuality and Disability*. Edited by Jonathan Cheu. Jefferson, NC: McFarland & Company.

**QUEER KINSHIP AND WORLDMAKING
IN BLACK QUEER WEB SERIES** /
DRAMA QUEENZ AND *NO SHADE*

Eric Darnell Pritchard

In his iconic essay, "Making Ourselves from Scratch," the
writer-activist Joseph Beam recalls, "It was imperative for my survival that I
did not attend to or believe the images that were presented of black people
or gay people. Perhaps that was the beginning of my passage from passivism
to activism, that I needed to create my reality, that I needed to create images
by which I, and other black gay men to follow, could live this life."[1] Beam
rightfully notes the limitations in the representations of Black queer lives
in media. He also speaks to the particular responsibility he felt to disrupt
those limited views by offering alternatives to the ways Black queer life was
being represented in mass media. Through these alternatives, Beam sought
to prepare the table for Black queer people of the future to live with more
satisfying depictions of Black queer life in media. He also provided a blueprint on which generations of Black queer people have continued to do their

own work as image-makers, storytellers, and activists on the matter of representations of Black gay men in mass media.

From the mid- to late 1980s, when Beam was writing and published his essay, through the early 1990s, when many other Black gay culture critics echoed Beam's critique and concerns, the very few depictions of Black gay men in mass media were the primary visions through which Black gay men were seen and understood. A noteworthy exception is the work of the filmmaker Marlon Riggs, a friend and contemporary of Beam's, who in his feature-length documentary films *Tongues Untied* (1989) and *Black Is, Black Ain't* (1994), as well as the short films *Affirmations* (1990) and *Anthem* (1991), examined the complexities of Black queer subjectivity, especially as it pertains to Black gay men. Despite the cultural criticism and artistic-activist interventions of Riggs, Beam, and other Black queer culture-makers who sought to render the multidimensional lives of Black queer people, the more highly visible images, though very few in number, were those prone to problematic caricature. This visibility and the regularity with which those images were created and disseminated made ever more urgent and raised even higher the stakes for interventions by Riggs, Beam, and others.

Inarguably, Black queer lives have certainly become more visible in U.S. popular culture since that time. But this visibility has not always resulted in a more diverse or less stereotypical depiction of Black queerness than that critiqued in the past. For instance, among the televisual images of Black queerness most debated and written about by Black gay culture critics and activists was the caricature of the Black gay "snap queen" popularized in the "Men on . . ." skits featured on the 1990s television program *In Living Color*. The skits were deemed dangerous by the vast majority of Black gay writer-activists such as Riggs, Beam, Essex Hemphill, and Ron Simmons, who all commented on the problematic representations of Black gay men on television.[2] Hemphill, for example, noted in the mid-1990s that "the representation of sexual, racial, ethnic, and gender identities in the context of media is one of the most critical debates the marginalized, the oppressed, and the disenfranchised groups in this country will contend with in this decade."[3] This critical debate about representation remains true for marginalized groups today. So powerful and politically impactful were the "Men on . . ." skits and the debates around them that they continue to be central to scholarly discussions about representations of blackness and queerness today.[4] More than two decades since the critique of these skits, the lack of growth in representations of Black gay men on television is evidenced by the dearth of narratives of Black queerness in various media generally and, particularly, in network television dramas and comedies in which Black gay men are absent save for the rare exception. Among these exceptions are the television show *Noah's Arc*, written and directed by Patrik-Ian Polk, as well as Polk's feature films, *Noah's Arc: Jumping the Broom*, *The Skinny*, and *Blackbird*, based on the Larry Duplechan novel of the same name. A more recent example is the Fox drama series *Empire* and the character of Jamal Lyon, a Black queer man played by Jussie Smollett, as well as the characters Pray Tell, Damon, and Ricky on FX's Golden Globe Award-nominated drama series *Pose,* played by Tony Award winner Billy Porter, Ryan Jamaal Swain, and Dyllon Burnside, respectively. Another example appears on OWN's family drama *Queen Sugar,* which features the character of Nova, a Black queer woman portrayed by Rutina Wesley. Even fewer television series and films focus on the lives of Black lesbians or transgender women and men. The ubiquity of the absence of transgender people on television was illuminated upon *Pose*'s June 2018 premiere. Set in New York City's house and ball culture in the late 1980s, *Pose* made history when it assembled the largest ever cast of transgender actors to star on a television series, including MJ Rodriguez, Indya Moore, Dominique Jackson, Haile Sahar, and Angelica Ross as members of the fictional House of Evangelista, House of Abundance, and House of Ferocity. Janet Mock, writer and Black transgender activist, also serves as a writer and director on the series. Still, even with these major steps in the twenty-first century, there remain too few depictions of Black queer life and culture on the big and small screens. In fact, the two areas of television where Black gay men are being shown more frequently, though not necessarily any less problematically, are reality television and talk shows.

In the twenty-first century, many Black queers find, as Beam notes, that they too must make themselves from scratch given the absence of Black queer people in mass media. They find that they must seek to create images of Black queer life apart from the very few depicted in traditional mass media (i.e., television, film, popular magazines), which does in many ways still rule the roost of representation. What Beam could not have anticipated, however, was the emergence of twenty-first-century digital technologies that have allowed for the proliferation of representations of Black queer lives by Black queer people who are independent of traditional mass media. As Simone Drake has noted, representations of twenty-first-century Black culture have "been influenced heavily by the digital age. . . . The Internet and the availability of social media and digital downloads have expanded the production of Black popular culture, as well as its audience."[5] These digital spaces have been so successful that traditional mass media depends on these twenty-first century technologies, especially courting digital social networking sites to promote their works. Christine Acham argues that web series are a powerful "tool for the expression of Black voices, as empowerment for Black creative forces, and as a potential site for creating Black community" and that these series "tackle stories that are representative of various demographics within the Black community" that are otherwise overlooked. The popularity of the web series medium is evident in that, according to Acham, "African American webisodes from both amateur and professional producers have thrived, and at the beginning of 2011, over 125 series appeared online."[6] Among these productions, Faithe Day and Aymar Jean Christian find that within Black queer web series "indie producers and fans collectively create new performances of blackness and queerness via open networks online, in response to legacy broadcast and cable television networks that ignore and normalize intersectional Black identities through closed development processes."[7]

The proliferation of Black queer web series necessitates an analytic of the critical possibilities these texts, and the digital sphere, offer for Black popular culture studies to undertake an assessment of the state of representations of Black queerness through twenty-first-century technologies. This includes an analysis of how twenty-first-century Black queer culture workers are using digital technologies to continue the representational activism of their Black queer ancestors. This essay contributes to this project by using two Black queer web series to examine the ways Black gay image-makers and storytellers draw on the digital sphere to create texts we must engage in any analysis of twenty-first-century Black popular culture. I contend that Black queer web series are a mechanism through which the Black queer people Beam was writing in anticipation of labor to create new ways in which they might see themselves, ponder how to "live this life," and create their own realities and worlds. Black queer web series are, thus, counter-storytelling from a counterpublic sphere about life in the twenty-first century through the lived experience of individuals who are not represented as fully realized human beings in the images and storytelling that are created and disseminated by the dominant culture. These image-makers and storytellers are, in effect, engaging in practices of queer worldmaking.

Queer worldmaking, writes José Esteban Muñoz, "delineates the ways" individuals and groups "have the ability to establish alternate views of the world. These alternative vistas are more than simply views or perspectives; they are oppositional ideologies that function as critiques of regimes of 'truth' that subjugate minoritarian people," creating "oppositional counterpublics" or "'worldviews'" that reshape as they deconstruct reality." Within

Black queer web series, the creators take real-life oppressive, discriminatory, and ultimately marginalizing ideologies and politics that underpin those discourses, and engage them dialectically to critique them. Doing so, these creators simultaneously create space for a multiplicity of representations. These image-makers and storytellers thus restructure old and create anew the very vocabularies and grammars in which Black queerness is represented in mass media, which establishes a platform for the diverse stories to be told about Black queer people that are absent or misrecognized in popular culture. These texts give "access to queer life-worlds that exist, importantly and dialectically, within the future and the present."[8] Viewers are invited to look at issues affecting Black queer people in the context of the present through a lens focused on race(d) and queer(ed) senses of being. Through this same lens viewers can also engage in a critique of the oppressive systems that are relevant to the stories being told, while simultaneously co-creating Black queer futures that are distinct from the oppressive ideologies that are resistant to Black queerness in any context.

Analyzing two web series, *Drama Queenz* (2008–12) and *No Shade* (2013–14), I examine how the image-makers and storytellers behind both series are engaged in Black queer worldmaking. A primary site of counter-storytelling is the family. I choose the family because its central role in representing and affirming regimes of the normal make it especially significant to the ways in which the web series forge their interventions. Each series queers family in ways that honor the diversity of kinship formations. Marlon Bailey writes that "queer kin are" families "established out of necessity and on their own terms, while exposing the fallacy of dominant family ideologies by doing the kin labor that many biological families fail to do. Moreover, kinship among Black LGBT communities makes clear that heterosexuality is not the *sine qua non* of family. Instead, family is about and based on the kin labor that members choose to undertake."[9] These queer kinships are often invisible or disregarded by the dominant culture. By disrupting traditional notions of family through emphasis on queer kinship, Black queer web series are creating the world as they see it or would like it to be, even as they critique the present representation of Black queer life that serves the interest of oppression and marginalization.

All in the Family: Queer Kinship and Black Male Intimacy

The queer kinships in *Drama Queenz* and *No Shade* are each examples of Black queer worldmaking. This worldmaking takes shape through characters and stories that critique dominant discourses of what counts as family defined through regimes of normativity. One of the ways the web series does this is by displaying a range of queer kinship formations among characters that are not biologically related. Another way is by exposing the failures of the traditional family to offer the material, emotional, and physical care and affirmation that queer kinship provides the characters. Illuminating this failure of traditional family, the web series challenge assumptions that the normative family is superior to those deemed nonnormative, including queer family and kinship formations. Indeed, the dominant discourse of family represents it as heteronormative, nuclear, and biological. Given the realities of heterosexism, homophobia, and cisnormativity that ignore or are hostile to same-sex and other nonnormative familial and kinship structures, the families queer people create are excluded from representation in mass media. The exception here is when LGBT families are depicted as closer to the heterosexual, nuclear family model, a neoliberal rhetoric of such families as being nonthreatening and *just like us.*

Emily Arnold and Marlon Bailey write that there is "a dearth of research on the kinship practices of African American gay, lesbian, bisexual, transgender, and queer (GLBTQ) people." Studies of Black or queer family and kinship that do exist tend to exclude Black queer kinship bonds, as "studies of African American kinship are almost exclusively heterosexual and the literature on queer kinship generally focuses on White gays and lesbians."[10] Representations of Black and LGBTQ family and kinship in popular culture, unfortunately, support this trend. For example, none of the major network television programs focused on Black families, few as they are as well, have ever centered on nonheterosexual Black families. Also, while in recent years more television programs (e.g., *Modern Family*) that prominently feature same-sex families have gained both critical and commercial success, the same-sex or queer family features white gay and lesbian couples to the exclusion of queer people of color. The impact is that LGBTQ of color families and queer kinship formations are being overlooked. By centering queer family and kinship powerfully in the narratives of Black queer characters, *Drama Queenz* and *No Shade* fill this critical gap.

Drama Queenz is a dramatic comedy produced and written by Dane Joseph, who is also one of the show's three stars. The web series revolves around three Black gay roommates living in Astoria, a neighborhood in Queens, New York. The three roommates are Jeremiah Jones (Dane Joseph), Preston Mills III (Troy Valjean Rucker), and Davis Roberts (Kristen-Alexzander Griffith). Each episode includes a narrated voice over by Jeremiah as the roommates navigate matters in their personal lives while pursuing their professional dreams as struggling theater actors. The spaces the three men share—their Queens apartment, the streets of New York City, casting call rooms, and a local bar where Preston works—provide many moments of interaction between them and the cast of recurring characters orbiting their world. Over the series' three seasons, Jeremiah's story focuses on his on-again-off-again relationship with Donovan, a piano player in many of the productions for which Jeremiah auditions. The central stories of the third season are Jeremiah's becoming an escort when he falls on financially difficult times and a story about domestic violence when a new love interest of Jeremiah's physically assaults him in that season's finale. Davis's initial story revolves around a shared attraction between him and Diego, a sexually nonconforming man who has a girlfriend. Later stories focus on Davis's abuse of the prescription medication he receives for injuries he suffers in a physical altercation in which he defends himself against antigay street harassment. Preston's story is centered between two key romantic relationships he has throughout the series, as well as his work as a volunteer at a center and shelter for queer youth in season 3.

The series tells us very little about the past and backgrounds of the three men. What we know is that none of them is a New York City native. In season 2, episode 7, which I will discuss in further detail shortly, we are introduced to their mothers, who pay the three men a surprise visit. We learn that Davis is a closet southerner and that Jeremiah's mother is a recovering addict of either alcohol or drugs. This limitation on background details is useful to seeing the ways that the characters' relationships with one another and others support my argument that queer kinship in *Drama Queenz* is one example of the worldmaking Black queer creators enact through web series.

In season 2, episode 7, titled "In My Own Little Corner," the introduction of the three mothers provides some insight into the kinds of connections the three men draw with their families of origin. Because we do not meet any other family members, I argue that the mothers stand in for their respective larger families. As a result, the ways each roommate connects or disconnects from his mother is intended to suggest to the viewer a larger story about how each roommate relates to the rest of his family of origin. By episode's end, all three men have had one or more tender moments that display the very real connections they have to their mothers. However, within this same episode each roommate confronts his mother about some way he feels neglected, judged, or otherwise disconnected, even when the mothers are demonstrating concern or what they perceive as care. For example, Jeremiah's mother tells him his life appears to be imploding and that he has not been meeting his goals. This discussion is a clear source of frustration that sends Jeremiah running away from her and into the street, where he is almost struck by a vehicle. When Jeremiah does voice his frustration with his mother, the conversation quickly turns to him providing emotional care for her regarding her struggles with addiction. The mother-and-son dialogue ceases to be an opportunity for an expression of Jeremiah's grievances that need healing. Scenes of Preston show him dodging his mother, who is extremely judgmental of him and others. Davis's mother takes this same judgmental approach and goes a step further by taking him to a life coach while insisting that his life is lacking direction.

This episode shows us why the close connections Jeremiah, Preston, and Davis share might be better understood as an example of the queer "families we choose," to borrow a phrase from the anthropologist Kath Weston. The three men are more than roommates or people who share a racial and sexual identity that is dwarfed by their families of origin.[11] *Drama Queenz* could easily have had the surprise arrival of the mothers be a story about how the mothers possess some insider knowledge integral to the lives of these men as we have come to know them that their roommates and viewers do not possess. This would have indicated that the relationships with their families of origin were more significant in knowing who these men are than their relationships with each other or the connections viewers forge to the characters. This does not take place. Instead, Jeremiah, Preston, and Davis continue to lean on each other. The interactions with their families of origin instead solidify why each of them treats his roommates as the family he chooses. This point is best illustrated by a voice-over from Jeremiah in season 2, episode 1, when he says, "As the world goes round and round, spinning our lives into all types of drama, it concurrently orchestrates beauty, laughter, and friendship, introducing us to those people who are special to us, and whom we are special to, who know that we are standouts amongst the millions and millions and millions of people scraping by in the city, in the world. These friends and people are just—they're good company."[12]

Jeremiah describes his relationships with Preston and Davis as a safe place away from the drama of life, as built on a foundation of shared affirmation and care. Each character fulfills the kind of connection that is usually assumed by families of origin. This connection between the three roommates operates as a family of choice to stand in the gaps where connections to their families of origin are assumed to exist. Jeremiah, Preston, and Davis have formed a bond through which they uplift one another because of the totality of who they are as Black gay men. Their bond does not occur *despite* any aspect of their identities or lives that anyone else may use to judge them unfairly. Their connection queers family and forges queer kinship as a praxis of Black gay male worldmaking. The relationships between these men critique the institution of family as we are expected to consume it, exposing its heteronormative and respectable trappings as disconnected from these characters. Simultaneously, the relationships show the alternatives that presently exist for some Black gay men by using the web series to promote a future in which intimacy between Black men is possible, necessary, and happening.

Another example of Black gay worldmaking through queer kinship in *Drama Queenz* focuses on Preston and a gender-nonconforming teen who is introduced to Preston as "Tranny Boi," played by James E. Lee.[13] Tranny Boi lives at the homeless shelter for LGBTQ youth where Preston volunteers. In Season 3, episode 7, "Ease on Down the Road," Tranny Boi is shown in a video on a blog post having a rage-filled fit in a business establishment.[14] This event occurs after Preston, in the previous episode, "When It Ends," found the teen at the pier in NYC doing sex-work, negotiating with an older man with whom they planned to leave the pier.[15] Preston chases the older man away and brings the teen home to his apartment when the teen informs him that the shelter does not permit anyone to enter after their eleven o' clock curfew. The next day, Preston brings Tranny Boi back to the shelter. When they arrive Preston's colleague and love interest, who has been wanting Preston to commit to regular volunteer hours, flirtatiously tells Preston that he will not report him as "harboring Tranny Boi" if he will come back to volunteer daily. When Tranny Boi sees Preston and the shelter employee flirting with one another they get upset and run away. We next see Tranny Boi in the business establishment where they are enraged and subsequently featured on the local news for having a fit. Preston decides to go on a search for the youth and asks his love interest to join him.

While looking for Tranny Boi, Preston and his love interest have a discussion about whether or not looking for the teen is the right thing to do. While Preston is certain they should be searching for Tranny Boi, his companion believes his employer would say they should *not* be looking for the teen. He argues that it is up to the teen to make their own decision. The two finally locate the address of Tranny Boi's mother, Celeste, and go to talk with her to find out if she might know where they could be hiding out. In the conversation, they discover that when Tranny Boi was younger and living at home, their mother had been hitting them for years because she did not approve of the child being effeminate. The conversation reveals her homophobia, effemiphobia, and transphobia. She tells Preston and his love interest that Tranny Boi may be at the clubs or wherever they might dance, which Tranny Boi loves to do. She says if she sees Tranny Boi again she will slap the teen again. This statement leaves both Preston and his companion disappointed and saddened for the teen. Leaving her apartment, Preston is even more committed to finding Tranny Boi and suggests that he and his boyfriend go look in local clubs until they find them. This suggestion returns Preston and his colleague to their earlier debate about whether or not they should be looking for Tranny Boi at all. Ultimately, Preston's love interest determines this is not his responsibility as an employee of the shelter, and he leaves Preston alone. So Preston decides to continue to look for Tranny Boi on his own.

In this storyline we see the remaking of family through queer kinship as Black gay worldmaking in multiple ways. First, take Preston's love interest's refusal to look for Tranny Boi. He knows Tranny Boi more intimately than Preston does, so his reluctance to look for the teen and decision to give up shows the ways the state conspires to constrain the empathy, affirmation, and care this Black queer man has for a Black queer youth. This is evident when he repeatedly returns to what the shelter, a presumably state-funded and -governed institution, dictates as justification for why he does not feel they should be looking for Tranny Boi. Still, he joins Preston on the search for a great portion of the time. Though no one is forcing him to stop looking for the teen, the disciplining gaze of the state is evident in his arguments with Preston about whether looking for the teen is right or wrong. We know Preston's ethics are invested with a commitment to care for other Black queer people. This ethics is best evidenced in his relationships with Jeremiah and Davis, as well as his insistence that he will look for the teen with or without his love interest's or the shelter's approval or assistance. Preston's persistence exposes the state's ethics as lacking empathy and failing in its moral responsibility to the teen. Preston's reasoning and morality further expose the failure of family as an institution in ways promulgated by the state, as it is a Black gay man, an aberrational subject within the normative conceptions of family, that proves to be the more empathetic, careful, and socially responsible actor on behalf of the teen. It is the queer kinship Preston has with Tranny Boi that possesses the true qualities of affirmation, care, and safety that one assumes of the normative family or of the state-sponsored shelter.

Preston's actions also exemplify Black queer worldmaking in that the queer kinship is intergenerational. This a reality that too few Black queer people experience due to the many, many Black queer people of previous generations lost to bias-motivated death and the AIDS epidemic, to name two primary causes that ravaged almost a generation of Black queer people.

Relatedly, it is worth noting that worldmaking is also present in that Preston, a gay adult, takes interest in a queer youth that is not his biological relation in the face of a state that is not itself assuming that responsibility, but imposes normative belief systems that make suspect his care for the youth as sexual or problematic. Thus Preston's actions both critique the state and its ethics of benign neglect toward the teen and provide a vision for the role of Black gay men in the surviving and thriving of queer youth.

A heteropatriarchal reading of Tranny Boi's story might view it as the expected outcome given that they come from a single-mother-headed household. Such a claim comes out of the pathologizing and demonizing discourses of the household led by single Black mothers, infamously reinforced in the Moynihan Report, a study whose findings have been widely discredited.[16] However, Preston's care and concern for the teen is informed by one Black queer connecting to another. I contend, as informed by Cathy Cohen's cogent arguments in her trailblazing essay, "Punks, Bulldaggers, and Welfare Queens: The Radical Potential of Queer Politics?," that in the eyes of racialized heteropatriarchal structures, Black single mothers are also queer subject given the pathologized and demonized, racialized sexual and gender discourses projected onto them and their families.[17] The outcome of these discourses is that they are constructed to position the state's ideas of a heteropatriarchal, nuclear family as normal, one built for optimal success and thriving, as superior above all others. Thus Preston's intervention because of the queer kinship he shares with Tranny Boi disrupts the lazy reading of the teen's mother as a failure and the state as morally upright. Rather, it is a queer person (Preston) and queer kinship formations that provide the empathy, care, affirmation, and safety the teen needs. Ultimately, by showing a representation of the present that is an alternative to how Black gay men are seen televisually, the image-makers and storytellers that made *Drama Queenz* also create a future where queer kinship is not abnormal on screen. Rather, queer kinship is a source of the survival and flourishing of Black gay men in the realities they create on the screen and in the world.

The web series *No Shade* further demonstrates how such series use queer kinship as a way of Black queer worldmaking. Created by Sean Anthony, *No Shade* is also set in New York City (Brooklyn and Manhattan). It focuses on the everyday life of four friends: Noel Baptiste (David Brandyn), Kori Jacobs (Donny DuRight), Eric Stone (Terry Toro), and Danielle Williams (Tamara M. Williams). Each of the four main actors is also credited as a writer on the series, with Anthony credited as primary scribe. The show departs from *Drama Queenz* in several ways. One difference, crucial to my argument, is that, in *No Shade*, the cast of Black gay friends are joined by a Black transgender woman. *No Shade* also tends to focus more on the personal than the professional lives of its main characters, with only a few scenes devoted to Kori's and Danielle's work and career.

Where *No Shade* is similar to *Drama Queenz* is that we know very little about the background and past of the characters. This a creative choice that allows for the writers to draw from the relationships between the four main characters and a recurring cast to inform us who the individuals are at present. With the exception of Noel, we do not meet any of the characters' families of origin. One effect of this choice is that the four friends operate as each other's primary familial relationship. Examining these relationships highlights how queer kinship in *No Shade* evidences Black queer worldmaking.

Noel's relationship to his family of origin is a primary storyline through the first (and only) season of *No Shade*. The show's pilot begins with a slow-motion shot of the four characters walking fiercely, though glumly, through the entrance of a public park. Viewers learn from a voice-over that they are coming from the funeral of Noel's mother. The next scene jumps two weeks prior to the opening scene and explains more about why Noel's mother passed away while introducing the main characters. In that same episode, and over those that follow, we learn that Noel's mother is antigay; she tells Noel to stop hanging out with those "sick gay people."[18] In episode 3, "No Roaches," Noel's mother again shows herself to be antigay, telling Noel to stay away from those "ungodly people." In that same episode, his mother calls her pastor, Melvin, and asks him to come help her get this "gay demon out of [her] son."[19] Pastor Melvin abducts Noel and brings him to the church. Noel is later rescued by Danielle, who reveals that the pastor secretly frequents the website *Trans-Chat*, where he has sent Danielle sexually explicit messages. Noel's relationship with his mother is vexed, to say the least. His relationships with his friends are his source of nurture, affirmation, and love. The queer kinship that exists between them, juxtaposed with Noel's mother and the church's actions, critiques families of origin as innately more supportive and safer.

Kori's storyline in *No Shade* further speaks to the role of queer kinship in Black queer worldmaking through web series. Kori is a dancer and dance instructor striving to become famous, though he lacks the motivation to be a full adult by getting a residence of his own, paying bills, and handling other responsibilities. A member of the NYC Ball community and the House of Alchemy, Kori is living with his "house mother," Patti Alchemy. In multiple episodes, Mother Alchemy is portrayed as throwing shade at Kori, regularly suggesting he should move. Mother Alchemy also takes the money Kori wins competitively at the Ball. By the season's end we learn that Mother Alchemy had not been taking his money as payment for his living with her. Rather, she has been saving the money so that Kori would have it when he was ready to stand on his own, fearing that he was not responsible enough to do it himself. Mother Alchemy, himself a Black queer man and not a biological relative of Kori's, serves as his parent, guardian, and mentor, evidencing queer kinship in the absence of traditional depictions of family.

The scenes with Mother Alchemy are also crucial in that they establish this queer kinship as crossing generations. When we are introduced to Mother Alchemy, he describes his role as mother by quoting directly the legendary Pepper LaBeija, who was a Mother of the House of LaBeija, as featured in Jenny Livingston's 1990 documentary, *Paris Is Burning*. It is worth noting that in many ways the television series *Pose* also depicts characters that are analogs of real people featured in Livingston's documentary, and that Livingston herself serves as a consultant on the FX series. Like *Pose*, the film documents Ball culture in New York City from the mid- to late 1980s. In having Mother Alchemy use LaBeija's words without attribution, the writers establish Mother Alchemy's role as part of a longer tradition of queer kinship that stretches back decades. In fact, that other viewers of the series and I can immediately recognize LaBeija's words demonstrates the ubiquity with which the role of queer kinship structures like the house and ball scene operate in the lives of many queer people. In addition, the historical continuity of this queer kinship solidifies the family of choice as a real part of Black queer people's lives that is worthy of representation. Yet it is still conspicuously missing from many representations of Black gay male life that are more interested in caricature.

A final way in which *No Shade* invokes queer kinship as a practice of worldmaking is through the character of Danielle, a Black transgender woman. As with *Drama Queenz*, the four main characters in *No Shade* are depicted as being the most important relationships in each other's lives. This is a significant part of the worldmaking through this web series because, prior to *Pose*, it was one of the only significant televisual depictions of Black gay men in relationship to Black transgender women in popular culture. While many Black gay men, myself included, have Black transgender and nonbinary people as part of our families of origin and of choice, this reality is often erased in narratives of Black gay life in popular culture. This erasure misses the opportunity to examine the complexities of community building across gender identity and expression that occurs among Black and other queer people. This makes the storytelling in *No Shade* that much more significant. This depiction of Danielle and her cisgender Black gay male friends serves as a form of critique in that it exposes, for those who see this as foreign or unrealistic, that there does still exist a cisnormative and transphobic disavowal of transgender people that makes the connection between Danielle and her Black gay male friends appear as fantasy. Thus, through a queer kinship formation that centers a Black transgender woman alongside her cisgender Black gay male friends, the web series offers a vision of not just what Black queer community sometimes is, but what it is not and must be for all.

Conclusion

This essay demonstrates the limitations and possibilities of the web series genre to increase the number of texts that portray and archive diverse representations of Black queerness compared to what we have seen in traditional mass media. Black queer web series demonstrate and forecast the possibilities of digital technologies and texts to document the past, present, and future of Black queer image-makers' and storytellers' worldmaking. Sometimes these images and stories counter what are the most visible representations of Black queerness. In other cases they bring into focus those aspects of Black queer life that are overlooked in public culture. The future of Black popular culture studies would be wise to continue looking to such texts as a site of analysis of the ways Black queer people have entered into the twenty-first century, (re)making realities on their own terms, creating a field of possibilities on which to build a world in which Black queer people of the future can, as we chil'ren say, get their life!

Notes

1 Beam, "Making Ourselves from Scratch," 261.
2 Hemphill, "In Living Color'"; Riggs, "Black Macho Revisited," 324–30.
3 Hemphill, "In Living Color," 400.
4 Johnson, *Appropriating Blackness*, 65–75; Acham, "Blacks in the Future," 67.
5 Simone Drake, email correspondence, August 28, 2013.
6 Acham, "Blacks in the Future," 65, 64.
7 Day and Christian, "Locating Black Queer TV."

8 Muñoz, *Disidentifications*, 196, 198.

9 Bailey, *Butch Queens Up in Pumps*, 93–95.

10 Arnold and Bailey, "Constructing Home and Family," 173.

11 Weston, *Families We Choose*.

12 NovoNovusProductions, "Drama Queenz, Episode 201: 'And the World Goes 'Round.'"

13 It is imperative to note that the word "tranny" is offensive to many transgender people and functions as a form of harm, degradation, and violence regardless of intent. The central characters in *Drama Queenz* are all Black gay men, as is the creator, writer, producer, and lead star of the series. Given this fact, I would be remiss if I did not note that this phrase calls attention to the realities of cisnormativity in real life and in the Black queer world created in the web series.

14 NovoNovusProductions, "Drama Queenz, Ep. 307: 'Ease on Down the Road.'"

15 NovoNovusProductions, "Drama Queenz, Ep. 306: 'When It Ends.'"

16 Ferguson, *Aberrations in Black*; Hill-Collins, *Black Sexual Politics*; Springer, *Living for the Revolution*.

17 Cohen, "Punks, Bulldaggers and Welfare Queens."

18 Slay TV, "No Shade, Pilot."

19 Slay TV, "No Shade, Ep. 3: No Roaches."

References

Acham, Christine. "Blacks in the Future: Braving the Frontier of the Web Series." In *Watching While Black: Centering the Television of Black Audiences*, edited by Beretta Smith-Shomade. New Brunswick, NJ: Rutgers University Press, 2012.

Arnold, Emily, and Marlon Bailey. "Constructing Home and Family: How the Ballroom Community Supports African American GLBTQ Youth in the Face of HIV/AIDS." *Journal of Gay and Lesbian Social Services* 21 (2009): 171–88.

Bailey, Marlon. *Butch Queens Up in Pumps: Gender, Performance and Ballroom Culture in Detroit*. Ann Arbor: University of Michigan Press, 2013.

Beam, Joseph. "Making Ourselves from Scratch." In *Brother to Brother: New Writings by Black Gay Men*, edited by Essex Hemphill. Boston: Alyson, 1991.

Cohen, Cathy. "Punks, Bulldaggers, and Welfare Queens: The Radical Potential of Queer Politics?" In *Black Queer Studies: A Critical Anthology*, edited by E. Patrick Johnson and Mae G. Henderson. Durham, NC: Duke University Press, 2006.

Collins, Patricia Hill. *Black Sexual Politics: African-Americans, Gender, and the New Racism*. New York: Routledge, 2005.

Day, Faithe, and Aymar Jean Christian. "Locating Black Queer TV: Fans, Producers, and Networked Publics on YouTube." *Transformative Works and Cultures*, no. 24 (2017). http://journal.transformativeworks.org/index.php/twc/article/view/867/826.

Ferguson, Roderick. *Aberrations in Black: Toward a Queer of Color Critique*. Minneapolis: University of Minnesota Press, 2003.

Hemphill, Essex. "In Living Color': Toms, Coons, Mammies, Faggots, and Bucks" (1990). In *Out in Culture: Gay, Lesbian, and Queer Essays on Popular Culture*, edited by Corey K. Creekmur and Alexander Doty. Durham, NC: Duke University Press, 1995.

Johnson, E. Patrick. *Appropriating Blackness: Performance and the Politics of Authenticity*. Durham, NC: Duke University Press, 2003.

Muñoz, José Esteban. *Disidentifications: Queers of Color and the Performance of Politics*. Minneapolis: University of Minnesota Press, 1999.

NovoNovusProductions. "Drama Queenz, Episode 201: 'And the World Goes 'Round.'" YouTube, December 1, 2009. https://www.youtube.com/watch?v=ouLTGiVViHI&index=2&list=PL90ED4112E04C17D1.

NovoNovusProductions. "Drama Queenz, Ep. 307: 'Ease on Down the Road.'" YouTube, October 30, 2012. https://www.youtube.com/watch?v=ei4hIm_1A2s.

NovoNovusProductions. "Drama Queenz, Ep. 306: 'When It Ends.'" YouTube, July 25, 2012. https://www.youtube.com/watch?v=F9O_uH8mgmI&list=PL707C62B49DBCE0A8&index=6.

Riggs, Marlon. "Black Macho Revisited: Reflection of a SNAP! Queen." In *Brother to Brother: New Writings by Black Gay Men*, edited by Essex Hemphill. Boston: Alyson, 1991.

Slay TV. "No Shade, Pilot." YouTube, February 13, 2013. https://www.youtube.com/watch?v=z22DtUGd5Q4.

Slay TV. "No Shade, Ep. 3: No Roaches." YouTube, March 13, 2013. https://www.youtube.com/watch?v=7R_UF63ofWw.

Springer, Kimberly. *Living for the Revolution: Black Feminist Organizations, 1968–1980*. Durham, NC: Duke University Press, 2005.

Weston, Kath. *Families We Choose: Lesbians, Gays, Kinship*. New York: Columbia University Press, 1993.

CH.8   **STYLING AND PROFILING** / BALLERS, BLACKNESS, AND THE SARTORIAL POLITICS OF THE NBA

David J. Leonard

Each year, with the arrival of the National Basketball Association (NBA) playoffs, comes a heightened level of scrutiny for the players' shot selection, defensive effort, and sartorial choices. Yes, the postgame clothing choices of NBA players anchor playoff coverage. Commentators routinely analyze, mock, and celebrate the fashion choices of Kevin Durant, James Harden, Stephen Curry, Russell Westbrook, LeBron James, and Dwyane Wade, turning postgame press conferences into the NBA's version of the red carpet, transforming their arrivals to each game into a catwalk. Donning elaborately designed shirts covered with polka dots, a circus theme, or fishing lures; plaid jackets, pink and green suits; an array of hats; bow ties; pink and yellow pants; and suits with capri pants, a myriad of superstars have pushed their own sense of style into the public square. In the face of widespread pressure and newly formed rules regulating their clothing choices, these players have extended a tradition of signifying and protesting through clothing.

While read against the NBA's dress code, which was enacted after the infamous "Palace Brawl"[1] and in relationship to the media "style wars,"[2] this chapter doesn't conclude that these stylistic choices are transformative forms of resistance and rebellion.[3] Reflecting the neoliberal logics of individuality, marketing, branding, and personal transformation, these player interventions are constrained by the logics of white supremacy and the limited possibilities of individualized protests. This is equally evidenced by the media's response to the players' sartorial choices in the wake of the dress code, which seemingly made them into "exceptions" to the authentic gangsta stereotype or children who are throwing a temper tantrum at the demands of professionalism. Part shock and awe, part celebration of the players' purported back-turning on pathological hip-hop styles, and part embrace of the fashion industry appropriation of a hip-hop or new black aesthetic, the sartorial choices of NBA players reflect the broader racial culture wars that have defined the NBA for three decades.[4]

Attention to the sartorial politics of the NBA landscape is an important contemporary phenomenon that works toward one way of understanding the complex relationship between blackness and popular culture. In spite of only a very small percentage of African American NBA players performing "nerd chic" through sartorial choices, the media pays significant attention to the phenomenon. This hyper attention given to these fashion choices and the social politics of the NBA that produced the performances represents an important public arena wherein the complexities of blackness are represented.

At one level, the players are challenging the narrowness of professionalism, respectability, and appropriateness through suits and other business attire. They are saying that there are many ways to be professional, to be marketable, and to be celebrated within the American landscape. At another level, the players' sartorial choices are resisting the narrow constructions of blackness that define authentic hip-hop styles and urban masculinities, those very aesthetics and styles used to demonize and pathologize black youth. They try to dismantle the dialectics that equate nerddom and whiteness and thuggery and blackness, that reduce black athleticism to body and physicality and white athleticism to intelligence and creativity. These sartorial choices work to disrupt the entrenched ideas that form the core of antiblack racism. And finally, the range of sartorial choices—Nick Young, Kevin Durant, and Russell Westbrook's nerd chic, James Harden, Chris Paul and Kyle Kuzma's stylish bags (or anything else for that matter), Dwayne

Wade's capri pants and Tim Duncan's flip-flops and jeans, Kobe Bryant's and LeBron James's jerseys and $5,000 suits—highlight the ways that players are complicating our understanding of the adorned black male body. The range of styles between players and from individual players signifies on the heterogeneity of black masculinity. The fact that Westbrook or Durant or Jimmy Butler or Harden or J. R. Smith or Kobe Bryant wears a jersey and baggy jeans one day, a designer suit the next, and a nerd chic outfit on the third spotlights the ways they perform multiple inscriptions of black masculinity. During the 2015 All-Star weekend, James put on a fashion show where participants dressed as they would for the boardroom, a night out, and arriving to the game. This juxtaposition highlights the multiple inscriptions of black masculinity at work.

Yet despite the diversity of styles, the NBA's black players have long been reduced not only to their clothing but also to a single part of their closet. As evidenced by the media response to NBA style choices and the broader cultural landscape, a flattened and narrow understanding of black masculinity can be seen in the reading of their sartorial choices. That is, despite the larger history of dandyism, which sought to disrupt white supremacist readings of blackness, the emergence of the NBA's nerd chic fails to disrupt hegemonic antiblack stereotypes and the logics that gave rise to its dress code. The dialectics between whiteness and notions of civilization, between blackness and constructions of thuggery, between whiteness and nerddom/ intelligence, and between blackness and unprofessionalism/pathology are held in place through the reading of NBA stylings, from the pre–dress code era right through to our current moment.

Within this context, this chapter looks at the ways that sartorial choices, constructions of black male identity, and commodity culture operate through, against, and within hegemonic definitions of blackness and whiteness. Both the dress code and the reaction to nerd chic operate in and through a hegemonic understanding of blackness. I examine how racial performance and sartorial choices within the NBA and hip-hop culture work through dominant stereotypes, existing amid persistent antiblack racism. Arguing that the fascination with nerd chic and the wardrobe of the NBA's stars embodies the fear and loathing, the demonization and racialization, the fetishization and commodification of black bodies, I explore the racial lessons offered amid the clothing commentary that has become commonplace within contemporary sporting culture. While a part of the chapter rests with contextualizing the sartorial choices of today's NBA stars, from LeBron James to Russell Westbrook, within a tradition of resistance, I am more concerned with the racial logics attached to the clothed black NBA bodies before and after the NBA's dress code. Still, it is important, even while acknowledging its limitations, to see the agency, to recognize the resistance, to see the broader history, and to otherwise not allow for the mainstream media and broader hegemonic discourses to overdetermine the meaning in their sartorial choices. Embodying a history of dandyism, today's black ballers are subverting the expectations of the NBA, and white America as a whole, remixing aesthetic demands in a way that illustrates their power, subjectivity, and agency. Irrespective of the media discourse, which will be a focus, that seeks to exceptionalize and individualize bow ties and backpacks, plaid and bright color schemes, the clothing choices must be seen within a larger history of black identity, the NBA, and the surveillance regimes of white supremacy.

Clothing Matters

The NBA's place on the fashion runway is long-standing. From Clyde Frazier's fur coats and fedoras to Dr. J's disco funk, from Michael Jordan's immaculate $5,000 . . . $10,000 . . . $15,000 suits to Allen Iverson's hip-hop gear, NBA players have always held a connection to fashion. In a GQ interview, Frazier discussed the expectations to perform off the court: "I first found out that I was an icon for blacks, say, like, we'd go to Detroit and after the game we're on the bus, and all the kids would go, Clyde, c'mon, man, where's the mink? Clyde, c'mon, man, we wanted to see you dressed up! That's when I realized that people were really into the way I was dressing. So that's when I went somewhere I made sure I was dressed up."[5] In a related piece, Steve Marsh argues that the centrality of NBA style, on and off the court, is not surprising given the ways the league has long marketed itself through individual stars and the ways that basketball itself is about creativity, individuality, and spontaneity.[6]

More than in any other sport, basketball showcases the individual; we can see each player's tics and idiosyncrasies when he's on the court, and that's how we begin to decide who we think he is.[7] At least as far back as Frazier, no sport has been more enmeshed in the allure of black culture and style.[8] The visibility, the primacy of a culture of cool, and the celebrity of NBA stars has compelled attention for more than three decades. The connection between the NBA and the city, between the basketball and urban black culture, and between 1970s black culture and the league's stars, fueled the crossover of these styles. Through the 1980s and 1990s, not only within the NBA but also in college with the squads at UNLV and Michigan, basketball would be instrumental in shaping clothing styles on and off the court. In recent years, the importance of the sartorial choices of NBA players has taken on greater meaning. Reflecting the cultural ascendance of sports media and new media technologies, which allows for a larger platform, the sartorial performance of today's NBA stars has emerged as almost as important as assist totals and championship rings.

As evident in the experiences of Frazier and the catwalk-like realities of walking from car to locker room, the players' clothing choices matter. They matter because of the place of the NBA within the cultural landscape given the NBA's racial demographics. Yes, the NBA's cultural power fueled the interest in "the style wars." The place of hip hop and the league's commodification of individual stars further the importance of style, aesthetics, and sartorial choices. With each, race, the white gaze, and signifiers surrounding blackness sit at the center; the meaning, spectacle, and fetish surrounding the clothing of NBA stars, from the 1970s through today, highlights the power in the staging of black masculinity within public discourse. Race and conceptions of blackness and whiteness fuel the interest in the clothes. The bodies that don these clothes further highlight the racial stakes, demonstrating the ways that clothes become a site for the contestation of racial meaning.

Race and the Politics of Adornment

It would be easy to simply read Frazier's coat, Jordan's tailored suits, Iverson's baggy jeans, LeBron's capri suit, Steph's trenchcoat and Timbs, or Westbrook's nerd chic as capitalism personified. Yes, the NBA's marketing of individual stars and the efforts of players to brand themselves in financially lucrative ways play out in important ways. Branding matters; so do commodity culture, neoliberalism, transnational capitalism, and the dialectics between cool, race, gender, and clothing. Yet the sartorial choices of NBA stars are also a story of resistance—they are part of the "hidden transcript" and the infrapolitics that disrupt the structures of racism.[9]

To understand these dimensions requires looking beyond the marketplace, beyond corporate culture, toward an understanding of resistance and the ways that race operates within American culture. The "politics of adornment" are shaped by America's racial history.[10] It is not just the clothing but the body wearing the clothes, a racial body imbued with meaning and signification in the dominant white imagination. As Herman Gray notes, "Self-representations of black masculinity in the United States are historically

structured by and against dominant (and dominating) discourses of masculinity and race, specifically whiteness."[11] To understand the NBA's clothing
politics, dress code, player resistance, and media discourse necessitates centering a discussion of racism as well as the signifying practices of blackness
and whiteness.

Whereas much media discussion of the outfits of the Oklahoma City
Thunder's Russell Westbrook and Kevin Durant and the eyewear of the
Miami Heat's LeBron James and Dwayne Wade focuses on individual branding, rendering their styles as depoliticized practices, as little more than a
personal expression, it is important to link their sartorial choices to a larger
history of race, racism, and the "politics of adornment." As noted by Tanisha Ford in her discussion of clothing and Freedom Summer, "Focusing on
the adornment politics of Freedom Summer does not trivialize its political
aims. It helps us broaden our understanding of 'black freedom,' moving us
beyond a definition that centers on the pursuit of equal access to public
facilities."[12] Noting that "black style attempts to escape stereotypes, fixity,
essentialization—signify on them—and functions as a process of identity
formation," Monica L. Miller argues that African American sartorial choice
is "a dialogic process that exists in relation to white dandyism at the same
time it expresses, through its own internal logic, black culture." Demonstrating the power in the clothes, the "politics of adornment," and the sartorial
stakes, Miller further argues that "the black body alone inside the material
will alter the fabric. . . . Black dandies continually 'repeat, revise, reverse, or
transform what has come before,' using clothing as a means to create new
images and identities and revise them yet again."[13]

As evident here, one of the primary areas of discussion concerned with
race, stereotype, and clothing has focused on the concept of black dandyism. Shantrelle P. Lewis, the curator for the exhibit *Dandy Lion: Articulating
Black Masculine Identity*, describes the "dandy lion" and "dandyism" in the
following way: "A dandy lion is a contemporary expression of black dandyism. It's a new statement on black masculinity within a contemporary
context. He is a man of elegance, an individual who remixes a Victorian era
fashion and aesthetic with traditional African sensibilities and swagger."[14]
Noting that the stakes and significance extend beyond personal style but
are wrapped in existing stereotypes, Lewis reflects on the significance of
clothing in the racialization of black bodies: "Especially for young people,
we are bombarded with this one sided, monolithic image of what it means
to be black and male, primarily around the United States and actually even
around the globe. The image is a negative one, images of black men are

not reaffirming and not positive. . . . Express creativity and individuality. That's what dandy lions seek to express, especially to a young generation that's also paying tribute to the older generation. Respectability was a way of life.[15]"

Although black dandyism has the potential to operate through a "politics of respectability" (I will return to this at the end of the paper) that requires blackness to disrupt antiblack stereotypes and buys into "the social engineering project," the importance here rests with the stakes and the power in these sartorial choices.[16] In other words, while the ability of clothing and stylistic choices to disrupt antiblack stereotypes is questionable, the demands that black bodies prove their worth, their desirability, their civility, and their place within the white imagination is part and parcel of white supremacy.

This is part of the history of the NBA. The dialogic performances and signifying practices on full display during press conferences and as most players arrive and leave the stadium highlight the ways they are staging black masculinity in their sartorial choices, and these choices cannot be read outside of a larger social-cultural-political and race landscape. While that was always the case, given the interest in Frazier's pregame dress or the fact that Jordan would rarely be seen off the court in something other than a business suit, the stakes and importance of player clothing took on new meaning by 2003.

NBA Dress Code

To understand the stakes, and the power in the sartorial choices of NBA players, it is crucial to look at the history of the NBA and its obsession with their closets. That is, the efforts to appeal to white fans and corporations, to contain the league's blackness, and to 'civilize' those unruly black bodies have focused on the players' clothes.

Not only unsuccessful on the court, the 2004 Olympic basketball team caused a significant amount of embarrassment for the NBA in the wake of its efforts to conceal blackness from the league. Prior to the games, members of the basketball team attended a dinner in their honor at a fancy Belgrade restaurant. While other guests, including members of the Serbian National Team, wore matching sport coats and dressed as others might describe as "appropriate," Allen Iverson, Carmelo Anthony, LeBron James, and other members of the American team showed up in sweat suits, oversized jeans and shirts, large platinum chains, and, of course, diamond earrings. Larry Brown, the team's coach and often celebrated benevolent white father figure of the NBA, was appalled, coming close to sending several players back to the hotel. Word of the fashion faux pas eventually made its way to the office of NBA Commissioner David Stern in New York, where concern was already on the rise about how some players were dressing and, more broadly, how the game's appeal was slipping.

In the aftermath of the Palace Brawl, which saw Ron Artest and the Indiana Pacers go into the stands, declining ratings, the sexual assault allegations against Kobe Bryant, the arrest of Allen Iverson, several high profile drug incidents, and the longstanding perception that the NBA was being overrun by "criminals," "gangstas," "thugs," and those otherwise prone to "bad behavior," David Stern announced plans for a league-wide dress code in October 2005.[17] As the cliché goes, clothing makes a man, and Stern sought to remake the NBA's black men in hopes of curtailing widespread animosity toward the NBA and its hip-hop ballers. Concluding that ad hoc policies and team-directed rules were incompatible with their efforts to "rehabilitate the image of a sport beset with bad behavior," the league instituted a dress code policy that governed players, all while sending a message to fans and corporate partners.[18] The dress code represented an effort to counteract the negative perception that had plagued the NBA through simply restricting, controlling, and regularing the assumed signifiers of blackness.

Specifically, the league office directed players to be more accessible through public appearances and signing autographs; it pushed players to participate in events that sought to diminish the? social distance between players and ticket holders. And, of course, they needed to dress in a more presentable way; they needed to appeal to Red State America (white America) in how they looked. The dress code, along with the NBA cares program and other changes, represented the NBA's effort "to look a little less gangsta and more genteel."[19] It was part of a public relations strategy that emphasized the quality and good nature of NBA players. "These guys are millionaires and should act like it. They stay in four-star hotels, go to the best restaurants, it's not appropriate to go to these places in a tracksuit," said Clyde Frazier, the one-time sartorial rebel of the NBA. "If they worked at that high a level for any other corporation in America, with their salaries, they'd have to wear a suit and tie. It's not too much to ask."[20] Their clothes needed to index their benevolence, professionalism, and desirability. They needed to be respectable and to appeal to a white gaze that would see them as desirable rather than threatening. The clothes draping their bodies needed to literally and metaphorically cloak—hide and conceal—their blackness, highlighting their proximity to whiteness.

Specifically, the NBA's dress policy required that players "wear business casual attire" whenever participating in league events or team functions or when conducting "team or league business," defined as any "activity conducted on behalf of the team or the league during which the player is seen by or interacts with fans, business partners, members of the public, the media, or other third parties." The policy restricted the clothing choices of players engaged in a number of tasks: participating in league events, promotional appearances, or media interviews; sitting on the bench when not in uniform; leaving or arriving at the stadium, and, potentially, riding on team buses or planes. In addition to regulating dress in particular (public and private) spaces, the policy also stipulated what constituted "business attire," specifying that to be in compliance players must wear dress shirts and/or sweaters, dress slacks, dress jeans or khakis, socks, and either dress shoes "or presentable shoes." At the same time the policy laid out a series of unacceptable clothing choices: "Headgear of any kind while sitting on the bench or in the stands at a game, during media interviews, or during a team or league event or appearance (unless appropriate for the event or appearance, team-identified, and approved by the team) is to be excluded."[21] Although Stern and others inside the NBA spoke of the policy in universal terms, as an effort to highlight the professionalism and "goodness" of all its players, numerous players saw the policy as something else: a racist assault on hip hop and yet another instance of the NBA attacking its young black male stars.[22]

Changing Clothes, not the Narrative?

The dress code, and the players' negotiation of the dress code, would spark ample praise from America's sport's media.[23] Such praise highlights the limitations of the signifying brought into focus from several NBA players. Despite asserting their agency and voices, and despite their disruption of the goals of the dress code, ultimately the rise of nerd chic left intact the hegemonic inscription of blackness and the NBA.

The media efforts to see the rise of nerd chic as the arrival of respectability, as connected to whiteness, spotlights the boundaries in these sartorial protests. At times, media discursive interest in the sartorial choices of black NBA players played into hegemonic stereotypes about the "selfish athlete," reinforcing narratives about NBA players being obsessed with "style over substance." Some within the media saw the clothing shift as further evidence of the problems of a league wrought with selfish, egotistical, and superficial athletes who were all about style and no substance. For others, it was a re-freshing change from the dysfunction of the hip-hop era. Still others would dehistoricize style and aesthetics as little more than individualized branding, as reflective of the power of social media, or a response to the sartorial surveil-lance emanating from the league.[24] Rachel Felder even concluded, "Fashion has become a virtual obsession for many players, presumably fueled in part by athletes' naturally competitive nature to outshine other peers."[25] Yet, nei-ther the dress code nor the shifting styles from jerseys and jeans to capris and backpacks disrupted the narrow and flattening definitions of blackness. Oscar Moralde makes this clear, questioning the possibility of sartorial trans-gression given white supremacist ideologies: "Ultimately, if the NBA dandy wishes to subvert the white-imposed league dress code, can he only escape by submitting himself to the authentication of a different dress code that remains coded white?"[26]

Interestingly, America's sports racial skeptics and those who celebrated the N.B.A.—the "New Black Aesthetic"[27]—among its elite ballers, shared a similar understanding of the ways that whiteness and blackness operated through these clothing choices. For example, noting how players wear "ging-ham and plaid and velvet, bow ties and sweater vests, suspenders, and thick black glasses they don't need," Wesley Morris, in *Grantland*, celebrated their stylistic stances as a stance against racial stereotypes. Seeing them as black dandies, Morris found power in the players' adjustment to the dress code era. For him, postgame clothing was not simply an outfit but an effort to stomp out racial bigotry: "Their colors conflict. Their patterns clash. Clothes that once stood as an open invitation to bullies looking for something to hang on the back of a bathroom door are what James now wears to rap alongside Lil Wayne. Clothes that once signified whiteness, squareness, suburbanness, sis-syness, in the minds of some NBA players no longer do." Seemingly accepting the premise that suits or ties are indeed the clothing of the white commu-nity, Morris argues that the NBA's new clothing era will spark a new level of acceptance of the NBA's black players and a reimagination of these sartorial choices through a colorblind lens.[28]

Similarly, NBA writer Sean Gregory identifies a player's sartorial choices as a window into his broader appeal and demeanor: "In Durant, African-Americans are blessed with an ideal front man: a seemingly humble super-star," evidenced by his "refusal to play the part of ego-driven hoops celeb" as well as his propensity to wear glasses rather than chains, a backpack rather than headphones, and a sweater in lieu of a hoodie.[29] If you didn't know that plaid and mismatched colors were a sign of humility and a lack of ego, now you know. Like Morris, Gregory sees shifting style as a tool used to disprove antiblack stereotypes.

This sort of sartorial respectability as antiracism was commonplace in the dawn of the NBA's sartorial revolution. Even glasses had the potential to convince America's racial skeptics that black NBA players were not thugs or gangstas but good, honest, and respectable people. Glasses were a game changer in America's long-standing racial struggle. Commenting about the popularity of nonprescription glasses among NBA stars, Dave Hyde, another of the NBA's litany of commentators, furthered the links between "nerds" and the sort of "style" embraced by several NBA stars: "That's just it. No one's sure what the statement these frameless glasses are other than, well, Urkel-R-Us. . . . But wear the non-glass glasses? You don't need to understand fashion to recognize a nerdy idea when it hits you right between the eyes."[30]

The efforts to celebrate what Gregory describes as "preppy-dress movement" and "nerd attire" are wrapped up in larger questions of identity. For several commentators, the shifting clothing choices punctuated an expanded definition of blackness common in contemporary America. Alongside the rise of NBA nerd chic, we also saw the embrace of postracial blackness articulated by Kanye West, Pharrell, and Touré, each of whom has spoken about a new blackness developing inside the walls of a postracism America.

Under this logic, our changing world allows for Allen Iverson and Kevin Durant, Kanye West and Lil Wayne, Brittney Griner and Nicki Minaj, Michelle Obama and Cory Booker all to exist under a larger umbrella of blackness, without any societal stigma, consequence, or problem. According to Touré, "I see [black irony] in NBA star Kevin Durant's penchant for nerd chic, wearing glasses and a schoolboy backpack and thereby taking the air out of the black male imperative to be masculine, tough, and cool."[31] That is, blackness exists without the mandate of respectability and the trappings of whiteness. The scrutiny directed at player clothing, at the sartorial choices of President Obama and the first lady, the existence of dress codes within not only the NBA but also public schools and nightclubs, and of course the criminalization of black youth, from Trayvon Martin to Michael Brown, for their clothing choices, all point to the ways that culture and clothing exist as a racial signifier, imbued with the logics of antiblack violence and white supremacy.

Here's where the argument falls apart: Touré and others see expanded performances available to black bodies as evidence of postraciality yet ignore the ways that certain bodies, performances, and styles are privileged as more desirable, respectable, and acceptable. Moreover, he cites nerd chic as ironic, seemingly normalizing glasses and nerd style as the purview of whiteness. At the same time, his argument ignores the ways that high fashion has embraced hip hop, selling certain styles at significant profit. Likewise, the commentary around nerd chic seemingly erases the historic specificity of these sartorial choices. The failure to account for dandyism, to look at the use of colors, spectacle, and flamboyance from these players, and the larger context of black dandies point to the ways that narrative seeks to see these players through a lens of whiteness. The irony emanates from not only the binary between whiteness=nerd and blackness=athlete but through imagining athleticism/blackness as disconnected from intelligence, logic, and books as those are part and parcel of the nerd/whiteness identity.

While oversimplifying black identity and reducing blackness to aesthetics, styles, and cultural practices and erasing the long-standing diversity within the black community, the celebration of nerd chic or "black irony" actually reinforces stereotypes. According to this logic, what makes their style noteworthy, what is worth celebrating and worthy of commentary is that Durant, Westbrook, James, and Wade aren't acting like "black men." What is unusual is that they are wearing the clothes and embodying the styles of someone else, someone they are not. Clothing change—check; stereotypes continue—check.

Morris makes this clear when he equates the nerd movement within the NBA to cross-dressing: "The cardigans and black frames, the backpacks and everything else: It's all as overdetermined as what happens on Project Runway with Lady Gaga and Nicki Minaj, and with the drag queens. 'Nerd' is a kind of drag in which ballers are liberated to pretend to be someone else." Morris, like so much of the celebration of the NBA's nerd chic, essentializes blackness as "thug" and "gangsta," so much so that shedding sagging pants for capris is imagined as a form of "racial cross-dressing." Such narratives see liberation as possible by pretending to be "respectable" and "sartorially white," which, in the end, holds up the logics of white supremacy, all while seeing change as possible with a simple shopping spree.[32] While the transformative possibilities of the rise of NBA nerd chic are overstated, given the entrenched nature of antiblack racism, given its neoliberal capitalist sensibilities, this is a sartorial intervention. Whereas Morris and others see these clothing changes through a binary that reifies whiteness and blackness, that juxtaposes an essentialized black and white style, it is clear that players are disrupting these binaries, playing with and undermining hegemonic under-standings of difference.

Shock and Awe

While much of the dominant discourse sees athletes "acting" like nerds, as if being athletic is the opposite of being smart and intellectual, this reflects the overall idea that the nerd look allows these black athletes to become white in the dominant imagination and therefore transcend the stereotype of young black males. This does little to transform the stereotype but instead leaves them unscathed as ties and cardigans remain as symbols of goodness and whiteness, whereas hoodies and beanies continue as markers of criminality, danger, and blackness. Robin D. G. Kelley suggests, "In these efforts to rep-resent body through dress, African Americans welded a double edged sword since the styles they adopted to combat racism all too frequently reinforced rather than challenged bourgeois notions of respectability."[33] In other words, "Black dandyism serves as both liberation and a mode of conformity."[34] The realities experienced in an NBA of the dress code era points to the limitations and false promises of a politics of respectability because of the investment in whiteness and white supremacy.

While seeing the rise of nerd chic within the NBA as part of a larger his-tory of black dandyism and understanding the liberatory possibilities, this example demonstrates the futility of a politics of respectability. According to Kobena Mercer, the "binarism of so-called positive and negative images" are "unhelpful." Mercer makes clear that the cultural yearning to replace "nega-tive" (racist) with "positive" (respectable) forecloses on endless posititibilies: "As black people, we are now more aware of the identities, fantasies, and desire that are coerced, simplified, and reduced by the rhetorical closure that flows from that kind of critique."[35] Cornel West, like Mercer, questions both the desirability and the plausibility of such a "social engineering proj-ect," arguing, "The social engineering argument claims that since any form of representation is constructed—i.e., selective in light of broader aims— Black representation (especially given the difficulty of Blacks gaining access to positions of power to produce any Black imagery) should offer positive images, thereby countering racist stereotypes. The hidden assumption of both arguments is that we have unmediated access to what the 'real Black community' is and what 'positive images' are."[36] The demand to disprove "negative" representations with "positivity" mandates that artists, practi-tioners, and others further centers the white gaze. Mercer, West, Patricia Hill

Collins, and countless others identify these representational movements as futile challenges to racism, which put the burden on African Americans to perform and embody a respectable and desirable image of blackness to be consumed by the public. Hats, bow ties, and $5,000 suits (or significantly higher), clothing from a fashion industry dominated by whiteness, are not sources of "liberation and a mode of conformity"; they offer no liberation from white supremacy; there is no challenge to the logics of white supremacy and a practice that gives legitimacy to the binaries of white supremacy, which furthers exploitation and abuse.

Although offering important interventions, and a symbolic challenge to the flattening of black identity, while playing with the binaries of "respectable" versus "thug," black versus white, and the racialized constructs of athlete versus nerd, NBA dandyism is not a tool of liberation or a pathway delegitimating dominant racial stereotypes. Even as an intervention, it is evidence of the profitability in antiblack racism. The allure of a "new black aesthetic" is understandable given the desire to challenge antiblack racism and its consequences inside and outside the sporting landscape. Yet in the end we see the power of commodifying both "new styles" and "transformative images." These interventions do more to line the pockets of the owners, sports media conglomerates, and clothing companies. At best, they offer narratives of "exceptions" to the narratives of blackness that center pathology, criminality, and danger. Yes, KD24 or LB6 are different from their friends back on the block. In their sartorial choices, they are the exceptions that normalize the rule and the associated violence. Nerd chic is profitable for the league all while sanctioning daily racial profiling. The dress code, the discourses surrounding players' sartorial choices, and the resulting nerd chic "gives credence to the deeply reactionary idea that you can profile antisocial behavior through clothes," writes progressive sports writer Dave Zirin. "If someone wears baggy jeans and a chain, they must be on drugs, packing a gat, or on their way to see one of their twenty babies. This is a slap in the face to every baller who lives clean and, as a grown man chooses to wear what he damn well pleases—not to mention the young urban audience that the NBA depends on."[37] Despite the promise of changing white hearts and minds, the nerd chic era gives credence to racial essentialism, the logics of racial profiling, and the false home of liberation through personal transformation. It anchors colorblind racism.[38] The importance of exceptional blackness in seeing certain bodies as aberrations results from the "illegibility" of black bodies not dressed in hoodies, jerseys, or (prison/athlete) uniforms.[39]

The spectacle of shock, which imagines the recent NBA stylings as an aberration, as "illegible," and seemingly incompatible with an authentic blackness, emanates from a failure to consider sartorial choices in relationship to a history of black resistance. It also rests on a refusal to see player agency, and a collective response to antiblack racism within the NBA and the broader social fabric. As Nicole Fleetwood asserts, "Authenticity is a highly racialized and complex term in American culture. In the context of race and masculinity, authenticity imbues the subject with a mythic sense of virility, danger, and physicality."[40] The sartorial choices and the performative exhibitions of these aesthetic markers from today's NBA players carve out a space of resistance to those regimes of regulation, whether in the form of a dress code or demands that certain styles are antithetical to an authentic black masculinity.

The discourse, thus, erases the racial history and the specifics behind the dress code and how the players responded in ways that asserted their subjectivity, individuality, and agency; it also erases the history of fashion within the NBA and even college basketball for that matter. From Wilt Chamberlin's unbuttoned silk shirts and Dr. J's Afro to Jordan's shaved head, from Slick Watt's headbans to the Fab Five's baggy shorts and black socks, from Allen Iverson's jewelry to Shaq's oversized suits, from Westbrook's construction uniform or distressed jeans to Kyle Kuzma's turtle neck and fur coat, NBA players have always embraced a fashion-forward sensibility on and off the court. To reimagine contemporary NBA stylings as progress, as a maturity, discipline, or understanding of what's appropriate to wear in a work place, as the result of David Stern's intervention, or as reflecting "their stepping up their game" requires erasing not only the history of fashion within the NBA but also the broader history of sartorial choices and resistance.[41]

In focusing on Stern, and how an intervention from the NBA's "great white father" led to the "style wars," the discourse once again reimagines black identity and resistance from the standpoint of a white savior. That is, it is because of Stern and his dress code that NBA players are dressing so "nicely" and receiving positive media attention, financial rewards, and cultural appreciation. Celebrating the potential and the necessity of disciplinary actions directed at the abject bodies, the dominant narrative around the stylish choices of today's NBA superstars embraces the trope of white saviors and the power of civilizing through coercion and power.

Despite efforts to dehistoricize and erase the political dimensions sewn into the social fabric, there is much at stake within the "style wars." Whether in the threats of fines from the NBA or the media commentaries about clothing, whether in accepted stereotypes or the daily realities of racial profiling, it's clear that there is much more at stake than a sense of style—the war is not simply about cool, the hottest designer, or appearing on some list of "the best dressed baller"; the war is over black bodies and their signification within the dominant white imagination.

The importance of clothing and discussions of American racism are fully evident outside the arena. The "politics of adornment" are not simply fodder for sports commentators but a site of profiling—violence and antiblack racism. Responding to the release of security footage of Trayvon Martin at a 7/11 on the night of his murder, Geraldo Rivera identified his "thug wear" as the reason he was profiled and ultimately killed by George Zimmerman: "I'll bet you money, if he didn't have that hoodie on, that nutty neighborhood watch guy wouldn't have responded in that violent and aggressive way."[42] In other words, had Martin worn Durant's backpack, Wade's glasses, or Amar'e Stoudemire's tie-cardigan combination (interestingly many of the players at the forefront of nerd chic also participated in hoodie protests within the NBA), he would be alive today? Beyond its simplicity and offensiveness, such a remark highlights that no matter how nerdy James, Harden, Curry, or Durant dresses, their blackness and its meaning remain fully present in the dominant imagination. The legibility of black criminality is entrenched within the dominant white imagination. Their sartorial choices are surely resistance efforts to navigate the NBA rules and entrenched antiblack racism, yet their meaning and the stakes can never be covered up.

Notes

1 Leonard, *After Artest.*
2 Marsh, "Inside the NBA's New Style Wars."
3 Leonard, *After Artest.*
4 Boyd, *Young, Black, Rich, and Famous.*
5 Marsh, "Legends of NBA Style."
6 Marsh, "Inside the NBA's New Style Wars."
7 Boyd, *Young, Black, Rich and Famous.*
8 Marsh "Legends of NBA Style."
9 Kelley, *Race Rebels*; Scott, *Domination.*
10 Ford, "The Politics of 'Freedom Summer' Style."
11 Quoted in Fleetwood, "Hip-Hop Fashion," 342.
12 Ford, "The Politics of 'Freedom Summer' Style."
13 Miller, *Slaves to Fashion*, 14.

14 Haque, "Black Men."

15 Haque, "Black Men."

16 Higginbotham, *Righteous Discontent*; West, "The New Politics of Difference," 130.

17 Philips, "The NBA's Bling Ban." See Leonard, *After Artest*, for discussion of the media discourse.

18 Philips, "The NBA's Bling Ban."

19 Eligon, "N.B.A. Dress Code Decrees."

20 Quoted in Critchell, "NBA Stars Up Their Style Game."

21 Morris, "NBA Dress Code Policy."

22 Leonard, *After Artest*.

23 Leonard, *After Artest*.

24 Ferrari-King "NBA Players Who Changed the Style Game for Good"; Graham "How David Stern's NBA Dress Code Changed Men's Fashion"; Cunningham, "NBA Style"; Lieber, "Inside the Symbiotic Relationship."

25 Felder, "N.B.A. Style."

26 Moralde, "The NBA Dandy Plays the Fashion Game," 70.

27 Ellis, "The New Black Aesthetic."

28 Morris, "The Rise of the NBA Nerd."

29 Gregory, "NBA Finals Profile."

30 Hyde, "Some Optical Delusions."

31 Quoted in Gregory, "NBA Finals Profile."

32 Morris, "The Rise of the NBA Nerd."

33 Quoted in Miller, *Slaves to Fashion*, 17.

34 Miller, *Slaves to Fashion*, 17.

35 Mercer, *Welcome to the Jungle*, 202

36 West, "The New Politics of Difference," 130.

37 Zirin, *Welcome to the Terrordome*, 116.

38 Bonilla-Silva, *Racism without Racists*.

39 Neal, *Looking for Leroy*.

40 Fleetwood, "Hip-Hop Fashion," 327.

41 Critchell, "NBA Stars Up Their Style Game."

42 Jonsson, "Geraldo Rivera."

References

Bonilla-Silva, E. *Racism without Racists: Colorblind Racism and the Persistence of* Racial Inequality. Lanham, MD: Rowman & Littlefield Publishers, 2006.

Boyd, Todd. *Young, Black, Rich, and Famous: The Rise of the NBA, the Hip Hop Invasion, and the Transformation of American Culture.* New York: Bison Books, 2008.

Collins, Patricia Hill. *Black Sexual Politics: African Americans, Gender, and the New Racism.* New York: Routledge, 2004.

Critchell, Samantha. "NBA Stars Up Their Style Game off the Court." *Associated Press*, June 9, 2013. https://www.apnews.com/a6de374ddcfd44cfb8e40b06b86 04db7.

Cunningham, Erin. "NBA Style: Full Court Dress." *Daily Beast*, May 11, 2014. http://www.thedailybeast.com/articles/2014/05/11/nba-style-full-court-dress.html.

Eligon, John. "N.B.A. Dress Code Decrees: Clothes Make the Image." *New York Times*, October 19, 2005. www.nytimes.com/2005/10/19/sports/basketball /19stern.html?oref=login.

Ellis, Trey. "The New Black Aesthetic." *Callaloo*, no. 38 (winter 1989): 233–43.

Felder, Rachel. "N.B.A. Style: How Players Showcase Their Fashion A-Game off the Court." *Vanity Fair*, June 5, 2014. http://www.vanityfair.com/online/ daily/2014/06/nba-style.

Ferrari-King, Giancarlo. "NBA Players Who Changed the Style Game for Good." *Bleacher Report*, April 7, 2017. https://bleacherreport.com/articles/2697208-nba -players-who-changed-the-style-game-for-good.

Fleetwood, Nicole R. "Hip-Hop Fashion, Masculine Anxiety, and the Discourse of Americana," In *Black Cultural Traffic: Crossroads in Global Performance and Popular Culture*, edited by Harry Justin Elam Jr. and Kennell Jackson. Ann Arbor: University of Michigan Press, 2005.

Ford, Tanisha C. "The Politics of 'Freedom Summer' Style." *New Black Man (in Exile)*, June 12, 2014. http://newblackman.blogspot.com/2014/06/the-politics-of- freedom-summer-style.html.

Graham, Zach, "How David Stern's NBA Dress Code Changed Men's Fashion." *Rolling Stone,* November 4, 2016. https://www.rollingstone.com /culture/culture-sports/how-david-sterns-nba-dress-code-changed-mens -fashion-104719/.

Gregory, Sean. "NBA Finals Profile: Inside the Mind of Kevin Durant." *Time*, June 12, 2012. http://keepingscore.blogs.time.com/2012/06/12/ profile-inside-the-mind-of-nba-superstar-kevin-durant/.

Haque, Fahima. "Black Men: Dandyism, Masculinity and Homophobia." *Washington Post*, February 2, 2012. http://www.washingtonpost.com/blogs/therootdc/ post/black-men-dandyism-masculinity-and-homophobia/2012/02/01/gIQA- fOffkQ_blog.html.

Higginbotham, Evelyn Brooks. *Righteous Discontent: The Women's Movement in the Black Baptist Church, 1880–1920*. Cambridge, MA: Harvard University Press, 1994.

Hyde, Dave. "Some Optical Delusions in NBA Playoffs." *Sun Sentinel* (South Florida), May 11, 2012. http://articles.sun-sentinel.com/2012-05-11/sports/ fl-hyde-miami-heat-0512-20120511_1_glasses-kurt-rambis-nba.

Jonsson, Patrick. "Geraldo Rivera (Again) Says Trayvon Martin's 'Thug Wear' Got Him Profiled." *Christian Science Monitor*, May 19, 2012. http://www.csmonitor.com/USA/Justice/2012/0519/ Geraldo-Rivera-again-says-Trayvon-Martin-s-thug-wear-got-him-profiled.

Kelley, Robin D. G. *Race Rebels: Culture, Politics, and the Black Working Class*. New York: Free Press, 1994.

Leonard, David J. *After Artest: The NBA and the Assault on Blackness*. New York: SUNY Press, 2012.

Lieber, Chavie. "Inside the Symbiotic Relationship between Fashion and the NBA." *Racked*, June 24, 2014. http://racked.com/archives/2014/06/24/nba-style-fashion-russell-westbrook-kobe-devin-durant-amare-stoudemire.php.

Marsh, Steve. "Inside the NBA's New Style Wars." *GQ*, March 28, 2013. http://www.gq.com/sports/profiles/201304/nba-fashion-style-dwyane-wade-lebron-james-russell-westbrook.

Marsh, Steve. "Legends of NBA Style: The GQ+A with Walt Frazier." *GQ*, March 28, 2013. http://www.gq.com/sports/profiles/201304/nba-fashion-style-walt-clyde-frazier-interview.

Mercer, Kobena. *Welcome to the Jungle: New Positions in Black Cultural Studies*. New York: Routledge, 1994.

Miller, Monica L. *Slaves to Fashion: Black Dandyism and the Styling of Black Diasporic Identity*. Durham, NC: Duke University Press, 2009.

Moralde, Oscar. "The NBA Dandy Plays the Fashion Game: NBA All-Star All-Style and Dress Codes of Black Masculinity." *Journal of Popular Culture* 52, no. 1 (2019): 53–75.

Morris, Wesley. "The Rise of the NBA Nerd: Basketball Style and Black Identity." *Grantland*, December 21, 2011. http://grantland.com/features/the-rise-nba-nerd/.

Morris, Wesley. "NBA Dress Code Policy." *Inside Hoops*, October 17, 20015. http://www.insidehoops.com/dress-code.shtml.

Neal, Mark Anthony. *Looking for Leroy: Illegible Black Masculinities*. New York: New York University Press, 2013.

Philips, Gary. "The NBA's Bling Ban: Looking Good." *Los Angeles Times*, November 27, 2005. https://www.latimes.com/archives/la-xpm-2005-nov-27-op-nbablingbling27-story.html.

Scott, James C. *Domination and the Arts of Resistance: Hidden Transcripts*. New Haven, CT: Yale University Press, 1992.

West, Cornel. "The New Politics of Difference." In *The Cornel West Reader*, edited by Cornel West. New York: Basic Civitas Books, 1999.

Wise, Mike. "Opinions on the NBA Dress Code Far from Uniform." *Washington Post*, October 23, 2005.

Zirin, Dave. *Welcome to the Terrordome: The Pain, Politics, and Promise of Sports*. Chicago: Haymarket Press, 2007.

**AN INTERVIEW WITH TRACY
SHARPLEY-WHITING /**
JANUARY 27, 2016

*What is the state of Black pop culture in the public sphere and as an
intellectual field of inquiry in the twenty-first century?*

I think we see it everywhere and nowhere in the public sphere. I say nowhere
specifically in reference to ways that it is elided, eclipsed, and repackaged as
American popular culture. In effect, the elision of Black contributions in the
making of America and our critical role in American history has the effect
of rendering those highly creative and appropriated aspects of Black popular
culture as white American–derived. It is, as the brilliant Greg Tate wrote,
an *everything but the burden* phenomenon. Here I am thinking specifically of
the very popular *New York Times* best-selling cookbook *Thug Kitchen* that perpetrated a serious fraud The cookbook tapped into the organic and whole
food movements deeply embedded in African American foodways and practices (though folks just want to think we eat all the bad stuff—history, and
my colleague Alice Randall's cookbook *Soul Food Love* and academic course,

Soul Food: African American Foodways, tells us that is not so!). Mainstream-ing/appropriation has often led to erasure and unwarranted compensation (monetarily and culturally—as these folks become tastemakers) for those other than the innovators of that cultural artifact or style. I am not opposed to cultural *metissage*—mixing, as the French say—but unfortunately, American culture, as hybrid as it is, via media and other powerful mediums for culture brokering, still stubbornly self-presents as "white." Intellectually, the field is thriving in journals and books. I would like to see even more histori-cal grounding in the approaches to Black popular culture. The long arc of history allows us to see its evolution.

> *How do you see Stuart Hall's theorization of the" Black" in Black popular culture influencing your intellectual engagement with Black cultural productions?*

I came to Hall through my training in French studies and Black Atlantic cul-tures and histories. For me, though, the "black" in Black popular culture was twinned specifically to gender and even class, so bell hooks, Audre Lorde, and Patricia Hill Collins were just as critical when I began thinking through how Black women were situated at a specific historical moment (early twenty-first-century hip-hop culture), what had changed historically in their situatedness, and how ideas of blackness and gender had changed po-litically in hip-hop culture. The gendered dynamics, performances of work-ing and middle-class femininity and masculinity, attempts to rethink/push the boundaries of conventional ideas about femininity, are critical parts of the cultural whole. For me, it was impossible to examine blackness without exploring gender and class. Hall's work treads the water of intersectionality. In effect, the work of Hall's contemporaries helps deepen his analysis. It for-tifies a critical foundation that had some blind spots—as all of our work does.

> *Do you feel the digital age affects the production, reception, and dis-semination of Black pop culture in ways that compel us to both continue revisiting Hall's piece but to also build upon it? If yes, how do you see contemporary theorists and critics building upon Hall's work given the changes the digital age has produced? If no, why do you feel the digital age does not compel scholars to revisit Hall and build upon his work?*

Absolutely. The digital era has rendered Black popular culture more easily accessible than ever; it has allowed synergies across vast distances. It also allows us intellectually to mine the global nature of blackness and race as historical terms, the meanings of blackness in different spaces, and even the ways that Black American popular culture, while marginalized but its wellspring of creativity deftly drawn upon at home, might also be viewed as hegemonic abroad. This last turn will be key, as the perception has not always been thus. How does a marginalized people from a global empire, which currently dominates the geopolitical landscape, parse intellectually/cognitively their perceived power/hegemony? For an example closer to home, that is, an academic one, I recall attending a conference on Black Europe—at the time an emerging scholarly field. There was palpable tension about the resources in the U.S. academy that some U.S.-located Black academics, who were all conflated into an African American identity, were able to access versus those available to Afro-European academics in Europe. Of course, some of this perception stemmed from a lack of understanding that the vast majority of Black faculty in the U.S. academy teach at HBCUs, many of which are underresourced; it was also understandably a linking to America as a capitalist, many-headed hydra with inexhaustible resources capable of exporting Black popular culture on a global scale, of producing scholarly monographs (a cultural product for the dissemination of much work on Black popular cultures), inter/national conferences (where the exchange of ideas about diasporic cultures occurs), and the most rarified of opportunities: research sabbaticals. Moreover, we were there in Europe, funded by our respective universities to attend the conference. We were inheritors of an imperial identity and culture. It was a stunning position to be in. And it pointed importantly to tensions in the African diaspora around "class" and "location" as well as a thick tethering to local/national identities versus racial identities—even in the face of social exclusion in Europe. In the United States, we often have a thin tethering to Americanness as a result of persistent racial exclusion. In the end, we had to grapple with that inherited imperial identity as well as the perceived and real strides made by African Americans in spite of American racism; I had to recognize my perceived position as an African American woman academic seemingly capable from my locale via a powerful cultural product/interlocutor—the book—to unintentionally direct even the discourse on black Europe—whether it be about popular culture or immigration.

Please describe how you would situate "the transnational" in contemporary Black popular culture, both as it is produced in the public sphere as well as in academic discourse.

Sonic transnationality comes to mind immediately, as well as the literary arts in the public sphere. And of course what is public has oftentimes crossed over into what is academic. Hip hop is everywhere, though associated primarily with the United States; we know its roots are more complicated in terms of the African diaspora. Beyoncé uses a clip from a TED talk on feminism by the Nigerian writer Chimamanda Ngozi Adichie on her trap song "Flawless." I am going to take the word "contemporary" to mean more than just the right now, but the past thirty to forty years. I remember reading Manthia Diawara's powerful memoir, *We Won't Budge: An African Exile in the World*, for the first time. It was for me stunning to read how influential Black American music and popular culture were in his life in Mali, how it shaped his ideas of America and his politics. And how even when in France, knowing the ins and outs of social exclusion with respect to Africans, he attempted to *pass* as African American. In effect, we see the back-and-forth, the fluidity of identity, as Black American musicians turned to Africa and the Caribbean for sounds. The Martinican Frantz Fanon inspires a rethinking of colonial models globally. I could go on and on and further back because transnational Black popular culture, diasporic Black expressive cultures and identities, in the public sphere and in academic modes of inquiry have been at work/play since the early modern era.

Your scholarship is consistently invested in examining transnational blackness through a feminist lens that reveals Black women are often in the vanguard of cultural movements. Can you discuss specific Black women cultural producers whose work is in the vanguard of transnational Black popular culture today?

One of my favorite transnational Black women cultural producers today is Rokhaya Diallo. She is a journalist, writer, filmmaker, and founder of Les Indivisibles. She wrote a wonderful and quite cheeky piece, "The Guerlain Affair: Odorless French Racism," which was translated and published in *Palimpsest: A Journal for Women, Gender, and the Black International* after Jean-Paul Guerlain said twice in an interview on French national television that he had worked "like a nigger" to build the luxury brand.

Do you foresee any critical shifts in Black pop culture as it relates to blackness and transnationalism in the next twenty years?

Certainly, the "black" in BRIC [Brazil, Russia, India, China] nations will have an interesting place in terms of academic comparative study and/or what we might stream most often on our various devices, if only because these are the spaces/places from where we sit in the United States in which a great deal of capital and negotiations is being expended; such outlay in places like India as a geopolitical counterweight to China cannot help but enter the public and academic discourse in interesting ways, especially as more work is done on the Indian Ocean world. But I really think fast-growing economies with vibrant youth cultures and populations in countries on the continent of Africa will be an interesting terrain for us to think about blackness and Black popular culture in fascinating ways. And here again, we will be reckoning with China intellectually and in the public sphere as it continues its soft-power incursions into places like Ghana, Nigeria, Senegal, and elsewhere, with flexible Chinese immigration policies and what some might call "integration," while others prefer the term "sexual colonialism"; the implications are that we will definitely be exploring Black popular culture and its manifestations among a growing and influential mixed-race youth population with Sino origins.

III. OWNING BLACKNESS

THE SUBALTERN IS SIGNIFYIN(G) /

BLACK TWITTER AS A SITE OF RESISTANCE

Sheneese Thompson

@DERAY: Twitter is home.
Facebook is grandma's house.
Snapchat is your best friend's house.
Tumblr is the lunch room.
Instagram is 24/7 prom.

· Tweeted by the user on November 8, 2015, at 11:31 a.m.

Freddie Gray, a twenty-five-year-old Black man from Baltimore, Maryland, was arrested "without incident" on the morning of April 12, 2015.[1] Cell phone footage of the encounter shows that Gray was not resisting arrest and that the lower half of his body was completely limp as he was being loaded into the police vehicle. Somehow, between the initial arrest and arriving at the Baltimore Police Department's Western District, where a medic was called,

Gray received fatal injuries to his spinal cord: three fractured vertebrae and a crushed voice box.[2] He went into a coma and died from his injuries on Sunday, April 19, 2015.[3] How Gray received those injuries is still a point of contention; however, it did become clear that, although Gray was handcuffed, he was not strapped in with a safety belt when placed into the police wagon.[4] Following Gray's death, the city of Baltimore erupted in civil unrest, which became known as the #BaltimoreUprising on Twitter and other social media sites.[5] It was in the midst of this series of events that Black Twitter responded to mainstream media accounts of Gray's story and the corresponding rebellion of Baltimore youth disgusted with state-inflicted violence against Black people.

DeRay Mckesson, an activist and Baltimore native, makes an astute observation about the kinds of behavior exhibited by users on various social networking websites and provides insight into the world of Black Twitter: it is home, a place where Black Twitter users can feel free to be themselves. Accordingly, users have been unabashedly taking on issues of race, racism, and police brutality as if the conversations were being held in their own living rooms. Departing from Henry Louis Gates's canonical text, *The Signifying Monkey: A Theory of African-American Literary Criticism*, this essay asserts that African Americans are using social media in general, and Twitter specifically, to contest mainstream media accounts of police violence against unarmed Black victims and advocate for change.[6] I assert that African Americans are using Black Twitter, a loosely formed but well-defined network of self-identifying Black users, to talk back, and further, that they are being heard. Black Twitter users are employing the age-old practice of signifyin(g) to revise biased news reports regarding police shootings of unarmed Black people and to address misrepresentations of corresponding Black Lives Matter protests that often criminalize victims of police violence; as they have done so, hashtags on Black Twitter have become catalysts for social change.

This essay homes in on the phenomenon of police violence because of the urgency of the issue, particularly in the way it sheds light on the long history of the normalization of violence against Black bodies. But I do not suggest that the content of Black Twitter is limited to this singular issue. I analyze tweets from two important hashtags as examples of what has been termed "Black Twitter activism": #BaltimoreUprising and #FreddieGray.[7] The hashtags themselves were used to detail and discuss the aftermath of Gray's death while he was in the custody of the Baltimore Police Department. The examples reproduced here are in response to two distinct news media gaffes regarding the case: first, the media's attempt to undermine the political nature of the Baltimore Uprising by employing the nonviolent ideology of Dr. Martin Luther King Jr.; second, CNN described Gray as the "son of an illiterate heroin addict" in an article about the jury selection for one of the six officers involved in the arrest that led to Gray's death.[8]

What Is Black Twitter?

The journalist Donovan X. Ramsey defines Black Twitter as an online platform "used to describe a large network of Black Twitter users and their loosely coordinated interactions, many of which accumulate into trending topics due to the network's size, interconnectedness, and unique activity."[9] The network that Ramsey references is indeed large, according to a 2015 Pew Research Center report on Twitter's demographics, twenty-eight percent of all Twitter users are Black, compared to only 20 percent who are white, which gives some credence to the existence of the online Black community.[10] In addition to the large number of Black users, Meredith Clark suggests that as Black people log on to Twitter, so do their "personal experiences with a shared historical legacy of marginalization, systemic and often subtle racism, and paradoxically, a denial of opportunity to interact with the dominant culture as individual actors uncharacterized by media stereotypes of Black people and Black culture."[11] When using the term "Black Twitter," however, it is important not to obscure the diversity of Black people that make up the online community. As Sarah Florini notes, Black Twitter "does not exist in any unified or monolithic sense. Just as there is no 'Black America' or single 'Black culture,' there is no 'Black Twitter.'"[12] The online community, then, like the offline one, is linked by shared experiences and perspectives of blackness in America and inclusive of the fact that those perspectives and experiences are diverse.

Florini also highlights an important feature of the online community: "When the body and corporeal signifiers of race can be obscured, the social and cultural markers of race take on great importance."[13] Therefore Black Twitter became not only a place for self-identifying Black people to convene but also a site of cultural performance. One example of this is the use of what Sanjay Sharma calls "blacktags," or black hashtags. More specifically, blacktags "are a particular type of hashtag associated with Black Twitter users (mainly African-Americans), because the tag itself and/or its associated content appears to connote 'Black' vernacular expression in the form of humor and social commentary."[14] In an interview with Donovan Ramsey for *The Atlantic*, Meredith Clark talks a bit about the need for cultural competency to participate in some hashtags (or blacktags) on Black Twitter: "Those hashtags in so many ways are indicators of a certain degree of cultural competency. To understand some of them, and I stress "some," you have to understand African-American vernacular English. To understand others, you need to have historical perspective on the issue. And so a lot of that rises out of a common experience of living as a black person, and specifically to living as a black person in the United States."[15]

Culture, then, is a more important factor in participation on Black Twitter than is racial phenotype since, as Florini made clear, phenotype can be obscured. This is particularly salient with the emergence of Russian bots and white supremacist users seeking to troll Black users on the site. Vann Newkirk, a staff writer for the *Atlantic* and a prominent Twitter personality, described identifying such accounts: "The thing that has tipped me off most is they often try to speak the way maybe someone who has never been engaged with Black culture thinks Black people talk. It's all very cartoonish."[16] This phenomenon evidences both the political and cultural utility of Black Twitter, since white supremacists have targeted it for disruption. Additionally, the ways in which these infiltrators are identified as imposters validates what Clark argues are a series of six steps that occur, in no particular order, and that create and sustain the phenomenon known as Black Twitter:

> It requires: 1) self-selection by users who 2) identify as Black and/or are connected to issues of concern among Black communities. It moves from the individual level of personal communities to collective action among thematic nodes via the 3) performance of communicative acts that are 4) affirmed online and 5) re-affirmed offline, leading to 6) vindication of the network's power through media coverage, attempted replication of the phenomenon within other demographic groups, and the creation of hashtags that serve as mediators of Black culture in the virtual and physical worlds.[17]

Because the cultural fluency of Black people follows them to Twitter through the process Clark outlines, trolls posing as Black Twitter users are often easily identified as devoid of the cultural competence participation requires, especially fluency in Black Vernacular English. Because of the complex cultural process that Clark outlines as the transference of blackness made virtual, it should be no surprise that the age-old practice of signifyin(g) is represented prominently on the social media site, and at times separates participants from provocateurs.

Why Signify? The Criminal Identity of Blacks in Mainstream News Media

Television news is particularly effective in dictating and/or perpetuating racial ideology because of its pervasiveness in American society. Unfortunately, the news often perpetuates racialized stereotypes and participates in the criminalization of blackness. William Barlow and Jannette L. Dates address the effectiveness of stereotypes in their book, *Split Image: African Americans in the Mass Media*, writing, "Stereotypes are especially effective in conveying ideological messages because they are so laden with ritual and myth, particularly in the case of African Americans, but invariably, the black representations are totally at odds with the reality of African Americans as individual people."[18] While these stereotypes are in opposition to Black people as individuals, such stereotypes are nevertheless of long standing. As such, the news media often employs negative stereotypes about Black people, such as with descriptions of hyperviolence, to fasten crime and other social pathologies to blackness. In so doing, the news media marginalizes crime (describing it as an aberration in American society) alongside blackness (another aberration), generating a narrative that social degeneration and danger come from the margins.[19] Carol A. Stabile explores the social implications of the news media's criminalization of Black people, writing, "By the late 1990s, the mainstream, national media rarely mentioned race without invoking the twinned themes of crime and black pathology."[20] Following up on Stabile's claim, Travis L. Dixon created an experiment to determine viewers' judgments about race in crime-related news reports and found that when suspects and arresting officers went unidentified, participants who were heavy news viewers were more likely to identify the suspect as African American and the officer as white. Similarly, when the race of the officer was identified, the participants were more likely to have positive perceptions of the officer if he was white and negative perceptions if he was Black.[21]

Stabile's assessment of mainstream news outlets' misrepresentations of Black people as criminals, in conjunction with Dixon's analysis of its impact, shows that the criminalization of blackness is continually being operationalized on television news (among other places). Because of this, the need for counternarratives to be written, or tweeted, arises. The portrayal of Black people as the source of social ills on television news informs the kind of victim-blaming that Black Twitter users often find themselves combating. Television coverage of the Black Lives Matter protests in various cities often treated them as anti-American riots, giving room for "All Lives Matter" sentiment to develop and eclipse the actual problem of police brutality. Despite evidence that all lives do not matter as much as others, taking the case of Freddie Gray as just one of many examples, the criminalization of Black people in the news media contributes to a narrative that both devalues Black lives and characterizes Black death at the hands of police officers as the removal of the criminal element to keep the lives that do matter safe. Dixon suggests this overrepresentation of Black criminals "activates" negative stereotypes.[22] Black Twitter activism undermines the activation of these stereotypes head-on. Like the online activism in response to the coverage of Gray's death that I discuss later, hashtags geared toward social action often make legible longstanding and troubling issues regarding how Black people are not afforded humanity or victimhood in life or after death.[23]

Signifyin(g) on Black Twitter

Many scholars have contributed to the body of work on Black rhetorical strategies and their usages for social critique.[24] Perhaps most relevant to this chapter, Gates concludes that "signifyin(g) . . . is a metaphor for textual revision," or repetition with difference.[25] This definition of signifyin(g) lends itself to use on Black Twitter, a web platform structured for repetition. Through the use of the retweet and quote functions, Twitter users signify on existing tweets, adding their own commentary and revising along the way. This kind of signifyin(g) happens in reference to the light-hearted, as well as in reference to serious issues that plague the Black community. To draw on one example of such social critique, Black Twitter broadly participated in the hashtag #IfTheyGunnedMeDown to bring awareness to the ways in which Black victims of police violence are depicted, usually in some way that criminalizes them. More often than not, a compromising image taken from social media or a mugshot would be used in lieu of a more appropriate and similarly available image, such as a graduation portrait. Because Black Twitter users participated in this hashtag, by posting two images of themselves and drawing out the difference that the picture chosen makes in the interpretation of one's life, or the circumstances of one's death, it trended on Twitter. The trend set the tone for other media sites to take up the issue as well, generating a large national discourse on victim blaming in police shootings and other tragedies.[26]

Signifyin(g) also plays a comedic role on Twitter. Sharma writes that black-tags "are distinctive because they curate and virally propagate racially charged messages expressing social critique through a particular acerbic style of humor which has been associated with elements of African-American culture."[27] Thus a hashtag like #ThanksgivingWithBlackFamilies that detailed the comedic events that frequently happen at Black Thanksgiving dinners trended all over Twitter. Similarly, #AskRachel, in response to news that Rachel Dolezal had been posing as a Black woman in Spokane, Washington (calling herself "transracial"), trended fairly quickly. The questions that emerged tested one's ability to participate in Black culture broadly and nicely frame Vann Newkirk's comments regarding fake Black Twitter accounts. #StayMadAbby began trending in response to Abigail Fisher's Supreme Court case to overturn Affirmative Action at the University of Texas.[28] It is worth noting that even though these hashtags employ humor as a rhetorical strategy, they are not without social critique. They do not, however, generate meaningful changes in outcomes that other, more targeted hashtags do. For that reason they should be delineated from hashtags that actually do the work of Black Twitter activism by changing narratives and pushing movements forward. Despite signifyin(g)'s long history as a means of communication among African Americans, somehow this method of signifyin(g) was widely misinterpreted. The two most notable articles to indict Black Twitter for simply being silly are Farhad Manjoo's "How Black People Use Twitter" and Dexter Thomas's "When 'Black Twitter' Sounds Like 'White Twitter.'" Both Manjoo and Thomas interpret Black Twitter as more comedic than political, instead of acknowledging what is probably more accurately described as a balance of both.

Dexter B. Gordon clarifies the import of humor in African American communication, writing, "Humor continues to be a relatively safe way to do violence to the oppressor in return for injustice." In what could be a direct response to the misreadings of Manjoo and Thomas, Gordon continues, "More pointedly, this humor challenges White oppression and promotes Black emancipation as a part of its effort to bring justice to the scene in which both groups have to coexist. African-American humor is neither innocent nor free from anger.... [It] is often sardonic and full of pathos and venom but always brimming with diversity, verve, and sophistication. Always making visible the invisible while masking its own anger and rage."[29]

In line with what Gordon describes, Black Twitter defended itself against Thomas's article, which is detailed in an article featured on *The Root* by Diana Ozemebhoya Eromosele. Challenging Manjoo and Thomas, Eromosele asserts that even though Black Twitter users disagree, joke, and jibe, they also launch social critiques, and further, one does not undermine the other.[30] I assert that the diverse population that composes the users on Black Twitter consider themselves dynamic human beings who can signify and laugh at the #PattiPies hashtag as well as signify and rally around the need to change the way Black victims of police violence are represented by mainstream media through the #IfTheyGunnedMeDown hashtag.[31] The online community is reflective of the humanity of its participants, and it is telling (and perhaps historically significant) that Black Twitter users are held accountable for the dynamism of their humanity in ways that are often dehumanizing. Black Twitter, like Black people, is multifaceted and will not be circumscribed by what critics think Black Twitter ought to be doing.

Signifyin(g) Meets Social Change: Black Twitter Activism

Although there were many attempts to delegitimate the salient message of the Baltimore Uprising, one worth mentioning is the frequent reference to Dr. Martin Luther King Jr. to decry the events in Baltimore.[32] CNN perhaps provides the landmark example of this when Wolf Blitzer tells the activist DeRay Mckesson, "I just want to hear you say there should be peaceful protests, not violent protests, in the tradition of Martin Luther King."[33] At the irrelevant though pointed question of what Dr. King would have thought about the riots, many Black Twitter users turned to Twitter to signify, mocking the question by calling attention to the state-sanctioned violence the champion of nonviolent direct action suffered, culminating in his assassination. This position can be seen in the tweets reproduced below, which call out mainstream media on its use of King as an attempt to decentralize the issues of poverty and police brutality.

@rob_theScorpion: A "RIOT" is the language of the "UNHEARD." #BALTIMOREUPRISING #MLK #REVOLUTION[34]

@harikondabolu: White people using MLK against Black people who respond to oppression with violence has been passed down for generations. #BaltimoreUprising[35]

@IamKINGKOKE: @deray @harikondabolu #MLK ASSASSINATED by Govt, mind you … proving our ENTIRE point in the first place! #BaltimoreUprising[36]

@BKTechNerd: Please stop trying to pacify the people with pictures and quotes from #MLK you know who I'm talking to. #BaltimoreUprising #NYCtoBaltimore[37]

Here, the users employ a more direct method to revise the narrative created by the mainstream media and take to task liberal notions of how social change should look. Perhaps inspired by the social media uproar, the journalist and senior editor for the *Atlantic*, Ta-Nehisi Coates, also took to the internet to address the glaring problems with King's sudden popularity beyond the months of January and February. Coates describes the terms upon which nonviolence was suggested: "When nonviolence is preached by representatives of the state, while the state doles out heaps of violence to its citizens, it reveals itself to be a con," reflecting the sentiments of many Black Twitter users and social media activists.[38] In conjunction with the work of Coates and other journalists, Black Twitter helped decentralize the mainstream media's indictment of the Baltimore Uprising as unduly violent and recenter the real issue: unbridled police brutality against unarmed victims.

In an article supposedly covering the trial of an officer involved in the Freddie Gray case, the CNN writer Ann O'Neill characterized Gray as "the son of an illiterate heroin addict."[39] Black Twitter users went into an uproar, often directly tweeting the author of the article and CNN when expressing their distaste.

@soso_southern: @AnnoCNN What a desperate attempt to marginalize, demonize, and berate this young brother and his mom. #sad #FreddieGray #justPlainEvil[40]

@KayKarter: The illiterate son of a heroin addict really CNN even in death we are not respected #Baltimore #FreddieGray[41]

Black users took to Twitter to revise the narrative on social media, and their actions had lasting implications. Other users were sarcastic in their response to O'Neill's characterization of Gray, employing the use of rhetorical questions about why that information would be important since the officer was on trial, not Freddie Gray's character or his mother's parenting.

@ChynaPoetic: It's funny how @cnn at 12:08am edited this article to remove "son of an illiterate heroine addict" #FreddieGray #CNN http://www.cnn.com/2015/11/30/us/baltimore-police-trial-freddie-gray-jury-selection/index.html[42]

@MsMakeda718: @AnnoCNN @cnn How r u certain that #FreddieGray was angry? You masked the dig at his mother but still defame the victim. U have no respect.[43]

@Knight3k: #CNN a violent death was inevitable? Are you basically calling #FreddieGray a #thug, which is the new N-word?[44]

@MsChanel09: #assholes @CNN what does illiteracy or drug addiction have to do with #policebrutality #unreal #FreddieGray[45]

Signifyin(g) on Black Twitter, or Black Twitter activism, forced O'Neill and CNN to make formal revisions to the biased article they created regarding the upbringing of Freddie Gray. Here, the repetition of Twitter users applying pressure to CNN produced a difference. Additionally, Black Twitter's response became the subject of articles from various media outlets, generating a counternarrative beyond the bounds of Black Twitter and social media, further discrediting CNN's racist commentary.[46] Black Twitter activism, then, is not just in the response to certain mischaracterizations of Black people or their suffering, or the racist remarks of a reporter. It is in the changing of outcomes and perspectives.

Sharma describes the function of blacktags in relation to activism, noting that "the intensive, imitative repetition of Blacktags [in this case #FreddieGray and #BaltimoreUprising] has the potential to interrupt the whiteness of the Twitter network."[47] These hashtags and tweets construct a counternarrative that affords the victim, Freddie Gray, and the protestors for his cause the humanity they deserve on and off Twitter. Appropriating a space that was intended for social networking, Black Twitter users have turned the site into a sounding board, giving voice to the voiceless and challenging mainstream media accounts of issues concerning the lives and deaths of Black Americans in ways that, before now, were nearly impossible. Although Black Twitter activism in no way replaces the serious work that is required to launch and maintain a protracted struggle against state-sanctioned violence perpetrated against Black victims, it does have import in this age of new media that should not be understated. These hashtags allow people to talk, mobilize, signify, and, as we have seen, revise the mainstream narrative being written about police violence and the victims of this violence.

Conclusion

As of July 27, 2016, all charges were dropped against the six officers involved in Freddie Gray's arrest and subsequent death.[48] Even after the civil unrest that occurred in the wake of Gray's death, the West Baltimore community and the larger Black community still find themselves wanting for justice. Although scholars and experienced activists alike have frowned upon social media activism as a passing fad, often characterizing it as lazy, the tweets reproduced in this essay and the change they created prove that Twitter provides a viable space for African Americans as subalterns to engage in social critique, create change, and demand the justice they deserve. After all, the Black Lives Matter movement started from a hashtag and tweets and became a national movement against police brutality and other forms of state-sanctioned violence. A protracted struggle against police brutality, racism, sexism, or any kind of oppression requires hard work and bodies on the ground, although as presented here, profiles on the internet certainly help. Additionally, taking one's thoughts to Twitter does not preclude one from taking them to the streets as well. In fact, it is precisely because of Twitter's ability to put various types of Black people in conversation with each other that makes it a useful tool to defend Black people's humanity in this historical and cultural moment. In defending blackness, Black Twitter users will continue to use the platform to revise mainstream media accounts and present counternarratives that shed light on the varying perspectives, perceived truths, and individual and collective realities of Black people.

Notes

1 Berlinger, "Police Release Timeline."
2 Graham, "The Mysterious Death."
3 Berlinger, "Police Release Timeline."
4 Linderman and Anderson, "Freddie Gray Was Handcuffed."
5 Grigsby Bates, "Is It an 'Uprising.'"
6 Gates, *The Signifying Monkey.*
7 Kang, "'Our Demand Is Simple.'" Here, Kang identifies social media activism as the marriage between initiating and participating in protests, and using social media to mobilize protestors in various cities and sometimes countries.
8 O'Neill, "First Officer Goes on Trial." The initial article was posted on November 30, 2015, but was updated on December 1 to remove the phrase quoted above.
9 Ramsey, "The Truth about Black Twitter."

10 Pew Research Center, "Mobile Messaging."

11 Clark, "To Tweet Our Own Cause," 64.

12 Florini, "Tweets, Tweeps and Signifyin'," 225.

13 Florini, "Tweets, Tweeps and Signifyin'," 234.

14 Sanjay Sharma, "Black Twitter?"

15 Ramsey, "The Truth about Black Twitter."

16 Quoted in Rashid, "The Emergence of a White Troll."

17 Clark, "To Tweet Our Own Cause," 87. Though it is beyond the scope of this essay, Clark elaborates on the implications of these steps.

18 Barlow and Dates, *Split Image*, 5.

19 Reeves and Campbell, *Cracked Coverage*, 41.

20 Stabile, *White Victims, Black Villains*, 173.

21 Dixon, "Black Criminals and White Officers," 283.

22 Dixon, "Crime News and Racialized Beliefs," 107.

23 Wanzo, *The Suffering Will Not Be Televised*, 5.

24 Roger D. Abrahams, H. Rap Brown, Dexter B. Gordon, Thomas, Kochman, Claudia Mitchell-Kerman, and Geneva Smitherman, just to name a few, have addressed the concept of signifyin(g), but Gates's seminal text synthesizes the information these scholars provide on the subject.

25 Gates, *The Signifying Monkey*, 88.

26 Ramsey, "The Truth about Black Twitter."

27 Sharma, "Black Twitter?," 59.

28 Barksdale, "18 Times Black Twitter Broke the Internet."

29 Gordon, "Humor," 269, 274.

30 Eromosele, "Black Twitter Defends Self."

31 Barksdale, "18 Times Black Twitter Broke the Internet." To be clear, I am employing Gates's definition of signifyin(g) as repetition with difference. Here Black Twitter users are using hashtags to repeat information already shared on the hashtag and to add their difference.

32 Rothman, "What Martin Luther King, Jr. Really Thought."

33 Craven, "Wolf Blitzer Fails."

34 Tweeted by the user on May 2, 2015, at 5:36 a.m.

35 Tweeted by the user on April 28, 2015, at 5:00 p.m.

36 Tweeted by the user on May 1, 2015, at 6:42 a.m.

37 Tweeted by the user on April 30, 2015, at 10:26 a.m.

38 Coates, "Non-Violence as Compliance."

39 O'Neil, "First Officer Goes on Trial."

40 Tweeted by the user on December 1, 2015, at 5:17 a.m.

41 Tweeted by the user on December 1, 2015, at 10:44 a.m.

42 Tweeted by the user on December 1, 2015, at 6:26 a.m.

43 Tweeted by the user on December 1, 2015, at 11:47 p.m.

44 Tweeted by the user on December 1, 2015, at 11:04 a.m.

45 Tweeted by the user on November 30, 2015, at 11:47 p.m.

46 Richards, "CNN Under Fire."
47 Sharma, "Black Twitter?," 63.
48 Stolberg and Bidgood, "All Charges Dropped."

References

Barksdale, Aaron. "18 Times Black Twitter Broke the Internet in 2015." *Huffington Post*, December 10, 2015. http://www.huffingtonpost.com/entry/18-times-black-twitter-broke-the-internet-in-2015_56686a65e4b0f290e5217d78.

Barlow, William, and Jannette L. Dates. *Split Image: African Americans in the Mass Media*. Washington, DC: Howard University Press, 1993.

Berlinger, Joshua. "Police Release Timeline of Events Leading Up to Freddie Gray's Death." *CNN*, April 23, 2015. http://www.cnn.com/2015/04/20/us/freddie-gray-baltimore-timeline/.

Clark, Meredith. "To Tweet Our Own Cause: A Mixed Methods Study of the Online Phenomenon 'Black Twitter.'" PhD diss., University of North Carolina Press, 2014.

Coates, Ta-Nehisi. "Non-Violence as Compliance: Officials Calling for Calm Can Offer No Rational Justification for Gray's Death, and So They Appeal for Order." *The Atlantic*, April 27, 2015. http://www.theatlantic.com/politics/archive/2015/04/nonviolence-as-compliance/391640/.

Craven, Julia. "Wolf Blitzer Fails to Goad Protester into Condemning Violence." *Huffington Post*, April 29, 2015. http://www.huffingtonpost.com/2015/04/29/wolf-blitzer-baltimore-protests_n_7168964.html.

Dixon, Travis L. "Black Criminals and White Officers: The Effects of Racially Misrepresenting Law Breakers and Law Defenders on Television News." *Media Psychology* 10 (2007): 283.

Dixon, Travis L. "Crime News and Racialized Beliefs." *Journal of Communication* 58, no. 1 (2008): 106-25.

Eromosele, Diana Ozemebhoya. "Black Twitter Defends Self from *LA Times* Columnist Who Says It's Not as Progressive as It Seems." *The Root*, July 16, 2015. http://www.theroot.com/blogs/the_grapevine/2015/07/l_a_times_columnist_dexter_thomas_argues_that_black_twitter_is_not_as_progressive.html.

Florini, Sarah. "Tweets, Tweeps and Signifyin': Communication and Cultural Performance on 'Black Twitter.'" *Television and New Media* 15, no. 3 (2013): 225.

Gates, Henry Louis. *The Signifying Monkey: A Theory of African American Literary Criticism*. New York: Oxford University Press, 1989.

Gordon, Dexter B. "Humor in African American Discourse: Speaking of Oppression." *Journal of Black Studies* 29, no. 2 (1998): 269.

Graham, David A. "The Mysterious Death of Freddie Gray." *The Atlantic*, April 22, 2015. http://www.theatlantic.com/politics/archive/2015/04/the-mysterious-death-of-freddie-gray/391119/.

Grigsby Bates, Karen. "Is It an 'Uprising' or a 'Riot'? Depends on Who's Watching." *Code Switch*, NPR, April 30, 2015. http://www.npr.org/sections/

codeswitch/2015/04/30/403303769/uprising-or-riot-depends-whos-watching.

Kang, Jay Caspian. "'Our Demand Is Simple: Stop Killing Us.' How a Group of Black Social Media Activists Built the Nation's First 21st-Century Civil Rights Movement." *New York Times*, May 4, 2015, http://www.nytimes.com/2015/05/10/magazine/our-demand-is-simple-stop-killing-us.html?_r=0.

Linderman, Juliet, and Curt Anderson. "Freddie Gray Was Handcuffed and without Seat Belt during Arrest Transit: Lawyer." *Huffington Post*, April 23, 2015.

Manjoo, Farhad. "How Black People Use Twitter." *Slate*, August 10, 2010. http://www.slate.com/articles/technology/technology/2010/08/how_black_people_use_twitter.html.

O'Neill, Ann. "First Officer Goes on Trial in Freddie Gray Death." CNN, December 1, 2015. http://www.cnn.com/2015/11/30/us/baltimore-police-trial-freddie-gray-jury-selection/.

Pew Research Center. "Mobile Messaging and Social Media 2015: Twitter Demographics." August 17, 2015. http://www.pewinternet.org/2015/08/19/mobile-messaging-and-social-media-2015/2015-08-19_social-media-update_11/.

Ramsey, Donovan X. "The Truth about Black Twitter." *The Atlantic*, April 10, 2015. http://www.theatlantic.com/technology/archive/2015/04/the-truth-about-black-twitter/390120/.

Rashid, Neha. "The Emergence of a White Troll behind a Black Face." *Code Switch*, NPR, March 21, 2017. https://www.npr.org/sections/codeswitch/2017/03/21/520522240/the-emergence-of-the-white-troll-behind-a-black-face.

Reeves, Jimmie Lynn, and Richard Campbell. *Cracked Coverage: Television News, the Anti-Cocaine Crusade, and the Reagan Legacy*. Durham, NC: Duke University Press, 1994.

Richards, Kimberley. "CNN Under Fire for Calling Freddie Gray 'Son of an Illiterate Heroine Addict.'" *Huffington Post*, December 1, 2015. http://www.huffington-post.com/entry/cnn-freddie-gray-son-of-an-illiterate-heroin-addict_565dafafe4b072e9d1c32a77.

Rothman, Lily. "What Martin Luther King, Jr. Really Thought about Riots." *Time*, April 28, 2015. http://time.com/3838515/baltimore-riots-language-unheard-quote/.

Sharma, Sanjay. "Black Twitter?: Racial Hashtags, Networks and Contagion." *New Formations* 78 (2013): 51.

Stabile, Carol A. *White Victims, Black Villains: Gender, Race, and Crime News in U.S. Culture*. New York: Routledge, 2006.

Stolberg, Sheryl Gay, and Jess Bidgood. "All Charges Dropped against Baltimore Officers in Freddie Gray Case." *New York Times*, July 27, 2016. http://www.nytimes.com/2016/07/28/us/charges-dropped-against-3-remaining-officers-in-freddie-gray-case.html.

Thomas, Dexter. "When 'Black Twitter' Sounds Like 'White Twitter.'" *LA Times*, July 15, 2015. http://www.latimes.com/business/technology/la-black-twitter-20150715-story.html.

Wanzo, Rebecca. *The Suffering Will Not Be Televised: African American Women and Sentimental Political Storytelling*. New York: State University of New York Press, 2009.

AUTHENTIC BLACK COOL? / BRANDING
AND TRADEMARKS IN CONTEMPORARY
AFRICAN AMERICAN CULTURE

Richard Schur

While some genres of music have had a more ambivalent relationship with branding, hip hop, through its moguls, has seemed to embrace it to an unusually large degree. These moguls see hip-hop branding
as a cultural success that is transforming American culture. Recent texts by
Dan Charnas (2010) and Steve Stoute (2012) revel in how African American
culture has mastered the marketplace and created a bevy of hip-hop millionaires, even if it is unclear how much money has trickled down to ordinary
African Americans.[1] The challenges provided by peer-to-peer file sharing
during the 1990s and the recent growth of streaming has forced hip-hop acts
to be creative and turn to auxiliary avenues for generating revenues. Hip-
hop stars have allowed companies to use their personas and street credibility
in order to gain income and visibility, while the companies have embraced
new identities and reached a broader range of consumers.

Hip hop's success in marketing and branding, however, may say less about hip-hop artistry or the creativity of contemporary African American culture than it does about the American cultural imagination. Seeing the co-optation resulting from branding, some critics have used such concepts as "underground," indie hip hop, or alternative hip hop to preserve what they perceive as hip hop's founding spirit. This makes sense, for in hip hop's early days, Chuck D boasted that "rap is Black America's CNN," the way for African Americans to gain real information about what is happening in their communities. Today, however, hip hop is just as likely to serve as an advertisement for luxury and consumer goods as it is a space to speak truth to power. One might argue that contemporary message rappers, the progeny of Public Enemy, have struggled to find both financial backing and an audience since the mid-1990s, while artists and acts more focused on materialism have increasingly dominated the scene.

This essay explores how trademark and branding are extending the life and meaning of race, racialization, and racial stereotypes in a putatively post-Black world. In particular, I examine how hip hop and its corporate sponsors seek to draw on concepts such as authenticity and Black cool, embodied in hip hop, to sell products.[2] The first part of the essay explores how trademark law, from its earliest days to today, empowers trademark owners to traffic in racial stereotypes, such as Aunt Jemima, Uncle Ben, the Morton Salt Girl, and Mia, the Land O Lakes Butter trademarked image. The second part examines the arguments in support of hip hop's marriage to branding, based on the idea that African American culture is authentic and cool. The third considers criticisms and potential costs of this marriage, exploring how branding may reify a problematic image of Black life. The essay concludes by questioning whether the branding success of hip hop, fostered by trademark law, achieves the cultural and political changes claimed by its proponents.

Trademarks and Racial Inequality

Unlike many areas of law, trademark has never undergone a revision or reconstruction based on the civil rights movement. In an earlier essay, I argued that the main concepts of trademark law—product origin, authenticity, dilution, and fair use—were products of a Jim Crow legal order that sought to classify people and objects through racial and cultural categories.[3] Here I want to consider how trademark law and branding work together to promote and regulate the performance, circulation, and meaning of Black identity. In other words, hip hop seems to embrace trademarked identities, such as Rocawear, Sean John, Akademiks, Yeezy, and FUBU, in which the trademark is intimately connected to a potentially narrow vision of blackness. These branding efforts have raised the visibility of hip-hop culture, enabled a handful of hip-hop moguls and millionaires to enter into the ruling capitalist class, and succeeded in diversifying the media and musical landscape. The use of racialized trademarks appears to strengthen the power of stereotyped images of Black life and increases their frequency as these trademarks circulate through American culture.

According to the U.S. Code, a trademark is "any word, name, symbol or device . . . [used] to identify and distinguish the services of one person, including a unique service from the services of others and to indicate the source of those services."[4] A trademark is officially granted by the U.S. Patent and Trademark Office (USPTO) and identifies the origin of an object or symbol. In effect, a trademark certifies the authenticity of whatever it marks. For example, a trademark assures consumers that a can printed with the name Pepsi is, in fact, a genuine Pepsi product and not a knock-off version. In the immortal words of Coca-Cola, a Coke is the "real thing," not a fake.

Trademark law gives the owner monopolistic control over the mark and enables the owner to protect its use and meaning. Transforming an image, word, or logo into private property through trademark law can insulate a mark from criticism by those who are harmed or offended by it. Consider Aunt Jemima. The trademark was created in the late 1880s after a small businessman attended a minstrel show. The mammy image complemented the concept of premixed batter he was developing because it created the illusion that purchasing the product put the consumer in the place of leisure occupied by white southerners who had Black maids. Later Quaker Oats purchased the fledgling company, and the syrup and its famous logo and have become a staple of American culture ever since.[5] For much of the mark's history, African Americans, including members of the Black Arts Movement, have protested and challenged Aunt Jemima. In response, the trademark owner has updated Aunt Jemima's look several times but continues to use the Black female body to sell pancakes.

The legal scholar Rosemary Coombe suggests this situation typifies how trademark law can be used to limit access to cultural symbols and signs and, in turn, harm democratic dialogue and the ongoing project of repairing the legacy of three centuries of legal racism.[6] Sonia Katyal makes a similar observation: "Although culture is shifting, dynamic, and fluid, property rights are often considered just the opposite: fixed, static, and concrete."[7] Historically, once a trademark owner produced a racial or racialized trademark, they owned that racialized image in perpetuity unless someone objected and persuaded the USPTO to cancel a mark that was scandalous or disparaging. The prohibition against scandalous and disparaging trademarks, enacted in the 1940s, allowed the USPTO to reject eight trademark applications, including one submitted by Damon Wayans, for racially insensitive marks, such as variants on the word "nigger"—even though most of the applicants were African Americans who sought the mark.[8] There have also been efforts to cancel the trademark of the Washington Redskins because it involves a stereotypical image of Native Americans.

In the 2017 *Matal v. Tam* decision, the U.S. Supreme Court held that the prohibition against disparaging marks violated the First Amendment because it would require the USPTO and courts to engage in viewpoint discrimination and limit free speech.[9] The effect of the case is that the Slants, an Asian American rock band, can get a trademark for their name, a term that the USPTO had deemed potentially disparaging and offensive. The Slants had chosen this name to challenge stereotypes of Asian Americans and reconstruct Asian American identity. While the Court's decision affirms the principle that racial and ethnic groups can name themselves and resignify potentially racist language, it also clears the path to further trademark, commodify, and circulate potentially disparaging terms related to race and ethnicity, without limitation on who may profit from these terms and regulate their use.[10] Trademark law thus will continue to accelerate the flow of racial imagery—no matter whom it benefits or harms—in American culture.

Branding and Hip Hop

A brand, while sometimes the same thing as a trademark, serves a different purpose than identifying the manufacturer. The brand tells the story of the product and in some cases offers cultural cachet or cultural capital; it is the branding that distinguishes an ordinary commodity from its competitors. Endorsements are frequently used in branding campaigns to connect a product to the style of the celebrity endorser. For example, when Beyoncé endorses L'Oréal products, the company is seeking to trade on her reputation and image, which emphasize both empowerment and feminism, to transform how consumers see their product lines. Being linked to a company associated with beauty also enhances Beyoncé's brand. Another way to think of this distinction between trademarks and brands is that trademarks protect and regulate *who* can invoke a particular corporate name, whereas branding aims to define the content of that brand identity and what that brand can do for consumers. While trademark law is well established, few laws regulate branding and businesses possess considerable freedom when shaping their brand identities. Trademark law (before *Matal v. Tam*) thus had been one of the few ways to legally challenge racial stereotypes involved in branding.

An example may illuminate the distinction between a trademark and a brand. Cadillac has manufactured cars since the early 1900s. The Cadillac trademark identifies which company produces its cars and allows the company to protect itself from counterfeit or fake goods. The brand has been organized around the concept of luxury. After World War II, Cadillac cars were popular with African Americans because they symbolized the benefits of American citizenship and connoted material success.[11] By the late 1990s, the Cadillac brand was floundering. The company responded by looking to how the urban consumer had been altering and transforming their cars, and then it built a car, the Escalade, that borrowed liberally from those practices.[12] The result is that Cadillac created a car that appealed, ironically, to both young urban consumers and suburban mothers. Escalades began appearing in videos by Ludacris and Big Tyme and became popular with professional basketball players, who tricked them out. The car's popularity with white suburbanites was linked to its ability to master the codes and styles of urban America. The car's appearance drew on ideas of luxury and conspicuous consumption, from fancy rims to high-end audio-visual systems in the backseat, popularized by hip hop, even as the Escalade was designed to chauffeur suburban children to soccer practice and school. Steve Stoute, who recounts these brand changes, argues that the Cadillac example shows how a company can change its brand identity by meeting consumers in a genuine dialogue without altering its trademarked symbol.[13]

For Stoute, Cadillac's brand transformation symbolizes the power of what he terms "the tanning of American culture." The success of the automaker's brand reimaging brought together demographics that marketers had viewed as distinct. To Stoute and others, the recent commodification of urban or Black cool constitutes a fulfillment of the civil rights movement because it is destroying the remaining vestiges of a Jim Crow mind-set that shaped American business practices. It might be a bit overstated, but not too much so, to interpret Stoute as saying that branding and consumerism have replaced civil rights activism as the primary way to challenge white supremacy, even as it allows hip hop's biggest names to profit and frequently allows corporate America to retain ownership of the newly enriched trademarks. Stoute is well aware that many African American leaders, scholars, and critics disagree with his optimism about marketing and branding. In his book he tries to persuade critics that economic self-sufficiency and success is a key element of hip-hop culture.

Stoute is a key player in translating the urban mind-set to corporate America. He got his start managing Kid 'n Play, the early hip-hop act, then worked in musical development at a major record label, and eventually got into marketing. According to his (self-promoting) book exploring how "hip-hop rewrote the rules of the new economy," Stoute pioneered the concept of 360 deals centered around marketing and branding, in which artists and record companies would view music as more than just a revenue source.[14] Working with Jay-Z, Stoute realized that Jay-Z's earning potential was much greater if he used his name-checking rap lyrics and videos to sell products. Corporate America has learned that branding products, especially luxury and high-end goods, through hip-hop and African American culture can increase sales, making elite goods desirable for a younger multiracial audience who aspires to wealth.

The rise of Armand de Brignac champagne illustrates this new marketing or branding paradigm. Since the early 1990s, rappers, including Jay-Z, had been bragging about buying and drinking Cristal champagne. In 2006, one of Cristal's corporate managers lamented that so many rappers drank their product. Jay-Z responded by promising to stop rapping about Cristal, which he had been doing for free, and began promoting another brand, in which he had an ownership stake.[15] While some might see Jay-Z's actions as being too opportunistic or materialistic, Stoute defends him from accusations of selling out because "it's not a sellout when it's authentic to your taste and style." In other words, what differentiates hip-hop branding and the urban mind-set from previous iterations of celebrity endorsements is authenticity. Early hip hop, along with African American culture more generally, saw certain brands as aspirational and carrying the hope for social and cultural improvement.[16] Products that connoted self-improvement were valuable and valued indices of personal success and talent. Even though his switch to Armand was likely the result of his receiving a financial stake in the brand, Jay-Z's endorsement did not seem contrived, merely an extension of his true self, who had always consumed high-quality champagne. Thus it was deemed authentic.

Dan Charnas largely agrees with Stoute's assessment and argues that hip hop has helped transform America. "From hip-hop, but even more so its diverse fan base, a vision of America's new Manifest Destiny: multiracial, multicultural, and willing to revel in differences rather than suppress them." Charnas further notes that "most of today's young hip-hop fans came of age after the decline of overtly political hip-hop. . . . Instead of political artists, hip-hop's businessmen and journalists now lead the practical political charge."[17] He then offers the election of Barack Obama, especially his popularity with young people, as evidence of the positive effect that hip hop has had on transforming the values, beliefs, and actions of ordinary Americans. Charnas narrates how artists, their managers, and their producers found ways to commodify and profit from hip hop. In his account, hip hop's history is largely a romantic tale in which a bunch of visionary and hard-working people—mostly from the "wrong side" of the tracks—became multimillionaires and tastemakers for the country. This is also the narrative offered by television shows like *Empire* and *The Get Down*. More than simply selling music, hip-hop culture triumphed at the cash register as hip hop's stars learned how to brand themselves. Through songs, videos, and other public appearances, the artists modeled conspicuous consumption for their fans.

The logic of branding and trademarks has become so pervasive and ubiquitous in hip-hop and contemporary African American culture that it has come to define it. Branding started out offering a narrative or image for a given product or company, and trademarks were used to identify the source of a product. Hip-hop culture and contemporary African American culture, however, have flipped these concepts upside down so that every person ought to be a source for products and be their own brand. Neither hip-hop nor African American culture created the concepts of trademark or branding, but a handful of hip-hop moguls and their corporate partners are profiting immensely from them. The net result is that the ownership of the styles and cultural practices of African American culture are transferred from the "people" to a few individuals who may or may not be connected to hip-hop culture. Furthermore, it risks transforming a vibrant culture into a series of trademarked properties, giving monopoly control to one person or company. Stoute and Charnas, along with Jay-Z, Dr. Dre, and 50 Cent, would likely respond to this critique by arguing that hip hop's emphasis on trademark and branding offers potentially positive role models of African American entrepreneurs who have mastered capitalism and accumulated tremendous wealth. Moreover, hip hop's very financial success, they would argue, has changed how the game has worked.

Branding and the Demise of Black Cool?

The movement toward trademarks and branding may have broad cultural consequences. The questions this movement provokes are how much the branding of hip hop has altered racial representation and whether hip hop's embrace of branding and trademarks merely strengthens racial stereotypes and increases their power? These are not new questions or ones that are unique to hip hop. Throughout American history, whites have borrowed from Black culture, and vice versa. The underlying issue, however, is not about identifying the proper origins of cultural practices, which has been the historical function of trademark. Rather, my concern here is how American law and business practice have ignored the ownership rights of African Americans in Black cultural practices and consistently found ways to "propertize" and then transfer "ownership" of these practices and products to white people and companies. The battles about hip-hop branding and the "trademarkization" of Black life seem to be the newest chapter of this long-standing debate over who owns Black cool.

In a series of articles from 2014, Questlove of the Roots argues that hip hop has lost its "cool" and lacks the very authenticity that set it apart from earlier forms of African American popular culture. In the early days, the brands mentioned (e.g., Adidas) and the narratives told in hip-hop songs, Questlove argues, were accessible to most hip-hop fans and created a bond between the performers and the audience because these brands were relatively accessible to all.[18] The luxury brands in today's hip hop (e.g., Bugatti, Maybach) now signal a fundamental break between emcees and their fans.[19] Although it once constituted a form of social and cultural protest, Questlove argues, hip hop today offers little "resistance," seemingly reiterating the values and beliefs of dominant America."[20] Elsewhere he writes, "Hip-hop, after beginning as a site of resistance, has become, in some sense, the new disco. The signifiers are different, of course. Hip-hop has come to know itself largely via certain notions of capitalist aspiration, braggadocio, and macho posturing, which are different notes than those struck in disco. But the aesthetic ruthlessness, the streamlining of concept, is similar. What began as a music animated mainly by a spirit of innovation now has factory specifications."[21]

While Questlove may be painting with too broad a brush here, the irony in this quotation is that, with respect to Stoute, hip-hop stars have become more bankable, in terms of sales and marketing, as they have embraced the very values early hip hop rejected. Hip hop's success seems to undermine the claims of authenticity at the center of hip-hop culture.

To understand Questlove's commentary, it is crucial to trace briefly the history of Black cool and how its creators and proponents sought to intervene in popular culture's representations of Black life. In 1949 and 1950, Miles Davis recorded an LP titled *Birth of the Cool*, which was released in late 1957. Davis's version of cool avoided the emotional extremes of those earlier forms of jazz. It also signaled a new persona for the jazz musician, who resisted the spotlight and the demands of the audience. The music was a clear response and rebuke to both big band and bop and dominant culture's view of African Americans. Joel Dinerstein traces the birth of cool to the influential saxophonist Lester "Pres" Young. [22] Young was more influential within jazz circles than he was famous. His influence, however, exceeded his idiosyncratic playing to encompass his then shocking decision to wear sunglasses indoors and speak in a hip code that was nearly incomprehensible to those unfamiliar with it. Young developed his persona as a form of resistance to and protection from white supremacy. As a marketing strategy, however, it proved a disaster and did not garner him commercial success.

The concept of cool offered by jazz artists such as Young and Davis quickly expanded beyond the Black community. In *The Conquest of Cool*, Thomas Frank argues that advertisers in the late 1950s and 1960s, drawing on the nonconformity of jazz and the Beats, created the idea of hip consumerism. The cool described by advertisers "deplored conformity, distrusted routine, and encouraged resistance to established power."[23] Authenticity, which was reframed as cool, served as an antidote to the mass appeal deployed by earlier advertisements that encouraged consumers to conform to community values and expectations. Advertising and branding brought American popular culture closer to trends within African American culture, but they did so in a way that erased the link to Black artists and Black cool. For example, both the Beat poets and the British Invasion (i.e., the Beatles, the Rolling Stones, the Who, etc.) drew extensively on Black culture, but did so in a way that rendered African American artists and poets mostly invisible. Nor did African Americans profit from these new branding strategies or gain any form of cultural ownership, including trademark ownership, over the new paradigm of cool. This white version of cool ignored the implicit critique of racism while embracing a depoliticized and deracialized nonconformity.

In the 1980s and 1990s, marketers and advertisers rejected white appropriations of Black cool and sought more "authentic" versions to sell to an American public that was (and still is) both fascinated by and scared of Black culture. Hanes and Nike, among others, used Michael Jordan's athletic and aesthetic prowess to transform the images of their companies. For Pepsi, Michael Jackson was the face of a new generation of consumers. At the same time however, Tipper Gore and the Parents Music Resource Center tried to constrain record companies who were selling gangsta rap to white suburban teenagers. The irony here has not escaped critics of African American culture. Donnell Anderson points out that while many whites want to purchase or experience Black cool, they don't want to live in the same neighborhood as actual African Americans. In other words, just because white Americans gravitate toward products marked as cool by African American culture, that consumption has not necessarily translated into either improved cross-cultural communication or enhanced status or wealth for many African Americans.[24]

Beyond Donnell's humorous critique, there is a potentially more ominous side to the marketer's embrace of Black cool; it may be reifying, through the power of advertising and branding violent and nihilistic behaviors and practices as essential elements of a Black identity. In her book *We Real Cool*, bell hooks describes in vivid detail how the quest for Black manhood, rooted in Black cool, has caused many African American men to mimic white men's strategies for achieving respect: perpetrating violence against the powerless. For hooks, the answer to building the self-esteem of young Black males and breaking the cycle of self-destructive behaviors rooted in Black cool is to engage spirituality and foster self-love. hooks, however, does not see hip hop as a cultural site where much healing or self-love is happening. Instead, "black male hip-hop artists who receive the most acclaim are busy pimping violence; peddling the racist/sexist stereotypes of the black male as primitive predator."[25]

Black cool, as a political and artistic aesthetic, was developed and nourished after World War II to challenge white supremacy and empower African Americans to withstand daily assaults on their dignity. While hip-hop enthusiasts, such as Charnas and Stoute, celebrate that hip hop has become culturally dominant through its assertion of Black cool in branding, Questlove sees hip hop, pace hooks, as offering nothing more than recycled imagery. Questlove argues, "What once offered resistance to mainstream culture (it was part of a larger tapestry, spook-action style, but it pulled at the fabric) is now an integral part of the sullen dominant."[26] For Questlove, art and culture ought to "humanize" and "open the circuits of empathy."[27] Charnas and Stoute interpret hip hop's embrace and engagement with the world of branding, trademarks, and marketing as transforming the business world and revitalizing cultural democracy, mostly because they conflate increased Black wealth with a more open and democratic society. Questlove, however, argues that hip hop has become "flat" and "meaningless" as it gains wealth and power because it no longer offers much critical commentary on American life. If Black cool is no longer a source of strength and criticism for the African American community, then it is no longer "cool"; it is just another resource to be mined, owned, and ultimately depleted.

Who Owns Black Cool? The Limits of Trademark Law

Over the past two decades, intellectual property law scholars have explored whether trademarks and branding enhance democracy and strengthen cultural traditions. In her study, Coombe documents many corporations' attempts to stifle dissent or criticism that may involve their trademarked properties or their brands. Coombe writes that "politics is a cultural activity; its practice demands appropriate access to the materiality of means and mediums of expressive communication."[28] Trademark law, however, can be used to limit access to those signs and symbols. This means that the monopolistic structure of intellectual property law affects the nature and outcome of these debates. For example, many hip-hop stars, including Ice Cube and Snoop Dogg, endorsed and made commercials for St. Ides Malt Liquor in the early 1990s. The brand wanted Chuck D to endorse their product and even used a sample of his voice in an ad without his permission. Chuck D then recorded "One Million Bottlebags," which criticizes how malt liquor producers targeted young African Americans. The song, however, did not call out St. Ides specifically, perhaps because to denigrate or criticize a well-known brand would have invited being sued. Trademark law, in effect, encourages artists to shout out to brands when praising them but protects those very trademarks or brands from being tarnished or diluted.

David Dante Troutt, a legal scholar and critical race theorist, imagines an elaborate hypothetical (that seems remarkably similar to what Jay-Z, Dr. Dre, and Sean Combs have been doing) in which an African American advertising executive sought to become the "first federally registered human trademark." Troutt demonstrates that trademark law would most likely allow such a trademark because of how publicity rights already allow famous individuals to control how their likenesses are used. He points out that any such individual brand must distinguish the advertising executive's brand as being unique from African American culture more generally. Troutt playfully imagines that the fictitious trademark application would claim a color-blind mark, even if it is connected to what I have been calling "Black cool." He ultimately concludes that his hypothetical individual could trademark his name and identity. The problem, however, would be that he could not change his core identity or he would lose his trademarked status.[29] In other words, to trademark or brand himself in this way would lock him into a relatively static identity that would over time lose its "cool" and ultimately harm his name and reputation rather than enhance it.

In many ways, Troutt underscores what is at stake in the debates about hip hop's use of branding, marketing, and trademarks and points us back to the problems with Black cool identified by hooks. Using trademark and branding to market and profit from Black cool locks it into place and tends to reify problematic images and stereotypes. As hooks points out, hip hop and other purveyors of Black cool as brands tend to emphasize consumerism, misogyny, and personal appearance over other values. More important, creating a trademark creates a de facto property interest for the trademark owner in a particular image. Rather than decrease the salience of race, such branding practices reinscribe racial and class differences on ordinary products from clothes, perfumes, and liquor to cars and fast food. While some of these brands and trademarked goods, such as Rocawear and Beats, may be owned by African Americans, much of Stoute's work helps corporate entities, such as Cadillac and McDonald's, that have relatively little connection to the Black community. Moreover, the version of Black cool being marketed and branded seems more connected to the self-destructive version described by hooks than the liberating and nurturing one she remembers from her youth. While all cultures possess distinctive patterns of consumption, cultures themselves ought not be reduced to forms of consumption.

In his analysis of the relationship between race and trademark law, K. J. Greene concludes that "although we have come far as a society in reducing racial prejudice, analysts note that our culture is still awash in negative racial stereotypes in popular media." He further notes that trademark law has been complicit in this traffic of stereotyped imagery.[30] Despite the claims of hip-hop supporters, there has not been a doctrinal shift in trademark or branding law because of their efforts. The recent U.S. Supreme Court decision in *Matal v. Tam* held that any limit on registering trademarks because of their disparaging nature would violate the First Amendment. This decision now allows racial and ethnic-based trademarks, even if they are potentially discriminatory or invoke stereotypes.[31] *Matal v. Tam*, along with hip hop's emergence and embrace of branding, marketing, and trademarks, will likely give hip hop more freedom to deploy potentially degrading or disparaging terms, such as earlier efforts to trademark variants on the word "nigger," and the USPTO and critics will have little power to challenge those trademarks.

There are some signs, however, that intellectual property activists are finding ways to challenge the power and reach of trademark law. Anjali Vats writes of the football player Marshawn Lynch's Beast Mode trademarked apparel, "Lynch uses trademark law to claim property rights in his body and . . . rewrites the narrative of the black beast and subverts the smooth operation of the NFL's money-making apparatuses."[32] Other scholars at the inaugural Race +IP Conference in April 2017 are developing strategies to deploy trademark to challenge racial, gender, and social class divides, including considering whether hashtags such as #BlackLivesMatter should be owned.[33] The challenge for the future is whether hip-hop moguls will embrace or reject these forms of trademark activism. It is also unclear who will benefit financially from these new approaches.

The commodification of Black cool has enhanced the visibility of hip-hop and African American culture and made a handful of African Americans exceptionally wealthy. This is not an insignificant thing and ought to be celebrated. However, what cannot be missed in the rush to celebrate the hip-hop mogul is that the very Black cool they are now selling may no longer help the community deal with the nihilistic forces that Black cool had historically kept at bay. Although Black cool seems to possess a rebellious and resistant core that promises social and cultural transformation, the very acts of branding and trademarking frequently produce caricatures of Black cool rather than the real thing. Trademark law promises control and ownership over words and symbols, but cultural meaning can easily shift from critical reappropriation to stereotype and back again. As long as we remember the cultural and social forces that animate the quest for authentic Black cool, we will not be fooled by trademarked imitations.

Notes

1 Charnas, *The Big Payback*; Stoute, *The Tanning of America*. In "Copyright and Distributive Justice," Hughes and Menges argue that IP has enabled the richest African Americans to gain their wealth. Their analysis, however, does not distinguish between IP and branding.

2 For discussions of authenticity in African American culture, see Favor, *Authentic Blackness*; Johnson, *Appropriating Blackness*.

3 Schur, "Legal Fictions."

4 "Trademark" 15 U.S.C. Sec. 1127.

5 Kern-Foxworth, *Aunt Jemima, Uncle Ben, and Rastus*, 65–66.

6 Coombe, *The Cultural Life*, 274.

7 Katyal, "Trademark Intersectionality," 1605.

8 Trademark Application Number 76639548, May 25, 2005.

9 *Matal v. Tam* 137 S. Ct. 1744 (2017).

10 I would argue that the Court arrived at the right result in this case but relied on flawed reasoning. The decision to find the entire statutory scheme unconstitutional overshot the narrower claim—that the Slants trademark was simply not a disparaging term. The Court then could have offered guidance for the USTPO about how to analyze these kinds of cultural reappropriations. The decision opened a potential Pandora's box that goes way beyond the Slants' initial claim.

11 Seiler, *Republic of Drivers*, 113. See also Mukherjee, "Bio-Brand in the Blacking Factory."

12 Stoute asserts that "urban" refers to a consumer mindset, rooted in dense, multicultural cities, rather than a specific racial or socioeconomic group; see *The Tanning of America*, ix.

13 Stoute, *The Tanning of America*, 213–19.

14 Stoute, *The Tanning of America*, 169.

15 O'Malley Greenburg, *Empire State of Mind*, 115, 112–18.

16 Stoute, *The Tanning of America*, 43, 35.

17 Charnas, *The Big Payback*, 636, 537.

18 In the early and mid-1990s, rappers such as Ice Cube and Biggie Smalls made advertisements for St. Ides Malt Liquor. At the time, they were criticized for not being aspirational enough for their fans; see Questlove, "Mo' Money."

19 Holmes Smith, "'I Don't Like to Dream.'" 681.

20 Questlove, "When the People Cheer."

21 Questlove, "Disco."

22 Dinerstein, "Lester Young," 266–67.

23 Frank, *The Conquest of Cool*, 9.

24 Anderson, "Are Black People Cooler."

25 hooks. *We Real Cool*, 4, 14, 142, 56.

26 Questlove, "When the People Cheer."

27 Questlove, "Does Black Culture."

28 Coombe, *The Cultural Life*, 274.

29 Troutt, "A Portrait," 1151, 1152–55, 1202–3.

30 Greene, "Trademark Law," 438, 441.

31 *Matal v. Tam*, 1765.

32 Vats, "Marking Disidentification," 1247.

33 See Vats and Keller, "Critical Race IP."

References

Anderson, Donnell. "Are Black People Cooler Than White People? The Racial Roots of Cool." *Utne Reader*, November–December 1997. http://www.utne.com/politics/are-black-people-cooler-than-white-people.aspx.

Charnas, Dan. *The Big Payback: The History of the Business of Hip-Hop*. New York: Penguin, 2010.

Coombe, Rosemary. *The Cultural Life of Intellectual Properties: Authorship, Appropriation, and the Law*. Durham, NC: Duke University Press, 1998.

Dinerstein, Joel. "Lester Young and the Birth of Cool." In *Signifyin(g), Sanctifyin,' and Slam Dunking: A Reader in African American Expressive Culture*, edited by Gena Dagel Caponi. Amherst: University of Massachusetts Press, 1999.

Favor, Martin. *Authentic Blackness: The Folk in the New Negro*. Durham, NC: Duke University Press, 1999.

Frank, Thomas. *The Conquest of Cool: Business Culture, Counterculture, and Rise of Hip Consumerism*. Chicago: University of Chicago Press, 1997.

Greene. K. J. "Trademark Law and Racial Subordination: From Marketing of Stereotypes to Norms of Authorship." *Syracuse Law Review* 58 (2007–8): 431–45.

Holmes Smith, Christopher. "'I Don't Like to Dream about Getting Paid': Representations of Mobility and the Emergence of the Hip-Hop Mogul." In *That's the Joint! The Hip-Hop Studies Reader*, edited by Murray Forman and Mark Anthony Neal. 2nd ed. New York: Routledge, 2012.

hooks, bell. *We Real Cool: Black Men and Masculinity*. New York: Routledge, 2004.

Hughes, Justin, and Robert Menges. "Copyright and Distributive Justice." *Notre Dame Law Review* 92, no. 2 (2016): 552–55.

Johnson, E. Patrick. *Appropriating Blackness: Performance and the Politics of Authenticity*. Durham, NC: Duke University Press, 2003.

Katyal, Sonia. "Trademark Intersectionality." *UCLA Law Review* 57 (2010): 1601–99.

Kern-Foxworth, Marilyn. *Aunt Jemima, Uncle Ben, and Rastus: Blacks in Advertising, Yesterday, Today, and Tomorrow*. Westport, CT: Praeger, 1994.

Mukherjee, Roopali. "Bio-Brand in the Blacking Factory." Plenary lecture. Race + Intellectual Property conference. Boston College, April 2017.

O'Malley Greenburg, Zack. *Empire State of Mind: How Jay-Z Went from Street Corner to Office Corner*. New York: Penguin, 2011.

Questlove. "Disco and the Return of the Repressed—How Hip-Hop Failed Black America Part IV." *Vulture*, May 13, 2014. http://www.vulture.com/2014/05/questlove-how-hip-hop-has-become-the-new-disco.html.

Questlove. "Does Black Culture Need to Care About What Happens to Hip-Hop?" *Vulture*, May 27, 2014. https://www.vulture.com/2014/05/questlove-part-6-does-black-culture-need-to-care-about-hip-hop.html.

Questlove. "Mo' Money, Mo' Problems: How Hip-Hop Failed Black America, Part II." *Vulture*, April 29, 2014. http://www.vulture.com/2014/04/questlove-on-money-jay-z-how-hip-hop-failed-black-america-part-2.html.

Questlove. "When the People Cheer: How Hip-Hop Failed Black America." *Vulture*, April 22, 2014. http://www.vulture.com/2014/04/questlove-on-how-hip-hop-failed-black-america.html.

Schur, Richard. "Legal Fictions: Trademark Discourse and Race." In *African American Culture and Legal Discourse*, edited by Lovalerie King and Richard Schur, 191–208. New York: Palgrave Macmillan, 2009.

Seiler, Cotten. *Republic of Drivers: A Cultural History of Automobility in America*. Chicago: University of Chicago Press, 2008.

Stoute, Steve. *The Tanning of America: How Hip-Hop Created a Culture That Rewrote the Rules of the New Economy*. New York: Gotham, 2012.

Troutt, David Dante. "A Portrait of the Trademark as a Black Man: Intellectual Property, Commodification, and Redescription." *University of California Law Review* 38 (April 2005): 1141–1205.

Vats, Anjali. "Marking Disidentification: Race, Corporeality, and Resistance in Trademark Law." *Southern Communication Journal* 81, no. 4 (2016): 237–51.

Vats, Anjali, and Deidre Keller. "Critical Race IP." *Cardozo Arts and Entertainment Law Journal* 36, no. 3 (2018): 736–76.

CH.12 **BLACK CULTURE WITHOUT BLACK PEOPLE** / HIP-HOP DANCE BEYOND APPROPRIATION DISCOURSE

Imani Kai Johnson

Cultural appropriation is currently a prominent topic of discussion, and at any given moment there are readily available examples of it in mainstream pop culture. From such infamous examples as Rachel Dolezal and her performed blackness to predictable practices like dressing up in ethnic costuming at Halloween or at frat parties, accusations of appropriation are actually being heard and discussions are gaining traction.[1] When I first started drafting this essay, Iggy Azalea's appropriation of hip hop—from her "blackcent" to her ignorance of its history—led to demands for greater accountability to the culture and the broader community.[2] While these discussions have not been exhausted, joining these debates seems exhausting because they are so oversimplified that people end up repeating themselves to those with no stake in listening. Therein lies the struggle. In my own work on breaking (also known as b-boying or breakdancing), the appropriation discussion is complicated by the realities of the culture itself: though born of African diasporic practices, it is a worldwide phenomenon dominated by nondiasporic practitioners whose whole lives have been shaped *by* hip-hop culture. Appropriation is not enough.

To appropriate speaks to both the fact of something being taken and to its being taken up in a certain kind of way: with the power to do so uncritically and unethically. Simply put, appropriation is colonialism at the scale of the dancing body or the sacred ritual object, its life and dynamism reduced to a thing for consumption or a costume for play. Though not exactly "theft"—and I am wary of thinking of culture through the lens of capitalist ownership—the presumption that one has the *right* to stake a claim to something and use it, buy and sell it, misrepresent it, and rewrite its history is colonial logic at work. With that said, appropriation only addresses one type of cross-cultural performance, one that perpetuates systems of power that marginalizes and excludes.

We are in a time when many millennials already know that appropriation is "problematic" or that they might get "dragged" on social media for it. Videos and articles from MTV and *Teen Vogue* distinguishing between appropriation and appreciation, while annual articles decrying black-, brown-, red-, and yellowface costumes attest to the changing terrain.[3] The clearest message in these forums is that it is wrong, and millennials appear to hear the message. What follows that acceptance though?

This question comes out of informal discussions during a lecture wherein my students already know what not to do, yet still question what it means when appropriation is not enough. I am interested in nurturing a discourse that attends to cross-cultural performances that are related to but different from appropriation, and possibly finding language that moves with, alongside, and yet away from appropriation (yes! like a dance). There is a difference between staking a claim to a culture (i.e., appropriation) and the culture's staking a claim to you, possessing you, moving you in unfamiliar and possibly uncomfortable ways that become essential to a person's existence. Hip-hop dance lends itself to expanding that discourse precisely because the spectrum of cross-racial performances is embodied evidence of something else. Thus this essay is not about appropriation, but about thinking of appropriation as part of a spectrum rather than a binary.

Within and across dance forms, movement communicates and transmits knowledge that allows people of different nationalities, ethnicities, and races to speak to one another less encumbered by the limits of verbal language. This matters in hip hop because, as I have argued in other work, breaking is fundamentally informed by Africanist aesthetics even as the faces of breaking are largely of those who are not recognized or might not identify as being of the African diaspora.[4] With particular attention on the dance circle, known as the cypher, key elements of Africanist aesthetics are organizing sensibilities.[5] In cyphers, one embodies lessons in call and response, polyrhythms, improvisation, trickster practices, and spiritual communion not merely as features of the culture but as fundamental dimensions to the practice itself. In learning how to cypher, one embodies Africanist aesthetics so much so that they may also acquire a legible understanding of aspects of other African diasporic ritual practices as well. Practitioners though identify themselves as hip hop (sometimes as hip hopppas, breakers, and the like). They recognize that with these identities come some degree of playing in and with African diasporic cultural elements, and thus blackness. Appropriation suggests that there is no cultural education in such performances. My ongoing research on breaking culture tells a different story, one that recognizes the capacity for dance to articulate a broader range of experiences than appropriation alone addresses.

While there are still places where black breakers figure prominently (cities like Philadelphia and Paris, countries like South Africa and Uganda), anxieties about claiming breaking's Africanist aesthetics comingles a dearth of black breakers with a fear of participating in a lineage of minstrelsy despite a commitment to hip hop—which still carries counter hegemonic politics despite its mainstream life. Shifting our attention to hip-hop dance means recognizing how cultural literacy and practice-based expertise are meaningful components of how bodies physically move in and through the world. If, as is the case in many communities, the manner by which you move your body demonstrates who your people are, then how does hip hop move people both literally and positionally in relation to blackness?

There are other terms that have been used (e.g., cultural exchange, cultural borrowing), yet they don't feel satisfying. "Borrowing" feels transitory, and "exchange" suggests a level playing field or equal sociopolitical standing, which is not always the case. Perhaps, though, a precise glossary of terms is not a satisfactory resolution anyway. What I am leaning toward is activating the nuance and specificity of experience through language that resists blurring the meaning of appropriation.

This essay is an exploration of dance and its discursive possibilities in understanding the convergence of race, performance, hip hop, and Africanist aesthetics practiced worldwide. I attempt to build on similar work from other scholars and bring their approaches to bear on my central questions.

What are the social politics of nondiasporic peoples embodying and circulating aesthetic sensibilities of the African diaspora? What is at stake when this happens in the absence of black bodies? This piece builds on work that attempts to move through, with, and past appropriation to look to hip hop's own cultural imperatives in order to facilitate a language that speaks to the nuanced complexity of cultural exposure, exchange, and belonging.

When Appropriation Is Not Enough

When breaking hit mainstream America in the early 1980s, it was frequently labeled a "black dance," not because it was solely practiced by African Americans but because of the way that blackness signified in pop culture. Multiple mainstream articles introducing its audiences to hip hop consistently represented practitioners as young, male, and black, while occasionally mentioning Puerto Ricans or Hispanics as secondary or parenthetical members of a "black youth." For example, in a 1983 *Time* magazine article titled, "Chilling Out on Rap Flash," Latino and white participants are prominent in the colorful pictures spreading across the opening pages. Yet the author only refers to their blackness. This was not an oversight; the author is not referring to national identity. Blackness signified the fear and titillation captured in the article's references to gangs, violence, crime, and a new style of cool.[6] Blackness was marked by the fact that it was a street dance dominated by African diasporic youth coming out of urban, working-class neighborhoods. That it was literally practiced on the street, outside of the institutions wherein dance is "supposed" to take place, is also symbolic of its otherness.[7] Breaking traveled with an aura of blackness that signaled coolness, youth culture, and counternarratives of socioeconomic marginalization that together contextualizes much of the black cultural production evident in pop culture.

In the mid-1980s, hip-hop films helped propagate narrow notions of blackness while also buttressing a developing discourse of breaking's multiculturalism in particular. Its selling point became its diversity, which still carries a sense of social possibility. As a consequence, blackness gets discursively resituated as both a source of innovative foundation and a racializing limitation, or the straw man to the promise of multiculturalism wherein race is politically meaningless costuming, "a kind of difference that doesn't make a difference of any kind."[8] While *Wild Style* (1983) gave us a peak into a still unknown culture, the commercial success of *Flashdance* (also 1983) and its two-minute scene featuring the Rock Steady Crew inspired youth nationwide and soon around the world. The multiracial and multiethnic group of young teenage boys dancing on cardboard in an alley surrounded by adults of different races clapping along set a precedence. Other films followed suit, depicting stories of a multicultural group of sometimes poor, ghetto kids doing good through hip hop, like *Beat Street* (1984), *Breakin'* (1984), and *Breakin' 2: Electric Boogaloo* (1984). Minor films like *Body Rock* (1984), *Flash Forward* (1985), and *Delivery Boys* (1985) also showcased moments of breaking among either multicultural or largely white groups. Black and white racial relations played a key role in some of these works, especially in the popular *Breakin'* franchise, whose central character Kelly—a white, upper-class modern dancer—sees a streetdance circle and decides to learn in hopes of distinguishing herself from other modern dancers to further her career. With very little actual breaking in it (popping and locking are showcased primarily), *Breakin'* uses the bodies of streetdancers of color to shore up the film's authenticity and mask Kelly's lack of skills. (Versions of this formula resurface in the *Step Up* franchise [2006–17].)

Popular storylines reek of appropriation and perpetuate narratives of newly welcomed white interlocutors who happily attempt to translate a culture that they have often *just* learned about for the consumption of mainstream audiences both within the films and literally at the box office. In these narratives, white people are typically the intermediaries between the subculture and the mainstream, thereby making it clear that signifiers of blackness (e.g., poor neighborhoods, black and brown practitioners, urban styles of dress and gesture, etc.) were performative not substantive. Simply put, in pop culture representations of black culture centered on nonblack people is our erasure; it is appropriation. Beyond these fictional narratives, though, are lived experiences of exchange that complicate these stories.

For example, I presented an earlier draft of this article at Emory University in 2016, and following the Q&A I was approached by a young Chinese American b-boy from Chicago, now going to college in the South.[9] He asked me how, within this political moment of Black Lives Matter activism, he and his largely white and Asian American crew should hold themselves politically accountable while loving and practicing an art born in black and brown urban, working-class communities? Additionally, going to college in Atlanta made him hyperaware of his own lack of connection to any black community, while espousing a history that he knew came from them. This tension compelled him to stay humble, especially in the face of his own urge to judge the growing competitive collegiate hip-hop "choreo" scene.[10] That is, to him. choreo did little to acknowledge hip-hop streetdance histories or connect to its current community-based manifestations, yet the choreo scene is also heavily Asian American in practice, forcing him to confront a version of hip-hop culture that was both an affront to his sense of cultural responsibility, and a mirror of his own anxieties about cultural appropriation.

I have worked with several students involved in choreo. A young, white, queer undergrad created a video project that paid homage to the form and expressed his love and commitment to his team and its founders. In a class I taught on global hip-hop dance documentaries, two women active in campus choreo (one black, one white) activated those experiences to engage the course materials. An indigenous woman form New Zealand was also in the class and explained that videos of an Australian hip-hop choreo team exposed her to hip-hop dance before coming to the States. I began to recognize that for women, queer, and international students choreo teams offered a place to enter and join communities of practice that supported their journeys through college life. They too understood that appropriation is bad, but nonetheless one asked, "But there's good appropriation too, right?," with a desire to understand how to account for his appreciation of and commitment to their campus teams. Appropriation does not exhaust our understanding of performances that traverse sociocultural and racial boundaries. Again, for these college practitioners, Africanist aesthetics are embodied, not costumes.

While my students helped clarify my questions, Dark Marc really embodied my struggle with appropriation. Dark Marc was a funky dancer whose musicality and soulfulness were as unexpected as his name. When I first saw him one Saturday afternoon at a dark New York City club in 2006, the then twenty-four-year old, 5'9," blond-haired Scandinavian man shimmied and bounced his way into the circle to James Brown's "Give It Up, Turn It Loose." He ignored the emcee's double-take when the name "Dark Marc" was announced, and his talent got spectators on his side. He nonetheless suspected that when people said that he danced well for a "white boy," it was a backhanded compliment. As far as his name was concerned, he chose it after watching Star Wars, alluding to "the dark side," arguing (however naïvely) that Scandinavians did not immediately associate "dark" with skin color.[11] He intended no offense; he just thought it was cool. Yet in New York, though white breakers are common, Dark Marc's whiteness stood out because of his name.[12] As a consequence, he became a nexus of discourses on race, national difference, hip-hop culture, and an appropriation of blackness itself—discourses that linger beneath the surface of the scene but do not often take center stage.

Ultimately, East Coast audiences appreciated his capacity to groove in synchronous harmony with the music rather than to just do a bunch of breaking moves to impress the judges without regard for the song. In an interview in 2006, Dark Marc told me how his appreciation for funk, soul, rock, and jazz music developed out of his having grown up listening to his father's record collection—some of which has since been canonized among breakers—and appreciating James Brown the most.[13] His father, a drummer, had a vast record collection, and Dark Marc got a distinct education from it. Embedded in his personal history are lessons that lent themselves to breaking. One came from learning drumming at a young age, which taught him about polyrhythms in a black music. A second lesson came from exposure to musicians jamming at parties in his home, which facilitated an understanding of improvisation, another central Africanist aesthetic. These details are neither prescriptive nor indicative of a kind of exceptionalism, but particular to Dark Marc's specific experiences with black aesthetics in music and dance before and subsequently within breaking.

In New York, though, Dark Marc activated several points of tension that could be analyzed just in reference to the "You dance good for a white boy" comment. Instead I want to pay attention to his relationship to breaking. Like other breakers around the world, Dark Marc did not just do the dance; he lived as a b-boy. He saved money to travel, he competed in battles for international respect, and he pushed himself to create and express himself within the form, while continuing to learn the dance's history because *it was his history too*. And that is what gave me initial pause. When I met him, he had traveled to New York City to learn firsthand about the roots of his adopted culture, a shared history with African diasporic, working-class American communities. He went to the South Bronx and Brooklyn to learn from first- and second-generation breakers and uprockers, these days mostly older Puerto Rican men, to teach him about his adopted culture.[14] In my interview with him, Dark Marc goes into some of those lessons, particularly around the rock dance, a battle dance born in New York (some say Brooklyn; some say the Bronx) where breaking adopts its toprock or upright dancing style.

DM: People, I think, people that know, older people that can really see if you know what you're doing, or if you just do it because you seen someone else doing it. If you know the history behind the move and you know the meaning of the move, you do it with much more . . . I don't know how to say . . . you do it much more, uhh, execution because then

you're sure of what you're doing. . . . If you know the meaning behind
a lot of the thing then it's easier to also create your own style. Because
that's maybe one of the most important things, also too: to learn the
dance, the foundation, and then try to do it your way. And, I think
a lot of new b-boys that want to try to [say], "Okay, I want to have
my own style right now." And then they kind of skip the hard work
with the foundation stuff. Then they're original but they don't have
no good form, they have terrible form. Like, I think it's really important to know the history, know how the original move is. And then it's
much more easy to make your own out of it.

IKJ: So knowing the history of the moves, does it help you innovate?

DM: Yeah. It does help me a lot when I got interested in rocking. It's, uh,
let's say when they do the jerks for instance, it's seen when b-boys try
to imitate it as when they go 1-2-3-and-4 and they go down on the 4
and hit on 2. That's like the milder version of rocking. And then, when
I learned what the rockers described . . . that you grab the opponent
and then breaking them on the hips, and then they went down to drop
the remaining of the opponent. And then when I learned *that* I was
like, "Hmm. That was a cool thing." Then it helps me to like, uh, try to
think in different ways . . . and make it my own. . . . I think it's a good
help to like open your mind.

Let me explain. Unlike breaking battles, where one person enters the circle
at a time and dances in a back-and-forth exchange to breakbeats, uprockers
form two facing rows and dance against the person standing opposite them
to entire songs while pantomiming stories of dominating their opponent.
Not unlike playing the dozens, wherein *how* you insult is more important
than the fact of insulting someone, rockers dance out intricate narratives of
dismemberment, beheadings, shootings, or breaking backs. The story told
is as creative and expressive as a rocker's imagination. So when these moves
are acquired as steps rather than individual stories, a gesture of breaking
someone at the hips just becomes a squat to the ground.

When Dark Marc talks about learning that the "go down" part is not in
fact just a part of a count—as if everyone should drop on the 4—his self-
assigned history lesson did more than satisfy a curiosity; it changed how
he understood his own practice. Moreover, it opened his mind to thinking
differently. This is not to absolve Dark Marc of any responsibilities that
come with adopting a culture, nor is this a fantasy of transracial progress
through dance. In fact, it is really not even about him. In meeting him, it

struck me that if I take Dark Marc's and my students' depth of commitment to hip-hop dance seriously, then the culture has claimed them. This alone compels a shift in discourse because those experiences are worthy of further exploration.

Inappropriable Discourse

In an effort to speak to the lived experiences of my interlocutors, I looked to work on cultural production (performance, fashion, theatre, ritual) to offer tools for moving the discussion forward. For example, in one case study featured in *Appropriating Blackness: Performance and the Politics of Authenticity*, E. Patrick Johnson writes of an all-white Australian gospel choir—many of the singers themselves atheists. In an analysis of the choir's performance at a Harlem church, he argues that in one moment they "became black," Johnson's way of accounting for the sonic achievement of what gets read as blackness in the voices of a choir. Some members were so moved in fact that they subsequently converted to Christianity. Johnson provocatively engages the language of race to speak to what a depth of performative investment can make possible. His goal is to make the language of race and particularly blackness more porous in order to undermine notions of authenticity, an essentialist discourse that buttresses intraracial practices of exclusion, such as homophobic and heteronormative black masculinities that exclude queer-identified black men. Johnson argues for "embodiment as a way of 'knowing' . . . as a way to disrupt the notion of authentic blackness." Embodiment also becomes a precondition for intersubjectivity and intercultural exchange. Performance allows us to see ourselves in Others and "engage the Others' political, social, and cultural landscape, and contextually constituted subjectivities within contested spaces."[15] Thus, between self and Other are powerful, dynamic, and transformative liminal spaces that performance opens up.

While Johnson's is an explicit engagement with African diasporic aesthetics rather than an implicit engagement mediated by hip hop, there is something to considering what embodied practices make possible. "Becoming black" is not unlike "being hip hop," which is an understanding in hip-hop circles that is all about a deep cultural investment that is lived every day and not merely put on for show or for exploitative profit. It is achievable not in biology but in practice.

Other approaches to embodied cross-cultural performances can be found in different areas of study. For example, Minh-Ha T. Pham's discussion of appropriation discourse in the fashion industry critiques the language's too easy collapse into binary oppositions (e.g., good/bad, respectful/not respectful, high/low culture, first/third world), which maintains existing power structures even within efforts to critique the fashion industry's repeated appropriative transgressions. Pham makes a case for "inappropriate critique," or that which cannot be appropriated while "continu[ing] to maintain the existing power structure."[16] In her primary example of a plaid design prominent among certain migrant worker groups "poached" for European runways as many critics argued, Pham brings attention to the design's seventeenth-century history left out of the appropriation discourse, which did nothing to undermine the implicit high/low cultural bifurcation that posited that the style was born in slums and elevated by innovative European designers, "obscure[ing] the actual diversity and complexity of the cultural object being copied."[17] Inappropriate critique might instead consider how statelessness and fashion industry wealth might intersect at various points of production, allowing us to ask different questions about who benefits and how.[18]

Works by historian Ivor Miller and performance anthropologist Dorinne Kondo also offer up new frameworks for consideration. Miller considers the participation of white elite Cuban practitioners of African-centered Palo Monte, expounding on the language of ritual to capture cultural identities through initiation, producing what he calls a "spiritual ethnicity" or ritual kinships in a tradition that requires years of study within a community to master an understanding.[19] Kondo centers cross-racial theatrical performances by Anna Deavere Smith and Culture Clash that interrogate the limits of racial discourses of multiculturalism and critiques of "identity politics." Kondo argues that "unfaithful" impersonations in each artists' works—the purposeful gaps between performers and the "other" that they portray—"disrupts audience complacency" by drawing attention to the performative aspects of identity and de-essentializing them.[20]

Though only Johnson and Pham explicitly unpack "appropriation," together these scholars' examinations open up alternative discourses worth exploring. In Kondo's examples, cross-racial performances employ racial signifiers in order to destabilize them, disrupting familiar racial scripts or stereotypes by demanding audiences experience the seemingly familiar differently. Breaking has its own moments of shaking up audience expectations, lending itself to potentially more nuanced discussions of appropriation, which I discuss further below. The language of initiation allows Miller to consider how deep, long-term study of communal practices offer ways to read Dark Marc's cultural adoption in earnest and studied terms. By drawing attention to inappropriate questions, Pham implores us to reframe appropriation debates so as to not reaffirm power structures of "white Western domination . . . over everyone else." This might, for example, allow us to shift our perspective from whether Dark Marc appropriates hip hop to hip hop's seduction of him, calling to question the capacity for commercial hip-hop industries to supplant embodied hip-hop identities (and thus Africanist aesthetics) with consumer identities. Johnson's analysis makes room for these very engagements, ones that acknowledge the profound impact of performance and the creation of new subjectivities as a result.

These strategies produce their own kind of dance, where counter discourses move with, alongside, and yet away from appropriation. Performance and dance are powerful starting points to ask different kinds of questions and perhaps represent different kinds of relationships within cross-cultural performances and in relation to appropriation. For example, learning how to break necessarily involves some degree of *biting*: stealing or mimicking someone else's style as if one's own. Biting alone is not okay; by definition it is appropriation. Yet beginning breakers typically put someone else's movement onto their bodies as part of their learning process. Insofar as biting is a form of learning, it is also a kind of enactment whose antithesis speaks to how one participates. Hence the cry among breakers: "Don't bite!" To *not* bite—to abstain from the mere consumption of another's style—means that one must respectfully name one's direct and indirect teachers, those who helped to make one's movements possible. As well, hip hop's Africanist cultural logic also necessitates that one must add their own flavor to the style adopted, making for an original style. It is a problem if one fails on either or both fronts. So appropriation is mitigated by cultural imperatives that recontextualize it as learning and even innovation, all while upholding hip hop's history and foundation.

Read symbolically, biting is a couple's dance in a rhythmic negotiation. One partner is present, moving in and through an invisible partner's path. And while one can attempt to embody the style of another—making the invisible present in the dancing itself—the gap between that re-performance and the original is always evident because the originality that birthed that style (necessarily within a particular historical context) is inappropriable. It is precisely in efforts to not bite and add one's own style that shifts away from discourses of "theft" and erasure to an act that conjures up and makes ever present one who is not physically there. It becomes an act of communion and community building, adding new dimensions of style into the dance's expanding repertoire overall.

Breaking also has its own ways of disrupting audience complacency. For instance, there are moments in breaking when uprocking battles occur. Unlike traditional rocking battles structured in two facing lines, uprock face-offs in breaking happen in large groups enmeshed in cyphers. They are structured by contrapuntal exchanges while moving circularly around one's opponent, filling the surrounding space with a pantomimed story of dominating, outwitting, and out-dancing the other without ever really touching. When I first witnessed this moment at a breaking battle, I became immediately alert, somewhat confused, and thoroughly sucked into the drama. At the same time, the "go down" part that Dark Marc mentioned—when it is *not* done to a count but in the context of an individual dancer's story—the "go down" part turns the seeming chaos into rhythmic waves of up and down movement that happen at differential moments yet remain collectively in sync, perhaps enabled by a polyrhythmic enactment of the music through dance. The result is simultaneously funny, disjointed, ordered, and frenzied. Grasping the whole is impossible and watching is a potentially disorienting act. With that said, to be in sync rhythmically is community in action, which is evident in Gena Caponi's discussion of polyrhythms in the introduction to *Signifyin(g), Sanctifyin', and Slam Dunking: A Reader in African American Expressive Culture*: "Polyrhythmic and polymetric music creates interdependence, because it forces all participants to be aware of each other—of their place in the rhythmic field in relation to others and to the whole."[21] Simply put, it is a communal mode of interaction, and participating in it requires deep listening and bodily awareness of the whole. It necessitates recognizing the central rhythmic thread within the multiplicity, even when it is not being played. Being in sync adds to it rather than disrupts it. As a metaphor, polyrhythms might represent varying depths of cultural initiation, giving us room to talk about different frequencies of participation.

Conclusion

Dance gives us insight into different cultural rhythms. Someone like Iggy Azalea can mimic the sound but this sonic costuming does not mean she is in sync with hip hop as a culture, despite hitting all of the beats of mainstream commercial rap music. Yet for a while she still had the influence to distort the notions of cultural responsibility. Dark Marc dances to a different rhythm, one that builds on the foundation of his adopted culture. This is a testament to the reality that how we connect to hip hop matters. Yet positionality complicates the matter.

In "What Is This 'Black' in Black Popular Culture?," cultural studies scholar Stuart Hall clarifies why positionality is unstable ground: "We are always in negotiation, not with a single set of oppositions that place us always in the same relation to others, but with a series of different positionalities. Each has for us its point of profound subjective identification. And that is the most difficult thing about this proliferation of the field of identities and antagonisms: they are often dislocating in relation to one another."[22] Since social identities are multiple, complicated, and always shifting, a "profound subjective identification" with hip hop is always alongside other equally or more profound identifications with race, nation, sexuality, gender, and class, as each continually shift our positionality relative to others. There is no stable, static, or singular positionality from which to locate ourselves that resolves everyday and individual experiences of potentially appropriative acts once and for all. Similarly, appropriation might locate or signal "fields of identities and antagonisms" precisely because our relations to each other via particular modes of expressive cultures are too dynamic and unfixed.

Labeling appropriation on its own does not fix anything (and I mean "fix" as both to resolve and to make stable). Performances that can alter our perceptions and foster deep connections to others can shape discourses that speak to under examined dimensions of lived experiences. Regardless, if cultural exchange (rather than cultural appropriation) truly only happens when groups of people are on equal footing—as dance artist and scholar Ananya Chatterjee argued in her keynote lecture, "Of Thievings, Essences, and Strategies," presented at the 2016 Congress on Research and Dance, on "Beyond Authenticity and Appropriation"—then we have to consider the reality that the terrain of exchange is always shifting and equal footing might not be possible or last.[23] By moving away from the binary of "Is it appropriation or not?," we can consider the polyrhythmic flows of cross-cultural performances: What is inappropriate? What disrupts complacent expectations? What's achievable through sustained study of embodied practices?

It goes without saying that the political stakes of appropriation remain important. So too are approaches to interpreting cross-cultural performances beyond appropriation. Dance allows us to engage these debates differently, just as it allows practitioners like Dark Marc to move differently in relation to and in proximity with others, and to embody an identity that entails responsibilities to a larger collective. Next steps then might entail staying vigilantly attuned to shifting positionalities within larger structures of power, which opens up even more ground for expanding the discourse now couched (and erased) in appropriation discourses. That alone might not be everything, but it can potentially move us toward a better understanding of our relations to each other.

Notes

1 Even in such extreme cases as Rachel Dolezal, who morphed her desire to be black into identifying as a black woman, the degree of attention and debate that followed her being "outed" as white further signals how conditioned we are to accept the erasure of black people even from our own identities. Nothing is actually ours.

2 Cooper, "Iggy Azalea's Post-Racial Mess." On Twitter in December 2014, the rapper Q-Tip from A Tribe Called Quest took Azalea to task for her lack of awareness of hip-hop history, leading to lengthy exchanges with her label boss and fellow rapper T. I. See Williams, "Q-Tip Offers."

3 MTV's *Decoded* video "7 Myths about Cultural Appropriation DEBUNKED!" and *Teen Vogue*'s video "How to Avoid Cultural Appropriation at Coachella" are just two examples that reveal countless additions to these debates.

4 Johnson, "B-Boying and Battling."

5 See Johnson, "Dark Matter."

6 Cocks, "Chilling Out on Rap Flash."

7 Bragin, "Global Street Dance."

8 Hall, "What Is This 'Black,'" 23.

9 Johnson, "Breaking Beyond Appropriation Discourses."

10 "Collegiate hip-hop choreo" refers to campus-organized dance teams that perform choreographed shows on stage, and compete with other college teams.

11 Ironically, even though Dark Marc appropriates *Star Wars* in his name, it is still racialized because the film captures the dark side in the iconic sonic force of James Earl Jones's voice, and then displaces this black man's body with that of an old white man. Race matters.

12 While it is common for breakers to give themselves comedic or self-ethnicizing names (e.g., AsiaOne, Casper), ambiguous cross-racial names are not common.

13 Personal interview 2006; Schloss "'Like Folk Songs.'"

14 Uprocking is a battle streetdance genre from which early breakers borrowed heavily in their own upright dancing styles. Uprocking has experienced resurgence in the b-boying scene in the past decade. Joseph Schloss discusses uprocking's relationship to b-boying history at length in *Foundation*.

15 Schloss, *Foundation*, 230, 213.

16 Pham, "Fashion's Cultural-Appropriation Debate."

17 Pham, "Fashion's Cultural-Appropriation Debate."

18 Pham, "Fashion's Cultural-Appropriation Debate."

19 Miller, "The Formation."

20 Kondo, "(Re)Visions of Race."

21 Caponi, "Introduction," 10.
22 Hall, "What Is This 'Black,'" 28, 30–31.
23 Chatterjea, "Of Thievings, Essences, and Strategies."

References

Bragin, Naomi. "Global Street Dance and Libidinal Economy." Paper and lecture, SDHS/CORD 2015 Dance Studies Conference, Athens, Greece, June 7, 2015.

Caponi, Gena Dagel. "Introduction: The Case for an African American Aesthetic." In *Signifyin(g), Sanctifyin', and Slam Dunking: A Reader in African American Expressive Culture*, edited by Gena Dagel Caponi. Amherst: University of Massachusetts Press, 1999.

Chatterjea, Ananya. "Of Thievings, Essences, and Strategies: Performative Cultures in 2016." Keynote address. Congress on Research in Dance annual conference. Pomona College, November 2016. https://www.youtube.com/watch?v=2TgRvee2gqc.

Cocks, Jay. "Chilling Out on Rap Flash." *Time*, March 21, 1983.

Cooper, Brittney. "Iggy Azalea's Post-Racial Mess: America's Oldest Race Tale, Remixed," *Salon*, July 16, 2014. http://www.salon.com/2014/07/15/iggy_azaleas_post_racial_mess_americas_oldest_race_tale_remixed/.

Hall, Stuart. "What Is This 'Black' in Black Popular Culture?" In *Black Popular Culture: A Project by Michelle Wallace*, edited by Gina Dent. Seattle, WA: Bay Press, 1992.

Johnson, Imani Kai. "B-Boying and Battling in a Global Context: The Discursive Life of Difference in Hip Hop Dance." *Alif: Journal of Comparative Poetics* 31 (2011): 173–95.

Johnson, Imani Kai. "Breaking Beyond Appropriation Discourse." Race and Difference Colloquium Lecture Series. Emory University, October 2016. https://www.youtube.com/watch?v=8aTze_N-o6k

Johnson, Imani Kai. "Dark Matter in B-Boying Cyphers: Race and Global Connection in Hip Hop." PhD diss., University of Southern California, 2009. http://digitallibrary.usc.edu/cdm/compoundobject/collection/p15799coll127/id/265317/rec/1.

Kondo, Dorinne. "(Re)Visions of Race: Contemporary Race Theory and the Cultural Politics of Racial Crossover in Documentary Theatre." *Theatre Journal* 52, no. 1 (March 2000): 87–107.

Miller, Ivor L. 2004. "The Formation of African Identities in the Americas: Spiritual 'Ethnicity.'" *Contours* 2, no. 2 (Fall 2000): 193–222.

MTV *Decoded*. "7 Myths about Cultural Appropriation DEBUNKED!" YouTube, November 11, 2015. https://www.youtube.com/watch?v=KXejDhRGOuI.

Osumare, Halifu. "Beat Streets in the Global Hood: Connective Marginalities of the Hip Hop Globe." *Journal of American and Comparative Cultures* 24, nos. 1–2 (Spring–Summer 2001): 171–81.

Pham, Minh-ha T. "Fashion's Cultural-Appropriation Debate: Pointless." *The Atlantic*, May 15, 2014. http://www.theatlantic.com/entertainment/archive/2014/05/cultural-appropriation-in-fashion-stop-talking-about-it/370826/.

Schloss, Joseph G. *Foundation: B-Boys, B-Girls, and Hip Hop Culture in New York City*. New York: Oxford University Press, 2009.

Schloss, Joseph G. "Like Folk Songs Handed Down from Generation to Generation: History, Canon, and Community in B-Boy Culture." *Ethnomusicology* 50, no. 3 (Fall 2006): 411–32.

Teen Vogue. "How to Avoid Cultural Appropriation at Coachella." YouTube, April 20, 2017. https://www.youtube.com/watch?v=GwV3LApkKTk.

Williams, Brennan. "Q-Tip Offers Iggy Azalea a Hip Hop History Lesson, T. I. and Azealia Banks Respond." *Huffington Post*, January 5, 2015. http://www.huffingtonpost.com/2014/12/22/q-tip-iggy-azalea-hip-hop-history-lesson-ti-azealia-banks-_n_6367046.html.

AT THE CORNER OF CHAOS AND DIVINE
/ BLACK RITUAL THEATER, PERFORMANCE,
AND POLITICS

Nina Angela Mercer

> We cannot abdicate our culture to those who sit outside of us. We
> should guard and protect our culture viciously, and work juju on
> those who screw up. · LARRY NEAL

I enter here, at the corner of chaos and divine, between the sticky place
where monster consumerism strangles all art that does not conform to its
conventions and the place where that monster gets funked into submission
under a blue light at the basement party. I enter here, at the corner of chaos
and divine, troubling the contradictions between corporate monopolies and
culture; between award committees and those street-corner review boards,
where the people sit wide-legged on milk crates out front the bodega—a
head-nod could mean you cool, but you'd have to stop often and shoot the

shit to know. I enter here, between monolithic metanarratives of blackness and the truths blaring just beyond my window on East 196th Street in the Bronx, or any city any black heart beat any black trip to the future from the ocean's deep blue-black-rooted past of brine and bones. I enter here, at the corner of chaos and divine in my womanist way, because I can't keep my hand off my hip and all the mothers before me whisper blood secrets, survival stories, and ways to stand without stooping inside this room, askew, in a house called these United States of America.

I enter as a Black womanist theater practitioner who understands my writing as a sacred act of resistance that is inextricably linked to the rituals, songs, and parables of Hoodoo, Yoruba, and Bantu cosmologies as they have evolved through the Black diaspora's survival of the transatlantic slave trade's Middle Passage. I work my practice from the inside. I write because I am called away from that illusion of safety made by a self-imposed distance from other human lives. I must share what I see and break into new light to see again through the lives of those who come to join me; it is a communion of souls meeting as many and one. Together, we testify and bear witness. Together, we hold the potential for transformation through the shared ritual in performance. It is a subversive potential. It is urgently real. We light candles and move counterclockwise in the ring shout. And some of us don't. We burn white sage sometimes. And some of us get cleansed at the sacred grove, the hush harbor, the temple and juke-joint, even when it all happens in the theater. Every place is the same space, sanctified by our soul. There are those of us who mark off the four corners and draw a circle on the floor, conjuring the Kongo cosmogram.[1] We may dance and call our ancestors by name. We retell the many possible stories of the twenty-one cowrie shells that may fall on the divining mat, always leaving space for improvisation. And even when we don't know that science, our cellular memory invokes it, disturbing the critiques that claim this is cultural appropriation. It is blood memory lived and practiced through recurring experience that happens across and through history and geographic divides. This is Black ritual performance. This is also the Black avant-garde, and it happens wherever we demand the space and are welcomed:

I. We surrender and bear witness, striving to tell our stories with raw, honest, and bold voices, working toward the space where the sacred meets the profane, where the absolute imperfection of humanity circles back into the divine.

We get free
Seeking

Conjure our own holiness
Touching mirrors
Soul deep
We a prismatic people
One

*

But how, you may ask, can Black ritual theater be considered in any discussion of African American popular culture, when that popular culture has become an industry that is bound by capitalism, defined by corporate acceptance, control, and distribution?[2] We recognize Beyoncé, Jay-Z, and Kevin Hart as icons of African American popular culture. We know that Kendrick Lamar, Rihanna, Nicki Minaj, and Cardi B are highly relevant hit-makers on the American popular culture scene because of the sales of their artistic products and the proliferation of their images bearing viral "likes" and "shares" throughout social media's virtual landscape. They are brands in a marketplace that seems to hold no allegiances, except to the almighty dollar.

Truth be told, the roots of Black performance as an industry in the United States are tainted. From the very first time a white owner of an enslaved Black person received monetary compensation for that Black person's artistry in music or dance as a commodity for trade, Black labor's relationship to the economy of performance in a white supremacist and capitalist economy has been shaped by a certain exploitation that emancipation only partially diffused. But our culture has never been dependent on this paradigm for its existence. Our ring shouts and secret dances under the cover of night always happened independent of the industry that sought to benefit from it. And that is still true today. Though Black popular culture as an industry may be subject to trends governed by corporate interests that are often antithetical to the cultural resistance we must summon to move our community forward, there is always an "underground" movement to disrupt its seeming domination.

We get free
Underground, seeking
Ritual soul deep inside
The over yonder space.

We sweat, bodies breaking
Every rule; we pop-lock,

Spin, defying
Gravity's law.

Our sacred kisses
The profane creating freedom
Over and over
Again.

Black ritual theater exists outside of what we understand African American popular culture to be today in the terms that have been placed upon us, terms that we have often helped to maintain as participating artists and as consumers with millions of dollars in buying power. Only a relatively small number of people attend theater compared to those who consume Hollywood's alternately saccharine and garishly violent buffet of entertainment, and it is generally accepted that theater audiences are mostly individuals of a privileged economic class and white. Furthermore, though the United States boasts an increasingly ethnically diverse population of people, such diversity has not been successfully replicated in the season line-up of theaters across the country, though progress is undeniable.

And though there are certainly more African American producers of theater than there have ever been, we must constantly challenge ourselves by questioning what role we play in the evolution of the industry. Barbara Ann Teer, who founded the National Black Theatre (NBT) in Harlem in 1968, cautions us with this reminder:

> Essentially there is no difference between the psyche of a white businessman [sic] and a black one. In this country, their sole concern is to make money. They stick to what has been tried and proven: the safe way; the easy follow-the-leader way. These narrow concepts have apparently, until now, been the code of ethics of the American businessman [sic]. So in planning [her] own businesses, the black performer must be very careful to analyze [her] thought patterns so that [she] will not make the same errors.[3]

Teer certainly dug her hands into the rich soil of Black culture and held true to her words. Because of her indomitable commitment, as well as the commitment of new leadership, NBT has produced theater for over forty-seven years, despite fluctuating economies, continuing to thrive largely because the demand for such a space for Black theater, its practitioners, and audience remains acutely necessary in the splintered landscape of American theater. NBT is an institution where Black ritual theater practitioners are welcome.

Still, many African American playwrights write American realism, creating inside the most recognizable narrative form in this country. In choosing the linear and well-ordered form of realism, these undeniably talented playwrights are often more likely to gain the enthusiastic support of the commercial theater industry as it currently exists. And yet those of us creating Black ritual theater are doing so outside of the expectations and trends dictating what commercially viable American theater should be. We are transgressing, choosing nonlinear narrative forms that emphasize disorder, hybridity, mystery, "magic," and the unpredictable. These are dangerous creative choices for an industry that rarely takes risks. This means that Black ritual theater practitioners often engage in a struggle for major institutional and financial support in an industry that has been tightening its purse strings for years. What becomes popular is often what bodes well for capital investment, "the tried and true" Teer cautioned us about. And while there has been more investment, and therefore more popularity, ascribed to experimental forms created by Black theater practitioners, we must continually affirm our presence. We must continually claim space, because it is not guaranteed. We must write and tend to our own ever-evolving archive so that we are not dependent on what any industry defines as "popular" or worthy of support.[4]

But at its very root, the word "popular" should refer not *only* to how much money a cultural product generates but to that cultural product's *relationship to the people*, the masses, the everyday folk who make this world, not a handful of corporate monopolies and fat-pocket individuals ready to triple investments. That means that if we are courageous, our work should be to create populist culture that resists the status quo by protecting our transformational ritual performance in its most potent forms. Black ritual theater and its practitioners do that work, putting the controlling interest of our culture back with the people. Our juju is resilient; we keep on.

II. Our performance is ritual/Our ritual is performance: We be go-go music and its all-night jam sessions. Jazz, the call, the response. Carnival, playing Mas, getting free and reborn. Block parties, praise, and spirit cyphers. We be street festivals, the corner, the blues and bodega, the kitchen, the porch, and the dance hall. We be the rap battle and the rhythm's pocket. Roll call. The stoop, our shrine, our temple, always then and now. We Be.

Raw and funky
Sanctified
Flash/light

Working the between space
The inside over yonder space
The getting over
And sacred
Kissing the profane
So divine.

*

My first experiences of Black ritual performance came to me in my youth, growing up in Washington, DC, when it was still considered the Chocolate City, because of its predominantly Black population. DC was, and remains, home to an indigenous Black American music and culture known as go-go, a heavily percussive music with a tradition of transformative ritual. Go-go music was ushered onto the scene in the late 1970s by "the Godfather of Go-go," the bassist, blues-man, and lead-talker Chuck Brown, when he led his band the Soul Searchers. Many bands would follow, creating a movement and culture with a loyal fan base spanning generations. Growing up as a Black girl in DC meant holding my stance at The Go-Go, getting knocked around a bit, and claiming a space where there seemed to be none in the crowd. When I am conceiving and writing ritual theater, I'm always coming from there.

Go-go connects me to the continuum of ritual performance born from the African diaspora, that intricate web of cultures that finds kinship in familiar percussive rhythms, stylized movements, repetitions, shouts, and call-and-response chants that have come with us across big water, now wearing a new language but recognized as our truth all the same.[5] It is our language, our legacy, our wealth; it is our resistance to all that seeks to shut us out and down, the evidence that we Here. It is the musicians, the lead talker, the congas' steady pocket, the cowbell and the snare, that go-go twang plucked from bass strings, the horn section's wail for glory. It is those of us in the crowd, standing, and tunneling our way through many bodies to get right in front of the stage as we reach our arms up in solidarity, jumping over the bullshit that may have clamored for our submission before we got to the venue. We defy gravity at The Go-Go. We get back home and our ears ring for hours. We get back home transformed and understanding freedom in our cellular memory; it is a blood recognition in a funky bass line. Church.

But the go-go don't just happen at The Go-Go. We carry it with us in how we walk, in how we say what we say and how we reason. It is how we stand, a rebel stance that refuses to be relegated to the shadows of the U.S. Capitol. Not even the White House is enough to satisfy us. We've been taxed without representation for so long that we cannot possibly trust the status quo to heal us of the weary blues. We know the time. It is now, right where our feet are planted. It pushes back against hostile attempts of takeover or absorption, ever transforming, and becoming new while defiantly holding onto roots grown deep in the soil at the banks of the Potomac and Anacostia Rivers. If go-go is a place, it is inside of us.

There is something remarkably resilient about a culture that endures over decades, despite the lukewarm attentions of the American music industry, its merchandising and many fans. In fact, go-go generates its own sustainable economy through live performances that do not rely on record sales or radio airplay. All of this is evidence of our ability to alter how capitalist power constructs and confines culture. We are able to think and act independently as a communal body that understands its own worth. We have the ability to persist and thrive, despite gentrification and political mandates that attempt to silence who and how we be. It is our Black caucus without buttons and lace, our baptism, and our power, whether Congress recognizes us or not.

The call and response that is critical at The Go-Go is embodied power and community engagement. It is intuitive. No one has to teach us how to be in that space, actively receiving and giving. It is both church and corner, sacred and secular, inclusive and liberating. When the go-go band Junkyard performed *The Word/Sardines and Pork 'n' Beans* in 1986, it was a public acknowledgment of the volatile connection between federal power and our local lives. Junkyard's lead talker chanted, "Reagan make the bombs [sic] Reagan gave the Pentagon the food stamp money."[6] The young artists beat this truth out on plastic buckets, hubcaps, crates, and discarded kitchen pots and pans. And we danced, shouting back in agreement, understanding we were not alone in our experience of inequality or injustice. We found recognition in the call. We found community in our response.

This is the same call and response of our Praise House. It is the call and response of our ring shouts in the sacred grove, and it is certainly connected to the tradition of "breaking the fourth wall" in ritual theater so that the actors and audience can dislocate the traditional divide between them, interacting in intimate ways, no longer ascribing to the belief that the urgency of the performance is separate from the audience sitting a cool and comfortable distance away from the fray. Ritual theater practitioners must push past this convenient and familiar way of experiencing art, inviting the audience to defy the usual parameters governing the theatrical experience. Amiri Baraka makes it plain in his essay "Bopera Theory":

Theatre in the United States is obstructed in its development by the same forces that obstruct general positive development of human life and society. Frequently, we are stalled by our very amazement at the rulers of society, shrieking for years of this "superiority," when one has only to look around to see what a mess they have made of everything and what a bizarre lie this "superiority" is. We must step outside the parameters of this society's version of just about everything. Often I seek to use, as one alternative, practices found in the oldest root of performance: ritual, but not in a frozen or atavistic way. We take the wholeness, the freshness, the penetrating emotionalism and spiritual revelation and renewal, the direct connection with what the ancients meant. We want to educate but we want to do that through the transformation of the human consciousness.[7]

Baraka is calling us out to move beyond entertainment and its industry. He is talking about "transformation" and spiritual awakening. He is asking us to call down the ancestors by name and make a healing that is urgently necessary for our survival and well-being, if we are ever to be well in this place at all.

If we take Baraka's "Bopera Theory" as a creed for Black ritual theater practitioners, we know that we must continue working for its fulfillment. Years after the seeming come-up for African American playwrights in American theater as a result of progress made during the civil rights, Black Power, and Black Arts movements, and further evolution reached through campaigns for diversity in regional theaters throughout the late twentieth century and continuing into the twenty-first, we are still hungry for the space and support to create Black ritual theater with a freedom and authenticity that commercial American theater has yet to fully embrace. But we need not wait for that. Teer did not wait for that. Woodie King Jr. did not wait. He established New Federal Theatre at Henry Street Settlement in New York. And Baraka certainly did not wait. He and his comrades in art pooled resources to stage plays on their own terms, and Baraka continued to demand this self-determined approach to art-making far into his senior years. The last time I saw him speak to an audience before he transitioned to the ancestral realm was at the Labyrinth Theater in the West Village after a stage reading of his play *The Dutchman* in the early spring of 2013. When an audience member asked him what younger artists could do to sustain Black theater financially, when major funders fail to reward us with the means to produce our work, he turned his fierce eyes in her direction and commanded that we just do it with what we have collectively; he was impatient with the idea that we would wait for anything.

III. For us, theater is not just what happens in a building that holds a traditional stage with a paying and well-mannered audience filling the seats. Theater is every day and everywhere there are lives touching other lives. Audiences may shout, jump up to kiss and dance with a neighbor, scream out of anger, or take over the "scene" with their own urgent selves in the making.

> *Our tongue is tree root*
> *And street market*
> *The boom bap and high hat*
>
> *The congas break us free*
>
> *We soul cipher*
> *And Mother Ship*
> *Back bone dip and real cool*
> *Block party and that bar*
> *At the corner of Chaos and Divine*
> *(You know that spot)*
> *Graffiti tag every name*
> *Once whispered*
> *Every voice*
> *Once hushed*
> *Now blazing hot fire*
> *Blue black blessing*
>
> *Oranges float down*
> *The river, an offering*
> *To beat back hurt*
> *With love*
> *Sweetness to counter*
> *The bitter fruits life*
> *Sometimes shakes*
> *From its tree*
>
> *This is grace*
>
> *A riotous yellow umbrella*
> *In the hands of a woman*

Wearing deep crimson-wine silks
She plum skinned
Call her Sunshine
And dancing down
Bourbon Street, remembering
Someone recently departed
This our sorrow and sweat
Coming undone
A celebration
A healing

*

In August 2002, my understanding of where I fit in relationship to my community and the world shifted drastically. And I entered at the corner of chaos and divine. I could no longer immerse myself in stacks of books, avoiding the real-life implications of our nation's dependence on the cultures of addiction and poverty. The War on Drugs was waged on my household, training its infrared spotlight on someone too necessary to how I understood reality for me to ignore. This also meant that a war was waged on my daughters' sense of safety and self-worth, as they struggled through the fallout of our family's fracture. This violent shift pushed me to reassess what it meant to be an actively engaged member of my community as mother, artist, and cultural worker, because I understood that work as Toni Cade Bambara defined it.

I first encountered Bambara when I was a nineteen-year-old undergraduate student at Howard University. I sat at her feet in the Blackburn Student Center, hungry for the secret to a wordsmith's brilliance. I listened to her words with awe, though there was much in the meaning I could not have understood because I hadn't really lived yet. I had no idea how close to transitioning she was. I knew only that I found home in her cadence, the weaving of her thoughts and imaginings in language, her magic, her truth. I returned to her novel *The Salt Eaters* when I was a divorced mother of two daughters years later, and I was immediately struck by the way Bambara's novel emphasized the vitality found at intersections of life for women cultural workers and artists. Through the journey of her characters, Bambara affirmed that the healing we took on for ourselves as individuals was a healing our community would experience with us. Like Teer and Baraka and so many of our predecessors, Bambara understood that we could not approach art from the very Western and modernist organizing principle of binaries, because life and art are not separate; neither are community and the self. Any attempt to compartmentalize these ways of being and knowing could lead to dysfunction with many real lives at stake.

Bambara's body of work as a novelist, short story writer, filmmaker, and self-defined cultural worker pushes those of us who find kinship with her mission and work to locate our belonging within the sociopolitical and economic life circumstances of the communities in which we exist. If our community is oppressed, we must locate our work within that community's reality. In her interview with Kay Bonetti in 1982, Bambara provides an analysis of the purpose and challenges of cultural workers: "As a cultural worker who belongs to an oppressed people, my job is to make revolution irresistible. But in this country [the United States] we're not encouraged and equipped, at any particular time, to view things that way. And so the art work or the art practice that sells capitalist ideology is considered art and anything that deviates from that is considered political, propagandist, polemical, or didactic, strange, weird, subversive or ugly."[8]

So I set about claiming my belonging because the revolution was urgently necessary to me and my community. There was no denying it. And while Bambara laid out the challenges to opposing the capitalist agenda in our artistic production, doing anything other than that felt like certain death. I chose to be subversive, political, and weird. I chose to be strangely unpretty and unsafe. I accepted that I lived most powerfully at the intersections of the personal, the political, and the public. My healing belonged not only to me. And even in my most vulnerable moments of seeming isolation, art was being made that had a direct message for my community, if I chose to share.

The urgency with which my family experienced this shift in our well-being was the same urgency with which I wanted to speak to my block. And I wanted that conversation to be live, intimate, reciprocal, and transformative. I was shaken to my roots, and down there in that messy excavation of self and soul, I returned to what resonated most for me at my core: my youth's most powerful survival tool as experienced at The Go-Go, the ritual of live performance. And I began writing Gutta Beautiful, the first ritual theater offering in what would become a cycle of plays, including *Racing My Girl Sally, Itagua Meji: A Road and a Prayer, Gypsy and the Bully Door, Mother Wit and Water-Born, Charisma at the Crossroads*, and *A Compulsion for Breathing*.

But the transformation moved in more ways than through the writing. My ways of seeing, knowing, and being were unhinged. Every truth connected to the way of living that ushered forth such a painful breaking of my family structure shattered too far into my chest, too close to necessary organs, and I eventually found myself sitting across the table from a Lukumi priest, being read through the twenty-one cowrie shells known as the Diloggún.

I will not give details of my reading, nor can I recount every ritual I have experienced as a practitioner of the Lukumi and Ifa cultures and as Yayi Nkisi Malongo of Palo Mayombe.[9] These are secret rites. But in exposing when and where I enter as a Black ritual theater practitioner, I must explain how my identity as a Black woman, mother, cultural worker, and artist merged with my need to transform and heal. I could not transform and heal through the most popular Western cultural systems and traditions any more than our community can expect to create progressive systemic change through our relationship to consumerism's pop icon worship. These intersections—the personal and political, the sacred and secular—all conspired so that the ritual practice required of me through my intimate involvement with the African diaspora's matrix of cosmologies became an offering for my community as artist and cultural worker toward collective transformation.

My entry through these systems is not a definitive step in the development of all Black ritual theater practitioners. Everyone enters from where they happen to be on the road that is life. Besides, a ritual is not necessarily tied to any one particular system. It is simply a series of actions performed according to an order prescribed by a community of people who agree on the efficacy of these repeated acts. These rituals shift over time. They can be linked to specialized bodies of knowledge, or they can be as ordinary as brushing one's teeth in the morning or playing dominos outside on a folding table on the sidewalk.

Hoodoo, Bantu, and Yoruba rituals are relevant to my work as a practitioner of Black ritual theater because of the required act of making objects that serve as divine creations leading to transformation. We make the sacred beaded necklaces that invoke the protection of forces of nature (*orisha* or *nkisi*). We make the space for the veneration of ancestors in our homes. We make offerings (*ebo* or *nsara*) to propitiate energies we need in our daily life. This process of making becomes a meditation on a specific change that one wants to experience in life to evolve or progress. For me, part of the ritual of making through these systems depends on the work of creating theater.

We conjure
Ourselves mirrors,

Prismatic, one and many
Underground seeking inside
The over yonder space.

We sweat, pop, unlock that other
History's law, spin our sacred
Knowledge, kissing the profane
Into a new vision of freedom
Over and over again.

In *Mojo Workin': The Old African American Hoodoo System*, Katrina Hazzard-Donald provides a thorough exploration of Hoodoo as a system of knowledge and cultural practice connected to the more actively studied and publicly recognized systems of Ifa, Lukumi, and Palo Mayombe. The latter three systems all became more prevalent in the United States long after slavery ended as practitioners migrated from the Caribbean, where religious and cultural systems with origins in African communities were able to flourish, despite slavery. Because the United States took such a violent stance against African cultural retentions, Hoodoo had to mask itself over and over again to survive. However, through careful research, Hazzard-Donald uncovered a system that persisted with a stubbornness that is testimony to our ancestral will. In particular, Hazzard-Donald notes the persistence of the sacred spoken word and the ring shout as aspects of Hoodoo that crossed the bridge from the sacred to the secular through a continuous flow between the two realms, defying Western binary divisions: "Since the spoken word was believed to embody spiritual potency, sacred remarks in the form of incantations and prayers were a significant component in African traditional medicine and would later perform a similar function in Hoodoo. Words were power."[10] And regarding the ring shout:

> In the American mainstream, the rapid commercial secularization of HooDoo's sacred dance the Ring Shout would give America the foundation for dance ritual[s] translated into secular dance steps. But more important, African American sacred dancing postures, gestures, and movements would influence all American theatrical dance and would eventually dominate American urban popular dancing even more thoroughly than it had dominated some of the older plantation country dance forms.[11]

I had my first experience of a sacred ring shout in 2004 at an *egun bembe* in the Bedford Stuyvesant area of Brooklyn, where my first spiritual home as a Lukumi practitioner was located. An egun bembe is a ritual ceremony honoring the ancestors through drumming, song, and dance. The ritual that happens at the egun bembe is sacred. It is a way to celebrate those who came before us, letting them break free through our bodies as we lean into the rhythmic patterns of the drums, singing and moving counter-clockwise in a circle around a center pole adorned in multicolored fabrics and raffia to invoke the presence of the ancestors. Our bodies move inside cellular memories as we become vessels for the presence of those whose lives paved the way for our own journeys through this world. Still, before the sacred, came the secular—I had my first intimate experience with the ring shout as a modified secular dance form through childhood games, and later as a young adult in the dance cyphers formed at nightclubs where house music played.

This merging of sacred and secular forms with origins in the African di-aspora's matrix of cosmologies is evident in Ntozake Shange's choreopoem *for colored girls who have considered suicide when the rainbow is enough.* Shange's choreopoem is a necessary and much revered Black womanist ritual theater experience, which had its first New York City production in 1976 at Joseph Papp's Public Theatre. In fact, *for colored girls* opens with a ring shout known to most as a children's game. The women of the choreopoem form a circle and chant:

> *little sally walker, sittin in a saucer*
> *rise, sally, rise, wipe your weepin eyes*
> *an put your hands on your hips*
> *an let your back bone slip*
> *o, shake it to the east*
> *o, shake it to the west*
> *shake it to the one that you like the best.*[12]

The children's ring shout is our entry point for ritual transformation as we bear witness to the women's most intimate testimonies and revela-tions about life as Black women in the United States through dance and spoken word, two of the most important elements of Hoodoo as a system of knowledge and power. My understanding of Black ritual theater as a womanist is in keeping with the tradition as it evolved through Shange's courageous pen, as well as through the confluence of the African diaspora's cultural matrix. With this understanding, I embarked upon my own inti-mate journey of elevating my ancestors, cultivating a greater awareness of my head and its divine power of choice, and deepening my connection to the earth. *Gutta Beautiful* sprang from the labyrinth of my mind near the start of that journey.

Gutta Beautiful (2005) was developed through an artistic partnership with the director Eric Ruffin and the dramaturge Sybil Roberts. The play emphasizes the ritual of rebirth possible as we navigate the psychological wounds of displacement common among many descendants of the peculiar institution of slavery, when we are confronted by the virulent implications of America's reliance on racist and classist paradigms used to subsume our individual wills beneath systemic and violent injustice for profit. This possibility for a ritualized rebirth through the recognition of our ancestral triumphs, which forms an unbreakable bond between the living and our ancestral freedom fighters through the cellular memory of our DNA, is one way to create holistic well-being. It is a psychological reinvention rooted in historical fact. Such a ritualized remembering creates a counternarrative through which blackness holds redemptive and revolutionary power over seemingly unbearable injustice spanning generations.[13]

This ritualized remembrance is made possible in the play through a nonlinear narrative structure that is in alignment with Yoruba and Bantu cosmologies, collapsing any perceived boundaries between the future, past, and present time. The city block of right now becomes the dungeon inside Elmina Castle in Ghana, where enslaved Africans were imprisoned prior to crossing the Atlantic Ocean during the Middle Passage and into this "New World" consciousness; this location, in turn, becomes the Delta swamp, our Hush Harbor, where plots for rebellion emerged alongside sanctified prayers for spiritual sustenance, and then the location returns to the city block again. In fact, we were there all along at the same time that we were in locations of the past. It is not nostalgia that governs this collapse of boundaries in time but an ability to connect to historical consciousness, memory, and meaning-making that creates the possibility for understanding and fortitude, despite chaotic life circumstances.

> IV. We make theater for the living. Let the audience shout. Be moved to dance in the aisles. Let it happen, because it already does.

> *We make*
> *Room for the living,*
> *A refuge.*

In *Gutta Beautiful*, this ritual is shared with the audience through an interactive relationship with the ensemble cast, led by the lead talker, or griot, so that the fourth wall is consistently broken, drawing the audience into a participatory role that is beyond mere spectatorship. The audience's participatory relationship with the world of the play and its ensemble cast includes call and response, but it goes beyond that as well. At key moments in the play, cast members enter the house, speaking directly to individual audience members, and there are also moments when audience members are brought into the actual performance space as active and performing participants in the ritualized drama.

The vigor with which *Gutta Beautiful* involves the audience was not limited to the play's performance on stage in the theater during its 2005 and 2006 productions in Washington, DC.[14] There were multiple spatial and cultural interventions born from the play. These interventions challenged the routine flow of our community in public spaces, asserting a ritualized rebirth and critique of Black lives' relationship to the state and its normative cultural projections on our identities.

A crew of artists came together to support the play's multimedia component. We descended upon Georgia Avenue, a major thoroughfare in DC, where the photographer Charisse Williams stood on the yellow line in the middle of the street to capture footage that the mixed-media artist Ayodele Ngozi would later photoshop into a montage projected during the play, featuring the performing artist Cher Jey Cuffie Samateh, who played Lola, the lead character. In the process of creating that montage, we had to break the law, risking arrest to tell our story and capture images, disrupting the order enforced by the yellow line, as a police officer, using the loudspeaker in his patrol car, commanded that we "get out of the street." Our art was an act of resistance to the state's control.

In 2006, as we sought ways to promote the show on a shoestring budget for the second workshop production, we brought the theater to 18th Street in Adams Morgan and down at the Waterfront in Southwest during club hours. The actors performed scenes from the play while walking alongside lines of people waiting to enter the hot night spots down by the river, and they stopped traffic while crossing 18th Street to stand on the steps of a local bar called Heaven and Hell. These disruptions were successful at removing spatial limitations of the ritual performance as it exists when confined to the theater. In a world where Black bodies are often controlled, disciplined, and terrorized, such collective action through performance ritual proves that we can take up space in profound ways without permission. This is important work. We also brought meditation and art workshops to women served by the DC Crime Victims' Compensation Unit and participants of Barrios

Unidos–Virginia Chapter's Youth Summit in partnership with the production, further extending the work beyond the theater.

■   ■   ■

Before these performances and interventions were able to happen, though, I stood, a bit uneasily, at the corner of chaos and divine, where culture-making meets the need to own the means of production. In 2004, I found myself holding a completed script that I was hungry to share with an audience, but I did not have a producer. I had joined an informal theater collective a year earlier. In that collective, we read through one other's scripts with the intention of producing a stage reading of our work at a local theater where one of the collective members held an executive position. But when I returned from a trip to Ghana in late August of 2004, I discovered that the collective had changed its shape. The original plan was no longer possible. Though collective members Cheles Rhynes and Gesel Mason of Mason-Rhynes Productions agreed to provide technical support to me at no cost, I needed a coproducer who had a sincere belief in the project's urgency. I must have troubled that need for all of two days.

After arriving at my parents' home looking down in the mouth about what I imagined was the end of my life in theater before it even got started, my father looked back at me and asked, "So, are you gonna shit or get off the pot?" It was his way of telling me to do something, or nothing. He advised that I incorporate a nonprofit arts education organization that could serve as a producing entity. My years of witnessing the go-go community create its own sustenance through collective action made the choice less daunting. In a matter of days, I gathered the paperwork necessary for incorporating a nonprofit organization and set about choosing a name for the organization to make it all real.

Simultaneously, my mother was deep inside her own ancestral history project. She was combing through archives and calling relatives, having photographs scanned and sent from the South to the North, and recording her own mother's memories on audiotape. She discovered a story about an ancestral foremother the elders in the family called Ocean Ana. My mother told me that Ocean Ana was born on the Middle Passage; her mother died shortly after her birth. Ocean Ana lived, though, giving birth to a line of survivors. So, when faced with the need to name the organization that would produce *Gutta Beautiful*, I thought about Ocean Ana, her lineage, and the countless others from whom we have all descended. I thought about the endurance, persistence, and creativity they had to maintain to survive and thrive on this side of their crossing over. I recalled the energy I felt in the dungeons of Elmina and Cape Coast, Ghana, and how that energy helped to inspire me to push forward in my life, connecting me to the continuum of rebirth and communal uplift that has been our inheritance. And I decided that I wanted the nonprofit organization to bear the name and mission of that collective legacy, its tenacity and deep-rooted love. I knew then that Ocean Ana Rising would help to birth many artistic projects by emerging and seasoned women artists. I believed we could respond to the communal need to sustain the lives and stories of Black women in the tradition of our ancestral mothers.

*

We make our own room.

> *Over yonder is the living*
> *Room and free space.*
> *We build circles,*
> *Defying capitalism's control*
> *Over our bodies' labor,*
> *A refuge, hush harbor,*
> *And jam session.*

In late 2009, I sat in a conference room at the Brecht Forum in the West Village of New York City. The Brecht Forum served as a safe space for cultural workers, activists, educators, and artists. It was home to popular education workshops, panels, and cultural events from October 1975 to May 2014. My introduction to the Brecht Forum came through my participation in the Theatre of the Oppressed Laboratory (TOPLAB) that held workshops to teach Augusto Boal's Theatre of the Oppressed technique. A friend and former member of the same theater collective through which *Gutta Beautiful* was born, Tracie Jenkins, had recommended that I travel from DC to NYC to take these workshops during the summer of 2004; she felt that studying Boal's pedagogical and aesthetic approach to community theater was a necessary alternative to what some considered the counterproductive, bourgeois tendencies of mainstream commercial theater. I hoped that my participation in these workshops would serve my own need to engage my community in urgent conversations about the economic, sociopolitical, psychological, and spiritual malaise impacting the most intimate aspects of our lives as a result of a toxic relationship between the people and the state.

Visiting the Brecht Forum during those crucial years in my development as a ritual theater practitioner affirmed my understanding of live performance as a ripe opportunity for a very necessary exchange, one through which the audience could not be expected to sit passively while enjoying entertainment from a safe emotional distance.

It was there, during those TOPLAB workshops facilitated by Claire Picher and Kayhan Irani, that I realized the political power of the call and response between performers and audience-participants as an essential ingredient to creating a space for transformation. It was also the place where I was able to connect my understanding of sacred communal ritual rooted in my study and practice of Hoodoo, Lukumi, and Bantu systems of knowledge to my work as a theater practitioner, because each workshop opened with a ritual in which we created a community altar and dedicated our work to a particular individual or purpose.

By the time I sat in that meeting at the Brecht Forum in 2009, I had moved from DC to the Bronx with a preexisting relationship with the organization, though they had moved from the humble loft in the Garment District to a much larger space in the Westbeth Artist Housing Building, across from the Hudson River, in the West Village. At that meeting, I met with Ebony Noelle Golden, CEO and visionary of Betty's Daughter Arts Collaborative (a company honoring Ebony's mother, the scholar and cultural worker Dr. Betty E. Simms), and Kazembe Balagun, who worked as the community outreach and programs director at the Brecht. Kazembe called the meeting because he understood that culture had to be at the center of any transformative movement toward greater justice. He understood that without a safe space to develop and share art uninhibited by the demands of capitalist consumerism, authentic voices intent on freedom and truth-telling would never be heard, witnessed, and experienced by the people for whom we create. So he invited me and Ebony to develop a cultural arts program in honor of Black History Month, created by and featuring the artistic labor of Black women artists in particular.

In this way we were able to cultivate a space for Black womanist culture to thrive without being ensnared by the inflexible demands and trends of consumerism. We were able to recover a transformational, bold, uncut, uncensored art with a special emphasis on the voices and lives of Black women who have often been relegated to positions far inferior to our worth as a result of the misogynistic and hypermasculine trends running rampant in the mainstream popular culture machine of the United States. We called this safe space the Women on Wednesdays Art and Culture Project (WoW). It ran at the Brecht Forum for three years, and it included a month-long performance series, alongside community art residencies for Black girls facilitated by women who performed during the performance series, and a teach-in and healing cipher for Black women who serve the community as cultural workers. Eventually some of these programs would extend beyond the month of February.

This experience helped to further my understanding of what it means to be an institution builder and womanist playwright practicing Black ritual theater with a heavy lean into the avant-garde. It is a knowing and a calling that has come down on me over many years, each play a new lesson, a new ritual, and a transformation meant to be shared. For us to share our culture on our own terms, we must not wait for mainstream cultural gatekeepers to give us permission. We must constantly push ourselves to write against inhibition and censorship. We must claim our spaces, even if it means creating outside on the city sidewalk.

■　■　■

We enter here, at the corner of chaos and divine, between the sticky place where monster consumerism strangles all art that does not conform to its conventions and the toe jam that funks that monster into submission under a blue light in the basement. We enter here, at the corner of chaos and divine, troubling the intersections between corporate monopolies and culture; between award committees and those street-corner review boards, where the people sit wide-legged on milk crates out front the bodega. We enter here, between monolithic metanarratives of blackness and the wild, free truths blaring just beyond our windows on any city any black heart beat any black trip to the future from the ocean's deep blue-black-rooted past of brine and bones. We enter here, at the corner of chaos and divine in our womanist ways, because we can't keep our hands off our hips and all the mothers before us whisper blood secrets, survival stories, and ways to stand without stooping inside this room, askew, in a house called these United States of America.

Notes

Epigraph is from Larry Neal, *Juju Research Papers in Afro-American Studies* (Spring 1975), iii.

1 Hazzard-Donald, *Mojo Workin'*, 35.

2 I want to clarify that I am using the term "African American" to emphasize the multiple histories of geographic crossings, trade routes, and transcultural points of contact between Africa and the Americas. I am not specifying the countries of either continent because there are many. I am not using "African American" as a container for those people or that culture that is specific to the United States of America. I am extending this term to include cultural forms and people from throughout the diaspora in the Americas. I recognize that this is not a popular usage of the term; it is not universally embraced in such a way. This is simply how I am using the term for the purposes of this exploration. Notice that I am also exchanging the term "African American" for "Black" when I am not emphasizing the popular culture industry. Again, this is for the purposes of organizing information. Thus "African American" is a term that harnesses the labor, commerce, and geography of the Black diaspora.

3 Teer, "Needed," 84.

4 Here, I want to acknowledge the scholarship of Dr. Omi Osun Jones. Her book *Theatrical Jazz: Performance, Ase, and the Power of the Present Moment* illuminates a kindred community of artists and work which "challenge the traditional western theatre making in general, and Black U.S. theatre aesthetics in particular" (5). Jones writes that theatrical jazz artists "have been relegated to the relative obscurity of avant-garde or experimental status," which means they are often "invisible in the Black Theatre world that resists the expansive Blackness and queer realities that characterize much of their work. In an avant-garde context, the Black aesthetics remain appropriated, fetishized idiosyncrasies rather than historically rooted through the resistive, feminist, antiracist paradigms they employ" (5). In acknowledging my own resonance with Jones's theatrical jazz scholarship I am also noting that I came to *Theatrical Jazz* after writing "At the Corner of Chaos and Divine." I first met Dr. Jones in New York City at The Lark, where her long-time collaborator and partner Sharon Bridgforth was sharing her theatrical jazz installation *River SEE* for Keith Joseph Adkins's New Black Fest. I did not read *Theatrical Jazz* until a couple of years after meeting her. I provide these details because of the deep *simpatico* I feel with Dr. Jones's work. We all arrive in our own ways. Mine is one. There are many.

5 Harrison, "(Re)Branding Black Theatre."

6 Junkyard Band, *The Word/Sardines and Pork 'n' Beans* (New York: Def Jam, 1986).

7 Baraka, "Bopera Theory," 378.

8 Toni Cade Bambara, interviewed by Kay Bonetti, *American Audio Prose Library*, Columbia, Mo, 1982.

9 In Palo Mayombe, which has its origins in Bantu cosmology, a Yayi Nkisi Malongo is a female priest.

10 Hazard-Donald, *Mojo Workin'*, 28.

11 Hazard-Donald, *Mojo Workin'*, 86.

12 Shange, *for colored girls*, 20.

13 In 2004, I took a trip to Ghana led by Dr. Wade Nobles, Dr. Naim Akbar, and Dr. Marimba Ani. On that trip, we retraced the journey taken by enslaved Africans

from the north of Ghana in Paga to the dungeons further south in Elmina and Cape Coast, where the enslaved Africans were held in bondage until they embarked on ships that sailed across the Atlantic Ocean to the Americas during the transatlantic slave trade. The scholars leading this journey organized our movements through Ghana as a physicalized reenactment comprising a series of rituals that could create psychological wholeness for descendants of the scattering of a people and their cultures. This journey made a crucial impact on my identity reformation and on my artistic practice.

14 Company members during the 2005 and 2006 productions of *Gutta Beautiful* included the following designers and artists: Eric Ruffin, Sybil Roberts, Cher Jey Cuffie-Samateh, Jalila Smith, Isaiah Johnson, Robin Marcus, Vanya Michelle Robinson, Sofale Ellis, Marcel Taylor, Robert "Bobby" Hogans, Tosha Grantham, Shi-Queeta Lee, Reggie Ray, Luqman Salim, Charisse Williams, Ayodele Ngozi, Kamau Donadelle/The Original DJ Silver, Karma Mayet Johnson, Roxi Victorian, Chaela Phillips, Anna B. Christa Severo, Mathew Miller, Jali D, Candice Adkins, Kiyanna Cox, Kyle Jones, Cynthia Brown. Each of these individuals was invaluable to the development of the play and its performance life as it moved on to New York City, where it was produced by Woodie King Jr.'s New Federal Theatre at Abrons Arts Center (2007), and then to Woodbrook, Trinidad, where it was produced by Isoke Edwards's Griot Productions at the Little Carib Theatre in 2011.

References

Bambara, Toni Cade. Interview by Kay Bonetti. *American Audio Prose Library*, Columbia, MO, 1982.

Baraka, Amiri. "Bopera Theory." In *Black Theatre: Ritual Performance in the African Diaspora*, edited by Paul Carter Harrison. Philadelphia: Temple University Press, 2002.

Harrison, Paul Carter. "(Re)Branding Black Theatre." *Black Renaissance Noire* 13, 2/3 (Fall 2013) 70.

Hazzard-Donald, Katrina. *Mojo Workin': The Old African American HooDoo System.* Urbana: University of Illinois Press, 2013.

Jones, Omi Osun Joni L. *Theatrical Jazz: Performance, Ase, and the Power of the Present Moment.* Columbus: Ohio State University Press, 2015.

Neal, Larry. *Juju Research Papers in Afro-American Studies* (Spring 1975): iii.

Shange, Ntozake. *for colored girls who have considered suicide/when the rainbow is enuf.* New York: Scribner, 2010.

Teer, Barbara Ann. "Needed: A New Image." In *SOS—Calling All Black People: A Black Arts Movement Reader*, edited by John H. Bracey Jr., Sonia Sanchez, and James Smethurst. Amherst: University of Massachusetts Press, 2014.

AN INTERVIEW WITH MARK ANTHONY NEAL / JANUARY 9, 2016

What is the state of Black pop culture in the public sphere and as an intellectual field of inquiry in the twenty-first century?

There is a certain kind of richness to this stuff that is being produced now, particularly in the mainstream. And now with all these different platforms, there is so much more stuff that is being produced that we get to see, that we get to hear. I worry with you [Lisa B. Thompson] particularly about the public realm and the quality of the criticism that we see. There are scholars now who are writing about popular culture and get to write about it in public spaces. What Brittney [Brittney Cooper] has been doing with *Salon* is a good example of that, but there are too many folks who are writing, repping their journal, magazine, website, writing about popular culture, and there is just no historical context. Can you write about a Spike Lee film and talk about how odd the filmmaking is if you have never actually watched other Spike Lee films? So that you would know that that is his style. That is what he does, right? There is nothing crazy about it. It is the reason why he calls it a Spike Lee joint. Too often folks, because they are trying to hit deadlines and their magazine wants a piece up tomorrow, they will review albums and things like that and not actually have listened to the previous work of the artist. I think there is a lot of that that goes on, and it becomes very troubling—whereas, when as scholars, obviously, but even those of us who have been writing for public realms, we're not putting too much work out there that is not in conversation with a broader archive, right? That—that is how we work. I'm not sure writers are feeling that they have the time or necessarily even the tools to be able to do that kind of work in this particular environment.

> *How do you see Stuart Hall's theorization of the "black" in Black popular culture influencing your intellectual engagement with Black cultural productions?*

I always loved that particular piece of his, particularly because midway through the essay, he talks about thinking about blackness in different realms. And particularly when he talks about style. When he talks about folks who think that is just a mere covering, a mere husk, but some of the real richness of blackness is occurring around these elements of style. I think in terms of theorizing about popular culture, Black popular culture, twenty-five to thirty years ago that was really a game-changer, because it gets us into this conversation about form versus content. We all think we know what blackness looks like in terms of the content of Black popular culture, but what does that look like in terms of form? How do we talk about folks who are working in the abstract? How do you talk about folks who are doing more experimental work, Spike Lee being one example of that? How that experimentation is actually something that is actually black in the context of trying to push the contours of what blackness is. I think about some of the work Margo Crawford is working on now—so much of the work I think we do on Black popular culture now is framed by some of the demands of the Black Arts Movement. And very often we read about the Black Arts Movement thinking that blackness was a known entity—like the end game was to know this thing that was black, as opposed to thinking about blackness as something that was ever-changing, that was something that was more fluid. And what the Black Arts Movement was, was to create a space to have the freedom to deal with that fluidity as opposed to the freedom to say "We're Black" and "Black is this" and then police that space of what we think of as blackness. I think that's part of what Hall is pushing at, in a very different context. . . .

Do you feel the digital age affects the production, reception, and dissemination of Black pop culture in ways that compel us to continue revisiting Hall's piece but to also build upon it? If yes, how do you see contemporary theorists and critics building upon Hall's work given the changes the digital age has produced? If no, why do you feel the digital age does not compel scholars to revisit Hall and build upon his work?

In some ways I think about, how do we think about Hall within this context, right? There is a way in which the Stuart Hall that circulates as cutting-edge Stuart Hall in this moment is not really talking about popular culture, and in some ways not really talking about race. It is like Stuart Hall has been embraced by folks who do not have interest in Black studies and popular culture. The fact that he is included in that early reader [edited by Michele Wallace and Gina Dent] was a way in which Black intellectuals were embracing Stuart Hall before some of the other folks were, so I think about it in that context. I wonder who is teaching Stuart Hall on race and popular culture now. We know there are grad students who are coming through doing work on cultural studies who do not know that Stuart Hall essay. I'm just being honest. So that is one piece of it. I think the digital turn is important, because what it has done is it has made the archive more explicit and more expansive. There is material now that we can go recover that we could not have recovered twenty years ago. What it allows is for us to make theoretical interventions from the contemporary into the past, because now we know there is material in the past where we can make those interventions that could not have been made before. Think about all the work being done on late nineteenth-century and early twentieth-century Black queer identity that could not have been done without access to these digital archives. If you think about a piece like Treva Lindsey and Jessica Marie Johnson do on the sexuality of someone like Harriet Tubman, because there is now more of an archive, both digital and otherwise to think about those kinds of questions. I think it changes the nature of the work, and I think that is one of the reasons why Hall still remains very relevant within that context. . . .

I think it is safe to say that one of the reasons you founded the Center for Arts, Digital Culture and Entrepreneurship at Duke University was because you believe social media plays a critical role in the contemporary academic study of Black lives. Popular culture has occupied a thorny space in the academy because, for some academics (and taxpayers), popular culture is not a legitimate field of academic inquiry. Do you see (Black) social media playing a role in expanding the academic legitimacy of popular culture studies since Ray Browne's inauguration of the field in 1973, when he founded the one and only department of popular culture?

So, you know, a couple of things. I think the value of social media to Black studies is that it builds connections between scholars working in the field and actual people. I think it breaks down some walls that are important. I always describe social media—Black Twitter in particular—as a space that is hungry for information. And in the absence of good information, folks will take whatever information they can get, so I think it is actually very important for Black scholars to be in that space to provide that kind of access to information. The value of it in the long run is that you get to see clearer the way that the work that we are producing in the academy can actually impact people in everyday places. All the syllabi that came out of the aftermath of Charleston and Ferguson was a way—and then suddenly all this work that was getting produced in the academy was suddenly accessible to people who just do not have access to the academy in the same way. I often get into conversations with the media folks at Duke News and Communications because they will often describe things that I do as Black popular culture. And I always issue a corrective that pop culture, Black or otherwise, is sort of ephemera. It is "Kanye and Kim went to Whole Foods," and someone will write a piece about that and it will get 100,000 views, whereas popular culture or Black popular culture is an actual field of study. And we have to be very clear to make those kinds of distinctions, because what you hear—very often the scholars who do public work around Black popular culture—is that they're thinking too much about it. That they're taking it too seriously. And that is an issue, because their model for it is this other stuff that kind of just passes it on. So I think we always have to be clear about drawing those clear lines about work being generated from a field of study and a field of inquiry that is very different than what essentially comes down to Black celebrity reporting. When you look at some of these major online sites—Black ones—whether it's *Ebony* or *The Root*, they are all trying to find a balance. A balance that justifies what they do, that produces certain kinds of pieces that get a whole lot of eyeballs, but then also creating a space where you can have a little bit more of a critical view of some things. Ironically, I think *Ebony* does that balance more successfully than *The Root* does.

*For those who register popular culture as the culture of the
people and a site where democracy is interrogated, the art of "branding" occupies an important space in how scholars theorize the relationship between race, citizenship, and neoliberal consumption. Can
you discuss the vicissitudes of branding in Black popular culture—
what are its benefits and pitfalls in the twenty-first century?*

I always want to be careful to make a distinction between thinking about
popular culture and thinking about corporatized youth culture. So we have
these conversations all the time about what hip hop is. What you hear on the
radio is a very small percentage of what is being produced in the name of hip
hop. The vast majority of it you never hear. What you do hear is very care-
fully curated by very successful commercial entities for the purpose of consuming it. Call that what it is. It is corporatized, commercial culture. The
seven or eight rappers that you see all the time are very lucratively rewarded
for their work, but they do not make up the totality of what is being produced. So I think we need to make those very clear distinctions. Popular culture is something that is popular; it resides with the people. Very often it is
not going to be something sanctioned and branded by corporations, because
that is doing a different kind of work. So how do we find a way in which we
do critical interventions that take on corporatization but also build community for the work outside of the mainstream, much more on the margins?
I think the best scholars are able to go in and out of those conversations. To
understand the interventions like, why work on Jay-Z as opposed to Tef Poe?
Because Jay-Z is recognizable to a broader population of folks, so if you bring
a critical lens to that it does a certain kind of work, but that also means you
try to bring that critical lens to someone who is not on the landscape. It is a
both/and dynamic.

*Do you foresee any additional critical shifts in Black pop culture, as it
relates to social media in the next twenty years, or do we even have a
language to discuss the future changes in technology and their effect
on Black popular culture?*

It's so fast. The thing that has changed so powerfully, at least in this moment of social media and technology, is the platforms on which people can
produce. Folks can make very quick interventions that demand our attention in ways that were not the case when folks would make interventions
twenty-five years ago; we would not find out about those for five years. It is

very different now, so I think, given who has access to the technology and what they are bringing to the table, there are so many different interventions that can be made now. I think it is hard to predict what the culture is going to look like. I imagine if you were to go to some cultural workers—Black cultural workers—thirty years ago, as they were thirty years ago and presented them some of the interventions that have been made in the contemporary moment, it would be foreign to them. Because interventions have been made that they could not even conceptualize. They would not have been able to conceptualize a Black trans presence in mainstream culture thirty years ago. It just would not make any sense to them. When Lisa [Thompson] talks about the proliferation of a Black stage presence on Broadway in terms of playwrights, for those folks who were producing *The Wiz* forty years ago, they cannot even conceptualize that. And so I think it is hard even for us now not knowing what kind of new technology is going to emerge, what kind of new platforms are going to emerge—to really even imagine what that is. It is difficult enough now hanging on. I was just going to add, in terms of my own practices as a scholar and someone trying to theorize about the culture, I recognize, for instance, that I do not have a grasp of all the language to talk about how a younger generation of theorists are talking about gender. When I hear references to cisgender and transgender, this is not—for lack of a better way to describe it—it is not my native language. So I find myself even in that regard trying to learn the new theoretical languages around thinking about Black identity. At the same time, I am trying to keep up on what seems to be a hyperreduction of texts both in the literal sense but also in terms of cultural texts that we have to respond to.

IV. LOVING BLACKNESS

THE BOOTY DON'T LIE / PLEASURE, AGENCY, AND RESISTANCE IN BLACK POPULAR DANCE

Takiyah Nur Amin

And the booty will always tell the truth of a given situation. *You can always tell what a community or a person truly believes by studying the actions of their booties at any given time.* They can claim to love this other person or culture or believe in this peaceful god, or really want freedom but do their actions prove it? Their actions, what their booties do, or don't do, that tells you the truth. · JANELLE MONÁE (Emphasis added)

People are known by the records they keep. If it's not in the records, it will be said that it did not happen. That's what history is, a keeping of records. · ALICE WALKER

Black Dance: Beyond Taxonomy, Beyond Pathology

Black dance—both concert and vernacular, sacred and secular—has been explored in a variety of ways in contemporary scholarship. Citing Black dances in the diaspora as a repository of African aesthetics, Kariamu Welsh, Brenda Dixon-Gottschild, and others intervened in dance studies by situating the movement vocabularies of Black dancing bodies at the center of scholarly inquiry to expose African retentions and characteristics, both subtle and overt.[1] Susan Manning, John Perpener, and Thomas DeFrantz have engaged Black dance—particularly as it relates to the landscape of twentieth-century American concert dance—as a crucial site for historical research and the development of new considerations in performance theory.[2] Notably, as Black choreographers began to create for the concert stage, many celebrated artists imported, restaged, and made use of Black vernacular or popular dance forms in their work. Katherine Dunham's *Barrelhouse Blues* (1938) made use of popular dances of the period and is centered around the "Slow-Drag," a pelvis-to-pelvis couple's dance made popular in jook joints at that time. Alvin Ailey's *Blues Suite*, his first evening-length work, premiered in 1958 and showcased stylized versions of Black popular dances derived from his youth in rural Rogers, Texas. The staging and repurposing of Black popular dance informs much of the backbone of contemporary Black concert dance today, with the work of Camille A. Brown, Rennie Harris, Ronald K. Brown, and others as testimony. Similarly, familiar movement traditions that are today celebrated as theatrical dance forms, including tap and jazz dance, are rooted very specifically in the social dances that emanated from newly emancipated Black communities in the United States, as seen in the work of Jacqui Malone and Katrina Hazzard-Donald.[3] Hip-hop dances have had a similar migratory path, from the urban Black and Latino communities of their origin to the concert stage, music video, film, and television.

Despite the pervasive presence and generative impact of Black popular dance, it is often cited as confirmation or evidence of Black deviance and the unsuitability of Black people for the project of citizenship. The ongoing push to criminalize Black youth for breakdancing in subway cars, for example, is justified by highlighting the dance as the domain of vagrants who endanger passengers with their antics.[4] Similarly, the suspension and punishment of students from a San Diego high school for creating and posting a video of students twerking suggests the heightened anxiety that Black popular dance can bring to those in mainstream positions of authority: surely, dancing *that way* is evidence of the students' aberrant and hypersexual behavior.[5] Even the National Football League has taken a stand on the matter, updating their 1984 rule to decry "choreographed celebrations" or "excessive celebration" on the field when a player has had a successful outcome or touchdown, suggesting that the presence of popular dance is read as unsportsmanlike behavior. Players have been punished with fines and other penalties for ignoring this rule.[6] These readings of popular dances that emanate from Black communities affirm the notion that Black bodies, in which these dances have their genesis, are best understood as the site and source for every negative human behavior; these readings suggest that bad habits or behavior somehow reach their zenith in the very personhood and physicality of Black people. Undoubtedly, racism and white supremacy hinge on the notion that it is not structural or political barriers that impinge on Black life but the very culture and habits—dance included—that reside within Black bodies that are, in fact, the problem. To that end, Black bodies are always already wrong—troubled, tainted, unworthy, dispossessed. By extension, Black dancing bodies are an even larger problem as both the dances and the bodies in which they find their origin are deemed pathology in motion. The terror and indignities of kidnapping, chattel slavery, lynching, stop and frisk, mass incarceration, and misogynoir are all forms of violence levied against the very being and materiality of Black flesh as a way to tame, discipline, and/or punish Black bodies for being purveyors of deviant culture; they are convicted by their speech, dress, hair, skin color, and dance. Perhaps the lack of sustained critical engagement with Black popular dance in both public and academic scholarship is rooted in the collective trauma of the shaming, exploitation, and abuse of Black bodies. *Why, after all, would anyone want to study something that emanates from a body so worthy of ridicule and disdain?* When this perspective is considered in light of the Western notion that dance is a "feminized" act and therefore inherently less valuable as a site of knowledge production, it is not a surprise that discussions of Black popular dance very seldom find themselves at the center of rigorous public scholarship or thoughtful public discourse.[7]

I contend that there is another way. Building on the existing work of dance scholars noted above, I posit that we might understand Black popular dances and the possibility they embody by moving beyond taxonomy, beyond pathology. Writing about Black popular dance for the sake of cataloguing its characteristics is perhaps too simple; the act of merely looking at the body to truncate and disassemble it can rob us of the dance and leave our understanding in tatters. This act of classification and dismemberment (i.e., What is the head doing? What are the hips doing?) distills Black dances into easily consumable parts that belie the complexity of the whole and obscure any sense of the ideas that are residing within the movement. Engaging Black popular dance demands resistance to the tendency to boil the dances down to a laundry list of cultural characteristics. These aesthetic markers are points of departure for sure, but what needs tending is the ways in which Black popular dances embody ideas, concepts, and memory. What are the ideas that are implicated and alluded to when we "pop, lock, and drop it"? What ideologies are implicated in a body roll? Beyond any negative readings that have been projected onto these movement vocabularies and the bodies from which they emanate, it is possible to read Black popular dances as more than confirmations of cultural deviance. I propose that these dances are sites for bodily enactments of pleasure, agency, and resistance, and consider that moving one's body in the manner of one's choosing is perhaps as revolutionary an act as many others. Black popular dances are resistive precisely because they push back against that idea that Black bodies are best when used to service the needs of a system that has little regard for their existence. These dances are a harvest, a bounty of meanings that require thinking beyond thick movement description or the mere capture of dance on film or video. Engaging and perpetuating the value of Black vernacular dance requires a consideration of the ideas and meanings therein and an intimacy with the nuances that the dances themselves represent.

Black Popular Dance as Possibility

I define "Black dance" as the multiple movement idioms that arise in Black African culture and those that emerge as they are filtered through the experiences of Black people as a result of assimilating various cultural influences. I understand social and popular dances to be those that are generally recognizable, easily accessed, and widely acceptable, even if that last descriptor is up for some debate when considering Black popular dance.[8] When I think of my own experiences doing Black popular dances, those movements are tethered inextricably to memories—places, sensations, experiences whose meanings ultimately become a part of the "stuff" of the dance itself. As the sociologist Paul Connerton writes, "the past, as it were, [is] sedimented" in the body.[9] Gesture, movement, and dance are ways to get at, to reengage, to remember; dancing is an act of putting the body back together, from a truncated analysis into a complex, integrated whole, composed of an ever-changing flurry of ideas that are at once deeply personal and informed by the contexts from which they emanate. The anthropologist Janet Goodridge explains that "kinesthetic memories . . . may range from snapshot impressions to short or longer sequences of movement" and that "kinesthetic memory of movement behavior [can arise] from what is learned in social and ritual contexts."[10] This suggests that there are other ways of knowing and of accessing knowledge that resides in the body, a notion that highlights Brenda Farnell's idea that "memory [or the past] remains with us not only in words but also in our neuromuscular patterning and kinesthetic memory."[11] Without a consideration of the ideas and knowledge that reside in the dancing body, understandings of Black popular dance are rendered incomplete. Beneath imposed readings of Black bodily enactment lie memories and experiences that exist within those movements. Critical engagement with Black popular dance becomes a way to challenge prevailing assumptions, reshaping collective narratives and equipping one to get in between, up under, around, and through the readings of Black popular dance that are meant to devalue and oversimplify. In this sense, the record or history of both individual Black and collective experiences, memories, and knowledge resides within the body and is manifest, in part, through Black popular dance. The dances become a way to give voice to Black dancing bodies as repositories of trauma and pleasure, abuse and agency. Popular dances function as a means by which to connect across history and diaspora through the recognition of diverse cultural experiences. Dance challenges the contours of what we know, of what is knowable, of how we know. As human beings shape and inform cultural systems and processes through their practices, Black popular dances must be considered as formative, not just as reactive or as unchanging archives. The question becomes: How do Black popular dances shape, inform, and record experiences and speak ideas? What new possibilities are presented as movement vocabularies continue to emerge?

Pleasure, Agency, and Resistance

Given that Black dance has and continues to be a source for mainstream conceptions of the popular, it is all the more important not to diminish it in its vernacular form as a pop fad that can be reduced to a singular narrative or experience. There is no one single authoritative reading of any particular dance, and contested meanings might reside within the same embodied enactment, juxtaposing hot and cool, pleasure and pain, and conflicting representations of the self. No single story is sufficient for the understanding of

Black popular dances, and the presence of tensions and dichotomies needn't be reconciled; all can arise in time and space to occupy the dance. No single narrative encompasses the lived experiences of Black people, and as such, no single story is our dancing. As a scholarly project, engagement with Black popular dance must be expansive, challenging the false boundaries of nation, geography, and academic discipline. By rethinking disciplinary and national boundaries we have the potential to engage with Black popular dance as "vital acts of transfer, transmitting social knowledge, memory and a sense of identity through reiteration." If we accept that performance—the repetition of acts that constitute our citizenship, gender, ethnicity, sexual identity, and so on—functions as epistemology, then dance specifically offers a way of meaning-making.[12] Dance can communicate concepts, deliver pronouncements and indictments of social structures, embody memories, and carry within it the possibility of shaping and reconsidering notions of the self. The Black popular dances twerking, the Harlem Shake, and J-Setting embody these possibilities.

While twerking only recently entered mainstream consciousness, its roots stretch back to at least the early 1990s in Black communities in New Orleans. It was 1993 when DJ Jubilee first made use of the term in the New Orleans bounce anthem "Do the Jubilee All," directing partiers to "twerk baby, twerk baby, twerk, twerk, twerk" in response to his music. Later popularized by queer artists Katey Red and Big Freedia, twerking as an accompanying dance to the Big Easy's indigenous bounce music was familiar to many well before Miley Cyrus's attempt to perform the dance on MTV's 2013 Video Music Awards. Popularized a decade earlier by Atlanta rap duo the Ying Yang Twins in their debut single, "Whistle While You Twerk" and by other hip-hop artists, including Cheeky Blakk, Bubba Sparxxx, and Timbaland, mainstream pop artists such as Justin Timberlake and Beyoncé referenced twerking in their song lyrics as well.[13]

While variations on the dance abound, the execution of twerking requires bent knees and the relaxed but persistent and jubilant shaking of one's backside; alternatively, one's buttocks may be alternated and isolated in twerking. Twerking can be executed in standing, squatting, or bent-over positions and in some instances is carried out standing on one's head. The dance's iconic movement demonstrates kinship with West African movement aesthetics and shows a strong resemblance to Mapouka. Known in Côte d'Ivoire as "la dance fussier" or the dance of the behind, Mapouka is executed in both traditional and ceremonial contexts and more recently as a popular dance among Ivoirian youth. Of Mapouka, Maureen Monahan writes:

The more modern version—and the one most closely related to twerking—is considered obscene and suggestive by some, and its traditional roots haven't immunized it against controversy. In fact, the public performance of modern Mapouka by groups such as Les Tueuses (The Killers), was outlawed in the 1980s; the Ivoirian government cited lewdness as the reason for the ban. After that government was toppled by a military coup around 2000, Mapouka performances were rendered legal once again. However, despite (or possibly due to) its prohibition, the infectious dance style had already spread throughout coastal West Africa and even taken up roots in the U.S.[14]

Similar indictments of twerking have not been enacted in the United States, though "twerking" was added to the Oxford English Dictionary in 2013.

Beyond the booty shaking that is central to twerking, it is a dance that, due to its concentration in the lower regions of the body, upsets traditional Black respectability politics that privilege chastity. Hampton University went so far as to use a PowerPoint slide during a student orientation stating that "ladies do not twerk" and that "Hampton men do not take twerkers home to their mothers."[15] In a blog post on the Crunk Feminist Collective on August 29, 2013, the feminist scholar Brittney Cooper (Professor Crunk) writes, "There is [a] time and place for sexy gyration with wild abandon, and Black folks should never concede that this isn't a part of our inheritance. We recognize as we participate that ratchet is a part of who we are, but not the whole picture. And it is a part of our experience that made the blues and jazz and hip hop necessary, not just for entertainment but for survival."

Cooper's words animate some of the ideas and possibilities within twerking. The persistent presence of this kind of movement evidences an understated truth: *this dance feels good.* The relaxed posture of the lower body needed to execute twerking liberates the body from being tightly held at the base of the spine. Twerking expresses a connection to the diaspora through movement with its emphasis on polycentrism in the body (movement emanating from multiple centers), polyrhythm, and the use of a bent or soft knee posture to execute the dance. Black dance scholars have written at length about the ways in which these markers of African-derived movement vocabularies find themselves remixed and recycled within the context of Black social dance and movement practice.[16] It is plausible that the currents that suggest a connection between Mapouka and twerking in terms of their execution are not necessarily a result of immigration or U.S. residents traveling to the continent per se, but are more likely the result of the persistence of West African movement aesthetics surfacing and resurfacing in social dances in the United States, as with the movements that made up jazz dance at the turn of the twentieth century. Moreover, this insistence in twerking on "freeing up" the parts of the body—the release of the spine and freedom of the hip girdle and pelvis—needed for reproduction and regeneration of a community hints at a kind of resistance to persistent puritanical ideals about sex that suggest the body as the site for deviance: twerking often literally turns this notion upside-down by privileging the unfettered movement of the body below the navel. Given the ways in which Black reproduction has been controlled, exploited, and commodified through enslavement, forced sterilization, and other means of violent control, it is perhaps no wonder that these same communities would develop—as a resistive technology—movement vocabularies that celebrate their ability to reproduce themselves, even within the context of state violence and inhumane treatment. In the twerk there is a possibility for pleasure, for cultural connection, and for freedom of movement that pushes back against social domination. While such meanings may not be articulated by all of its practitioners, the dance itself suggests a complexity that is about much more than the shaking of one's backside.

Similar to the mainstream fascination with twerking, the Harlem Shake is a dance form that has recently captured imaginations, albeit as a result of gross misrepresentation. In 2013, short videos were posted to YouTube of riotous, often costumed partiers shaking and bouncing their torsos to the song "Harlem Shake" by Baauer, an electronic musician from the United States. As these viral videos caught the attention of news stations and college campuses across the country, residents of Harlem and others familiar with the dance's origins and iterations began to speak out on YouTube and in interviews about the history of what was being touted as a "new" dance form.[17]

The Harlem Shake was initiated by Albert Leopold Boyce, a resident of the northern city, on basketball courts some three decades before its recent resurgence. Boyce would perform the dance as a part of half-time entertainment at basketball tournaments at the world-famous Rucker Park. In a rare interview, Boyce noted, "It's a drunken shake, it's an alcoholic shake, but its fantastic, everybody loves it and everybody appreciates it. And it's glowing with glory. . . . It was a drunken dance, you know, from the mummies, in the tombs. That's what mummies used to do. They was all wrapped up and taped up. So they couldn't really move, all they could do was shake."[18]

Boyce, who died of heart failure in 2006, suggests that while the dance began with him as a drunken reverie it also hinted at the way mummies would move if awakened from death, trying to remove their bandages. The dance includes popping-style movements in the upper body, with emphasis on the shoulder and side-to-side locking movements. Practitioners may infuse other movements on top of the basic Harlem Shake structure, including splits and isolations of the head and neck. First known in the community as the "Al. B.," the Harlem Shake first garnered broader recognition in G. Dep's music videos for "Special Delivery" and especially "Let's Get It." Both videos featured Harlem native, music mogul, and G. Dep's former producer Sean "P. Diddy" Combs executing the dance. The Harlem Shake has also been referenced in music lyrics by hip-hop artists Missy Elliott and Nelly.[19]

The persistence of Harlem community residents in decrying the meme-style iteration of the Harlem Shake first popularized in 2013 suggests that the dance itself is about more than Boyce as an individual; that it is a dance that represents community identity. Taken together with other dances emanating from Harlem in the past three decades, including the Chicken Noodle Soup, the Harlem Shake functions as a text for what it means to be from that particular community. While the dance is surely executed by persons from other locales, its origins were critical enough for community members to declare it as their own and dismiss the meme as "inauthentic." This dance is intimately tied to "place"; it "belongs" to a community that in the past thirty years has seen the worst of urban blight and gentrification. Extending Boyce's drunken-mummy-shake metaphor the dance embodies a desire to shake loose what is holding one in, to throw off one's constrictive bandages and receive new life. The Harlem Shake suggests an act of claiming one's beloved origins while embodying a desire for self-determination and a breaking of boundaries, self-imposed or otherwise. This embodied push to combat being held back or held down points to an embodied agency in the dance; the Harlem Shake becomes emblematic of the capacity of a particular community to act independently and make their own choices.

Originating in the 1970s, J-Setting is another increasingly popular Black dance form. The name is derived from the majorettes at Jackson State University, known as the Prancing J-Settes. Originally known as the Prancing Jaycettes, the group was first developed under the leadership of Shirley Middleton, who sponsored and advised the group from 1970 to 1975. Middleton, a former majorette and ballet dancer, approached the university's sixth president, Dr. John A. Peoples, to ask that the majorettes be allowed to "put the baton down," removing the centrality of twirling from their routines to focus on developing and executing more intricate dance routines. Referred to as "the thrill of a thousand eyes," the Prancing J-Settes have performed on national television, and their dance style has spawned today's J-Setting dance phenomenon.[20]

J-Setting has a call-and-response structure, whereby the leader of the group initiates dance steps first and is then joined or followed by the others. The dance performance includes intricate formations, similar to those used by a collegiate marching band; the group will also march in rows organized by height. One critical aspect of J-Setting is marching with high knee lifts or "high stepping": in this style of march, alternating legs lift with a bent knee but the foot must be brought up to the height of the opposite knee before returning to the ground. J-Setting also makes use of what the Philadelphia-based choreographer Jumatatu Poe calls "sharp explosive movements choreographed in tightly executed routines."[21]

While J-Setting has found its way into the mainstream, being deployed in music videos by Beyoncé ("Single Ladies") and on the Lifetime Channel's popular show *Bring It!*, the dance has become popular as a kind of competitive dance among men in the gay African American club scene. During the late 1970s, male students observed the practice sessions and performances of the Prancing J-Settes, bringing the dance movement back to their own local communities. Today groups like the Prancing Elites compete in J-Setting dance-offs with groups at various gay cultural events across the country.

What to make of the J-Setting phenomenon, which finds its genesis on an HBCU campus and moves into Black queer club culture? When Middleton took over sponsorship and advising of the Prancing J-Settes in 1971, she established requirements for the team such as academic standards, attire, and deportment; no member of the all-female auxiliary was allowed to "display any mannerism and stature of anything less than a model citizen."[22] This remains a core value of the Prancing J-Settes today. By promoting perfection and precision in both the dance routines and public demeanor of the auxiliary members, Middleton inculcated within J-Setting culture an emphasis on crisp, high-quality execution of steps, good-natured competition, and a focus on self-presentation as art. The existence, predominantly in the South, of Black, all–male J-Setting groups alongside the presence of the original Prancing J-Settes and other female teams of varying ages suggests that the dance creates a space for the queering of gendered identities. Male J-Setting teams wear costumes that are very similar to the ones worn by the women's group, including knee-high white boots, capes, and leotards. The dance opens a space to resist socially acceptable and stereotypical notions of gendered identities: Black gay men who J-Sett can push back against social scripts about what is appropriate or suitable for men to engage in. Similarly, the hyperstylized, hyperfeminine deportment of Black women who J-Sett (as evidenced by the emphasis on long, flowing hair and movements designed to highlight the curvature of the hips, buttocks, and breasts) creates a space where they can access markers of beauty and femininity that are often reserved for non-Black women.

While the presence of predominantly Black, gay male J-Setting groups has grown to include the widely known Prancing Elites as well as the Memphis Elite, J-Phi (Atlanta, Georgia), X-Men (Grambling, Louisiana), and Detroit Danz Zone, their presence hasn't eclipsed Black women who are proficient in the form. The Prancing J-Settes at Jackson State University have maintained their visibility for over thirty years and have performed not only at football games with the JSU marching band but also in music videos and at the NAACP Awards. Similar groups abound at other historically black colleges including Howard University's Ooh La La! Dance Line, which performs movements similar to the classic interpretation of the Prancing J-Settes. The popular television show *Bring It!* showcases the work of the entrepreneur, teacher, and choreographer Dianna Williams and features the Dancing Dolls and other predominantly Black girl dance teams in the U.S. South competing in hip-hop, J-Setting, and other dance vocabularies.

The J-Setting done by the all-male Prancing Elites and similar groups shouldn't be read as merely an appropriation and reembodiment of Black female performance. It is important to remember that at its origin, the context out of which J-Setting emerges privileges the space as single-gender and homosocial. Moreover, the aspects of J-Setting that privilege hyperstylized deportment is perhaps better understood when taken on by gay men as a desire to embody and express this aspect of southern football culture. As J-Setting becomes a site where dancers are celebrated and accepted by viewers willing to be entertained and inspired by the form, it is telling that gay men who may be perceived as deviant take up the dance to challenge the boundaries of social acceptance. Read in this way, the existence of the Alabama State University Honey Beez, a group of plus-size Black women dancers who perform with the school's marching band, suggests that J-Setting can function as a site whereby those considered outside of or beyond the confines of narrow readings of beauty can challenge those dominant social assumptions.

Taken collectively these readings of specific Black popular dances, though not exhaustive, demonstrate an interest in the meanings and ideas embodied in the movement of these vernacular dances. More than "steps," Black popular dances can function as a site for multiple representations of pleasure, agency, and resistance.

Conclusion

Black dances are more than a repository of aesthetics or cultural characteristics. They are ideas and meaning in motion. Sustained, critical engagement with Black vernacular dances is an opportunity to consider those ideas more thoroughly and access the collective meanings they embody, not in an effort to reassert some grand narrative to which all Black people ascribe but as a means by which we might uncover voices and experiences that have been understudied or undertheorized. Whose voices and experiences have been left out of the dominant narrative? Dance is an act of remembrance, a chance to incorporate ideas from the fringes of our consciousness into our understanding of Black life, past and present, without sacrificing the complexity of our own lived experience. In endeavoring to write about Black popular dance, we have a ripe possibility to reassemble ideas and ways of knowing that are articulated beyond language. In writing about Black vernacular dances in particular—street dances, bad dances, nasty dances—there is an opportunity to consider not only the ideas embodied therein but what aspects of ourselves we might have overlooked, ignored, or disavowed. Who might we disinherit by not including these dances in the grand project of thinking seriously about Black history in general and Black popular culture in particular? Our embodied ideas, memories, and experiences act as a counternarrative to oversimplified, derisive, watered-down, and inaccurate tellings of Black people's story. We should take seriously what the author Jonathan Holloway, writing on the work of choreographer Alvin Ailey, called "embodied retellings of collective memory," not as a confirmation of the sameness of all Black people but as a means by which to question that which is silent in the usual retelling of our history. In this way, sustained engagement with Black popular dance functions as a way to push the boundaries of community to be more inclusive and to wrestle with complex ideas. By approaching Black vernacular dance as a site for ideas, experiences, and memories, one can pull in from the edges of one's awareness those persons, places, things that one might rather turn away from because the complexity therein troubles notions of identity and the self. Sustained engagement with Black popular dance is a subversive act because it offers up other ways for thinking about bodily enactment, with all of its complexity and tension, as sources of new ways of conceiving of ourselves, of reconstituting the Black (dancing) body, of rescuing the embodied archive from pernicious attacks on its existence. In this sense, we might proceed by dancing, writing, and documenting ourselves into the future.

Notes

Epigraphs are from "About Janelle Monáe" and "A Keeping of Records."

1 Welsh-Asante, "Commonalities in African Dance," 71–82; Dixon-Gottschild, *Digging the Africanist Presence.*
2 Manning, *Modern Dance*; Perpener, *African-American Concert Dance*; DeFrantz, *Dancing Many Drums.*
3 Malone, *Steppin' on the Blues*; Hazzard-Gordon, *Jookin'.*
4 Smith, "Yes."
5 Garcia, "Twerking YouTube."
6 Jones, "So You Think You Can Dance?"
7 Burt, *The Male Dancer*, 22.
8 Vissicaro, *Studying Dance Cultures.*
9 Connerton, *How Societies Remember*, 72.
10 Goodridge, "The Body," 121.
11 Farnell, " Moving Bodies," 353.
12 Taylor, *The Archive*, 2, 3.
13 Lynch, "A Brief History."
14 Monahan, "What Is the Origin."
15 Jacobs, "Hampton University."
16 See Dixon-Gottschild, *Digging*; Hazzard-Gordon, *Jookin'*; Malone, *Steppin' on the Blues.*
17 Schlepp Films, "Harlem Reacts."
18 "Inventor of Harlem Shake Interview."
19 Gregory, "It's a Worldwide Dance Craze."
20 "Origins and Development."
21 Quoted in Alvarez, "How J-Setting Is Changing Pop Culture."
22 "Origins and Development."

References

"A Keeping of Records: The Art and Life of Alice Walker." Accessed May 15, 2014. https://www.theguardian.com/books/2009/apr/28/exhibition-color-purple-walker.
"About Janelle Monáe." Accessed May 15, 2014. https://www.laphil.com/musicdb /artists/3679/janelle-monae.
Alvarez, Alex. "How J-Setting Is Changing Pop Culture." *ABC News*, April 26, 2013. https://abcnews.go.com/ABC_Univision/Entertainment/sette-dance-moves -loved-knowing/story?id=19041546.
Alvin Ailey American Dance Theater. "Ailey Repertory: Blues Suite." Accessed May 24, 2014. http://www.alvinailey.org/about/company/ alvin-ailey-american-dance-theater/repertory/blues-suite.

Burt, Ramsay. *The Male Dancer: Bodies, Spectacle and Sexuality.* New York: Routledge, 1995.

Connerton, Paul. *How Societies Remember.* New York: Cambridge University Press, 1989.

DeFrantz, Thomas F. *Dancing Many Drums: Excavations in African-American Dance.* Madison: University of Wisconsin Press, 2002.

Dixon-Gottschild, Brenda. *Digging the Africanist Presence in American Performance: Dance and Other Contexts.* Santa Barbara, CA: Praeger, 1998.

Dunham, Katherine. "Barrelhouse Blues." In *Dancing in the Light: Six Compositions by African-American Choreographers.* DVD. 1938; Red Bank, NJ: Kultur, 2007.

Farnell, Brenda. "Moving Bodies, Acting Selves." *Annual Review of Anthropology* (1999): 341–73.

Garcia, Saudi. "Twerking YouTube: San Diego High School Students Suspended for Twerking Video." *Arts.Mic*, May 2, 2013. http://mic.com/articles/39229/twerking-youtube-san-diego-high-school-students-suspended-for-twerking-video.

Goodridge, Janet. "The Body as Living Archive of Dance/Movement: Autobiographical Reflections." In *Fields in Motion: Ethnography in the Worlds of Dance*, edited by Dena Davida. Waterloo, Ontario: Wilfrid Laurier University Press, 2011.

Gregory, Kia. "It's a Worldwide Dance Craze, but It's Not the Real Harlem Shake." *New York Times*, February 28, 2013. http://www.nytimes.com/2013/03/01/nyregion/behind-harlem-shake-craze-a-dance-thats-over-a-decade-old.html?pagewanted=all&_r=1&.

Hazzard-Gordon, Katrina. *Jookin': The Rise of Social Dance Formations in African-American Dance.* Philadelphia: Temple University Press, 1990.

"Inventor of Harlem Shake Interview." *Inside Hoops*, August 13, 2003. http://www.insidehoops.com/harlem-shake-081303.shtml.

Jacobs, Peter. "Hampton University Allegedly Lectured New Students About the 'Dangers' of Twerking." *Business Insider India*, August 29, 2013. https://www.businessinsider.in/Hampton-University-Allegedly-Lectured-New-Students-About-The-Dangers-Of-Twerking/articleshow/22148733.cms.

Jones, Jonathan. "So You Think You Can Dance? NFL Coming Down Harder Than Ever on TD Celebrations." *Sports Illustrated*, September 23, 2016. https://www.si.com/nfl/2016/09/23/nfl-excessive-celebration-penalties-antonio-brown.

Lynch, Joe. "A Brief History of Twerking." *Fuse*, August 28, 2013. http://www.fuse.tv/2013/08/brief-history-of-twerking.

Malone, Jacqui. *Steppin' on the Blues: The Visible Rhythms of African American Dance.* Champaign: University of Illinois Press, 1996.

Manning, Susan. *Modern Dance, Negro Dance, Race in Motion.* Minneapolis: University of Minnesota Press, 2006.

Monahan, Maureen. "What Is the Origin of Twerking?" *Mental Floss*, July 27, 2013. http://mentalfloss.com/article/51365/what-origin-twerking.

"Origins and Development of the Prancing J-Settes." Sonic Boom of the South. Accessed July 15, 2014. http://websites.one.jsums.edu/sonicboom/?page_id=522.

Perpener, John O., III. *African American Concert Dance: The Harlem Renaissance and Beyond*. Champaign: University of Illinois Press, 2005.

Schlepp Films. "Harlem Reacts to the Harlem Shake. Do the Harlem Shake. Harlem Shake Dance Original (v1)." YouTube, February 18, 2013. https://www.youtube.com/watch?v=IGH2HEgWppc.

Smith, Mychal Denzel. "Yes, Arresting Subway Dancers Is Still a Way of Criminalizing Black Youth." *The Nation*, July 8, 2014. http://www.thenation.com/blog/180569/yes-arresting-subway-dancers-still-way-criminalizing-black-youth#.

Taylor, Diana. *The Archive and the Repertoire: Performing Cultural Memory in the Americas*. Durham, NC: Duke University Press, 2003.

Vissicaro, Pegge. *Studying Dance Cultures around the World: An Introduction to Multicultural Dance Education*. Dubuque, IA: Kendall Hunt, 2004.

Welsh-Asante, Kariamu. "Commonalities in African Dance: An Aesthetic Foundation." In *African Culture: The Rhythms of Unity*, edited by Kariamu Welsh-Asante. Trenton, NJ: Africa World Press, 1989.

HE SAID NOTHING / SONIC SPACE AND
THE PRODUCTION OF QUIETUDE IN BARRY
JENKINS'S *MOONLIGHT*

Simone C. Drake

Well after a year since the release of Barry Jenkins's *Moonlight*
(2016), a film adaptation of Tarell Alvin McCraney's play *In Moonlight Black
Boys Look Blue*, Black cultural and Black queer studies scholars remain en-
amored with a film that made a host of critical interventions in how Black
cultural productions influence how society imagines, represents, sees, and
empathizes with Black boys. One of those interventions is its break from
protest rooted in macho, heteronormative representations of Black masculinity. This is not to propose that heretofore there have never been breaks;
rather, the point is that Black masculine sensibilities of disruptiveness and
protest have largely been understood as inherently physical and vocal acts.
This phenomenon has held true even when critical attention is paid to sexual
identity, when vocality around LGBT rights politics has also demanded vocal
disruptiveness, particularly in the context of lesbian and gay AIDS activists

in the late 1980s articulating that Silence = Death.[1] This understanding can make it difficult to *see* Black boys as children—as innocent and worthy of protection—and as not yet possessing a sexual identity, therefore associating Black boys with a Black manhood that is always already vocal, reactive, and heteronormative.[2] Such an understanding can also limit discourse on resistance and Black boyhood. *Moonlight*, then, is situated within and also intervenes in a genealogy of disruptive Black cultural productions through a protagonist who says little and, with the exception of one reactive act of violence, also does little throughout the film.

Few contemporary visual culture productions have imagined a boyhood or "coming of age" for Black boys that is situated outside of the 1990s urban, hip-hop-themed cinema that offered familiar yet static images of Black masculinity.[3] Attention to the urban, or the city, in Black cinematic productions prompted the film scholar Paula Massood to identify within such narratives "conflicted attitudes toward the city as either promised land or dystopian hell." The city therefore functions as a pivotal site of representation and identity formation in African American cultural productions that, as Massood notes, "explore[s] themes of hope, mobility, and escape."[4] Within the context of the intersection of race with gender and sexuality in contemporary Black cultural productions, the city is symbolic of a space where Black boys become a particular type of Black men against a backdrop in which violence is foregrounded and encapsulated by sound—sounds of hip hop, sounds of the city, and dialogue.[5] *Moonlight* stands in contrast to this popular trope by troubling narratives that cast Black boys as already men, rethinking the heteromasculinist coming-of-age narrative and privileging *quiet*.

In a political climate framed by violence, marginalization, and incivility, it is striking that an image of Black boyhood and masculinity steeped in quietude would interrupt, if ever so briefly, what have become everyday instances of terror in the United States since the 2016 presidential election. As a screen adaptation of McCraney's play *In Moonlight Black Boys Look Blue*, Jenkins's *Moonlight* set the film world abuzz. In spite of an unimaginable blunder at the 2017 Academy Awards ceremony, the film won three Academy Awards, for Best Picture, Best Supporting Actor, and Best Adapted Screenplay.[6] *Moonlight* is the coming-of-age narrative of a poor, gay, Black boy growing up in the Liberty City neighborhood of Miami during the Reagan era. Set against the backdrop of crack-cocaine indiscriminately ravaging the lives of Black Americans, Chiron, a timid, neglected child, desperately attempts to navigate his mother's substance abuse problems, violence inflicted by other children, and a social life stifled by his precarious queer positionality.

This is not a Hollywood story of happy endings—it is, rather, a story that begins and ends mired in the complexities of growing up Black and queer in a society with limited ways of *seeing*, or registering legibility in Black boys and Black men.

Each stage of Chiron's life—childhood, adolescence, and young adulthood—is framed by how the cultural studies scholar Kevin Quashie defines *quiet* in the context of the lived Black experience.[7] Chiron says little and little is said to him. Although his life being marked by vulnerability is undeniable, vulnerability and quiet converge to reveal a Black queer interiority that locates some degree of agency and self-fashioning within the depths of verbally saying little. In this essay, I juxtapose sonic space with quietude and the Black queer interiority that is produced within little dialogue. What is to be gained by the absence of *saying* anything? I also emphasize the distinction Quashie makes between silence and quiet, especially as so many reviews of the film use the language of silence. According to Quashie, "The notion of quiet . . . is neither motionless nor without sounds. Quiet, instead, is a metaphor for the full range of one's inner life—one's desires, ambitions, hungers, vulnerabilities, and fears." He extends this explanation further, insisting, "Silence often denotes something that is suppressed or repressed, and is an interiority that is about withholding, absence, and stillness. Quiet, on the other hand, is presence . . . and can encompass fantastic motion."[8] Thus even when Chiron does not speak, I would argue, the interiority revealed through his quietude is indeed full of desires, ambitions, hungers, vulnerabilities, and fears that make him fully human in ways that public performances of resistance cannot render fully.

The idea of Chiron saying nothing that is posited in the title of this essay is inspired by Gayl Jones's novel *Corregidora* (1975), a narrative of intergenerational violence. The mother of Ursa, the protagonist, offers the refrain "I said nothing" as a space between narrative and interiority. When recounting her own story of physical trauma framed within her mother's and grandmother's stories of sexual trauma, both Ursa's mother and Ursa herself take turns saying nothing, not only creating moments in which the narrative is suspended but also creating moments when the gravity of the situation is emphasized by quiet—not silence, because there is a phenomenal presence in those moments of quiet, particularly in a novel framed by the blues. In a film focusing on so many social and ethical wrongs—the drug trade industry, economic disparities, bullying, and homophobia—it is logical to expect a trope of resistance in *Moonlight*. The audience, no doubt, hopes and wishes Chiron, or even someone functioning as an advocate, will resist or be *loud* about the wrongs. Instead, Chiron's penetrating gazes and assessment of situations is almost always performed through shrouds of quiet. Within that space of quiet, of saying nothing, of inaudibility, the musical score stands in for dialogue, for rage, and for disruptiveness as a sonic space that takes viewers deep into the interior life of a queer Black boy coming of age in Reagan-era Miami.

Named Chiron (the name I will use throughout) at birth but also called Little (Alex R. Hibbert) and Black (Trevante Rhodes), Chiron (Ashton Sanders) lives in low-income housing with his mother, Paula (Naomie Harris), who quickly escalates from being employed and invested in her son's well-being to becoming ravaged by drug addiction. In the second scene of the film, the camera follows the blurred image of a group of kids running. One yells, "Get his gay ass!" Chiron, who is being chased, takes refuge in an abandoned housing tenement with boarded windows and drug paraphernalia littering the floor. Juan (Mahershala Ali), a neighborhood midlevel drug pusher, rescues Chiron from the crack house and takes him to the home he shares with his girlfriend, Teresa (Janelle Monáe), where they feed him and attempt to get him to tell them where he lives. The film focuses on Chiron's developing relationship with Juan until Juan's abrupt and unexplained death; his volatile relationship with his mother; his friendship and budding sexual interest in a schoolmate, Kevin (Jaden Piner/Jharrel Jerome/Andre Holland); and his often unsuccessful attempts at avoiding homophobic bullies. After being placed in a juvenile detention center for attacking the bully ringleader, Terrel (Patrick Decile), Paula and Chiron move to Atlanta, where the grown-up Chiron emerges as "Black," Kevin's nickname for him during adolescence. Black is dieseled, "traps," and lives in both solitude and a sonic space reflective of his contradictory metamorphosis.

Although *Moonlight* opens to the lyrics of Boris Gardiner's old-school "Every Nigger Is a Star" (1973) as entrée for Juan, who rolls up on one of his street corners in a blue Chevy to check in with one of his dope boys, the sound track and sonic space after that point in the film is wholly invested in Chiron. Chiron, however, does not speak until over nine minutes into the film. After much cajoling, he tells his unconventional caretakers, Teresa and Juan, "My name is Chiron, but people call me Little." He will not speak again until five minutes later, when he encounters Kevin at a makeshift football game, where the laughter and sounds of running are accompanied by Nicholas Britell's arrangement of Mozart's *Vesperae Solennes De Confessore* in C Major, K 339—"Laudate Dominum" (Psalm 116). The majority of Chiron's expressiveness from childhood through adulthood is articulated through nods and penetrating gazes—gazes reminiscent of Kehinde Wiley's portraiture of young queer Black men who stare out from the canvas, refusing to avert their gaze. It would seem difficult to develop a plot with little dialogue, but Jenkins already demonstrated his acumen with such tasks in his first film, *Medicine for Melancholy* (2008), which also incorporates sound simultaneous to being entrenched in frequent moments of quiet. The sonic space Jenkins has created aligns with Elizabeth Alexander's definition of art: "Art is where and how we speak to each other in tongues audible when 'official' language fails. It is not where we escape the world's ills but rather one place where we go to make sense of them."[9] The narrative and language racing through Chiron's mind is made audible through the vibration and oscillations that produce sound through instruments rather than voice in much of *Moonlight*.

Chiron struggles to make sense of his life through observation, vigilance, and quiet. Music is the art form that allows him to speak "in tongues audible." Just as Little becomes Black, producing consternation for his childhood love interest, Kevin, who does not attempt to hide his shock and disdain when the adult Chiron reveals he's "trappin'," Britell's frequent orchestral interludes offer a narrative in the absence of dialogue. The string orchestra is initially heard when Chiron spends the night with Juan and Teresa for the first time. The violin solo frames what I call an "aesthetic of care." In spite of Juan's troubling occupation, his home functions as a safe space for Chiron, where he is fed, provided a clean bed, and often given money. Accordingly, the violins abruptly stop when Chiron's mother enters the scene, when, after their initial encounter, Juan returns Chiron to her apartment.

In what is arguably one of the most notable and powerful scenes in the film, the string orchestra again conveys an aesthetic of care during the swimming lesson in the ocean. Although Juan's Cuban ancestry comes across as rather random, if not forced, his articulation of Black heterogeneity through his lesson on blackness and diaspora operates as a counterdiscourse to the public and domestic ridicule directed at Chiron by his peers and his own mother. As Chiron enters the ocean, violin arpeggios—short, fast strokes of the bow—emit rich, muted sounds of long strokes across the strings of a cello, and the soft splashes of water produce a textured sound that at once captures Chiron's apprehension and resoluteness. The orchestra plays as Juan cradles Chiron's head in his hand, encouraging him, "Let your head rest in my hand. Relax. I got you. I *promise* you, I'm not gonna let you go." The swimming lesson solidifies one of the most unlikely of relationships, in spite of the fact that the only words uttered from Chiron's mouth during the entire scene are "So, your name Blue?" During this scene, however,

FIG.16.1 Swim lesson. *Moonlight*. Dir. Barry Jenkins. 2016.

sound is multimodal. It is the sound of the waves, the sound of Juan's voice, instructing and affirming, and it is the sound of the string orchestra interlude that begins as they enter the water and plays until they exit the water. Paul Gilroy has noted the lack of critical study of how the body physically transforms when it encounters musical sound. Played against the backdrop of the string orchestra, Chiron transforms into a boy who is free, with arms and legs flailing with the rhythm of the ocean waves. This scene in particular gives meaning to Gilroy's insistence that sound is more complex than simply what we hear and how we interpret it. For Gilroy, "remembering the physical inscription of sound in matter provides a useful warning against the over-aestheticization of music."[10] Thus the cellular structure of the flesh itself is inscribed with the literal sound of waves in the water as those sounds are juxtaposed to the sound waves produced by the vibration of bow against strings and strings compressed by fingers. During and in spite of Chiron's quiet, then, sound is produced through the vibration and oscillation of both the waves and the orchestra. It is, in fact, his quietness that allows viewers to hear these things, but also, importantly, allows Chiron to receive instruction as we—Chiron and the viewers—learn how to listen in the break.

The orchestra also captures the challenges of caring for others when you yourself are broken and searching for self, as is the case with both Kevin and Paula. When Juan pulls Paula out of a car where she is free-basing crack cocaine, she confronts him about his own hypocrisy as her dealer. The strings begin playing as Juan dejectedly returns to his business practices, and they play through Paula's returning home and, assumedly, at some point calling Chiron "faggot" due to his inquiries about the term in the scene that followed at Juan and Teresa's home. The fact that it is easy to accept that "faggot" is indeed what Paula mouths speaks to the power of silence, or suspended dialogue, in the film as it forces the audience into a space in which the emotive is relegated to gestures and what is heard (or not) through the quiet. Unlike the orchestral arrangement during the swimming lessons, the tempo of the violins in this scene is faster and slightly frenetic, until the moment when Paula, framed by a doorway, squarely faces Chiron at the end of the hallway and leaning forward silently mouths "Don't look at me!" It would seem that Paula, who is high and already feeling the guilt imposed by Juan earlier that evening, registers Chiron's quiet, penetrating gaze as condemning her as a mother. At that point, only the lower tones of the cello are heard as Paula is literally muted. Here the strings express many forms of pain: the pain and rejection felt by Chiron when his mother fails to care for him; the pain produced from Paula's loving her son and wanting to care for him but being unable to stave off addiction; and the complexity of Juan's relationship with Chiron, given Juan clearly has no interest in terminating his business yet cares deeply for a child that no one else (other than Teresa) seems capable of loving.

The string orchestra also features prominently when Chiron, as Black, reconnects with Kevin, which will be analyzed shortly. But that moment of reconnection is the culmination of what began as an aesthetic of care on a football field, when viewers learn that although the speech is somewhat clipped, Chiron does indeed talk to Kevin. Kevin's own challenges with both loyalty in friendship and acceptance of his own queer identity, however, betray Chiron in their youth in spite of another notable and powerful scene offering hope for a different direction in their friendship. Another beach scene involves Chiron and Kevin. The familial intimacy of Juan functioning as surrogate parent is replaced by sexual intimacy between Chiron and Kevin. That intimacy, however, is not restricted to the sexual, and it is the longest point of sustained dialogue Chiron has with anyone. In this moment, both boys delve into their interior lives that society fails to register, discussing the "lot of things" Chiron wants to do "that don't make sense." In the midst of near constant conversation, though, there is quiet too, as it becomes central to their conversation. While noting the breeze on the beach, Kevin says the same breeze runs through their neighborhood: "It comes through the hood, and it's like everything stops for a second, 'cause everyone just wanna feel it.

FIG.16.2 Paula. *Moonlight*. Dir. Barry Jenkins. 2016.

Everything just gets *quiet*, you know?" (emphasis mine). Chiron responds, "And it's like all you can hear is your own heartbeat. Right?" Kevin concludes, "Shit make you wanna cry, feels so good," which prompts Chiron to ask Kevin if he cries. Kevin says he does not, but the quiet makes him want to cry. Chiron freely shares that he cries so much he feels like he is going to turn into drops, then becomes quiet and shakes his head. Listening to Chiron in the quiet of that space, Kevin deduces that Chiron wants to "roll out into the water like all these other motherfuckers around here trying to drown they sorrows." Although Chiron did not say that, Kevin explains that it "sounds like something you want to do." Quiet, then, is not always without dialogue or vocality. What is communicated through the breaks in Chiron's speech, the breeze, and the motion of the water allows both boys to access and assess "the full range of one's inner life—one's desires, ambitions, hungers, vulnerabilities, and fears."[11]

It is significant that string rather than brass orchestra is employed. Sonically, there is quite a difference in the acoustics produced by both style and aesthetic. The strings, and particularly Britell's arrangements, embody quietness and intimacy that speak to interiority in a way that brass instruments would not. Moreover, a musical form mostly associated with European culture is a curious inclusion in a film set in an urban context during the public rise of hip hop. Perhaps the strings orchestra was necessary. Hip hop, after all, has operated as a public, resistant blackness. But, as Quashie asserts, "all living is political—every human action means something—but all living is not in protest; to assume such is to disregard the richness of life."[12] Michael Gillespie argues about Black film that it "must be understood as art, not prescription," as he etches an argument that calls for "a more expansive understanding of blackness and cinema," posing questions such as "What if black film could be something other than embodied?"[13] Rather than encapsulating Chiron's coming of age in the sounds of hip hop, *Moonlight* quiets what might be understood as a logical soundtrack for Black urban life in the 1980s and 1990s and, instead, fills in what is inaudible with sounds that through Chiron's quiet speak "to a metaphor for the full range of one's inner life—one's desires, ambitions, hungers, vulnerabilities, and fears."[14] Beethoven and Mozart, conducted through the vibrations and oscillations of a "physical inscription of sound in matter," become just as much a metaphor for Chiron's inner life as will Jidenna and Goodie Mob. The "quieting" of hip hop in the first two-thirds of the film is not easily polarized, however, which is evident when Britell composes various "chopped and screwed" tracks—an important one being during the swimming lesson ("The Middle of the World") and another being a second version of Chiron's theme in the chopped and screwed style.[15] Thus Chiron's becoming Black in the third sequence of the film embodies a syncretic quality captured through the soundtrack, making the transition a logical progression rather than bifurcated.

Chiron reaches a breaking point with the bullying. After being physically assaulted by Kevin at the command of the homophobic school bully, Terrel, Chiron returns to school, storms into his classroom, drops his backpack at his desk, picks up a wooden chair, and slams it across the back of Terrel and then once more over his unresponsive body as Terrel lies on the floor. Chiron says nothing prior to or during the attack. There is no soundtrack. Only once he is pulled away from Terrel does he say anything, repeatedly directing those who intervened, "Get the fuck off me, niggas!" The string orchestra resumes when Chiron is being escorted in handcuffs out of the building and past Kevin, who stares as the police cruiser takes Chiron away. A frenetic orchestra plays as the scene cuts to a nightmarish dream in which Chiron revisits the painful eve in which his mother screams at him not to look at her and perhaps, off-screen, calls him a faggot.[16] As Paula screams, "Don't look at me!," the strings abruptly stop and a grown Chiron, with gold fronts, diamond stud earring, and a black doo rag bolts up in bed, breathing fast and hard. He gets out of bed and dunks his head in a bath of ice cubes, symbolizing a new birth and a new sound.

FIG.16.3 Déjà vu. *Moonlight*. Dir. Barry Jenkins. 2016.

FIG.16.4 Chevy. *Moonlight*. Dir. Barry Jenkins. 2016.

As he finishes the ice-cube bath, Goodie Mob's "Cell Therapy" begins to play and the scene cuts to Chiron driving; as the camera pans out, a small gold crown is seen adorning his dashboard, just as in Juan's Chevy in the opening scene of the film. It is in fact a scene of déjà vu, as Chiron, a trap king, checks in with one of his runners. And within the hip-hop anthem both sonic and spoken by Chiron, blackness here becomes expressive and even dramatic as, coincidentally, part 3 of the film introduces viewers to Black. As Black, Chiron not only speaks; he even has a sense of humor. After accusing Travis (Stephon Bron), one of his runners, of being short, Chiron jokes, "Nah, I'm just fuckin' with you." Like Juan, Chiron gives business lessons to his runners. But the hip-hop soundtrack is displaced whenever Chiron is drawn back into the quietude of his interior life—the life that connects directly to his childhood. A voicemail from his mother reignites the orchestra. Similarly, when Kevin calls out of the blue, the soft sounds of R&B on a jukebox play in the background on Kevin's end as Chiron searches for words.

The new audible tones and vibrations of Chiron's adult life expand the musical genre of his interiority. Just as in his youth the string instruments evoke the tenderness and intimacy of Juan's care for Chiron, the scared little boy, grown-up Chiron's willful and tender embrace of his repentant mother is accompanied by Caetano Velosa's rendition of "Cucurrucucu Paloma." The song continues as Chiron drives the long stretches of green, tree-lined highway and as the frame fades to Black children playing in the ocean during his journey from Atlanta to Miami for an impromptu rendezvous with Kevin. The song title references the cooing sound of a dove and the lyrics address lovesickness, making this Mexican folk song (Huapango) appropriate for expressing Chiron's quiet and the potential for rekindling the relationship that never developed beyond the beach makeout years earlier (a moment notably without instrumental sound and instead filled with dialogue and the ocean waves as background sound).

The song lyrics could, however, be multilayered, speaking also to Chiron's conflicted love for his mother. After repeated unanswered calls on his end, Chiron gives in and stops to see his mother before leaving town. At this point, Paula has completed a drug rehabilitation program and is clearly in a continued state of recovery. In fact, when Chiron asks her when she plans to leave the facility and "go home," she articulates it as a safe space, reflecting, "Home? This is home. I mean they allowing me to stay and work as long as I like. I figure might as well help other folks. Keep myself out of trouble." During this conversation, Paula scolds Chiron for "still being in them streets," and he is irritated by her seeming hypocrisy and rises to leave. Upon her pleading, he sits back down and listens to her acknowledge how she messed up both of their lives, telling Chiron, "But yo' heart ain't gotta be black like mine, baby. . . . I love you, Chiron. I do. I love you, baby. But you ain't gotta love me. Lord knows I did not have love for you when you needed it, I know that. So you ain't gotta love me, but you gonna know that I love you." After her repentant speech, she asks him twice if he heard her, as a tear runs down his face. And then, in a scene equally as tender as Juan's swimming lesson and making out with Kevin on the beach, Chiron takes a cigarette and lighter out of his mother's shaking hands, lights the cigarette, and wipes a tear from his mother's eye, prompting her to say, "I'm sorry, baby. I'm so sorry." It is an utterance that brings Chiron quickly to his feet and reaching across the table to embrace his mother as "Cucurrucucu Paloma" begins to play. Chiron says little during this exchange—Paula does almost all of the talking—but it hearkens back to another time, many years earlier, when he sat at Juan and Teresa's dining table and blurted out, "I hate her [Paula]!" Juan responded by saying he also felt that way about his mother when he was Chiron's age, but he now sure does miss her. Thus, in the quiet of the exchange, the embrace, and the thoughts of reconnecting with Kevin, there would also seem to be a lovesickness for his original love—for his mother, the sole person he seems with certainty to want to love and be loved by throughout all three vignettes of his life.

Upon arriving in Miami, viewers see the complex interiority of Chiron's quiet when the softness of Velosa's folk song fades and, ever so briefly, just before entering the diner where Kevin works, a chopped and screwed version of the refrain of Jidenna's "Classic Man" plays, defining Chiron within a theme song that he performs more than he speaks. "Even if she go away, even if she go away/Even if she go away, even if she go away/I'm a classic man/You could be mean when you look this clean." Chiron has become—no more coming of age. And his becoming is just as complex as Juan's aesthetics of care and as complicated as Stanford-educated Jidenna's explanation of his classic sartorial style situated within the hip-hop genre. By adopting "Classic Man," and this version in particular, as his theme song, similar to Juan's "Every Nigger Is a Star," Chiron remains illegible. Mark Anthony Neal refers to the challenges encountered when society provides only one legible means of reading Black men—as criminals, thugs, and general problems—whereas queerness, for example, renders Black men illegible.[17] To push Neal's point further, Chiron complicates both the legibility and illegibility factor, as he straddles the heteronormative, hypermasculine realm of hip hop and urbanity at the same time that his sexual identity expels him from such spaces.

As quickly as "Classic Man" begins to play, it stops, and Chiron enters the diner with Aretha Franklin's "One Step Ahead" (1965) filtering through the doorway. A relatively unknown song from Franklin's chart-topping oeuvre, this throwback speaks through the quiet of the scenario of both Chiron's and Kevin's pasts and the precarious space each lives in as Black men trying to stay not just one step ahead of their economic and social circumstances but also one step ahead of keeping quiet their same-sex desires. Kevin emphasizes the reality of Chiron's quiet when he good-heartedly concludes, "You ain't changed one damn bit. You still can't say more than three words at a time, huh?" Chiron replies that Kevin had said he would cook for him, that he knows how to say that, alluding to his first meal with Juan and Teresa and Juan's conclusion that even if Chiron says nothing, he sure can eat.

FIG.16.5 Diner. *Moonlight*. Dir. Barry Jenkins. 2016.

Following that brief exchange, Kevin cares for Chiron through his culinary skills, and amid the quiet between the two men, the orchestra plays, creating an unanticipated montage of soul music and classical strings.

Again the soundtrack goes to the archives of soul, pulling out "Our Love" by The Edge of Daybreak, a song recorded in 1979 in Powhatan Correctional Center in State Farm, Virginia. It functions as background sound to actual dialogue between Kevin and Chiron, although Kevin, as always, directs the conversation. Noted as a dance groove, "Our Love" speaks to the lost love of what could have been between Chiron and Kevin and it also hearkens back to a primary school scene in which Chiron was at school having a ball dancing to The Performers' "Mini Skirt." Digging even deeper into the archives, Kevin plays the song he says reminded him of Chiron and prompted his phone call after ten years of separation. Barbara Lewis's "Hello Stranger" (1963) offers lyrics of intimacy when Chiron says nothing beyond his pointed inquiry about why Kevin called him. Letting lyrics and doo-wop backup by the Dells reverberate through the diner, the stereophonic sound fills in for Kevin's unspoken acknowledgment of the wrongs he knows he did. The two men stare into one another's eyes as Lewis's rich vocals speak for them: "It seems like a mighty long time . . . I'm so glad you stopped by to say 'hello' to me/Remember that's the way it used to be."

When they leave the diner, Kevin is forced once again to come to terms with the Chiron he once knew and the Chiron who traps, wears gold fronts, and drives a late-model Chevy Impala. As they approach the car, Kevin inquires with a tone simultaneously dubious and impressed, "This you?" Chiron, as expected, says nothing, but he smiles both bashfully and proudly. Kevin enters the car, concluding, "You wasn't playin' 'bout dem traps, huh?" As the engine revs to a start, the lyrics "You look this clean/I'm a Classic Man" belt out as Chiron smiles shyly and Kevin grins, acknowledging, "Ridin' dirty, huh?" Chiron quickly and quietly replies, "Somethin' like that," as the soundtrack continues: "Calling on me like a young OG/I'm a classic man/Your needs get met by the street elegant old-fashioned man." Yet Chiron's contemporary theme song and Juan's throwback theme song, "Every Nigger Is a Star," speak to the hyper-heteromasculinity that both Juan and Chiron find nearly impossible to speak about. When Chiron pointedly asks Juan if he sells drugs, it is a moment when, aside from his affirmative response, Juan falls quiet, unable to say anything. Juan represents the epitome of "hard," yet he does not hesitate to care for a young boy who is gay, answering another one of Chiron's pointed questions, "What's a faggot?," by assuring him he does not have to try to classify his sexual identity at this stage of his life. Juan's relationship with Chiron seems to embody the bridge of his own musical theme song: "They got a right place in the sun/where there's love for everyone." This bridge signifies further on the old school/new school aspect of the relationship between Juan and Chiron when considering that Kendrick Lamar samples "Every Nigga Is a Star" in the intro of the first track on *To Pimp a Butterfly* titled "Wesley's Theory." The lyrics of Lamar's song employ the actor Wesley Snipes as a stand-in for the way Black people, and Black men in particular given the gendered language employed, get "pimped" by the entertainment industry and the government when they have financial success by legitimate means rather than the underground economies Juan and Chiron partake in.

During Reagan's extension of Nixon's war on drugs, drug dealers are easily seen as scourges of society. Ironically, during that era, gay men and gay sexual activity are not thought of that differently from drug dealers and drug usage. News and popular media during the 1980s and 1990s widely implicated gay men as criminals, as one of the primary parties guilty of producing the HIV/AIDS epidemic. It is within this precarious space that a Black drug dealer decides to be a guardian of sorts to a stigmatized gay Black boy. Jenkins constructs a sonic space of redemption around two flawed figures and renders them human, even as they do things that suggest an utter disregard for humanity. In the sonic space of quietude, an orchestral score, R&B, and hip hop converge to trouble the heteromasculinist attitudes that make *quiet* a safe space for Chiron to sort through who he is—for claiming an interiority that society is unwilling to imagine for him.

Notes

This essay began as a conference paper for a *Moonlight* panel at the 2017 American Studies Association annual conference. I am grateful to Maurice Tracy for inviting me to participate and to Jeffrey Q. McCune for feedback as respondent. Terrance Dean, Valerie Lee, and Terrance Wooten provided thoughtful feedback on the expanded essay, for which I am also grateful.

1 McCraney wrote the original play following his mother's death from AIDS-related complications.

2 Numerous social scientific studies have found that Black children are often registered as being older than they are. For more detail, see Goff et al., "The Essence of Innocence."

3 Two films that stood out for breaking from the urban, hip-hop-themed trope of Black boyhood during the 1990s are Matty Rich's *The Inkwell* (1994) and Kasi Lemmons's *Eve's Bayou* (1997).

4 Massood, *Black City Cinema*, 8, 2.

5 For more on how northern migration created spaces of possibility for Black men's agency, see Griffin's *"Who Set You Flowin'?"*

6 Reading the wrong card, Faye Dunaway and Warren Beatty mistakenly announced *La La Land* as winner in the Best Picture category for 2017.

7 I am not the only scholar to recognize Barry Jenkins's penchant for employing limited dialogue in his scriptwriting. In his chapter on Jenkins's *Medicine for Melancholy* (2008) in *Film Blackness* Gillespie also turns to Kevin Quashie's distinction between silence and quiet when analyzing *Medicine for Melancholy*.

8 Quashie, *The Sovereignty of Quiet*, 6, 22.

9 Alexander, *The Black Interior*, ix.

10 Gilroy, "Between the Blues," 298.

11 Quashie, *The Sovereignty of Quiet*, 6.

12 Quashie, *The Sovereignty of Quiet*, 8–9.

13 Gillespie, *Film Blackness*, 2, 5.

14 Quashie, *The Sovereignty of Quiet*, 6. It was common during the 1980s and 1990s for films focused on urban Black life to be accompanied by hip-hop soundtracks. Films such as *Boyz N the Hood* (1991), *Juice* (1992), and *Menace II Society* (1993) are well-known examples.

15 "Chopped and screwed" is a technique developed during the 1990s in the Houston hip-hop scene by DJ Screw. When applying this technique, DJs change the texture of the music by slowing down the tempo and warping pitch. The remix effect is said

to enable listeners to not only hear the lyrics fully but to also allow a relaxed rather than hyped experience with the music. In this regard, then, there is a certain brilliance on the part of Britell and Jenkins in wedding classical music and the chopped and screwed technique.

16 Interestingly, in spite of the contempt Chiron might have for his mother, he keeps a photograph on his nightstand of her holding him when he was a baby.

17 Neal, *Looking for Leroy*, 4, 8.

References

Alexander, Elizabeth. *The Black Interior: Essays*. Saint Paul, MN: Graywolf, 2004.

Gillespie, Michael Boyce. *Film Blackness: American Cinema and the Idea of Black Film*. Durham, NC: Duke University Press, 2016.

Gilroy, Paul. "Between the Blues and the Blues Dance: Some Soundscapes of the Black Atlantic." In *Media Studies: A Reader*, edited by Sue Thornham et al. 3rd ed. New York: New York University Press, 2009.

Goff, P. A., et al. "The Essence of Innocence: Consequences of Dehumanizing Black Children." *Journal of Personality and Social Psychology* 106, no. 4 (2014): 526–45.

Griffin, Farah Jasmine. *"Who Set You Flowin'?" African-American Migration Narrative*. New York: Oxford University Press, 1995.

Massood, Paula. *Black City Cinema: African American Urban Experiences in Film*. Philadelphia: Temple University Press, 2003.

Neal, Mark Anthony. *Looking for Leroy: Illegible Black Masculinities*. New York: New York University Press, 2013.

Quashie, Kevin. *The Sovereignty of Quiet: Beyond Resistance in Black Culture*. New Brunswick, NJ: Rutgers University Press, 2012.

CH.17 BLACK WOMEN READERS AND THE USES OF URBAN FICTION

Kinohi Nishikawa

Teri Woods, Vickie Stringer, Nikki Turner: their names won't be familiar to academics, and you won't find them featured on Oprah's Book Club. But these women invigorated the African American reading public at a time when critics were fretting over the demise of the book in the digital age. Noting a dearth of leisure reading for black women, Woods, Stringer, and Turner began writing their own works of fiction in the 1990s. To get into print, Woods and Stringer first tried submitting their manuscripts to major publishing houses. They were rejected by every one, with some editors practically scoffing at the idea that black women's popular fiction could be profitable. Despite this setback, Woods and Stringer stood by their work and devised an alternative. Using print-on-demand technology, they published their books in cheap paperback editions, which they then sold in their communities, relying on face-to-face interactions and word-of-mouth hype. Bypassing the publishing industry allowed them to tap into the market they knew had been there all along. Soon Woods's *True to the Game* (copyrighted 1994, published 1998) and Stringer's *Let That Be the Reason* (copyrighted 1999, published 2001) became underground sensations. The success of their business model encouraged them to publish other writers, as Stringer did for Turner by bringing out *A Hustler's Wife* in 2003. That year the publishing industry recognized the extraordinary popularity of these books by giving them a new genre designation: "urban fiction."[1]

Colloquially, urban fiction went by names like "street lit" and "hip-hop fiction." The references were fitting insofar as urban fiction circulated within the broader media culture of hip hop, specifically gangsta rap, a genre known for its hardcore aesthetic. Characters referenced chart-topping hits by title, and storylines resembled the narratives of inner-city life that gangsta rap had popularized. The novels' packaging also took its inspiration from hip hop. Most notably, publishers created eye-catching front covers that resembled album cover art (minus the parental advisory label) or music video images, as figure 17.1 demonstrates.

Yet, though they were complementary in many ways, street lit was unlike gangsta rap in one important respect: its stories were told from the point of view of girls and young women, and the obstacles highlighted therein were distinctly gendered. From date rape and domestic violence to family care and teenage pregnancy, street lit tackled issues that hip hop wasn't likely to address. Thus, if gangsta rap's misogyny and masculinism were core influences on black popular culture in the 1990s, urban fiction gave girls and young women a means to shape black popular culture in their own image in the twenty-first century.[2]

In the early 2000s, the original "queens" of street lit signed book deals with the very publishers that had once rejected them. As part of those deals, they were given the opportunity to develop series in new imprints dedicated to the genre. For their part, publishers facilitated the genre's mainstreaming with mass-market distribution. No longer confined to beauty shops and fold-out tables in black neighborhoods, titles could be found in retail outlets across the country, including chain bookstores in predominantly white suburbs. But with increased visibility came heightened scrutiny from critics. In a continuation of criticism leveled against hip hop during the previous decade, writers took urban fiction to task for perpetuating stereotypes that African Americans were oversexed and prone to violence. Often pointing to the books' salacious covers, they were quick to call the lot "trash," an indulgence of readers' worst impulses. Urban fiction weathered the criticism and, over the next decade, became a multimillion-dollar niche

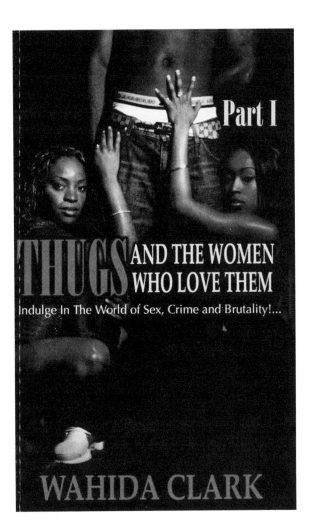

FIG.17.1

Wahida Clark, *Thugs and the Women Who Love Them*, front cover, 2002.

in the literary marketplace. Some would argue it's stronger today than it's ever been.[3] Still, despite being a genuine black entrepreneurial success story, the genre remains dogged by accusations that it's deleterious to "the race," a failure of literary standards that redounds to the group as a whole.

This essay moves beyond the aesthetic elitism and ideological moralism of such standards. I propose instead an examination of urban fiction on its own terms, that is, according to its own norms of reception.[4] To conduct my analysis, I bracket what critics have said about the genre and attend to how readers themselves have described engaging with these books. My analysis is not a qualitative ethnography of readers' experiences, nor is it a statistical measure of their responses. The data set is small, and it exists solely in an online social network. This essay is not the place where I solve the problem at the heart of Robert Darnton's oft-cited claim, "Reading remains the most difficult stage to study in the circuit followed by books."[5] Still, my sense is that the intertwining of popular culture and social media in contemporary black life makes it possible to outline something like urban fiction's grassroots reception. If social media has afforded young African Americans unprecedented access to the public sphere, it has also documented the tremendous complexity of their reading practices, including their reflexive engagements with genre.[6] In this essay, I track online reviews of a popular novel to show how urban fiction's readers make use of the genre in far more complicated ways than the protocols of professional criticism would allow.

■　■　■

The question of why black women read urban fiction has been addressed with a mixture of incredulity and despair in popular media. In 2009, for example, the journalist Juan Williams took to the pages of the *Wall Street Journal* to complain, "Much as rap music—also fascinated with predatory sex, anger and violence—has displaced jazz or soul singers on the black music charts, gangster lit now overshadows the common late 20th-century theme of black middle-class striving." Acknowledging that "middle-class black women" were the primary audience for these books, Williams nonetheless worried that the genre promoted "the worst of black life" rather than qualities that are readily associated with racial uplift.[7] Whatever had driven them to read urban fiction, he implied, was not in keeping with their class status. Williams's conservative opinion was not confined to the corporate elite. A year earlier, in the NAACP's *Crisis* magazine, the literature scholar Eisa Nefertari Ulen warned that urban fiction reinforced the racist stereotype that "Black people *are* hypersexual, *are* pathological; they feel but don't think." More pernicious was how "we," African Americans, were "actually starting to believe these stereotypes about ourselves." Ulen concluded, "We're literally buying into the mythology."[8] From this angle, urban fiction was not only a problem of content—of, say, unsavory characters and outlaw exploits. It was a problem in itself—an indication that self-denigration could be sold as escapist fodder to the masses.

The false consciousness attributed by Williams and Ulen to black women readers found its most disparaging expression in Nick Chiles's 2006 *New York Times* op-ed piece, "Their Eyes Were Reading Smut." The title's cheeky pun (on Zora Neale Hurston's 1937 novel *Their Eyes Were Watching God*) turned a reflection on spiritual meaning into a fixation on pornography, a fall from the sacred to the profane. In the piece itself, Chiles recounted entering a Lithonia, Georgia, Borders bookstore, where, to his chagrin, he had stumbled upon an "African-American Literature" section overrun by street lit. "I felt as if I was walking into a pornography shop," he wrote, "except in this case the smut [was] being produced by and for my people, and it is called 'literature.'" Chiles had seen how his books, along with novels by Terry McMillan, Toni Morrison, and Edward P. Jones, were forced to share shelf space with *Legit Baller* (2005) and *Chocolate Flava* (2004). Prior to this visit, he had witnessed urban fiction take over book-buying outlets in black neighborhoods. Now, though, it was obvious the genre had also invaded (white) suburbia by way of his beloved Borders—"as if," he posited, "these nasty books were pairing off back in the stockrooms like little paperback rabbits and churning out even more graphic offspring that make Ralph Ellison books cringe into a dusty corner."[9] Chiles's choice of metaphor was not incidental to the argument. Imagining urban fiction's rise as (animalistic) sexual reproduction gone amok was his way of casting aspersions on black women readers. Their unruly desires, he implied, threatened to cancel out what cultural respect "the race" has earned through an award-winning novelist like Ellison.

Not everyone agreed with Chiles, of course. In fact, urban fiction has had its share of defenders over the years, many of whom are professional critics themselves. In a 2009 article, for example, the respected literary and cultural historian Gerald Early ventured, "Urban literature has democratized and broadened the reach and content of African-American literature." By rejecting the dictates of the lettered class, street lit, according to Early, demonstrated "the maturity, not the decline, of African-American literature."[10] The editor and journalist Danyel Smith went one better, suggesting that the very comingling of the respectable and the lowdown that Chiles had decried ought to be celebrated:

> Black literary fiction and street lit should embrace in a rowdy, passionate, illicit love affair—very Romeo and Juliet minus the star-crossed thing. The two genres should hole up for a long weekend of wet, buck-naked lovemaking, and then part as the rare kind of lovers who remain acquaintances, but respect the other's skill and heat. In a perfect world, the two genres, each gangsta in its own way, would get together often for fun and pleasure, and, truly, for some respite from those who would try to erase them.[11]

Smith countered Chiles's nightmare of unbridled reproduction with a steamy scenario of casual sex. In her extended metaphor, "serious" fiction and street lit should hook up and stay in touch, with neither side evincing jealousy or passing judgment ("the rare kind of lovers who remain acquaintances"). Under this arrangement, the genres would see each other as equals ("respect") but would not have to commit to the other's way of being in the world.

In tone and figuration, Smith's scenario seemed to offer a genuine alternative to Chiles's critique. Where he saw only an invasion, she located the possibility of a tryst. Yet Smith rounded out her fantasy in a way that showed she agreed with Chiles on at least one key point. The scenario continued: "From such a hot hookup (imagine the gymnastic lust, the hair pulling, the scratching, kissing, and conversations), there might evolve love." If that should happen, Smith gushed, "there'd be many, many children—each freaky and bold and wonderful in his or her own blessedly ensured way."[12] The metaphor of sexual reproduction thus came back into the picture, only this time it sealed the bond between literary art and urban fiction. Granted, the offspring Smith dreamed up was distinct from the infestation that Chiles had imagined. However, the fact that, even in a sympathetic account, black women's reading practices were metaphorized as a sexually reproductive act is, I think, the problem with the whole debate about urban fiction. To the question What do black readers want?, defenders and detractors alike seemed able to think only in terms of good and bad mothers.

This point of overlap suggests that, despite their evident differences, Chiles and Smith viewed urban fiction in a surprisingly similar way: namely, by its relationship to the canon of African American literature. Chiles argued that the genre had occluded the canon and, with it, values that constitute symbolic, antiracist capital. Smith, on the other hand, contended that urban fiction and canonical works can mutually inform one another, and in so doing diversify the canon even further. But a question for both is this: Why must the canon of African American literature be the yardstick by which we measure the value of urban fiction? Each side committed a category error by either judging the genre unfavorably (Chiles) or comparing the genre favorably (Smith) to a body of literature to which it simply doesn't belong—and has never pretended to be part of. (This point also underscores the absurdity of Early's claim that street lit signaled the "maturity" of the African American literary tradition—Ellison, Morrison, and Whitehead be damned.) By assuming and/or conceding the ground of legitimation to the kind of institutionalized reading practices that value canonicity, Chiles and Smith embedded urban fiction in a framework that, by definition, cannot recognize it.

■ ■ ■

A major problem with the aforementioned accounts is that they keep urban fiction at arm's length, forgoing an accurate description of its formulas, even when they claim to appreciate it. By not engaging the genre's particularities, the accounts maintain a level of discursive abstraction that ends up revaluing institutionalized reading practices. I take the opposite approach here, detailing the reception norms for a representative book of the genre. That book is Wahida Clark's 2002 debut novel, *Thugs and the Women Who Love Them*. Clark's narrative follows the misadventures of three young black women—Angel, Kyra, and Jaz—who approach men as they do consumer goods: when they like what they see, they do whatever it takes to get it. Angel commits serial check fraud to secure the latest designer brands; she falls for the flash and dazzle of Snake, a local pimp. Fourteen-year-old Kyra is lured away from her boyfriend by a twenty-two-year-old dealer named Marvin; he seduces her with Foot Locker gear that matches his own. Completing the trio is Jaz, a student who starts a meth-cooking operation for ostensibly noble reasons: "She was able to stash twenty-four grand a week, hoping to use some of the money to retire her parents to a nice, big house down South some day."[13] But as Jaz rises to the top of the drug trade, the Armani-clad, Escalade-driving entrepreneur sheds her ideals for the pleasures of the fast life.

Thugs is set in central New Jersey, between hardscrabble Trenton (Clark's hometown) and tony Princeton. Refuting the assumption that urban fiction is always about lower-class people in the inner city, Clark's narrative shows how black women from different walks of life get caught up in bad situations—no matter their class status, family background, or educational history. As Snake's girlfriend, Angel gives up on her dreams of success and rationalizes the abuse he visits upon women, including herself. It's only when one of his prostitutes says enough is enough and poisons him that she escapes his influence. Kyra, meanwhile, becomes addicted to Marvin's heroin. Her old beau, Tyler, saves her from an overdose after he thinks he has killed Marvin in a sneak attack. Kyra and Tyler's romance is rekindled for a time— until, that is, she welcomes Marvin back into her life (he survived the attack, after all) and turns the other cheek when he exacts revenge on Tyler. As for high-flying Jaz, her white business partner, Brett, turns state's evidence, exposing the secret drug business to the authorities. Jaz's boyfriend, Faheem, thinks he's come to her rescue by successfully coordinating Brett's murder. But their hope is short-lived: even without Brett's testimony, Jaz is found "guilty on all counts" and receives a seventeen-year sentence.[14] She is five months pregnant.

Clark wrote *Thugs* on yellow notepad paper while serving nine and a half years in a women's federal prison. In the acknowledgments section, she recognizes inmates as her first readers, friends on the outside as her typists, and "C.O.'s," or corrections officers, as her copyists "when the raggedy ass inmate copy machine was broken (which was all of the time)."[15] Clark was incarcerated after being convicted of money laundering, wire fraud, and mail fraud in Georgia, where her husband had been serving time in an Atlanta prison. She began writing because she needed the money and had heard about another inmate's experience doing the same. Clark was already a fan of Donald Goines and Iceberg Slim, pulp writers from the late 1960s and early 1970s who had adapted aspects of their criminal pasts into the stuff of popular literature.[16] Realizing she had enough material from her own past to cook up a page-turner, Clark set to work on her first book.

Clark sent the manuscript of *Thugs* to the romance writer Carl Weber. His Brooklyn-based Black Print Publishing offered an alternative path to publication for little-known authors. Her manuscript was accepted, and the book followed shortly thereafter.[17] Sales were phenomenal, not least because of the cover art. A sequel, *Every Thug Needs a Lady*, appeared in 2003. By the time Clark was released from prison in 2007, she had a successful brand and two popular book series to her name. At that point, she decided to make good on a business plan she had shared with another inmate at the women's prison camp in Alderson, West Virginia. With Martha Stewart's blessing, she started Wahida Clark Presents Publishing in the late 2000s. Like Woods and Stringer before her, Clark had gone from street-lit author to street-lit publisher, bringing in more readers and talent along the way. Full incorporation into hip-hop media culture followed in 2012, when she signed a book deal with Cash Money Content, a Simon and Schuster imprint associated with Cash Money Records, the label for hip-hop acts such as Drake, Lil Wayne, and Nicki Minaj.[18]

Thugs exemplifies what has made urban fiction a popular yet controversial genre. Narratively, it puts black girls and young women at the center of the reading experience. For many, this is the most valuable thing the genre provides: a mirror held up to lives that are overlooked or occluded in male-dominated popular culture. Relatedly, because Clark drew heavily from personal experience to write *Thugs*, the assumption is that girls and young women can more readily identify with her writing. The book becomes more real, in other words, when readers understand that she *lived it*. Yet *Thugs* is ultimately a work of fiction and, as such, reflects choices Clark made in scripting her characters' lives. To that point, it's hard to deny that Angel, Kyra, and Jaz are recklessly dependent on male lovers or that they are enthralled by the temptations of criminality and commercialism. With that in mind, it's reasonable to ask whether Clark is playing to what already sells in hip-hop media culture. That is, instead of conveying the truth of her experience, she may be peddling the most commodified images of blackness in American popular culture.[19]

These position-takings are familiar. They reflect the debate over urban fiction that's been going on since the early 2000s. But what happens when we listen to *Thugs*'s "non-critical," everyday readers? Do they confirm the views of one side or another? In fact, we get far more complicated responses like Corinne's: "ok if this book didn't have drama, i don't know what drama is, this book was the bomb. I would love a thug but only in my dreams. big ups to ms clark."[20] Corinne's candid appreciation of "drama" belies the notion that readers approach *Thugs* as if it were documentary truth. On the contrary, she proves that she is well aware of the fictionality at the heart of Clark's enterprise. Yet it's also the case that she tacitly acknowledges the truth *behind* that enterprise when she says "big ups" to Wahida Clark. Corinne recognizes that Clark's life story informs her writing and the compliment intends to give credit where it's due, even if the book itself is a mass-market product. But the assertion that confounds any prejudgment is, of course, Corinne's admitting she would "love a thug . . . only in [her] dreams." Deftly toeing the line between hard-nosed reality ("thug") and whimsical fantasy ("dreams"), she playfully confesses to finding pleasure in suspending the distinction between the two.

Corinne is a user on Goodreads, the world's largest website devoted to reading and reviewing books. A cataloguing application, Goodreads allows users to create virtual bookshelves, complete with personalized annotations, ratings, and reviews. It also allows everyone—users and nonusers alike—to browse these data and share information within and outside of the platform. Indeed, many users access the website via the world's largest social media website, Facebook. Thus, even as a massive online book catalogue, Goodreads functions as a social media network that brings readers together to talk about books and anything to do with reading (or wanting to read) them. As of this writing, the website has 40 million user members worldwide, though that number does not include someone like me, who "uses" Goodreads (by accessing and looking at its data) without having signed up as a member. The online catalogue includes 1.3 billion titles, and users have published 47 million reviews since the company's launch in January 2007.[21]

To be clear, I do not think that Goodreads provides unmediated access to reader response or to the reception of any book or literary genre. The website's goal always has been to collect user-generated data and turn them into a revenue stream—by way of targeted advertising, for example. So I take to heart the new media theorist Lisa Nakamura's warning that the hidden cost of Goodreads's open-access policy has been "loss of privacy, friction-free broadcasting of our personal information, the placing of user content in the service of commerce, and the operationalization and commodification of reading as an algocratic practice."[22] All of which helps explain why Amazon, the largest retailer—online or otherwise—in the world, acquired the company in March 2013.[23] The algorithmic formulas in place at Goodreads were attractive to Amazon's awesome and ever-growing capacity to commoditize user-generated content. Thus one should have no illusions about Goodreads: it's there to sell us things.

Even so, I do not believe the website's commercial interests ruin the qualitative validity of all the data on the website. While we may not trust Goodreads's data in the aggregate, I think the website, on a smaller scale, does serve as a forum for readers to share their reflections on what they've read and why. At any rate, it's not as though the choices we make in reading are ever entirely free from commoditization or from the innumerable ways the market invisibly steers us toward one thing rather than another. Mediation is a constitutive part of the way we live now. Rather than bemoan that fact, I identify what this social network affords: a window onto experiences, like Corinne's, that have largely gone unnoticed in previous work on reception.

Taking a closer look at the Goodreads data, we can see that Corinne's response is hardly unique. As of this writing, *Thugs and the Women Who Love Them* has an average rating of 4.59 out of 5 stars, based on 3,878 ratings. Seventy-three percent of users, or 2,835 members, gave the book 5 stars, while only 1 percent, or 55 members, gave it 1 star. Underneath the title of the book, there's a hyperlink: "(Thug #1)." This takes you to a webpage that brings together all the titles in Clark's thug love series. The second installment, *Every Thug Needs a Lady*, has the highest average rating of the group (4.69/5), but all of the books have high scores, including the sixth and most recent title, *Honor Thy Thug* (2013), which has an average rating of 4.51 out of 5 stars.

A brief glance at other pages on the website shows that Clark is not just one of the highest-rated street lit authors on Goodreads; she outperforms even the most broadly popular authors in the United States. That is the case, for example, with the young-adult novelist Suzanne Collins (*The Hunger Games*; 4.37/5), the fantasy writer George R. R. Martin (*A Game of Thrones*; 4.44/5), and perennial favorite Harper Lee (*To Kill a Mockingbird*; 4.24/5). Finally, it probably goes without saying that Clark's ratings easily surpass those of any so-called canonical figure, from Aeschylus to Yeats. While it's undoubtedly true that Goodreads encourages niche segmenting among readers, such that any rating is relative to scale and is in no way absolute, this sorting-out process does make room for nonmainstream readers to have their opinions appreciated by others online, via social media. In this sense, while comparing Clark to Conrad on Goodreads would be like comparing apples to oranges, what one can find *within* Clark's pages on the website should tell us a lot about her books' reception norms.

■ ■ ■

What do online reviewers have to say about *Thugs and the Women Who Love Them*? Praise like this is typical: "These ladies are off the chain and in love with some ruff riders. Angel, Jaz, and Kyra go hard and love even harder. The action is fast and the storyline has numerous twists and turns. This is a classic urban lit tale. I'm off now to find the sequel" (Monique). The first thing that makes this review representative is its equal treatment of characters. Readers consistently identify the trio's romantic lives as their primary investment in the novel. Even more, they usually name the characters as a definable set—"Angel, Jaz, and Kyra"—before going on to address individuating traits. This suggests that Clark's thug love series is constructed to appeal broadly to black girls and young women as a demographic. The author spreads attention across three characters to mime the social dynamics of sisterhood that defines black female friendship and intragender relationships. Unsurprisingly, then, the vast majority of Goodreads users who have rated or reviewed the novel appear to be or identify explicitly as black girls and young women. In this sense, *Thugs*'s braided plotline mirrors the real-life social network to which it appeals.

At the end of her comments, Monique mentions her eagerness to pick up the sequel. Seriality is the second structuring factor in black women's demand for urban fiction. Her point is echoed by another user, Cheri Cromartie, who bemoans, "Barnes & Noble is closed and I'm on the edge with Jaz being sentenced to seventeen years!!" By leaving the reader with a cliffhanger—What will happen to Jaz as she finds herself on the threshold of prison and motherhood?—the author not only creates anticipation for the narrative's continuation but encourages a practice of serial reading among her fans. There are, of course, a handful of users who complain that the novel does not have a clear-cut ending. But most of them pick up on the idea that the entire point of the first book is to read on. DoLL puts this point nicely when she claims, "The only problem I had with this book is that it was too short. I literally read this book in one day." This "problem," uttered with tongue in cheek, is a welcome one insofar as she recognizes that *Thugs* "has just the right amount [of] drama to keep you wanting more." Rather than see the book's brevity as a deficiency, this user lauds it as Clark's way of extending, or indeed drawing out, readerly pleasure. In her account, serial reading is interwoven with black female desire, and "wanting more" is valued in its own right.

Readers operating within street lit's genre parameters of sisterhood and seriality find much that's usefully illuminating in *Thugs*. Take these highly positive assessments:

> Throughout the book the girls express how they want to get out of the hood. I applied that to me. (Dominique)

> They were all focused on not letting the hood define them and making something of themselves. (Kitani)

> They are not going to let the ghetto turn them out as in make them change the way they game and turn into girls with no class. (Leanna Armstrong)

Somewhat counterintuitively, these users talk about Angel, Kyra, and Jaz in *inspirational* terms. That reading goes against the critical tendency to frame urban fiction's characters in apologetic (at best) or pathological (at worst) terms because of their involvement in criminal activity. Readers don't approach the novel with such a moralizing lens. They would rather acknowledge the motivation behind such activity: a desire to escape the environs into which they were born. Seen from this angle, it makes sense that characters' actions would be flawed or compromised. When the point is to get out by any means necessary, one's hands are bound to get dirty. The question for these readers, then, isn't "Are these women doing something illegal?" but "Can these women escape difficult circumstances using the tools available to them?"

From that basis of understanding, Goodreads users are then able to craft nuanced responses about the role of men in the narrative. For many of them, black women's desire for social mobility exists in tension with their desire for the proverbial "bad boy." As they make clear, this isn't a conflict between love and money, nor is it a conflict between go-getters and triflers. (All of Clark's male characters are go-getters in their own way.) It's a conflict, really, within the women themselves, and it's based on the following interior assessment: Will this man help or hinder my goal of reaching a better life? Goodreads reviewer Lisa Moulton posits that question in this way: "Very motivated ladies getting ahead in life while yet trying to be in a relationship with their thug boyfriends . . . [But] my question is how will they break free from the thug life if they love a bad boy too much to walk away?" The narrative of *Thugs* is defined by what Moulton calls the "while yet" of loving someone who threatens to stymie your dreams. For her, Clark offers the goal of simultaneously loving someone and dreaming of a better life, but she also shows how these things are constantly at risk of becoming incompatible. Mirrlees states the matter bluntly: "Angel in love with a pimp but attending school to be an atty, what's wrong with that picture. huh????" Between them, and characteristic of a lot of the reviews on Goodreads, Moulton and Mirrlees identify the conflict at the heart of Clark's narrative.

The particular uses to which women put this act of reading—of working through narrative conflict—are as varied as one might expect from a critical reading of any text. Several reviewers attest to how the novel sheds light on real-life experiences, especially when it comes to relationships. Dominique, for example, confesses, "I would relate [to] the character's attitudes, and also the settings of each book. This book affected me as to how I look at any male." By placing herself in the fictionalized circle of friends, this user devises strategies for how to view men in her own life. Other reviewers are more explicit about what those strategies entail. Telivia Talley, for example, writes, "I can relate to Jaz just a little, recently my sister broke up with her boyfriend that shes been with for years just to be with someone that was just fun for the moment. now shes some were stuck wanting her old life back just like how Jazz was when her an her man broke it off." And Aneyah, in reflecting on Angel's relationship to Snake, says, "This connects to the world because domestic violence happens every day. Some women don't fight back like the character in the book and die in these situations." Crucial to point out here is how these readers relate not to specific characters as ego ideals but to specific *situations* that they or somebody else or black women in general have experienced. Far from idolizing criminal activity, urban fiction's relatability is about making sense of a world in which black femininity is routinely victimized.

That *Thugs* elicits situational understanding from readers helps explain why many of them are drawn to the narrative's romantic plotline. The point is not to demonize black men but to underscore the fact that they too need love. Again, this reading goes against the critical tendency to describe street lit's readers as falling prey to a kind of animal lust. In fact, Goodreads users demonstrate that they are quite adept at teasing out the affective nuances in these fictional relationships. Kitani, for example, states, "So much drama was occurring and no matter what each thug was involved in, it didn't stop the women from loving them. . . . Thugs and the women who love them proved things will never be easy but with the right one by your side you can withstand anything." Shaybb elaborates, "wahida brings da thugs and their woman to whole new different level becuz thugs need a woman to love them." And, not least, Dcakes101 clearly emphasizes, "THIS BOOK REALLY JUSTIFIES THAT EVERY MAN NEEDS THAT 1 WOM[A]N IN HIS LIFE TO BE WITH HIM TILL DEATH [DO] YOU PART." At no point do these reviewers excuse men's criminal activity or domestic violence. They are clear about the fact that male love interests do Angel, Kyra, and Jaz wrong. However, neither do they cast criminal activity or domestic violence as *inherent* qualities of black masculinity. If the female characters struggle to reconcile loving and dreaming, the decisive question for the male characters is whether they can reform and become the embodiment of that sought-after reconciliation. This is par for the course in the good girl–bad boy love story, and it's a meaning to which everyday readers of urban fiction are clearly attuned.

Of course, situational understanding need not always be "positive." In fact, some readers view the book as a cautionary tale, wherein the female characters realize "their choices in men didn't reflect the change they were seeking" and that "crime doesn't pay" (Destiny). In one case, a reviewer plaintively observes, "I found myself relating [to] the characters . . . unfortunately, not in good ways" (Imani Phillips). Yet even this cautionary use of the novel does not preclude enjoyment on the part of the reader. Time and again reviewers stress how much they like the book *while* articulating a harsh judgment against some of its characters' actions. "This was an awesome book," writes Tasha, even though it "gives you an ugly look at how raunchy and gutter the streets can be." Rakia is blunter: "Despite the stupidity of the characters this book is addicting." And April Sherman sums up the contradictory feelings with a very personal take on the novel: "Off the chain . . . Brought back memories . . . (sigh) may my boo Rest In Peace." What I find most fascinating about these responses is exactly how caution is expressed. Some, like Sherman's, are tinged with loss and regret or "relating . . . not in good ways." Others, like Rakia's, evince a clear sense of what the reader would never do or not relating with the characters at all. Taken together, these cautionary responses do not establish a consensus about readerly identification. Instead, they reveal how *Thugs* opens up fictive space for black women to find their own voice within *or* outside of the narrative, and as such, to make up their own minds about what they like about the book. This structured optionality is, I believe, what readers find most pleasurable about reading urban fiction.

My analysis of the Goodreads data follows Kenneth Burke's influential call to conceive "literature as equipment for living." In the essay titled after that phrase, Burke proposes to view literary expression as "*strategies* for dealing with *situations*. Insofar as situations are typical and recurrent in a given social structure, people develop names for them and strategies for handling them." By reframing literary expression in this pragmatic vein, Burke hopes to determine not what literature is (a task that he thinks is fruitless) but what literature *does*. In place of the question of literary quality or value, he would like to examine the question of literary activity. In this sense, Burke is interested in restoring the dynamism of reading to the study of literature. Such is the object of what he calls "sociological criticism," a project that "would seek to codify the various strategies which artists have developed with relation to the naming of situations."[24] Crucially, that criticism would not reduce literature to sociology. Rather, it would free up the *uses* to which readers put any given work, regardless of content or quality.

Burke admits that his sociological criticism would "violate current pieties, break down current categories, and thereby 'outrage good taste.'" "But," he continues, "'good taste' has become *inert*. The classifications I am proposing would be *active*."[25] Here Burke outlines the necessity of focusing on everyday use. Limiting our understanding of literature to critical legitimation has the effect of turning literature into a dead letter. The appeal to taste, Burke suggests, ensures that literature can exist only in a hermetic, highly exclusive realm. By contrast, the study of literature's usefulness expands not only the range of what can be deemed "literary" but the potential for literature to *act* in the world. Far from being a domain of disinterested reflection, the literary imagination, for Burke, is something to put into practice, whose value resides in its utility for living.

It's telling, I think, that the handful of one-star reviews of *Thugs and the Women Who Love Them* come from those who concede they have no use for urban fiction. Sarah, in fact, admits this right off the bat: "I write this review with the caveat that I am not the target population for this type of novel. I read this for a class." That she goes on to offer a dismal view of the novel is unnecessary, of course. She has already assured us that her whiteness and the fact that this was required reading for her make this book anathema to her interests. Far from being an outlier, the rhetoric of Sarah's first sentence is echoed in other one-star assessments:

> I didn't give it much more than a cursory pass-through because there was too much meaningless sex, language, and it really didn't go anywhere. (Alicia)
>
> I'm not wasting my time reading this. (Laura)
>
> Definitely not the target demographic—shocked at how fast I read it though. (Marian Buck)

Consider that these are the reviews' first lines (or the only line, in Buck's case). Again, there's no need to read further since these readers start off by disavowing any real use for the book. The fact that the reviewers here are white women is not coincidental. The low ratings bespeak their refusal to see, or even consider, the usefulness of street lit to readers who are not like them.

▩　▩　▩

It's important that we not mime the logic of these responses in our own critical approaches to the genre. Urban fiction does not need to appeal to bourgeois tastes or to rhyme with canonical black writing in order to be taken seriously. As I have tried to show in this essay, black women readers *already* take the genre seriously—and that, on its own, should suffice to command our attention. In this light, one way of reframing the urban fiction debate is to retire the depth-model, vaguely psychoanalytic question, "What do black readers want?," and replace it with the site-specific, properly Burkean question, "What do black readers make of their books?" The latter opens up the critical imagination to uses of literature it could hardly conceive. Even more, it supposes that readers do not need to be told why they value what they read; Burke might say they enact or "do" it as a matter of course. Examining the Goodreads data on *Thugs and the Women Who Love Them* is my imperfect effort to model this kind of inquiry. However persuasive it may be judged, I'm confident its premise—that Wahida Clark's novel is useful to readers who are not like me—is a methodological necessity for future work in the field.

Notes

1 Patrick, "Urban Fiction."
2 On the specifically gendered appeal of gangsta rap in the 1990s, see Cheney, *Brothers Gonna Work It Out*.
3 Rosen, "Ashley and JaQuavis Coleman."
4 See Jacqueline Bobo, *Black Women as Cultural Readers*. This objective owes much to Bobo's critical example. Though we focus on different readerly investments, and though much has changed in the quarter-century since her book came out, Bobo's effort to assess black women's complex engagements with popular culture is an inspiration for my work here.
5 Darnton, "What Is the History of Books?," 74.
6 Allen and Light, *From Voice to Influence*.
7 Williams, "'Precious' Little of Value."
8 Ulen, "The Naked Truth," 18.
9 Chiles, "Their Eyes Were Reading Smut."
10 Early, "What Is African-American Literature?," 20.
11 Smith, "Black Talk," 196.
12 Smith, "Black Talk," 196.
13 Clark, *Thugs*, 154.
14 Clark, *Thugs*, 209.
15 Clark, *Thugs*, vii–viii.
16 Cutler, "Q&A with Wahida Clark."
17 Sands, "Holler."
18 XXL Staff, "Cash Money Books Author"; Campbell, "Wahida Clark."
19 See Bragg and Ikard, "Feminism and the Streets".
20 In the analysis that follows, I have decided to cite online reviews without correcting spelling or punctuation, and without using the notation *sic*. In the spirit of taking these comments on their own terms, I want to refrain from imposing my sense of style onto their modes of expression.
21 "About Goodreads."
22 Nakamura, "'Words with Friends,'" 242.
23 Herther, "Goodreads."
24 Burke, "Literature," 296–97, 301.
25 Burke, "Literature," 303.

References

"About Goodreads." Goodreads, n.d. https://www.goodreads.com/about/us.
Alicia. Review of *Thugs and the Women Who Love Them*, by Wahida Clark. Goodreads, July 15, 2011. http://www.goodreads.com/review/show/185322994.

Allen, Danielle, and Jennifer S. Light, eds. *From Voice to Influence: Understanding Citizenship in a Digital Age*. Chicago: University of Chicago Press, 2015.

Aneyah. Review of *Thugs and the Women Who Love Them*, by Wahida Clark. Goodreads, November 9, 2012. http://www.goodreads.com/review/show/449465775.

Armstrong, Leanna. Review of *Thugs and the Women Who Love Them*, by Wahida Clark. Goodreads, February 6, 2009. http://www.goodreads.com/review/show/45567084.

Bobo, Jacqueline. *Black Women as Cultural Readers*. New York: Columbia University Press, 1995.

Bragg, Beauty, and David Ikard. "Feminism and the Streets: Urban Fiction and the Quest for Female Independence in the Era of Transactional Sexuality." *Palimpsest* 1, no. 2 (2012): 237–55.

Buck, Marian. Review of *Thugs and the Women Who Love Them*, by Wahida Clark. Goodreads, February 10, 2016. http://www.goodreads.com/review/show/1142019591.

Burke, Kenneth. "Literature as Equipment for Living." In *The Philosophy of Literary Form: Studies in Symbolic Action*. Baton Rouge: Louisiana State University Press, 1941.

Campbell, Rhonda. "Wahida Clark: The Story behind Her Successful Urban Publishing Business." *Madame Noir*, May 24, 2012. http://madamenoire.com/180241/wahida-clark-how-she-launched-her-publishing-business-from-behind-prison-walls/.

Cheney, Charise L. *Brothers Gonna Work It Out: Sexual Politics in the Golden Age of Rap Nationalism*. New York: New York University Press, 2005.

Chiles, Nick. "Their Eyes Were Reading Smut." *New York Times*, January 4, 2006. http://www.nytimes.com/2006/01/04/opinion/04chiles.html.

Clark, Wahida. *Thugs and the Women Who Love Them*. Brooklyn, NY: Black Print, 2002.

Corinne. Review of *Thugs and the Women Who Love Them*, by Wahida Clark. Goodreads, February 28, 2009. http://www.goodreads.com/review/show/47837678

Cromartie, Cheri. Review of *Thugs and the Women Who Love Them*, by Wahida Clark. Goodreads, December 11, 2015. http://www.goodreads.com/review/show/1462911629.

Cutler, Jacqueline. "Q&A with Wahida Clark: 'I Started Visualizing My Name on the Spines.'" *Newark (NJ) Star-Ledger*, June 2, 2013. http://www.nj.com/entertainment/arts/index.ssf/2013/06/qa_with_wahida_clark_i_started.html.

DoLL. Review of *Thugs and the Women Who Love Them*, by Wahida Clark. Goodreads, May 16, 2015. http://www.goodreads.com/review/show/990241376.

Darnton, Robert. "What Is the History of Books?" *Daedalus* 111, no. 3 (1982): 65–83.

Dcakes101. Review of *Thugs and the Women Who Love Them*, by Wahida Clark. *Goodreads*, January 20, 2011. http://www.goodreads.com/review/show/142290806.

Destiny. Review of *Thugs and the Women Who Love Them*, by Wahida Clark. Goodreads, December 16, 2013. http://www.goodreads.com/review/show/739181880.

Dominique. Review of *Thugs and the Women Who Love Them*, by Wahida Clark. Goodreads, January 11, 2009. http://www.goodreads.com/review/show/39149036.

Early, Gerald. "What Is African-American Literature?" *eJournal USA* 14, no. 2 (2009): 17–20.

Herther, Nancy K. "Goodreads: Social Media Meets Readers Advisory." *Online Searcher*, July–August 2013: 38–41.

Kitani. Review of *Thugs and the Women Who Love Them*, by Wahida Clark. Goodreads, May 31, 2015. http://www.goodreads.com/review/show/405727979.

Laura. Review of *Thugs and the Women Who Love Them*, by Wahida Clark. Goodreads, June 8, 2015. http://www.goodreads.com/review/show/1133506088.

Mirrlees. Review of *Thugs and the Women Who Love Them*, by Wahida Clark. Goodreads, April 6, 2013. http://www.goodreads.com/review/show/537112231.

Monique. Review of *Thugs and the Women Who Love Them*, by Wahida Clark. Goodreads, December 4, 2011. http://www.goodreads.com/review/show/227916431.

Moulton, Lisa. Review of *Thugs and the Women Who Love Them*, by Wahida Clark. Goodreads, July 18, 2013. http://www.goodreads.com/review/show/670856326.

Nakamura, Lisa. "'Words with Friends': Socially Networked Reading on *Goodreads*." *PMLA* 128, no. 1 (2013): 238–43.

Patrick, Diane. "Urban Fiction." *Publishers Weekly*, May 19, 2003: 31.

Phillips, Imani. Review of *Thugs and the Women Who Love Them*, by Wahida Clark. Goodreads, October 31, 2013. http://www.goodreads.com/review/show/722894345.

Rakia. Review of *Thugs and the Women Who Love Them*, by Wahida Clark. Goodreads, July 17, 2011. http://www.goodreads.com/review/show/181379467.

Rosen, Jody. "Ashley and JaQuavis Coleman: Kiss Kiss Bang Bang," *T Magazine*, May 3, 2015. http://tmagazine.blogs.nytimes.com/2015/05/03/ashley-jaquavis-coleman-profile/.

Sands, Darren. "Holler If Ya Read Me: African-American Writers—and Readers—Fret over the Future of Thug Lit." *New York Observer*, May 13, 2013. http://observer.com/2013/05/holler-if-ya-read-me-african-american-writers-and-writers-fret-over-the-future-of-thug-lit/.

Sarah. Review of *Thugs and the Women Who Love Them*, by Wahida Clark. Goodreads, October 5, 2012. http://www.goodreads.com/review/show/424300346.

Shaybb. Review of *Thugs and the Women Who Love Them*, by Wahida Clark. Goodreads, August 20, 2009. http://www.goodreads.com/review/show/68163769.

Sherman, April. Review of *Thugs and the Women Who Love Them*, by Wahida Clark. Goodreads, November 12, 2012. http://www.goodreads.com/review/show/454350613.

Smith, Danyel. "Black Talk and Hot Sex: Why 'Street Lit' Is Literature." In *Total Chaos: The Art and Aesthetics of Hip-Hop*, edited by Jeff Chang. New York: Basic-Civitas, 2006.

Talley, Telivia. Review of *Thugs and the Women Who Love Them*, by Wahida Clark. Goodreads, October 30, 2013. http://www.goodreads.com/review/show/738407469.

Tasha. Review of *Thugs and the Women Who Love Them*, by Wahida Clark. Goodreads, October 16, 2009. http://www.goodreads.com/review/show/74783378.

Ulen, Eisa Nefertari. "The Naked Truth." *Crisis* (Winter 2008): 18–21.

Williams, Juan. "'Precious' Little of Value in Ghetto Lit." *Wall Street Journal*, November 5, 2009. http://www.wsj.com/news/articles/SB10001424052748703740004574514260044271666.

XXL Staff. "Cash Money Books Author Wahida Clark Talks Prison, Inspiration, and Future Projects." XXL, May 2, 2012. http://www.xxlmag.com/lifestyle/2012/05/cash-money-books-author-wahida-clark-talks-prison-inspiration-and-future-projects/.

AN INTERVIEW WITH PATRICIA HILL COLLINS / APRIL 9, 2017

What is the state of Black pop culture in the public sphere and as an intellectual field of inquiry in the twenty-first century?

Black artists and intellectuals who use popular culture as the primary venue for their creative production, differ from critics and theorists in the academy who task themselves with discussing and analyzing this work. Often these are the same people, making it difficult to tell which hat a given thinker is wearing. But conflating the two endeavors masks the different contributions and limitations of creative production and of cultural criticism.

Black popular culture in the public sphere houses creative expression that is heterogeneous, richly textured, and contradictory. Gone are the historical straitjackets of searching for heroic positive images to stave off negative Black stereotypes. A plethora of representations of blackness, many of them crafted by African Americans and other people of African descent, coexist with many intractable historical stereotypes. Whenever I can, I watch and/or listen to a wide array of film, music, art, drama, best-sellers, and videos that engage social and political issues of anti-Black racism and that offer an array of representations of blackness. Independent films, reality television, and YouTube videos provide rich and contradictory depictions of African Americans among others as well as conceptions of blackness.

Yet Black popular culture is about far more than the content of representations. Evaluating representations of blackness in popular culture requires clarifying all aspects of the political economy of production, from the inception of ideas, which ideas become cultural projects and which do not, patterns of audience consumption, and the intended and unexpected effects on audiences. What makes Black popular culture "Black"? Is it seeing people who seemingly "look like us" in television shows, films, music videos, and graphic novels? Is it knowing that people of African descent wrote, produced, and/or directed these products? Individual African American artists have made tremendous strides in trying to bring quality experiences to the broader project of Black popular culture. Yet they do not work in a vacuum.

What makes Black popular culture "popular"? Success within popular culture requires popularity with an ostensibly general audience that far too often means white, male, and young American consumers. Representations of African Americans among others must be recognizable and palatable to this general public, or a specific film, video, or hip-hop superstar cannot be popular. Moreover, the speed with which images travel means that representations of blackness within popular culture also aim to speak to global audiences who bring their own distinctive sensibilities to American race relations.

When it comes to Black popular culture as an intellectual field of inquiry, especially in the academy, I value the new work in cultural studies, media studies, Africana studies, women's studies, and other places that currently house this far-reaching field of study. Yet popularity comes with caveats. Instant experts routinely show up in new fields that seem to be hot, and fields that appear to be popular because their material is familiar to the public run the risk of attracting opportunists. The field of education has long faced this problem—because most people have attended school or know someone who has, they see themselves as instant experts on what's wrong with schooling and what can be done to fix it. Cultural critics of Black popular culture face similar boundary issues, but with a twist. Producing and criticizing art in an era of consumer capitalism that markets unneeded products and services raises new questions about the integrity of our work. Is Black popular culture popular because it is good, or because it can be sold? Does Black popular culture as an intellectual field of inquiry exist as an extension of Black popular culture itself or as a savvy marketing tool where everybody gets paid?

If anyone can become an instant cultural critic of blackness, then what use is a field? What can and should fields do to protect the integrity of their core? My sense is that a book like *Are You Entertained?* reflects these kinds of questions. The field of Black cultural criticism, especially as organized within academic venues, might consider asking itself some hard-hitting questions: In what ways is the thoughtful, substantive analysis that characterizes much of this field, especially late twentieth-century scholarship, obscured by the mediocrity of others? How many more academic papers does the field need on movies, parts of movies, television shows, and characters on television shows, not to mention the intense scrutiny granted song lyrics? Stuart Hall and the other authors in the 1992 volume *Black Popular Culture* confronted the paucity of representations of people of African descent and blackness, not our current era of overload, and certainly not the excesses of consumer capitalism. Because they were at the front end of the explosion of representations of blackness in Black popular culture, they asked hard-hitting questions. The current challenge to the field seems to be analyzing the effects of the exponential growth of Black cultural products themselves on all consumers, but especially African American consumers and people of African descent in different national settings.

> *How do you see Stuart Hall's theorization of the "Black" in Black popular culture influencing your intellectual engagement with Black cultural productions?*

This question initially stumped me, because I honestly couldn't remember enough of Hall's arguments in that specific essay to trace the effects on my own work. Rereading Hall's essay did jar some memories about my initial reactions to this particular piece. When I first read the essay, I recall liking it in the abstract but felt that it spoke more to the concerns of Black intellectuals in New York who were developing a theoretical framework for the Black public sphere than it did to front-line actors like myself *within* African American studies who were defending programs and departments that were under assault. Hall wrote within a British context of anti-Black racism. The United Kingdom's pre–World War II Afro-Caribbean British citizens, more recent migrants from the Caribbean and continental Africa, and South Asian migrants aimed to forge a British identity around a shared political blackness. This socially constructed political blackness made intellectual and political sense in the British context of decolonization and migration. In this context, Hall's critical synthesis of poststructuralism and Marxist social theory in shaping British cultural studies spoke to many African American scholars who were interrogating the meaning of blackness.

That wasn't me. At that time, I remained skeptical that Hall's analysis was relevant within a U.S. context that was still struggling with the effects of official public policies of racial segregation. In the 1990s, African Americans faced serious social problems and also confronted a sustained backlash against the gains of the civil rights, Black Power, and similar mid-twentieth-century social justice movements. Because I was working in an African American studies department, I was preoccupied with more bread-and-butter issues than the meaning of Black culture. Mass incarceration, calls to dismantle social welfare policies, the fallout from the crack cocaine epidemic, the defunding of public education as well as sustained efforts to dismantle the very field in which I worked took all my time.

When it came to Black culture, those of us in Africana studies were fighting for the right to define ourselves as Black people. Much as the early twentieth century struggle to capitalize the word *negro* pivoted on capitalizing the term *Negro*, we capitalized the term *Black* in the phrase *Black people* as a gesture of self-definition. Capitalizing the word *Black* when describing various subgroups of Black people, for example, Black women or Black men, highlights the significance of Black people as a historically recognized population group. But during this time, struggles were more than semantic. In the United States, we also confronted the legacy of interpretations of Black culture as the cause of African American poverty and the rationale for African American disenfranchisement. From struggles to get the term "Black" capitalized in our publications to struggles to challenge the arguments about culture and Black people, Black culture was a site of political contestation, not a space of creative retreat.

Black cultural critics and I during the 1990s seemed to be running in very different circles. Despite the fact that I had a tenured job with benefits, I was underpaid, overworked, and associated with a disrespected field. Given these political, social, and intellectual assaults, the 1990s were a time of closing ranks for reasons of safety and protection. My concern lay less with investigating the meaning of blackness via abstract issues of identity and culture and more with the social problems confronting African Americans, Black people, and others who faced a similar anti-Black racism. Moreover, the uptake of Hall's work within certain Black intellectual circles left me wondering why some African American academics found this question of investigating Black popular culture so compelling. Were these people front-line actors in trying to build Black studies departments and programs, or was their involvement in blackness a sideline business?

Rereading Hall highlights what has changed in my thinking and what hasn't. By today's academic standards, my former perspective may sound harsh, yet the outcome and aftermath of the 2016 U.S. presidential campaign highlights how issues of Black popular culture remain deeply intertwined with bread-and-butter issues of anti-Black racism and political disempowerment. Closing ranks in the face of a threat to Black people as a collectivity, and arguing for the shared humanity of people of African descent in the United States, Canada, Brazil, the Caribbean, the many countries of continental Africa, as well as Europe, was essential then and remains so now. Yet developing solidarity in response to a global anti-Black racism also means crafting a more heterogeneous and inclusive conception of blackness within Black politics. In this regard, Hall pointed us in the right direction. His work foreshadowed the steady move toward intersectional analyses of race, class, and nation, as well as the centrality of intersectional frameworks for analyzing and responding to anti-Black racism. The Black Lives Matter movement, for example, embraces an expansive understanding of blackness that was virtually unthinkable when Hall issued his call to rethink Black culture. I remain open to any social theory that can connect the dots from the social issues that most concern African Americans and others who experience variations of anti-Black racism to political agendas and action strategies for empowerment. Yet because I remain angered by the deeply entrenched nature of anti-Black racism in the United States, I value the insights of frontline actors who do the dirty work of keeping African American communities going, as much as if not more than elegant abstractions about the meaning of blackness, including my own.

> Do you feel the digital age affects the production, reception, and dissemination of Black pop culture in ways that compel us to both continue revisiting Hall's piece but to also build upon it? If yes, how do you see contemporary theorists and critics building upon Hall's work given the changes the digital age has produced? If no, why do you feel the digital age does not compel scholars to revisit Hall and build upon his work?

Hall's work is extremely important in ways that go beyond his critical essay on blackness. I'm much more likely to engage the corpus of Hall's work in relation to intersectionality, namely, Hall's attention to race (here discussed through the lens of Black culture), but also to class, nation, and ethnicity. Given the suppression of class analysis in the United States, Hall remains on a short list of intellectuals who analyze social class by engaging the core ideas of Marxist social thought in *relation* to racism, nationalism, and colonialism. Hall's thesis of articulation foreshadows contemporary understandings of intersectionality as a form of critical inquiry and praxis. Moreover, Hall not only did top-notch cultural criticism, but he was also a major partner in shaping the Birmingham School of Cultural Studies. Hall was not just an armchair cultural critic—he helped institutionalize the field that made the work of his junior colleagues possible.

I neither feel obligated to revisit Hall's work on the meaning of blackness, nor do I think that the digital age necessarily compels scholars to do so. I do think that scholars in Black popular culture as a field of critical inquiry might place greater emphasis on two themes. First, we need a broader understanding of the corpus of Hall's work as well as how diverse intellectuals have used and appropriated various aspects of Hall's work. We can't cherry-pick one essay, in this case his essay on Black popular culture, ignoring the rest of his work. Reading beyond this one essay, it is apparent that Hall remained attentive to the structural shifts within capitalism, to British state policies regarding racism and immigration, and to how Black popular culture in the United Kingdom participated in those relationships. Black intellectuals in the United States must be mindful of Hall's expansive synthetic theorizing of anti-Black racism that contextualizes analyses of Black popular culture.

Second, building a field is hard work, especially in a digital era that raises entirely new possibilities concerning the politics of intellectual production and dissemination. Without sustained self-reflection that connects our work to the contemporary economic and political landscape, Black popular culture as a field of intellectual inquiry may fade away. The Birmingham School of Cultural Studies was dismantled in 2002. Yet Hall's ideas and those of others who were associated with that institutional location persist. Fifteen years from now, will the same be said of contemporary Black popular culture as a field of inquiry?

Your concern in Black Feminist Thought about the intersections of race, gender, and class in relationship to Black women's labor and the resulting suppression of their ideas or knowledge production remains

a relevant concern today, unfortunately. In what ways do you see
Black women utilizing popular culture as a site of resistance?

To me, popular culture is inherently contradictory. Depending on how cultural representations are used, they all contain potentially conciliatory and resistant dimensions. For Black popular culture, narrow understandings of resistance that assume that a given work or artist either collaborates with or resists the status quo miss the mark. The resistance lies neither in the intent of the artist—if we can in fact ever accurately ascertain an artist's intentionality— nor in audience reactions to music, film, fiction, and poetry. Rather, resistance occurs in the space of co-creation among artists, the cultural products they create, and how multiple audiences engage cultural productions. Resistance is something that is dynamic and always under construction.

One obvious site of resistance redresses Black women's historical exclusion from popular culture by enhancing our visible inclusion. Relying on the racial integration framework for measuring African American progress, we celebrate the hypervisible victories of African American women who seemingly desegregate Black popular culture. Black actresses who you wouldn't have seen several decades ago are increasingly visible in popular culture. We see so many Black women in popular culture that we forget that this visibility has been decades in the making. Julie Dash's 1982 independent film *Illusions* captures this issue of how talented African American women could not appear in front of the camera. In Dash's film, a white woman heroine appropriated the dubbed voice of a talented African American singer. The film invoked blackness without actually seeing Black people. Those days are over. Shonda Rhimes has had at least three successful shows on network television; director Ava DuVernay has entered the world of mainstream films and has made an Oscar-nominated documentary; comedian Wanda Sykes has expanded public space for intersections of sexuality, blackness, and gender; actress Viola Davis is finally receiving accolades; and arguments about whether Beyoncé's work contains Black feminist subtexts may continue for some time. This visibility can be read as resistance.

Yet there are dangers in interpreting simple inclusion as resistance. Popular culture is ever-evolving and any resistance associated with it changes in tandem. Bill Cosby's fall from grace should make us cautious about prematurely assessing the career, film, or corpus of any figure within popular culture as "resistance." Understanding how resistance may be working within ambiguous cultural products may be more important than a simple tally of visible representation. For example, how refreshing it is to see casting that rejects prevailing notions of racial, gender, and sexual order. The 2015 surreal film *The Fits* focuses on an eleven-year-old African American girl who excels as a boxer in an all-male environment. Yet when she aspires to join an all-girl dance team, her actions unsettle prevailing conventions concerning gender, sexuality, and appropriate transitions to womanhood. Initially, the director aimed to cast white girls in the film, yet ultimately used an all–African American cast and set the film in an inner-city Cincinnati, Ohio, neighborhood. These decisions changed the meaning of the film without making it a film about race. Similarly, work where representations of blackness seem to uphold prevailing stereotypes yet simultaneously undermine them point toward elements of resistance. Again, casting matters, but not due to inclusion. In countless television dramas, when police round up prostitutes for questioning or arrest, an African American woman is typically part of the group. If she were missing, her *absence* would constitute an anomaly that challenges the meaning of the category of prostitute. How might white audiences read the new casting? How would working-class or middle-class audiences? Or African American women, for that matter?

Black audiences who are differently situated within relations of race, class, gender, and sexuality bring cultural codes and patterns of interpretation that may be less visible if not completely misunderstood by non-Black groups. Black people often use cultural products toward resistant ends. All viewers can enjoy Netflix's 2016–18 series *Luke Cage* as a fun story of a Harlem superhero. Yet African American audiences can also enjoy the layers of subtext concerning representations of blackness regarding music, urban politics, masculinity, a revalorization of the meaning of the hoodie, and refreshing depictions of women who are not simply ancillary to the actions of men. Subversive readings of popular culture's subtexts can be as subversive as, if not more subversive than, simply celebrating images of inclusion precisely because visible representations of blackness can lead audiences to assume that equality has been achieved.

> *And what continuities or discontinuities do you see emerging between the public "talking back," or the Black social media "clapback," of contemporary Black women popular culture producers and the Black women scholars and writers who shaped the field of Black women's studies during the 1970s and 1980s?*

It all depends on how you conceptualize "clapback." Clapback as a digital update of playing the dozens may be entertaining, but to what end? I wonder how well that term actually travels in describing the experiences of African American women, Afro Brazilian women, Black women in South Africa, Black British women and the like. How does this particular cultural practice work among such a heterogeneous population? I also wonder how much that term reflects the experiences of a particular generation of African American women in the academy and in the United States who discover Black Feminism in a digital age.

Serious debates that aim to strengthen the intergenerational ties that have sustained Black Feminism are one thing. Clapback that invokes the wit and wisdom of playing the dozens certainly livens up staid academic discourse. They say, "I check you because I love you and know that you can do better." Yet disagreements that deteriorate into friction, conflict, and finger-pointing are another. Sadly, one common set of practices within academia lies in rewarding opportunistic people who try to build their careers in the here-and-now by trashing what was done in the past. This kind of cultural criticism panders to neoliberalism, the fallacy of thinking that you as an individual did it all, all by yourself, and that you can build a career criticizing everyone else with no regard for consequences. What sense does it make to take one of the worst features of the white male academy and uncritically incorporate it into Black Feminism? It is disrespectful—and I do mean to invoke the term *respect* here in Aretha Franklin's sense—to negate, ignore, and criticize the accomplishments of previous generations that made one's current accomplishments possible.

When it comes to conversations among African American women, as well as Black women throughout the African Diaspora, opportunistic cultural criticism is bad for Black Feminism. To reduce Black Feminism writ large to an internecine battle of "talking back" or "clapback" among ourselves is counterproductive. Fortunately, that's not what I see happening. Black Feminism is far from finished, and there is plenty of work to go around to keep it going. In the United States, African Americans and any other social group that consistently finds its members relegated to the bottom of hierarchies of race, class, gender, sexuality, age, ethnicity, and disability face precarious futures. The institutionalized violence that lies at the heart of anti-Black racism continues to normalize violence against people of African descent in the United States and in a global context. This violence takes aim at African American women, forces us to witness the violence experienced by our sisters, our mothers, our brothers, our fathers, and our children, and expects us to clean up the damage done in the aftermath. There is much joy in Black life, and I am not defending a humorless, pessimistic view of the world. From signifying to clapback, Black culture has an arsenal of tools to use for cultural critique. This is not the time to relax and pretend that racism, sexism, class exploitation, and homophobia are far enough in the past that we can mimic the adolescent rebellions of privileged white youth in relation to their powerful white parents. There's too much at stake.

Sirma Bilge, one of your collaborators, has argued that academic discourse on intersectionality and antiracism in the twenty-first century has become depoliticized and deliberately neutralized through neoliberal regimes. Similarly, debate about what constitutes Black Feminism in the contemporary moment has spilled into popular culture from the academic realm. Ultimately, in the twenty-first century, Black women producing popular culture are beginning to vocally and explicitly engage what it means to embody multiple identities and champion the social and political rights of women. In what ways do you see contemporary Black artists working to politicize intersectionality and antiracism activism? How do you see ideologies and theories of Black feminism manifesting in the popular realm?

I think that popular culture may be eclipsing the academy as the site of Black Feminism. Once I began looking for Black Feminism beyond the academy, I found exciting expressions of it within social media, the blogosphere, and within Black popular culture. Given African American women's history with the ideas of feminism (as opposed to specific communities of women who laid claim to those ideas as their property), the public and unapologetic reclamation of Black Feminism is refreshing. Black women are definitely more open and explicit about claiming Black feminism in popular culture than in the academy.

Beyoncé's 2016 work provides one provocative case. Beyoncé's career can be seen as a savvy set of choices about how to work a hegemonic popular culture that is trying to work you. I've been following Beyoncé for some time. I opened *Black Sexual Politics* (2004) with a brief discussion of the song "Bootylicious" by Destiny's Child. I situated the song both within and against a historical fascination with African American women's buttocks. What intrigued me about the song was how it encouraged multiple interpretations from different audiences. Their song "I'm a Survivor" was far more popular than "Bootylicious," primarily because many African American women claimed it as an anthem that described their survival despite exploitation and abuse. In the context of the image of the "strong Black woman" lauded in "I'm a Survivor," "Bootylicious" seemed more frivolous because it seemingly undercut representations of respectability. Instead, "Bootylicious" issued a clarion call concerning owning one's own self, enjoying the fruits of one's own labor, and celebrating the part of Black women's bodies that invoked blackness. To me, "Bootylicious," "Formation," and "Lemonade" constitute points along a trajectory of one artist's work in bringing Black women's body politics into view. Beyoncé's work on Black women's body politics is especially important because her body has been so prominently on display. Claiming her body in public, especially control over its sexualized parts as well as economic value within commodity capitalism, resonates with themes within *Black Popular Culture* (1992).

Beyoncé is a successful African American woman artist, but some ask, is she a "Black feminist"? For me, that's the wrong question. I want to know what contributions any artist makes to Black Feminism specifically and social justice projects in general. Critical commentary that begins with a preconceived notion of Black Feminism and then proceeds to evaluate how well a given Black woman artist measures up simply misses the mark. If we keep that kind of evaluation up long enough, we won't recognize true art when we encounter it.

> You have noted your persistent effort to place your academic work in service to social justice. Part of that work seems to be to push for analytical debates rather than prescriptive routes to follow. Prescriptive routes, such as the boom in African American self-help books you discuss in Black Sexual Politics, seem to be thought of as reparative for a people who continue to fight for full incorporation into the nation. Where do you see such analytical debates occurring in Black popular culture? And do you see any specific ways in which the analytical offers the repair so desperately sought?

I don't think that popular culture intentionally spends much time devoted to healing—the title of this volume, *Are You Entertained?*, speaks to the core mission of popular culture. People may use popular culture as such, but that's not what it's designed to do. The trope of the despondent individual who was one step away from suicide who decided against it when hearing a popular song grants far too much power to discreet representations to intervene in any real healing. These kinds of cultural productions may drive ratings and sales, but how effectively can they heal?

In this context, healing that engages Black culture can make a contribution. Music, dance, poetry, fiction, religion, and other aspects of Black culture have long served as venues for healing the damage done by anti-Black racism. Did the blues tradition heal, or did it enable Black people to retain our humanity in order to survive? Is hip hop a problem for Black people, or is it a release for Black people from the anger and frustration with bad schools, no jobs, sexual assault, and police misconduct? The Sunday morning gospel choir can be therapeutic, but can one ever really "heal" from these kinds of assaults of anti-Black racism, sexism, ultranationalism, and homophobia?

Healing can actually become the subject matter of entertainment, performed in popular culture quite admirably without much actual healing occurring. For example, the confessional talk shows—and of course *The Oprah Winfrey Show* was quite central to this popular culture trend—enhanced the visibility of domestic violence, incest, and other important social problems. Oprah is a savvy businesswoman who, I suspect, has never defined herself as an actual mammy but instead recognized the power of the controlling image of the mammy for her audience. Guests on talk shows such as Winfrey's confess all sorts of horrible problems to ostensibly warm, caring hosts. Yet the superficial solutions offered up by confessional talk shows often do not match the visibility granted important social issues, many of them raised by figures such as Oprah. Guests who cannot heal themselves by simply trying harder are advised to get professional help. Pep talks that counsel individual viewers that they are not alone because millions of viewers are rooting for them find themselves alone when they turn off the television and their imagined support group disappears. Individual viewers watching these televised morality plays are left to fall back upon their own devices. Social media often fills the void created by confessional talk shows. There everyone is encouraged to share and confess, looking away from television screens and toward computer and cell phone screens for compassion and understanding. The result of this drumbeat of shows on downtrodden women or the pervasive sharing with people who one is unlikely to meet in everyday life can be a collective numbness, one that can make healing from trauma even more difficult.

Individual trauma emerges from collective trauma, and American culture's predilection to look away from the damage done to individuals by racism, sexism, class exploitation, statelessness, homophobia, and religious intolerance contributes to the perpetuation of harm. That said, I remain heartened by the growing willingness of artists to engage questions of harm in ways that humanize the suffering of African Americans rather than turning that suffering into comedy or highlighting it for some broader political agenda. Black popular culture can make interventions in the status quo from unlikely places. For example, in the pre-2016 era when the picture-perfect Obama family served as a template for evaluating African American mental health and respectability, some shows explored the challenges of African American middle-class families. For example, a clip from *Black-ish* showed the difficulties that confronted middle-class African American parents who felt they had to talk with their kids about how to deal with the police to avoid individual harm. This episode on "the talk" was familiar to many African American families but came as a surprise to white families where no such talk was required. This segment inserted a powerful small moment of resistance into a standard sitcom. Mara Brock Akil's show *Being Mary Jane* tackled the theme of suicide, not exclusively through the trauma of the individual but through the structural web of what may have contributed to it and how those left behind experienced this loss. Akil's characters are clearly in the upper echelons of American wealth. Yet they are depicted as real people with real problems that mandate healing. Black suffering and healing need not be exploitative.

Focusing on the humanity of people of African descent, taking responsibility for the ways in which we harm one another, understand each other's struggles, and the support we can give one another in grappling with the collective trauma of anti-Black racism is vital to individual and collective healing. In this regard, the growing corpus of films that work within this frame of the realities of Black people's lives provide a series of texts for understanding anti-Black racism and healing from it. We've come a long way from the groundbreaking film *Nothing But a Man* (1964) to *Moonlight*, the 2016 Oscar winner for best picture. The films that explore the humanity among Black people with an eye toward healing come with increasing frequency, *Pariah* (2011), *Middle of Nowhere* (2012), and *Twelve Years a Slave* (2013) come to mind. Films such as these come from different eras, but the ethos is the same. When we care for ourselves and others, we heal ourselves and others.

Popular culture can provide texts for healing, yet people need to look to one another for healing to occur. African Americans and our allies need to build community capacity that supports this endeavor. There are simply some things that cannot happen in cyberspace nor solely in our own heads. Popular culture is good for raising awareness but is no substitute for looking each other in the eye within families, communities, schools, and workplaces, recognizing each other for who we are in the context of what we confront.

CONTRIBUTORS

TAKIYAH NUR AMIN is a dance scholar, educator, and consultant. Her research focuses on twentieth-century American concert dance, African diaspora dance performance/aesthetics, and pedagogical issues in Dance studies. Her research has appeared in several academic journals including the *Black Scholar, Dance Chronicle, Dance Research Journal, Western Journal of Black Studies,* and *Journal of Pan-African Studies.*

PATRICIA HILL COLLINS is Distinguished University Professor of Sociology Emerita at the University of Maryland, College Park, Charles Phelps Taft Professor Emerita of African American Studies at the University of Cincinnati, and former president of the American Sociological Association. She is the author of numerous award-winning books, including *Fighting Words: Black Women and the Search for Justice* (1998); *Black Feminist Thought: Knowledge, Consciousness, and the Politics of Empowerment* (1990, 2000); *Black Sexual Politics: African Americans, Gender, and the New Racism* (2004); *From Black Power to Hip Hop: Racism, Nationalism, and Feminism* (2005); *Another Kind of Public Education: Race, Schools, the Media, and Democratic Possibilities* (2009); *The Handbook of Race and Ethnic Studies* (edited with John Solomos, 2010); *On Intellectual Activism* (2013); and *Intersectionality* (coauthored with Sirma Bilge, 2016). Her anthology *Race, Class, and Gender: Intersections and Inequalities,*

10th ed. (edited with Margaret Andersen, 2020) has been widely used in colleges and universities for thirty years. Her most recent book, *Intersectionality as Critical Social Theory*, was published by Duke University Press in 2019.

SIMONE C. DRAKE is the Hazel C. Youngberg Trustees Distinguished Professor of African American and African studies at The Ohio State University, where she also serves as department chair. She is the author of *When We Imagine Grace: Black Men and Subject Making* (2016); *Critical Appropriations: African American Women and the Construction of Transnational Identity* (2014); and book chapters and articles on African diaspora literature, Black popular culture, and visual and performing arts.

KELLY JO FULKERSON-DIKUUA is visiting assistant professor of English at Denison University, where she also teaches in the Black studies and Women's and Gender studies programs. Her scholarship focuses broadly on questions on race, gender, medicine, and literature. She is currently working on a book manuscript, tentatively titled "Racing and Erasing Consent: Reproductive Autonomy and Harm in (Post)Apartheid States."

DWAN K. HENDERSON is a writer, teacher, mentor, and scholar serving as a member of the English and American studies faculties at the Lovett School in Atlanta, Georgia. Her research is focused on the intersections and rhetoric of race, gender, and national identity in literature and popular culture. Her work has appeared in *Diverse: Issues in Higher Education* (formerly *Black Issues in Higher Education*) and the edited volume, *James Baldwin: Challenging Authors*.

IMANI KAI JOHNSON is assistant professor of Critical Dance studies at the University of California, Riverside, where she is currently completing her manuscript tentatively titled," Dark Matter in Breaking Cyphers: Africanist Aesthetics in Global Hip Hop," and coediting the *Oxford Handbook for Hip Hop Dance Studies*. Dr. Johnson is also the founder and chair of the Show & Prove Hip Hop Studies Conference Series. She has published in *Dance Research Journal*, *Women and Performance*, and the *Cambridge Companion to Hip Hop*.

RALINA L. JOSEPH is a scholar, teacher, and facilitator of race and communication. She is professor of communication and the founding director of the Center for Communication, Difference, and Equity at the

University of Washington. She is the author of *Postracial Resistance: Black Women, Media, and the Uses of Strategic Ambiguity* (2018) and *Transcending Blackness: From the New Millennium Mulatta to the Exceptional Multiracial* (2013).

DAVID J. LEONARD is a writer, teacher, and scholar. He is the author of several books, including *Playing While White: Privilege and Power on and off the Field* (2017) and *After Artest: The NBA and the Assault on Blackness* (2012). He is coeditor of *Woke Gaming: Digital Challenges to Oppression and Social Injustice* (with Kishonna Gray) and several other books. His work has appeared in *Black Camera*; *Journal of Sport and Social Issues*; *Cultural Studies: Critical Methodologies*; *Game and Culture*; *Simile*; as well as several anthologies.

EMILY J. LORDI is a writer, professor, and cultural critic whose focus is African American literature and Black popular music. She is associate professor of English at Vanderbilt University and the author of three books: *Black Resonance* (2013); *Donny Hathaway Live* (2016); and, forthcoming in 2020, "The Meaning of Soul." In addition to publishing scholarly articles on topics ranging from literary modernism to Beyoncé, she contributes freelance essays to such venues as New Yorker.com, the *Atlantic*, *Billboard*, NPR, and the *Los Angeles Review of Books*.

NINA ANGELA MERCER is a PhD candidate of Theatre and Performance at The Graduate Center, CUNY. She is an interdisciplinary artist, professor, and dramaturg, whose plays include *Gutta Beautiful*; *Itagua Meji: A Road and a Prayer*; *Gypsy and the Bully Door*; and *A Compulsion for Breathing*. Her writing has been published in the *Killens Review of Arts & Letters*; *Black Renaissance Noire*; *Continuum: The Journal of African Diaspora Drama, Theatre, and Performance*; and *Black Girl Magic* (2018), among other publications.

MARK ANTHONY NEAL is the James B. Duke Professor of African and African American studies at Duke University. Neal is the author of several books including *What the Music Said: Black Popular Music and Public Culture*; *Soul Babies: Black Popular Culture and the Post-Soul Aesthetic*; and *Looking for Leroy: Illegible Black Masculinities*, and coeditor, with Murray Forman, of *That's the Joint!: The Hip-Hop Studies Reader*, now in its second edition.

KINOHI NISHIKAWA is an assistant professor of English and African American studies at Princeton University. He is the author of *Street Players: Black Pulp Fiction and the Making of a Literary Underground* (2018) and is currently at work on "Black Paratext," a study of modern African American literature and book design.

H. IKE OKAFOR-NEWSUM (HORACE NEWSUM) is an independent artist-scholar working out of his studio in Delaware, Ohio. He is the author of *SoulStirrers: Black Art and the Neo-Ancestral Impulse* (2016). He is also an Emeritus Professor at The Ohio State University.

ERIC DARNELL PRITCHARD is associate professor of English at the University at Buffalo, State University of New York. He is the author of *Fashioning Lives: Black Queers and the Politics of Literacy* (2016), winner of three book awards, and editor of "Sartorial Politics, Intersectionality, and Queer Worldmaking," a special issue of *QED: A Journal in GLBTQ Worldmaking* (2017). His articles and essays on literacy, rhetoric, fashion, beauty, and Black queer life and culture have been published in multiple scholarly and popular venues including the *International Journal of Fashion Studies*; *Harvard Educational Review*; *Palimpsest*; *Visual Anthropology*; *Public Books*; Ebony.com, and *ARTFORUM*.

RICHARD SCHUR is professor of English and director of the Honors Program at Drury University. He is the author of *Parodies of Ownership: Hip-Hop Aesthetics and Intellectual Property Law* (2009) and coeditor of *African American Culture and Legal Discourse* (2009). His research focuses on the intersection of African American culture, popular culture, critical race theory, and law.

TRACY D. SHARPLEY-WHITING is the Gertrude Conaway Vanderbilt Distinguished Professor of African American and Diaspora studies and French at Vanderbilt University where she also chairs the Department of African American and Diaspora studies and directs the Callie House Research Center for Global Black Cultures and Politics.

VINCENT L. STEPHENS is director of the Popel Shaw Center for Race and Ethnicity and a contributing faculty member in the Department of Music at Dickinson College. He is author of *Rocking the Closet: How Little Richard, Johnnie Ray, Liberace, and Johnny Mathis Queered Pop Music* (2019) and coeditor of *Postracial America? An Interdisciplinary Study* (2017) with Anthony Stewart. He has published essays and chapters on popular culture in various peer-reviewed journals and edited collections.

LISA B. THOMPSON is professor of African and African Diaspora studies at the University of Texas at Austin. She is the author of *Beyond the Black Lady: Sexuality and the New African American Middle Class* (2009) and the play *Single Black Female* (2012). Thompson's other plays include *Underground* (2017), *Monroe* (2018), and *The Mamalogues* (2019).

SHENEESE THOMPSON is an assistant professor of Language, Literature and Cultural studies at Bowie State University. Her research focuses on Afro-Atlantic Religious Iconographies, particularly those related to Lucumí, Santería, and Candomblé in Black popular cultures.

INDEX

Bilge, Sirma, 297

"Billie Jean" (song), 2

Birmingham School of Cultural Studies, 293

Birth of the Cool (Davis), 182

biting: as appropriation, 201

Black Aesthetic, The (Gayle), 17

Black aesthetics, 8, 10, 16–17, 19, 58–59, 64, 66, 135, 138, 143, 197; anti-essentialist critiques, 18. *See also* Africanist aesthetics

Black art, 89

Black Arts Movement, 14, 16, 19, 77, 79, 177, 214, 230

Black athletes, 11–13; in corporate sphere, 2

Black avant-garde, 208

Blackbird (film), 120

Black bodies, 88; absence of, 194; Black dance, 239–41; clothing, significance of, and racialization, 139; demonization and racialization of, 136; nerd chic, as racial essentialism, 147; performance ritual, collective action through, 222; postraciality, 144–45; as troubled, 239; within white imagination, 149; and white supremacy, 140; women's bodies, 298

Black Broadway (revue), 71

Black cool, 93, 176, 182; branding of, 184, 186–87; and breaking, 194; commodification of, 179, 187; hip hop, 187; loss of, 185–86; marketing embrace of, 183–84; trademarking of, 187; white appropriation of, 183–84; white supremacy, challenging of, 184

Black cultural criticism, 290

Black cultural studies, 78

Black dance, 247; Black bodies, 239–41; Black deviance, evidence of, 238; collective memory, 248; concert dance, 238; cultural characteristics, 240; defining of, 240; diaspora, and African aesthetics, 238; as expansive, 242; and meaning-making, 242; memories, tethered to, 240–41; as subversive act, 248

Black dandyism, 143, 145–46; black masculinity, 139–40; politics of respectability, 140

Black diaspora, 208, 227n2, 241, 256. *See also* African diaspora

"Blacker the Berry, The" (Lamar), 5

Blackface, 4

Black Feminism, 296–98

Black Feminist Thought, 293

Black films, 91, 260. *See also* hip-hop films

Black folk culture, 16

Black identity, 2–4, 234; and branding, 176–77; trademark law, 176–77

Black intelligentsia, 78

Black Is, Black Ain't (documentary), 119

Black-ish (television show), 96, 300

Black Lives Matter, 80, 97, 102, 162, 166, 171, 187, 195, 292

Black masculinity, 12–13, 184, 199, 252–53; of boys, 253; and dandyism, 139–40; embodiment, as way of knowing, 199; multiple inscriptions of, 136; negative images of, 139–40; "phobogenic objects," 102; sartorial choices, 135–36; and whiteness, 138–39

Black nationalism, 68–70

blackness, 2, 22–23n6, 59, 66, 87, 97, 109, 193, 208, 230, 256, 261, 276, 294, 298; appropriation of, 196; authenticity, notions of, 32, 67–70, 148, 199; in Black popular culture, 157; Black superheroes, 104; Black Twitter, 163–65, 171; as blue, 9; and branding, 176–77; breaking, 194; and camp, 71–72; changing nature of, 6; and cinema, 260; clothing, as racial signifier, 144; clothing choices, 135, 138, 140, 143, 145–47, 149; complex subjectivities of, 7–8; concepts of, 19; criminalization of, 149, 165–66; cultural productions of, 21; defending of, 171; definitions of, 6, 18, 143–44; and diasporic, 20; disruptive trope of, 5–6; embracing of, 16; "exceptions" to, 147; and gender, 154; global nature of, 154–55; hegemonic blackness (cont.)

understanding of, 136, 142; in hip-hop culture, 259–60, 276; as lived experience, 19; meaning of, 290–93, 295; metanarratives of, 208, 226; mixed-race, 19–20, 30–38, 40–41; narrow conceptions of, 67–68, 135, 176–77; and NBA, 142; nerd movement, as cross-dressing, 145; as pansexual, 10; pathology, synonymous with, 11; as performed, 191; policing of, 67; politicizing of, 20; in popular culture, 289; as postmodern, 19; in public sphere, 91–92; queerness, intersection of, 60, 119, 121; as racialized, 194; region and class, linked to, 93; representations of, 3, 288–89, 295; as resistant, 5–6, 259–60; signifying practice of, 139, 141, 164–65, 195; as socially constructed, 290; social media, 163–65; in soul era, 69; in sports, 10; stereotypes of, 140, 165, 288; and thuggery, 135–36, 145, 263; traditional tropes of, 72; and transnationalism, 156–57; as unapologetic, 6; white gaze, 138, 149; whiteness, trappings of, 144–46. *See also* African Americans, Black popular culture

Black Panther (film), 7, 11, 23–24n21

Black Panther Party, 5, 68–69, 77

Black performance: roots of, as tainted, 209

Black Popular Culture (Wallace and Dent), 2, 22, 78–79, 290, 298

Black popular culture, 1, 18, 20–21, 78, 87, 91, 98, 155, 157, 209, 210, 232, 293, 294; "Black" in, 10, 19, 22, 95, 154, 230–31, 290–91, 289, 290; branding in, 233; "changing same" of white corporate ownership, 4; cultural memory, historical gulf in, 68–69; and cyberspace, 88–89; digital access to, 95; in digital age, 292; gangsta rap, 269; in mainstream popular culture, 2; political disempowerment, 292; as popular, 289; as profitable commodity, 3; in public

sphere, 153, 229, 288; and representation, 13; and resistance, 89; sartorial choices, 135; self-definition, 291; social media, 233–34, 271; transnational in, 156; underground movement, as disrupter to, 209; urban fiction, 269

Black popular music, 20; camp elements in, 66–67

Black Power Movement, 12, 16, 77, 214, 291

Black print culture, 8

Black Print Publishing, 275

Black protest movement, 83

Black queer lives, 21, 71; Black single mother, 128; the gaze, 255–56; as illegible, 263; and interiority, 254; kinship models, 123, 126, 128–31; in media, 118–20; and normativity, 122–23; queer identity, 231; on web series, 121–23, 131, 132n13. *See also* queerness

Black queer studies, 252

Black queer worldmaking, 121–22, 126–28; queer kinship in, 129–31

Black radio, 8, 20, 44, 46, 49, 54; in African American public sphere, 45, 51–52; "talking drums," 45. *See also* radio

Black radio albums, 46, 48; black economic nationalism, as model of, 54; concept album, revival of, 47; as source of collective promotion, 54

Black Radio (Robert Glasper Experiment), 44–47

Black Radio 2 (Robert Glasper Experiment), 45, 49, 55n23

Black Radio Society (Spalding), 54n3

Black reproduction, 244

Black ritual performance, 212; bearing witness, 208; blood memory, 208

Black ritual theater, 21, 209–10, 213–15, 217–18, 220–21, 226; space, claiming of, 211; struggle of, 211. *See also* Black theater

Black social media, 232. *See also* Black Twitter

Black social movements: political art of, 77–78

nerd chic: as cross-dressing, 145; as ironic, 145; racial essentialism, credence to, 147; and whiteness, 142, 145

"Never Give Anything Away" (song), 65

Newkirk, Vann, 164, 167

New Negro, The (Locke), 14–15

New Negro Movement, 14, 19

New Orleans (Louisiana), 242

Newton, Esther, 69

Newton, Huey P., 68–69

New York, 60, 62, 71, 196, 197; Ball culture in, 130; as epicenter of cabaret world, 61; integrated nightlife in, 69–70

New York Amsterdam (newspaper), 107

Nigeria, 157

Nike, 183

Nirvana, 49

Nishime, LeiLani, 34

Nixon, Richard M., 265

Nkisi: Head Hair (Okafor-Newsum), 83, 87

Noah's Arc (television show), 120

Noah's Arc: Jumping the Broom (film), 120

Nobles, Wade, 227–28n13

No Shade (web series), 122–23, 128–31

"Notes on Camp" (Sontag), 63

Notes on the State of Virginia (Jefferson), 13

Nothing But a Man (film), 300

Nottage, Lynn, 94

Nugent, Ted, 32

Nussbaum, Emily, 36

Obama, Barack, 29, 42n18, 144, 181, 300; as celebrity, 88; mixed race of, 19–20, 30, 33–35, 39–40; as "mutt," 30–34, 36–37, 41; sense of humor, 29

Obama, Malia, 30

Obama, Michelle, 42n18, 88, 144, 300

O'Hara, Frank, 70

Okafor-Newsum, H. Ike, 79, 83, 87

Old Negro, 14–15

Olympic basketball team (204), 140–41

Omi, Michael, 40

O'Neill, Ann, 169–70

O'Neill, Shaquille, 148

"One Million Bottlebags" (song), 185

"One Step Ahead" (song), 263

Ooh La La! Dance Line, 247

Oprah's Book Club, 268

Oprah Winfrey Show, The (television show), 299

Ormes, Earl Clark, 107

Ormes, Jackie, 20, 101–2; American education system, critique of, 112; Black womanhood, and fashion, 113–14; Black womanhood, imagining of, 115; characters of, 103–4, 107–15; characters, political and social mobility of, 108–9, 115; comic canon of, 103; gender and racial norms, breaking of, 106–7; white male space, appropriating of, 104–5

Ostberg, Daniel Mallory, 66

"Our Favorite Fugitive" (song), 53

"Our Love" (song), 264

OutKast, 66

ownership, 20–21

Palo Mayombe, 218–19

Parents Music Resource Center, 183

Pariah (film), 300

Paris (France), 60, 62, 193

Paris Is Burning (documentary), 130

Parks, Suzan-Lori, 94

Parlato, Gretchen, 49

Parliament (band), 46–47

Passing Strange (Stew), 94

Paul, Chris, 135

Peele, Jordan: as mixed race, 32, 35–41

Pence, Mike, 6

Pendergrass, Teddy, 46–47

Peoples, John A., 245

Pepsi, 183

Performers, 264

Perpener, John, 238

Perry, Tyler, 10, 95; as controversial figure, 11

Pham, Minh-Ha T., 199–201

Philadelphia (Pennsylvania), 193

Phillips, Imani, 281